Sean Dorney holds a peculiar distinction , deported from and honoured by the country he has specialised in reporting: Papua New Guinea. Deported in 1984 after a dispute between the ABC and the PNG Government, he returned in 1987, and was awarded an MBE in 1990 for 'services to broadcasting and sport'. Dorney has had a long and distinguished broadcasting career in the region for the ABC. There have been only rare intervals away from both the ABC and PNG, the longest during the years of his deportation when he worked as Chief Press Secretary to the Chief Minister of the Northern Territory. His first book was the successful *Papua New Guinea—People, Politics and History Since 1975*. Sean Dorney has two children. He and his wife live in Port Moresby.

*To: John
This is a fascinating place!*

The Sandline Affair

Politics and mercenaries and the Bougainville crisis

SEAN DORNEY

*Regards
Sean Dorney
10/10/98*

ABC BOOKS

Published by ABC Books for the
AUSTRALIAN BROADCASTING CORPORATION
GPO Box 9994 Sydney NSW 2001

Copyright © Sean Dorney 1998

First published September 1998

All rights reserved. No part of this publication
may be reproduced, stored in a retrieval system
or transmitted in any form or by any means,
electronic, mechanical, photocopying, recording
or otherwise, without the prior written permission
of the Australian Broadcasting Corporation.

National Library of Australia
Cataloguing-in-Publication entry
Dorney, Sean, 1951– .
  The Sandline affair: politics and mercenaries and the
  Bougainville Crisis.

  ISBN 0 7333 0701 9.

  1. Sandline International. 2. Civil-military relations—
  Papua New Guinea. 3. Mercenary troops—Papua New Guinea—
  Bougainville Island. 4. Bougainville Crisis, Papua New
  Guinea, 1988– . 5. Bougainville Island (Papua New Guinea)—
  Politics and government—1975– . 6. Papua New Guinea—
  Armed Forces. 7. Papua New Guinea—Politics and
  government —1975– . I. Australian Broadcasting Corporation.
  II. Title.

320.953

Maps by the Cartography Unit, RSPAS, Australian National University

Text designed by Jim Shepherd
Set in 11/14 pt Cambridge by
Midland Typesetters, Maryborough, Victoria
Colour separations by Finsbury, Adelaide
Printed and bound in Australia by
Australian Print Group, Maryborough, Victoria

5 4 3 2 1

Contents

Author's Note		6
Maps	PNG and its Provinces	7
	Bougainville–Island of Sorrows	8
	The PNG–Solomon Border–Points of Tension	9
	Operation Rausim Kwik–Critical Locations	10
Prologue	Operation Rausim Kwik	11
1	Caught Out in the Land of the Unexpected	15
2	The Bougainville War	37
3	An Undisciplined Force	57
4	Defence Systems Limited–The Forerunner to Sandline	82
5	Initial Contact	102
6	High Speed II Meets No Mercy	124
7	Orogen Opens the Window	145
8	The Cabinet Decision	164
9	Signing Up Sandline	182
10	Implementation and Exposure	205
11	Papua New Guinea Defiant	228
12	Undetected Manoeuvres	250
13	D-Day for Rausim Kwik	268
14	Days of Havoc	287
15	Parliament Under Siege	309
16	Consequences	333
Index		348

Author's Note

In March 1997 the ABC threw unprecedented resources into covering the PNG military's revolt against the Chan Government's hiring of mercenaries. The result was coverage that no other media organisation could match. I would like to thank the two ABC International Editors, John Tulloh (TV) and Tony Hill (Radio); the members of the hastily assembled ABC team—Craig McMurtrie, Sean Murphy, Marius Benson, Mark Corcoran, Geoff Clegg and Scott Taylor; Kawage, who kept the coffee flowing; and the locally hired camera crews, Frank Mills, Peter Dipp and John Philip.

There was one ABC staff member who was not part of the coverage team. Weni Singirok, the wife of Jerry Singirok, had worked with me for eighteen months prior to the crisis. Weni is an extremely competent journalist whom I knew and admired long before she and Jerry Singirok were married. However, in late 1995 when her husband was promoted to Commander of the PNG Defence Force we both knew that her professional career as the ABC's PNG journalist was going to become extremely difficult. It proved to be so, and far more than either of us could have suspected. Weni's loyalty to Jerry placed her in an impossible position. I could see how stressed she was after the Sandline deal became public, but she never let on to me what was about to happen. Weni's last working day at the ABC was Friday, 14 March 1997. She didn't turn up for work on the Monday, and late that morning I discovered why. Neither of the Singiroks has been prepared to talk to me during the preparation of this book.

Many others, though, have agreed to speak. Those willing to be quoted are acknowledged. The Australian National University's Research School of Pacific and Asian Studies provided me with a six-week visiting fellowship to help me begin writing, and I thank Donald Denoon and Mary for giving me lodgings in Canberra. Finally, I pay tribute to my wife, Pauline, who not only kept the ABC's PNG office functioning during the crisis but who has also stoically tolerated Sandline continuing to obliterate our life while I struggled to write this account.

Sean Dorney, July 1998

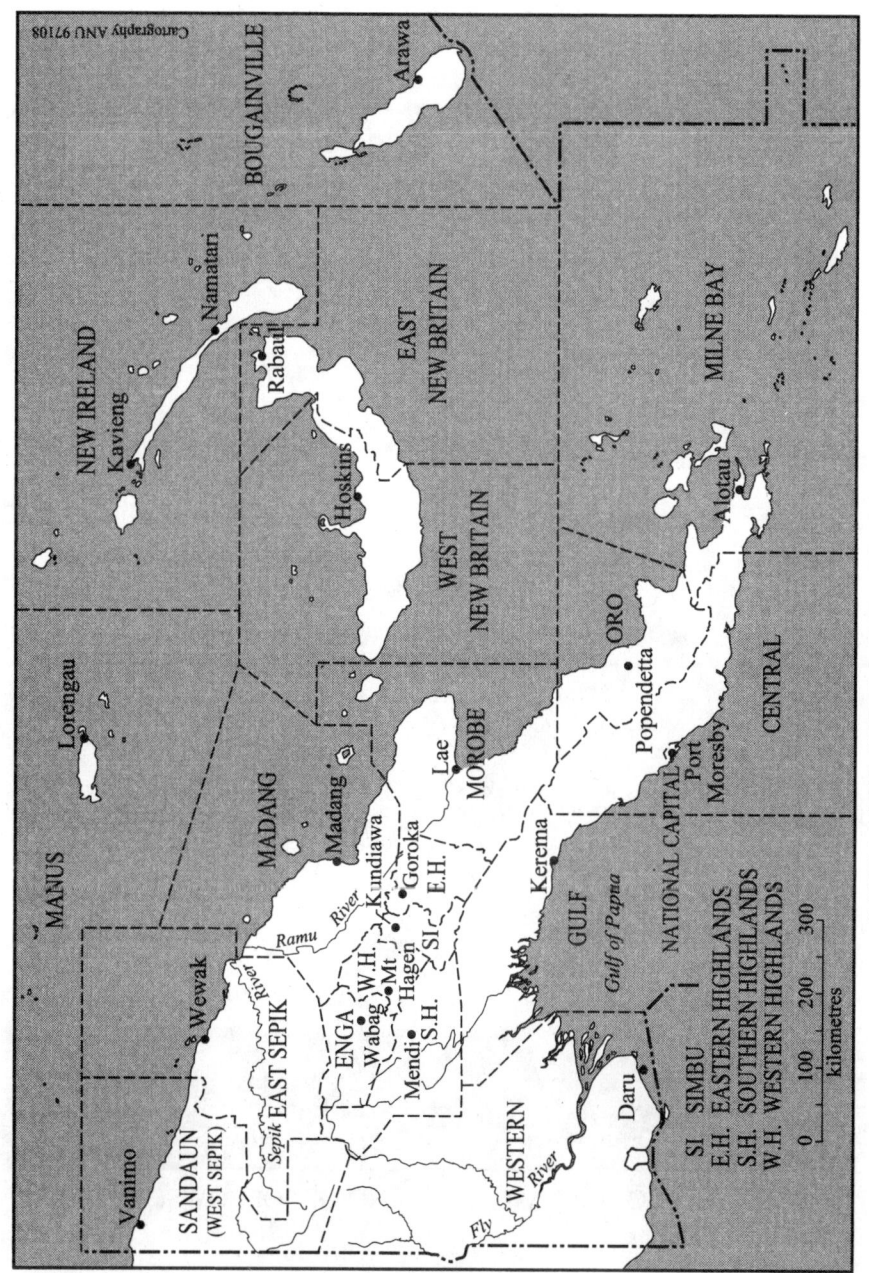

PAPUA NEW GUINEA AND ITS PROVINCES

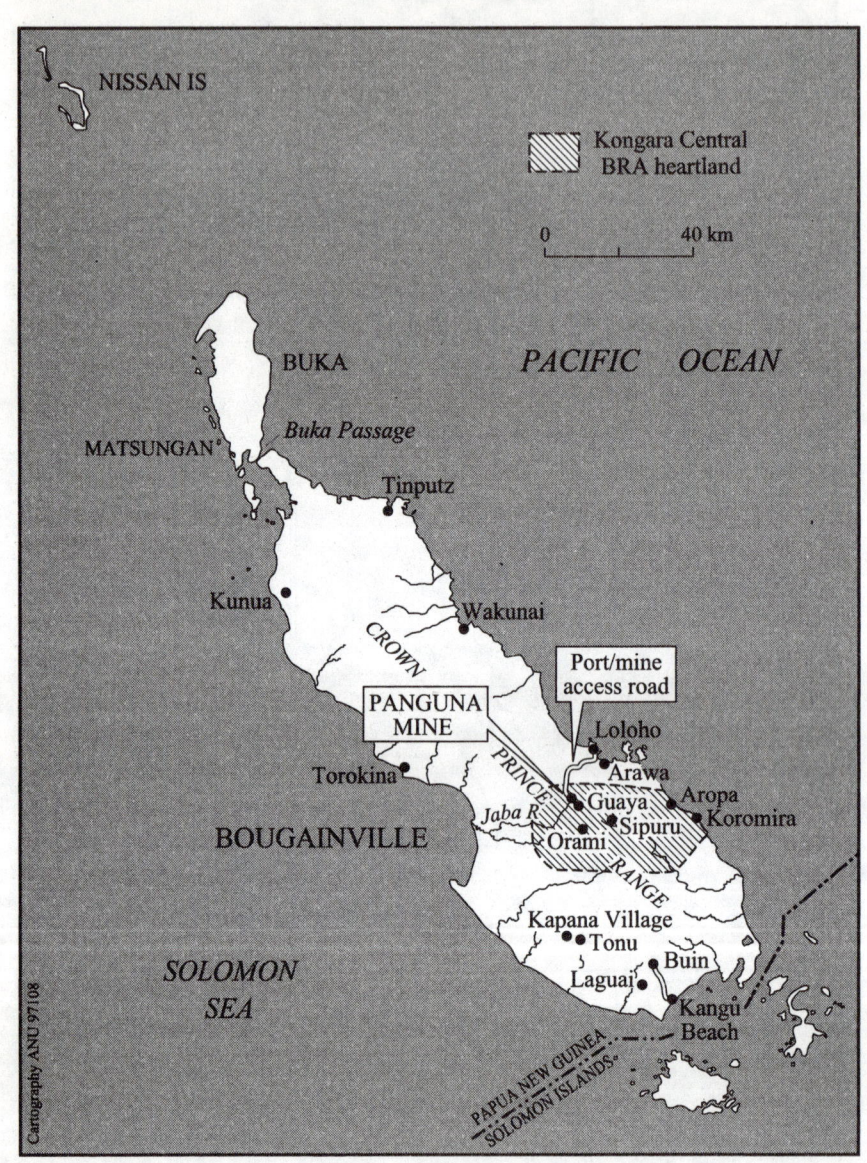

BOUGAINVILLE – ISLAND OF SORROWS

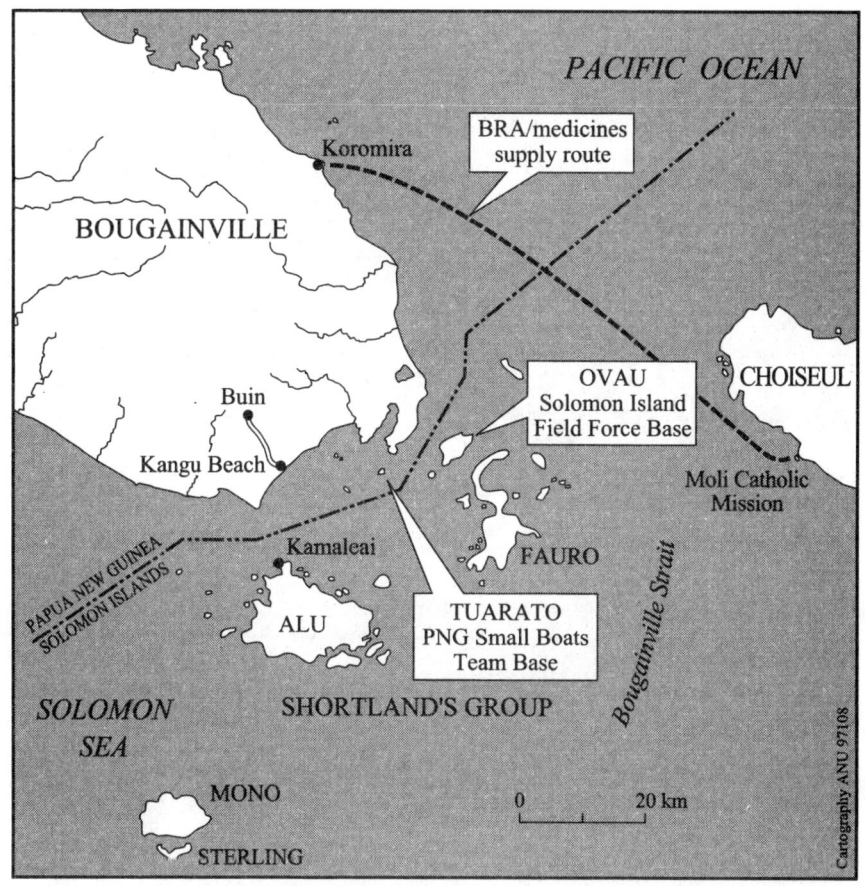

THE PNG-SOLOMON BORDER – POINTS OF TENSION

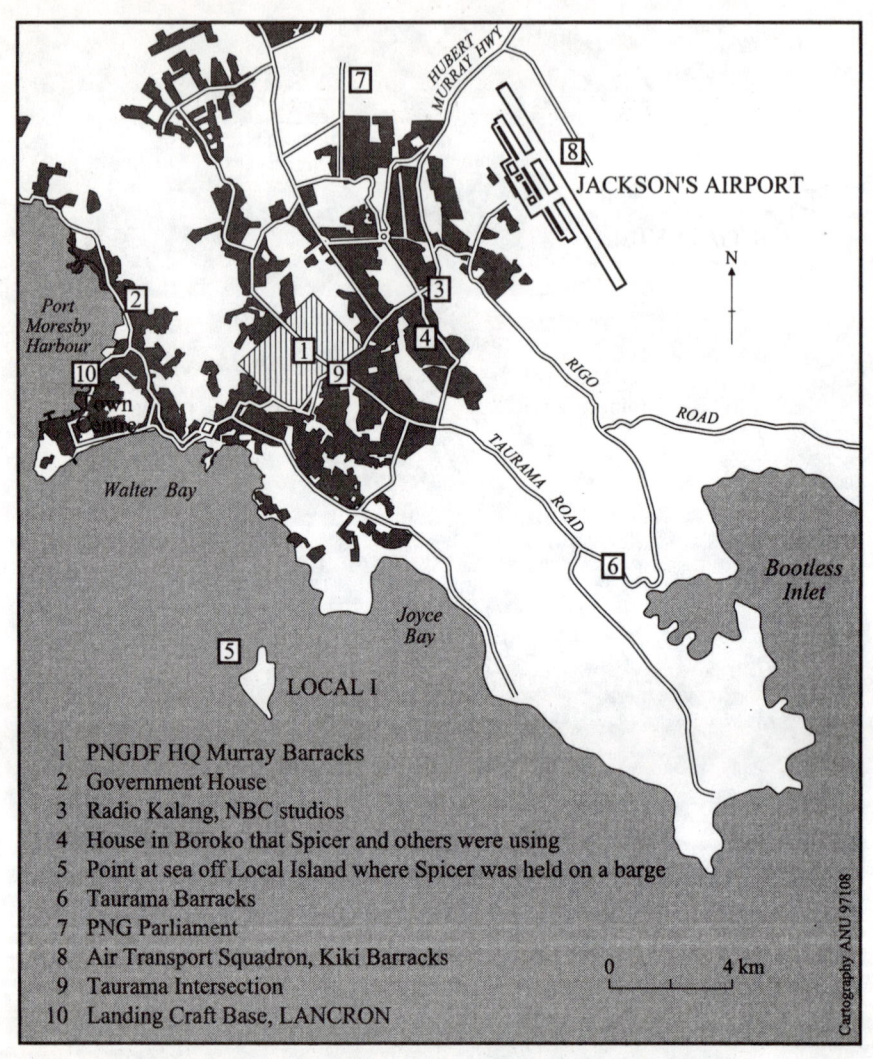

OPERATION RAUSIM KWIK – CRITICAL LOCATIONS

Prologue

Operation Rausim Kwik

'Hands up, gentlemen! Freeze!'

Furnace-eyed Papua New Guinea army Major, Walter Enuma, spoke menacingly to the two senior mercenaries from the world's most professional private army, Executive Outcomes. Startled, EO's local commander of the $US36 million Operation Oyster, South African Brigadier Nick Van den Berg, and his Intelligence Officer, Karl Deats, stared at Major Enuma and at the Browning semi-automatic 9 mm pistol he levelled at them. It was well after dusk, shortly before eight o'clock on a tropical Sunday night in Port Moresby.

That night, 16 March 1997, Van den Berg and Deats had come to the Commander's office at Papua New Guinea Defence Force (PNGDF) headquarters, Murray Barracks, for a meeting to confirm details of their plan for Operation Oyster—the recapture of the once immensely rich Bougainville Copper Mine. The mine had been out of operation for eight years. Closed down initially in 1989 by sabotage and terrorist attacks, it had been abandoned in 1990 after the anti-mine campaign had blown up into a full-scale secessionist war. Van den Berg's company, Executive Outcomes, was providing personnel and expertise for a contract that the military consultancy company, Sandline International, British-based and incorporated in the Virgin Islands, had signed just six weeks earlier with the PNG Deputy Prime Minister and Minister for Finance, Chris Haiveta.

As they were ushered into the room, Major Enuma had invited Van den Berg and Deats to sit down saying, 'I'll just get the Commander.' Enuma rapped on the door of the washroom attached to the Commander's office.

'Sir! Those gentlemen you were expecting? They're here to see you, Sir.' But it was not the PNGDF Commander, Brigadier General Jerry Singirok, who emerged. Instead, Captain Belden Namah and several other junior PNGDF officers armed with M16 carbines and military pistols burst the door open and charged into the room from the Commander's toilet. As they did, Major Enuma spun around and snatched up his own Browning from its hiding nook behind a pot plant.

'Welcome, gentlemen,' he continued. 'Welcome to the Land of the Unexpected.'

Major Enuma had planned to capture the whole of the mercenaries' command structure in the one swoop. However, the Director of Sandline International, ex-British Scots Guard Lieutenant Colonel Tim Spicer, had been delayed. He was seeing the Prime Minister, Sir Julius Chan, who was keen to have the Sandline and Executive Outcomes specialists give his senior Ministers and key officials a detailed briefing in the coming week; a briefing on what these high-cost 'military consultants' had planned for the rebel leaders on Bougainville, the 'criminals', as Chan called them.

Tim Spicer arrived only minutes after Van den Berg and Deats had been 'neutralised' and spirited away. Spicer was not so easily subdued. 'He gave me a bit of a problem,' Enuma said in recalling the incident in an interview. 'I was expecting the three to come in together. But somehow Tim was held up with the Prime Minister. So when the other two came in first, I had no option but to get them out quickly. And they were out of the way when Tim came in.' Enuma was worried that Spicer would realise there was a revolt under way and escape to raise the alarm. 'It was just by the skin of our teeth.'

On his way up to the Commander's office, at the foot of the stairs, an unsuspecting Lieutenant Colonel Spicer met the PNGDF's Acting Chief of Operations, Lieutenant Colonel Walter Salamas. Salamas had arranged the meeting but it was not turning out as he had expected. 'I convened the meeting because the Commander [Singirok] wanted another meeting with the Sandline executives,' Salamas told a subsequent inquiry. 'I took that as a normal meeting. We had not finalised the operation orders ... and I was hoping that meeting was to establish that. It came out to be a different exercise. I sensed that something unusual was happening.'

After bounding up the stairs and entering the Commander's office, Spicer asked, 'Where is everyone?' Repeating the earlier performance, Major Enuma said, 'The General is here. I'll just call him out.' And he rapped on the toilet door again.

'He was the only one who had a bit of fight,' Enuma said. 'I think it must be the self-confidence he'd built up over the years in various operations—the Falklands, Northern Ireland, Bosnia. And he was pretty high up with the Prime Minister. He was talking directly to Sir Julius Chan and the Defence Minister. Also to the Finance Minister. So Jerry [Singirok] was just like his mate. He had the attitude that they were more or less equal partners. That actually showed.' When Spicer asked where his 'mate' Singirok was, he was told, 'He's been taken care of.'

At first Spicer could not believe that what was unfolding was serious. He thought it was a practical joke. 'I half expected he might appear from the toilet door, laughing,' Spicer recounted later. But Major Enuma and the men following him were not playing games. 'I've got a lot of respect for Tim,' Enuma said. 'I mean, he's a military man. The same with Nick. They're professionals. And I could not pussyfoot with these guys.' Spicer admitted to being caught by surprise. 'If you're asking did we see this one coming,' he said when interviewed in April 1997, just before flying home to London, 'the answer is No! We expect to go and work with a government and a defence force. We don't expect them to be the people we end up having a problem with.'

There were to be two major commissions of inquiry into the Sandline Affair. During the first inquiry, Spicer was asked how he had been treated by the PNG military while he was under detention. 'Initially very aggressively, very aggressively. Thereafter I was not physically harmed but I was certainly intimidated.' Back in London, after his ordeal, Spicer told journalists he had feared for his life. 'I was physically assaulted, suffered intimidation and was subject to death threats. I had an automatic revolver put to my head on three occasions.'

Five PNG soldiers tackled Spicer in the Commander's office, knocking him to the ground. 'There was an altercation and I came off worst,' Spicer recalled. 'The belt was taken out of my trousers and my shoes were removed. They were all very tensed up and aggressive.' This time it was Captain Belden Namah who whispered into Spicer's ear as he lay pinned to the floor in the PNGDF Commander's office, 'Welcome to the Land of the Unexpected.'

That evening, the night before St Patrick's Day 1997, PNG soldiers also raided the house in the Port Moresby suburb of East Boroko that Sandline had been allocated as its operational command post. 'Boroko was their communications base,' Enuma said. 'It was our second objective.' On the other side of the country, 780 kilometres north-west of Port Moresby, soldiers from the PNGDF's 2nd Battalion ensured that the main body of mercenaries remained isolated. Those at the military barracks on Moem Point overlooking the Bismarck Sea near Wewak woke Monday morning to learn they were under detention. While inland at the Urimo jungle camp, five hours by four-wheel-drive away, the majority of the forty mercenaries who had been recruited from South Africa and Ethiopia blithely continued training with the PNGDF's Special Forces Unit (SFU) up until midday. When the Commanding Officer of the 2nd Battalion arrived at lunch time he informed them the training had been cancelled. They handed in their weapons.

Soldiers from PNG's much ostracised and denigrated army had captured their instructors, men who had helped turn wars in Angola and Sierra Leone. 'It was a precise military operation,' according to Enuma. 'All I can say is that they were simultaneously isolated. My biggest concern, though, was the command element. Their communications system, any gadgets they had in their hands that could activate a warning signal. That was my biggest worry. Surprise was the key. It was absolutely important to isolate the command element, to take them totally by surprise, give them no chance for any communications link with their men. So that operation on Sunday was absolutely important. That was critical. If I isolated the command and communications element without any leaks then the chance of success was ninety per cent.'

On that Sunday night, 16 March 1997, Papua New Guinea's post-Independence history took a dramatic turn. Tim Spicer's proposed Operation Oyster approved by the Government of Sir Julius Chan to retake the Panguna copper mine from the Bougainville rebels was aborted. And Major Walter Enuma's Operation Rausim Kwik (Pidgin for 'kick them out fast'), authorised by Brigadier General Jerry Singirok to defy the Government and expel Sandline's mercenaries from Papua New Guinea, was launched.

Chapter One

Caught Out in the Land of the Unexpected

*A Short Profile of Papua New Guinea;
The Corruption Issue; Sandline and Executive
Outcomes*

Papua New Guinea is not a country simply or easily understood. The PNG Tourist Authority's long-term slogan 'Land of the Unexpected' is a far more appropriate (and accurate) description than its late 1990s replacement 'Paradise Live'. As Australian journalist Richard Laidlaw wrote in 1990, PNG 'is a place that exacts a telling revenge on anyone with preconceptions'. Sandline's Lieutenant Colonel Tim Spicer learnt this to his cost. He did not get to know PNG very well at all. But that is hardly surprising. Spicer was from the other side of the world and had spent less than two months in the country when captured by those he thought he was helping. What is worrying is that there are very few people in Australia who understand PNG. 'Part of Papua New Guinea's problem is that its image in Australia has more to do with imperfect vision,' Laidlaw argued, 'than with a tutored understanding made deep by prolific exposure.'

With a few notable exceptions, the Australian media pays scant attention these days to Australia's former colony unless there is high drama such as during the Sandline crisis in March 1997 or a disaster relief effort such as the one in which the Australian Defence Force played such a high-profile role during the drought induced famine of 1997–98. The rest of the time it is the bizarre and tragic, especially violent crime involving expatriates, that fill the limited agenda. The last full-time staff correspondent that an Australian newspaper had based in PNG left in 1981. 'I know what the subs [sub-editors] want,' he confided a few months before he shut down the bureau. 'They want rascals, plane crashes and tribal fights! And that's what I'm giving them.' Perceptions are all. The correspondent he replaced, Gus Smales, who did understand PNG and covered its advance from the late colonial period through self-government to Independence exceptionally well, was told later by one of his bosses: 'Gus, you got out just in time. PNG's gone to shit since you left.'

However, it is not just sections of the media that fail to grasp the more complex reality. Perhaps what should disturb the Australian public most is the fact that, despite the massive amount of money that Australia spends on PNG each year—both in aid and on surveillance—this 'imperfect vision' is shared by many in Canberra advising and determining Australian policy towards its nearest neighbour. The friction in the Australia–PNG relationship will be evident in almost every chapter of this book and this theme of the dilemma which the Australian Government faces in properly understanding and dealing with Papua New Guinea will be developed further in the final chapter.

The chaos that was depicted in the television news footage beamed by satellite out of Port Moresby during the tumultuous ten days in March 1997, at the height of the mercenaries crisis, perhaps reinforced a common view in Australia that democratic rule in Papua New Guinea is perpetually on the verge of collapse. Some visiting journalists assumed that democracy had been overthrown, and that this was PNG's version of the Fiji coups of ten years earlier. To be fair, some others in the Pacific apparently thought it was too. Fiji's Prime Minister Sitiveni Rabuka (who as Colonel and later Brigadier Rabuka staged the two Fiji coups) asked Brigadier Jerry Singirok when they spoke on the telephone a few days into the crisis, 'Why did you stop?' However, the PNG Defence Force (PNGDF) Commander was not trying to take over the government. Despite some of the excited reporting at the time, the truth is that almost nobody in the PNG military seriously wants to take on the reponsibility of running what is an exceptionally diverse, challenging, difficult and perplexing country to administer.

The Australian colonisers had certainly found it so. The Australian Minister who did most to shape Papua New Guinea, the late Sir Paul Hasluck (Minister for External Territories 1951–63) wrote in his book, *A Time For Building*, that whereas he looked with pride upon what he achieved in the other responsibilities within his portfolio—the Northern Territory and the smaller island territories—Papua New Guinea 'was a task for Sisyphys'. Sisyphys was the character in Greek mythology who pushed the boulder to the top of the hill only to have it roll down the other side, from where he had to start pushing it up again. 'I think I did just as well as Sisyphys did,' Sir Paul said sardonically, 'and certainly got just as tired.' Australians who despair of present-day PNG public administration would do well to read Hasluck's book. Sir Paul wrote that on his first trip to PNG, the Acting Public Service Commissioner in the Territory, Mr E. A. Head, told him 'a disheartening story' about the state of the then Australian-dominated service and the incompetence of some of the key men. Head summed it up for Hasluck by suggesting that if the Australian Commonwealth Public Service was taken as a yardstick to be 100 per cent efficient, it would be 'an optimistic view' to think of the PNG service as being 25 per cent efficient.

Nevertheless, Australia did a fair job under trying circumstances and in a limited time frame to prepare Papua New Guinea for independence. But it is nostalgic rot to suggest that the Australians left behind a fully functioning, well-established and effective bureaucracy. The comments that Australian visitors often elicit from older people about how good things were when the Australians were in charge bear an uncanny resemblance to the way the people in the former German territory of New Guinea used to refer to the German reign (1884-1914) as the 'gut taim bipo'–the 'good times before' the Australians took over. In 1970, just five years before Australia granted PNG its independence, an area of some 170,000 hectares was still classified as not being under any Australian administrative control. When self-government (1973) and independence (1975) finally came with a rush, there was an understandable scramble by many Australians in the territory's public service to leave. This was, of course, encouraged by the rapid 'localisation' policy adopted by the first PNG Government, formed in late 1972 and led by Michael Somare. Too few Papua New Guineans had been trained to do the jobs they were quickly promoted to fill and some government departments have never recovered.

Of all the agencies which Australia handed over to PNG in the mid-1970s, the most crippled was the police force. Most of the country was still nominally under the care of patrol officers (kiaps). In the year of independence, 1975, police responsibility covered only ten per cent of the land area and forty per cent of the population. A PNG policy document produced just one month after Independence stated that the force had 'major problems' because of inexperienced and untrained staff. 'Of a total force strength of 4400,' it said, 'there are 239 commissioned officers, 96 below establishment strength.' The shortage of senior non-commissioned-officers (NCOs) was even more debilitating. There were only 149 sergeants, for instance, instead of 324. This was hardly the type of law-enforcement agency that one might wish upon a new nation with PNG's complex problems.

Of all the statistics that can be trotted out about Papua New Guinea, however, the most vital for any real understanding of the place is the fact that Papua New Guineans speak 867 languages. That is one third of the world's languages still in use. The population is about 4.3 million and there are upwards of one thousand indigenous ethnic groups, most quite small in number, who have been thrust together as a nation for less than a quarter of a century. One hundred years ago most of these tribal groups still did not know any of the others existed, apart from those who were their immediate, usually hostile, neighbours. This rapid transition from a thousand tiny society-states to a modern nation-state has its present-day political ramifications. 'The Papua New Guinean's loyalty is firstly to his parents,' wrote Yauka Liria, a former PNGDF intelligence officer in his remarkable book about PNG's secessionist war, *Bougainville Campaign Diary*, '... firstly to his parents, then his immediate relatives, then, in order, the clan, the village, the tribe, the district, the region, the occupational identity such as the Defence Force, and the nation-state PNG comes last. That's right, last of all!'

The absence of a popular perception of the primacy of the State—and the reality of the obverse of that, the general belief that your family and tribal group, your *wantoks* (Pidgin for 'one-talk'—people who speak your language) come first—is fundamental to what many outsiders see as some of PNG's biggest problems. The most notable of these are political instability caused by shifting loyalties in Parliament; corruption and the diversion of public money to benefit one's *wantoks*; poor land utilisation (ninety-seven per cent of the land remains in the hands of its traditional owners); gang crime; and a generally ineffective public service. However, there are many positive aspects to the make-up of this 'nation of a thousand tribes' as PNG has been called. More than eighty per cent of the people still live in their villages on their own land, many of them engaged in the informal economy in a state of what some commentators have described as 'subsistence affluence'. The *wantok* system of social obligations provides a safety net for tribal members, including those who have migrated to the towns, which saves the State from huge welfare payments it could never afford anyway. And the country is undeniably extraordinarily democratic.

The combination of this multi-fractured nature of society and the constitution that PNG adopted at Independence—a stunningly liberal document that emphasises the rights of the individual over those of the State—mitigate against the emergence of any despotic ruler. But equally they combine to inhibit the exercise of tough, single-minded leadership. A Prime Minister has to constantly shore up support in Parliament and disciplining Ministers can imperil continued survival. Its Constitution established PNG as a democratic, constitutional monarchy. Queen Elizabeth II of England is the powerless Head of State represented locally by a figurehead Governor General whose role is almost entirely ceremonial and who, unlike his Australian counterpart, has absolutely no latitude for independent action. PNG has a one-chamber Parliament that operates essentially, but at times erratically, in the British Westminster fashion.

There are 109 seats. The way these 109 Members are elected is a little like combining the Australian House of Representatives and the Senate into one. There are eighty-nine 'open electorates' of roughly similar population size (although, because there have been no boundary changes since 1977, some are now considerably larger than others); and there are twenty 'provincial electorates' (one per province including the National Capital District). Since the 1995 abolition of separately elected Provincial Assemblies these twenty Provincial Members are now also Governors of their provinces. Every elector gets two votes—one for the Open Member and one for the Provincial Member (or Governor). The number of seats per province ranges from two (Manus, which is the smallest, has only one Open Member as well as a Governor) to ten (Morobe, which is the largest, has a Governor plus nine Open Members).

Elections are held every five years. Although the Parliament can dissolve itself and move to elections at any time before the five-year term is up, that has never happened. And it seems unlikely that it ever will. This is because of the extremely precarious nature of political life in the PNG Parliament. Nobody wants to face the voter until it is absolutely necessary. In the 1997 elections fewer than half the outgoing Members were returned (just fifty-three). This high attrition rate has been a feature of all elections since Independence (in the 1992 poll the turnover was even higher—65 of the 109 Members voted in had not been in the previous Parliament). Fewer than one-fifth of the current Members have won more than twice (only twenty of them) and fewer than one in thirteen have been successful at more than three elections (just eight). The reason for the flushing out of over half the sitting Members at each poll is more complex than just voter dissatisfaction with performance, though undoubtedly that is a factor. Voter turnout is high—up to seventy per cent.

Political parties, though important in the Parliament, have been unable to establish much credibility in the electorate. Few have any grassroots structure. Those that have tried to build up party support at the provincial or local level generally have given up in frustration and left the party's branches to wither between elections. In 1997 forty independents were elected. The best any political party could do was sixteen seats. That was Sir Julius Chan's People's Progress Party (PPP) which had gone into the election with twice that number. Chan was among those to lose and, after his demise, the PPP split. The only other party to win more than ten seats was PNG's most enduring party, the Pangu Pati, which won just thirteen, its worst performance since it won eleven in its very first election in 1968, seven years before Independence. Ten other parties won seats but some of those parties quickly disappeared. At least three new political parties were created on the floor of Parliament in the nine months following the 1997 elections. One of those, Prime Minister Bill Skate's new party, PNG First, was formed out of the remains of several others, including his own People's National Congress which had won only six seats in its own right.

One crucial reason for this inability of political parties to take root is the very fractured nature of a society made up of so many language groups (an average across PNG of eight per electorate). Anthony Siaguru, a one-time Member, former Deputy Secretary of the Commonwealth, lawyer and newspaper columnist, explained it this way to the ABC some years ago: 'The peculiar situation existing in PNG is that when people go to vote, especially in the rural areas where the majority live, they consider themselves bound by social and family obligations to cast their vote for their relative or a person from their own clan, house line or language group. It might not be that that person is the best candidate in the judgment of the voter! But he or she is obliged because of social traditions to vote for him.' Most candidates are male and for ten years (1987-97) there was not a single woman in the Parliament. In 1997 two women were elected, Dame Josephine Abaijah, who had led the separatist Papua Besena movement at the time of Independence, and Lady Carol Kidu, the Australian-born wife of the late PNG Chief Justice, Sir Buri Kidu.

The system of voting encourages a proliferation of candidates. PNG has a 'first-past-the-post' voting system, so whoever scores the most on the first count wins. As the number of candidates has increased with each election, the proportion of the vote the winner needs to secure victory has kept falling. Democracy is rampant but the results show that it is becoming ever less representative. In 1997 a record-breaking 2372 candidates nominated for the 109 seats. This was a forty per cent increase on the record set five years before, despite the doubling of the already hefty nomination fee to K2000 per candidate (roughly the same in Australian dollars). More than half the members (sixty-one) were elected, despite getting the support of less than twenty per cent of the voters in their electorate. Throughout the country the average winning vote was just twenty-two per cent. In round terms, therefore, four out of every five voters in PNG backed losers.

The seat attracting the largest number of candidates was Oro Provincial, with sixty-one. Oro Governor Sylvanes Siembo won, scoring 3370, just 6.9

per cent of the total valid votes cast, meaning that 93.1 per cent of the voters in Oro saw their preferred candidate fail. But Siembo's percentage was not the smallest share of the total vote that a winning candidate received. In the seat of Gumine in the Simbu Province in the Highlands, Aulkupa Wamil scraped home with 2545 votes out of 38,267—a paltry 6.7 per cent. So more than 35,000 voters in Gumine would have been disappointed with the result. In the circumstances it is hardly surprising there is some post-election violence at the local electorate level.

One explanation for the explosion in candidate numbers is the widespread belief that almost anyone can win. If you do not need much more than five per cent of the vote to become an MP then it becomes a bit of a lottery, worth a K2000 bet. Prospective candidates are attracted by the rich rewards they have seen Members acquire in terms of status, power, privileges and money. The tenuous nature of a Member's hold on his seat contributes much to the way the Parliament operates. PNG's former Prime Minister, Sir Julius Chan, claimed to an audience in Brisbane some years ago that the bewildering nature of politics in PNG becomes logical if this lack of security is taken into account. 'Our politics [is] still regionalistic and tribally based,' Chan said. 'Each Member has a strong commitment to directly benefit his immediate electorate—much more so than in, say, Australia, where only a minority of seats are considered "marginal".'

Sir Julius said that commentators who bemoaned the lack of ideology in PNG political debate simply did not understand. 'Ideology is a luxury marginal Members cannot afford,' he claimed. 'It becomes a case of delivering the goods—a pragmatic approach, just as in marginal seats in Australia before election day with both sides offering election bonuses. The Australian parties play Santa at every Federal and State election. For us it is a full-time job!' This need to deliver to those who voted for you is one of the factors that led to the establishment of the notorious Electoral Development Fund (EDF), known popularly as the 'Members' slush fund'. Up until the abolition of separately elected provincial governments, each Member received K300,000 a year to be spent on 'development' projects of his choosing in his electorate. Following the constitutional amendment which disposed of the national MPs' political rivals at the provincial level, the system was changed so that a committee would decide on the spending of what then became classified as District Support Grants, one for each open electorate. But in mid-1998 Prime Minister Bill Skate was moving to change the Constitution again to give Members back control over half the District Support Grant while Governors were to get a new Provincial Support Grant of at least K300,000 each per year.

Part of Skate's motivation was to keep Members happy. With Parliament's term rigidly fixed, a Prime Minister has to be alert to regular challenge on the floor of the House through votes of no confidence. To ensure continuity, the Constitution says any no confidence motion must nominate an alternative Prime Minister. The incumbent is given no latitude to call a snap election. The Constitution does grant him, however, a limited period of grace to settle in–the first eighteen months after he is elected. Prior to a constitutional amendment in 1991, the guaranteed freedom from overthrow was only six months and so almost every session of Parliament was dominated by manoeuvring towards a threatened no confidence vote. In 1985, for example, there were three motions of no confidence in Prime Minister Somare. He fought off the first two, switching and changing his coalition partners. But in November of that year, exhausted by the process, he fell in the final session of the year and was replaced by Paias Wingti.

Party discipline is paltry because loss of endorsement and expulsion is no penalty. All of this elevates the power of the ordinary Member. As one Somare staff member put it in early 1985: 'PNG suffers from the dictatorship of the backbench.' Keeping Members on-side is an endlessly absorbing task. During his first term as Prime Minister (1980–82) Chan told a consitutional workshop that the PNG Constitution 'encourages corruption because a Prime Minister has to continually buy parliamentarians' support'. He said the system was a recipe for weak, unstable governments. 'People would be surprised if they knew how much of my time as Prime Minister was spent coping with requests for special favours of all kinds from individual politicians.' In 1981 Chan told a University of PNG student audience that as Prime Minister he regularly had to deal with political blackmail and that it was more sorrowful than amusing for him to relate that on several occasions Members had expressed loyalty to three political parties at the same time.

Of the seven changes in Prime Minister since Independence, three have come through votes of no confidence, three have come about as a result of elections and one resulted from an aborted attempt by Wingti to secure himself a second eighteen months in power by resigning in secret and then putting himself forward again. But it backfired. That led to Chan's re-emergence as Prime Minister in 1994 (a more detailed description of this event comes in a later chapter). Smooth flowing, no-nonsense government is a difficult proposition under the present system when no Prime Minister can ever be certain of the loyalty of any government backbencher or even, as has been proved repeatedly, members of his Cabinet. Attempts at reform have been made. But the problem is that while constitutional change in PNG requires the overwhelming support of the Parliament, most of the changes seen as vital are aimed at limiting the freedom and power of the very people who would have to vote those changes through—the backbenchers. Most constitutional amendments need either a two-thirds or a three-quarters majority, depending on the section, at two separate votes taken at least two months apart. This has stymied all efforts to overhaul the system.

Public disgust with politicians mingles with private expectation that your Member is beholden to you and will provide what you ask for upon demand. 'I think the greatest and most burdensome demand is the money demand,' the Member for Wewak, Bernard Narokobi, who became Opposition Leader after the 1997 elections, said in an interview for a Radio Australia program on the Members' slush funds in 1992. 'You're expected to give money for feasts, you're expected to give money for bride price, and you're expected to give money to buy tickets for people to travel ... the whole system is corrupt, inherently corrupt.' The Prime Minister at that time, Wingti, complained that the people looked upon their local Member as their banker. 'The demands that are put by the people on the leaders,' he said when interviewed for the same program, '[are] much greater than the amount of money [they've] got to give. So, in turn, the leaders are forced to look at other ways of looking after them. And that is the breeding ground for activities that are not proper.'

A major study into PNG's crime problem conducted in the mid-1980s commented on the widespread public perception that the country's leaders were by then already heavily involved in things improper. 'So much more is known about private lives here and so much more rumoured or suspected,' the Clifford Report stated, 'that the extent of corruption is difficult to hide. And if the official cases are no more than the crumbs from a table laden with corruption, the knowledge circulating amongst the public of the true size of this repast is exaggerated to lavish banquet proportions by their imagination.' It is a credit to Papua New Guinea's watchdog agencies, in particular the Ombudsman Commission, that so many official cases do come to light and are prosecuted. The Constitution lays down a Leadership Code and the Ombudsman has the task of safeguarding and enforcing it. Since Independence more than twenty Members have been thrown out of Parliament after major Ombudsman Commission investigations. Sir Julius Chan's Forests Minister, Andrew Posai, was one. In 1995 a Leadership Tribunal found Posai guilty of twenty-five charges of misconduct in office dating from when he was Minister for Home Affairs and Youth in 1992–93. Amongst the charges: transferring K400,000 of public funds into a private company of which he was board chairman.

In late 1996 the Member for Kagua Erave, Daniel Tulapi, claimed that for the benefit of PNG's international reputation the country's politicians should be immune from prosecution until their people rejected them at the polls and they returned to being 'ordinary' citizens. 'He's day-dreaming,' the Chief Ombudsman, Simon Pentanu, said when asked his opinion of Tulapi's suggestion. 'In effect what he's trying to say is that the Parliamentarians should, as a group, have a different set of laws from everybody else. I treat it with the contempt that it deserves.' Pentanu's Commission had a busy year in 1996. Six MPs went before Leadership Tribunals. Another, the former Health Minister, Yaip Avini, appeared before the criminal courts and was sentenced to six years jail for misappropriation. A report by the PNG Auditor General tabled in the Parliament in late 1996 stated that no fewer than forty-seven Members had failed to acquit their 1994 EDF allocations, amounts totalling K14 million. 'The Members of Parliament, in my opinion,' the then Auditor General, Makena Geno, said, 'have violated the Public Finances (Management) Act, the Leadership Code ... and the 1994 EDF Guidelines creating possibilities of huge sums of public funds being misappropriated.'

The report revealed that although the funds were supposed to be for local development projects, two Members of Parliament, brothers from the East New Britain Province, had together poured more than a quarter of a million kina into two companies, one a shipping company, to solve their cash flow problems and meet their debts and operational expenses. In another case the member for the Fly River Province had handed over practically his entire allocation to an agent who had converted it into Australian dollars to buy a twenty-metre barge. But there was no evidence that the barge had ever been delivered. One Member had allocated funds for an ambulance in his electorate but the Auditor General checked and found the vehicle registered in the Member's name. Another had provided five separate cheques totalling more than K20,000 for projects in his Southern Highlands electorate—projects for which the main activity, the Auditor General said, was the sale of liquor, in itself illegal, as there was a liquor ban in effect in the Southern Highlands at that time.

The years leading up to the Sandline crisis served up a bumper crop of astonishing deals in PNG ranging from a billion-kina Build, Operate and Transfer (BOT) contract with a Malaysian shelf company for the upgrading of Port Moresby's water supply to a twentieth-anniversary coffee table book that cost the State K2.5 million. The man who sold this ludicrously expensive publishing project to the Chan Government was from Iceland. Gudmundur Fridriksson had met and married an Air Niugini flight attendant who happened to be the niece of Sir Julius Chan's Chief of Staff. His proposal was to produce an expensive, glossy book to mark the twentieth anniversary of PNG's independence in September 1995, which Government Ministers could present as gifts to visitors. Some Ministers were apparently so taken with the idea that they ordered thousands of copies of the book, at K75 a copy, to be paid for by their departments. He produced 34,000 copies but the book was an embarrassment to PNG. It was full of factual errors and technically it was seriously flawed. Fridriksson had never produced a book before but he was given the job without any tenders being called.

Fridriksson hired another Icelandic gentleman, Jon Steinsson, to be in charge of quality control. They later had a falling out. Steinsson told ABC Radio/Television that neither he nor the writers he hired and brought to PNG knew anything about the country before their arrival. They were surprised at the hostility they encountered. 'We soon discovered that there were obstacles regarding this project because we found out that this was not a project that had everybody's backing.' Steinsson discovered there were serious concerns within sections of the bureaucracy about Ministers committing scarce departmental funds to a coffee table book. 'We got stonewalled almost everywhere.' One of the few Ministers to oppose the deal, Peter Barter, then Health Minister, found that his department has been signed up anyway. 'In the Health Department we had to chase the Minister for an interview for I don't know how long,' Steinsson said. 'We finally caught up with him and it was a great interview but I understood his dilemma. I think he had a bad conscience about taking part in this because at the time we were reading in the paper something that worried us all. There was no money available for medicine. People where dying. And here we were writing a book that was to be paid for by a government department that couldn't afford, you know, simple bandaids in rural Papua New Guinea.'

The production of *Destination Papua New Guinea*, as the book was called, turned into a fiasco. Fridriksson sacked Steinsson and his artwork production company before any of the finishing touches were put to the book. Steinsson locked up the computer disks which Fridriksson then paid someone in Malaysia to crack and the resulting jumble is clearly evident in the final product. The saga reached the point of high farce when, during the court case in Port Moresby between them, Fridriksson, under cross-examination in the dock, said he had taken over responsibility for all colour separations after he had sacked Steinsson. 'But you are colour blind aren't you?' asked Steinsson's lawyer. The reply from Fridriksson: 'Yes.' Fridriksson was paid the full K2.5 million even though the factually inaccurate and poorly finished book missed its deadline and was delivered three months after the Independence Day anniversary in 1995.

One deal very much in the news in 1995 and 1996 was the purchase in late 1994 by PNG's Public Officers Superannuation Fund (POSF) of a property in Cairns, North Queensland, for $A18.72 million from Katingo Pty Ltd, a company owned by the Australian property developer, Warren Anderson. The *Australian Financial Review* revealed that Anderson had bought the propery, the Conservatory, only one month before selling it to the POSF, for half what the PNG super fund paid for it. PNG's Auditor General launched a major investigation into the deal and in his report, tabled in the Parliament in 1997, Makena Geno found that the POSF had 'imprudently invested in an overvalued asset'. Geno was critical that the POSF had relied on valuations provided by the vendor. He asked the Australian Valuation Office in Brisbane for an assessment. 'As at period October–November 1994, the market value of the subject property,' its valuation report said, 'is considered to be Eight Million Dollars'.

Sir Julius Chan approved the property deal in late 1994 arguing that there was a Cabinet decision made in April 1994, when he was Deputy Prime Minister and Minister for Foreign Affairs, for a rationalisation of all PNG offices abroad. The idea was that the Cairns Consulate and the Air Niugini office in Cairns would be co-located and that the Government would take a headlease on the Conservatory. The Government signed up to take the headlease for seven years from early 1995 at $A700 per square metre. The Auditor General reported that this rental was twice what the PNG Consul said the Consulate was paying for its preferred office site located in another, more impressive building. In mid-1998 neither the Consulate nor Air Niugini had moved into the Conservatory and the arcade-like property was substantially vacant. However, the PNG Government still held the headlease and was paying the POSF $A2.1 million a year in rent. The POSF Board defended itself from attack claiming that the property was a good investment because the Fund was getting a healthy return. Indeed it was. PNG's taxpayers were the big losers.

In his report Auditor General Geno referred to the involvement of both Prime Minister Chan and the Deputy Prime Minister and Minister for Finance, Chris Haiveta, in the property transaction. 'A discernible nexus between politicians and public servants is clearly evident in the Conservatory building purchase saga,' he said. 'This relationship has resulted in incorrect economic and financial decisions being taken to the detriment of ... the country.' Although this report was not tabled until well after the Sandline crisis, the story that senior Government Ministers had played a major role in ensuring that the PNG public service superannuation fund had bought a property in Cairns allegedly for twice what it was worth was all over the PNG newspapers during 1996. By March of 1997 when Brigadier Singirok arrested the mercenaries, claimed the Sandline deal was corrupt and demanded that Chan and Haiveta resign, he was speaking to an audience ready to believe it.

Sir Paul Hasluck had never been keen on Papua New Guineans looking to Africa for examples to follow. In the early 1960s, as decolonisation swept across the African continent, Sir Paul was dismissive of many of the newly independent African states in which the facade of democracy quickly collapsed. In an address delivered at the end of his term as Minister for External Territories in 1963, he said his objective had been to create the conditions that would allow sustainable self-government for the people of PNG. 'For success a self-governing country,' he said, 'needs not only a parliament but also a competent public service; an independent judiciary and magistracy; a sufficient number of educated and competent men to become candidates for public office; and a sufficient number of knowledgeable persons to give popular leadership in the electorate ... Building a public service, helping a country to become economically viable and laying a broad base for political activity are all much more difficult than creating representative institutions or drafting constitutions.'

The late Sir Paul would have been horrified to learn that some thirty-four years after he delivered that speech, the Government of an independent PNG would hire mercenaries from Africa to help it try to crush a local insurgency. The full details of how that contract came about is the subject of the rest of this book. But who were they? Who were these 'diamond dogs of war' as some sections of the British media labelled them? Following the aborting of the Sandline contract there were two major inquiries conducted in Papua New Guinea. The first, before Justice Warwick Andrew, was established by Sir Julius Chan in an attempt to defuse the crisis and in response to Singirok's call for an independent inquiry. Justice Andrew held public hearings throughout April 1997 and presented his report at the end of May, just a couple of weeks before PNG held its five-yearly national elections. The second inquiry, with much broader terms of reference, was set up by the incoming government led by Bill Skate. It was a three-member commission of inquiry headed by Justice Kubulan Los who was assisted by two senior magistrates, Raphael Apa and Mekeo Gauli. The Los Inquiry began its public hearings in September 1997 and heard evidence on more than sixty days over the following six months. When this book went to press in July 1998, the release of the Inquiry's final report had been delayed yet again.

Justice Andrew devoted one whole chapter of his report to Sandline International and to Sandline's sub-contractor, Executive Outcomes. Quoting from Sandline's own corporate profile the Judge said it described itself as a 'stand alone' company 'established to offer military consultancy and related services'. Sandline claimed it sourced 'personnel and equipment from its own resources and from subcontractors such as Executive Outcomes (EO)'. Sandline was 'incorporated in the British Virgin Islands ... originally registered as Castle Engineering on 2nd July 1993 ... its name was changed to Sandline on 2nd December 1996'. Tim Spicer, the profile said, was 'authorised to act in the capacity of Chief Executive Officer (CEO) of the company'. For somebody occupying such a position, the ex-British Army Lieutenant Colonel seemed amazingly ignorant as to who owned Sandline. The information provided to the inquiry simply stated that Sandline International was 100 per cent owned by another company, Adson Holdings. But no information whatsoever was supplied about Adson, and Spicer told Justice Andrew he did not know who the beneficial shareholders were. The Judge went on to make his own findings based on the evidence he was able to unearth. But first a short profile of Timothy Spicer and a look into Sandline's origins.

'I spent twenty years in the British Army rising in a natural progression through the officer ranks,' Spicer said in an exclusive interview after the conclusion of his evidence to the Andrew Inquiry in April 1997. He had passed out of the Sandhurst Royal Military Academy in 1976, winning the Sword of Honour, and was commissioned into the Scots Guards. One fellow student was later to tell a diplomat at the British High Commission in Port Moresby he had been the most 'unpopular fellow' in the class. 'I had a very interesting and active career in the British Army,' Spicer said. 'I was involved in the Falklands campaign. I spent a lot of time in Northern Ireland. I was involved in the Gulf War and Bosnia.' Asked about the nickname 'Tumbledown Tim' a British journalist had given him, Spicer chuckled. 'I don't really know but it has some connotation with the Falklands campaign. I was involved in the battle for Tumbledown Mountain. I was the Operations Officer and involved in the planning and execution of the operation. I assume it came from there.' During the Gulf War, Spicer was Military Assistant (MA) to the Commander of the British forces in Operation Desert Storm, General Sir Peter De La Billiere. He was awarded the OBE by the British Government in 1993 and in 1994 was MA and spokesman for General Sir Michael Rose in Sarajevo, Bosnia.

'When I left the Army [in 1995] I spent some time working in the City, in London, for a financial institution,' Spicer said, 'and during that time some friends of mine who were involved with the concept of what was later to become Sandline asked me if I'd join them. It's obviously something that I enjoy doing and my military experience was useful in that regard.' Asked to elaborate on what this concept was, Spicer explained: 'The Sandline concept has evolved since the end of the Cold War, whereby the military capability of national governments is reduced as part of the so-called "peace dividend" while at the same time localised conflict has increased. And superimposed on that there is a lack of will for national governments to involve their own national forces, their rather smaller national forces, in conflicts that don't necessarily have anything to do with their own country. And you find a gap in which some governments, less well developed governments and military forces, require some expertise and support. The Sandline idea was to be able to provide that expertise and support whether it be consultancy, training, support for military operations or procurement of equipment.' Spicer paused. 'For legitimate governments,' he said, 'we will work only for legitimate governments.'

Two governments in Africa, he claimed, had already benefited from the assistance provided by the interests that eventually registered Sandline as a company. 'The concept was already there, it was instrumental in introducing military support in the guise of Executive Outcomes to both the Angolan and the Sierra Leone governments.' The British businessman, Anthony Buckingham, set up the first of these introductions in 1993. Buckingham, a former British soldier who had served in the Special Air Service (SAS), was the Chairman of Heritage Oil and Gas, a company registered in the Bahamas, which had millions of dollars worth of oil drilling and related equipment located in the coastal Angolan town of Soyo. Soyo had fallen into the hands of the UNITA rebels. Buckingham arranged for the Angolan state oil company, Sonagol, to contract the South African based Executive Outcomes to help recapture the port. 'In March 1993 EO's fifty men launched a surprise ground attack on Soyo,' Yves Goulet wrote in *Jane's Intelligence Review* (September 1997), 'supported by three helicopters and the unsuccessful amphibious landing of two brigades from the Angolan Armed Forces. The oil installations were seized after a week of fighting, although they were retaken by UNITA a few weeks after EO's withdrawal.' But not before Buckingham's company had recovered its equipment.

'EO's role soon came to the attention of the Angolan Armed Forces (FAA),' an Executive Outcomes brief carried on its own Internet site stated. 'By this time [mid-1993] UNITA had effectively beaten the government forces on the battlefield and had mustered rebel control over more than seventy per cent of Angola. EO was awarded with the contract to train the FAA's newly [re]established 16th Brigade, a brigade which had been virtually destroyed by the SADF [South African Defence Force] in the 1980s. This irony was not lost on EO!' The reason Executive Outcomes found it so ironic was that EO's boss, Eeben Barlow, had been one of the senior officers in the SADF's elite 32nd Battalion which had been operating in Angola under the name of the Buffalo Battalion in the 1980s in support of UNITA. Troops under Barlow's command had inflicted those heavy losses on the 16th Brigade. A lot had changed in ten years, however. South Africa had emerged from the apartheid era and the formerly Soviet and Cuban backed Marxist Popular Movement had won a national election in 1992. 'Elements of the newly trained brigade were soon rushed into action against rebel forces and excelled themselves in battle,' EO boasted. 'The brigade later captured strategic diamond mining areas held by UNITA, thus denying the rebels their major source of income.'

Executive Outcomes won two consecutive one-year contracts each worth $US40 million from the Angolan Government. It deployed up to 500 men who trained troops and pilots, directed the front line operations and fought alongside the men they trained. 'Angolan Armed Forces successes were overwhelmingly credited to EO-directed operations,' Goulet wrote, 'which included the disruption of UNITA's command and control centres, the exploitation of UNITA's rear area and its focus on the oil and diamond assets held by UNITA.' EO's own claim is that it was the actions of the 16th Brigade that 'marked the beginning of the end' for UNITA. 'Additional units, trained by EO, utilised new tactics and training, launching raids and strikes at UNITA troop concentrations,' it said. 'Growing FAA morale and heavy UNITA casualties soon led to the signing of the Lusaka Protocols [November 1994], effectively ending the long civil war in Angola.' The United States, which had poured $US15 million worth of CIA funds into supporting UNITA in the last years of the Reagan Administration, applied pressure and the Angolan Government officially asked EO to leave in January 1996.

Another company in which Buckingham held substantial interests, Branch Energy, became a diamond miner in Angola and it also obtained diamond concessions in the next country to which Buckingham introduced Executive Outcomes, Sierra Leone. In early 1995 Sierra Leone's former President, Valentine Strasser, contracted EO to help his forces hold off the rebel Revolutionary United Front (RUF) which had reached the outskirts of the capital, Freetown. 'At that time,' Goulet wrote, 'the RUF, in association with rogue elements within the country's army, was in control of the Sierra Rutile titanium oxide mine and the Sierramoco bauxite mine, which together accounted for fifty-seven per cent of the country's official export earnings.' In April–May of 1995, according to Goulet, 285 of EO's 'advisers' arrived in Freetown. EO's own account is that its men rapidly 'restructured and retrained' the Sierra Leone Defence Force (SLDF) and took the battle to the rebels. 'This caught the RUF off-guard and the SLDF rapidly gained the initiative, forcing the rebels to withdraw. Using different tactics,' EO said, 'the SLDF launched a series of strikes, raids, ambushes and offensives, inflicting heavy casualties on the RUF.' Elections were eventually held and Strasser's ruling military council handed over the government to a civilian president in 1996.

Executive Outcomes withdrew from Sierra Leone in February 1997 but the peace the company helped impose did not last. The civilian president, Ahmed Tejan Kabbah, was overthrown in late 1997 and in early 1998 Sandline International was heavily involved in helping restore him to power. Tim Spicer was back in the world headlines in May of 1998 after the matter became an international embarrassment for the British Foreign Minister, Robin Cook, because the United Nations had placed an arms supply embargo on Sierra Leone. Spicer, through his lawyers, claimed Sandline had received help from the Foreign Office. Cook set up an inquiry into the messy affair. However, a couple of years earlier, in 1996, when Spicer and Buckingham were trying to convince PNG Government Ministers of the benefits of hiring the Sandline-Executive Outcomes combination, the Sierra Leone adventure was still very much regarded as a success and it was one of their positive marketing points. Also, the way the government of Sierra Leone had paid for EO's services was suggested as an example PNG could follow. Sierra Leone had bartered mining concessions when it was unable to fully fund in cash its mercenaries' contract (reportedly worth $US15 million per year). Spicer and Buckingham were to suggest that PNG could do a similar deal to help pay for its far more expensive option (initially $US30 million– eventually $US36 million) to fix the Bougainville rebel problem.

Also in 1996, the activities of private military companies began attracting wider attention. During October 1996 a United Nations Special Rapporteur, Enrique Bernales Ballesteros, visited South Africa following reports that the Pretoria-based Executive Outcomes had 'allegedly been sending mercenaries to Angola and Sierra Leone under contracts concluded with the Governments of those countries in exchange for substantial cash payments and mining concessions'. Ballesteros spoke to Eeben Barlow and to various South African authorities. In his report, presented in February 1997, he raised a series of pertinent questions about this new phenomenon of privatising war. He presented a detailed account of his meeting on 25 October 1996 with Barlow and EO's Financial Director, Nico Palm. 'Mr Barlow said that his company had been established in 1989,' the Special Rapporteur noted, 'and was officially registered in Pretoria as a security service company.

It was, however, part of a holding company, Strategic Resources Corporation (SRC), which included companies with various social purposes that provided different economic services.' Ballesteros reported that Barlow claimed that the 'victory by the Angolan Government forces had marked the end of various kinds of illicit traffic in the country, such as traffic in marble, diamonds, weapons and munitions' but that it 'had earned Executive Outcomes many new enemies, especially among arms dealers interested in keeping wars going'.

However, Barlow told him business was booming and that SRC had received inquiries from no fewer than thirty-four countries. 'The other firms in the holding company provide various services, including medical and phamaceutical services, hospital construction and equipment, civil engineering, water purification, drinking water supplies, transport etc.' Ballesteros asked Barlow why he thought he, his employees and his company were regarded as mercenaries. 'He answered that his men never saw themselves as mercenaries: "We see ourselves more as soldiers and as Africans, out to help other Africans."' The UN Special Rapporteur was told by South African Major General Coetzee from the Intelligence Department of the South African Defence Force that once companies like EO had 'stabilised' the country they entered 'there were enormous opportunities for [them] to make money'. He also found that the South African authorities were concerned about how much Executive Outcomes could pay its employees. 'According to the information obtained, about 700 persons are regularly employed by this company (soldiers, police, doctors, pilots, engineers, technicians, etc.), with high salaries; the salaries of every rank from general to non-commissioned officer may be five times higher than in an army such as that of South Africa and definitely ten times higher or more than in other African States.'

Executive Outcomes is not shy about publicity and believes in promoting itself and its services. Its Internet site provides considerable detail about what it can do and is willing to offer clients. 'During its brief history,' it says proudly, 'EO has operated in support of Armed Forces, Law Enforcement Agencies and Private Corporations in Southern Africa, West Africa, South America and the Far East ... The men of EO are primarily ex-South African Defence Force (SADF), as well as ex-South African National Defence Force (after 1994), ex-South African Police (SAP) and ex-African National Congress (ANC) members. The criteria for prospective employees are that they must: have had military or police training; ... be prepared to work outside South Africa; carry "no political baggage"; [and] be prepared to work in high-risk environments.' And with the end of the apartheid era it has no shortage of manpower to call on. 'Due to the mass "down-sizing" of the Armed Forces of South Africa,' it says, 'EO is able to draw on a large, professional workforce and can call on over 2000 men at very short notice.'

Executive Outcomes even claims to have developed a new military term– discretionary warfare. 'During the early 1990s,' the company says, 'EO was also approached by a South American Drug Enforcement Agency (DEA) to provide them with advice on countering the growing drug trafficking problem in South America. EO's advice was "take the problem to the producers"– a strategy which led to the formation and training of a highly specialised team of soldiers who would operate outside the normal military brief, working closely with the host DEA and police intelligence. These troops deployed clandestinely into drug-growing areas and conducted raids and strikes against the drug lords with great success. This term of counter-drug operations later became known as Discretionary Warfare.' In a section headed 'What the Corporation can offer' EO touts its 'success' record. 'Employing a highly professional workforce, with more than 5000 man-years of military knowledge, combat and training experience, the corporation is probably the largest of its type in the world.' And it supplies details of twenty-three assistance packages EO can provide, ranging from 'Basic Infantry Training' to 'Discretionary Warfare'.

The United Nations Special Rapporteur posed a number of difficult questions for members of the United Nations in his report. 'Can it be,' he asked, 'that the mercenaries' behaviour is changing so profoundly that they now constitute the rank and file of the personnel recruited by private companies to contract with African Governments to provide internal security services, safeguard public order and even put an end to internal armed conflicts? If such contracts are, indeed, being concluded, the Governments signing them must be doing so on the basis of a sovereign decision; but ... responsibility for a country's internal order and security [is] an inalienable obligation that a State fulfils through its police and armed forces,' he said. 'Is it not a grave infringement of that State's sovereignty to hand over such responsibilities to companies registered in third countries which sell security services staffed by foreigners, presumably mercenaries? Who will be responsible for any repressive excesses that the security companies may commit against the civilian population? ... Who will take responsibility for any violations of international humanitarian law or human rights they may commit?'

'It is obvious that the ambiguity of existing provisions,' Ballesteros went on, 'the gaps in national legislation and the insecurity which prevails in many countries, as well as the end-of-century tendency to privatise everything in sight, have created the conditions for the establishment of this new type of company, which is organised to sell security in the international market to client countries from which it obtains contracts worth millions, protection and links to powerful companies dealing in oil, minerals and precious stones; the results are the growth and expansion of these companies and their presence in the countries with which the contractual relationship has been established ... The point is that there is now a type of company which offers full security services on the free and globalised international market that have till now been the exclusive responsibility of each State's own internal security system. If States are prepared to give up an intrinsic element of their sovereignty, this is something which should be clearly stated and which the United Nations should analyse in depth because it really would affect and change the nature, structure and functions of the State, while, at the same time changing the nature of international relations.'

A major feature of the operation of Executive Outcomes and its holding company, Strategic Resources Corporation, is that once the job of cleaning up the civil war is done, other companies in the group move in to reap the benefits. Goulet argued in his article in *Jane's Intelligence Review* that: 'The genius behind EO is that, with the help of its "associate" companies, it can barter its services for mining or energy concessions, security contracts, air transport licences and other business opportunities. This flexibility is probably its greatest asset, since these kinds of arrangements are often the only way for governments of poor countries like Sierra Leone, which had domestic revenues totalling only $US60 million in 1994 and 1995, to get the protection they desperately want.' Goulet claimed that 100 of the 285 EO operatives remained in Sierra Leone after EO pulled out and were hired by a sister SRC company, Lifeguard.

Before the Andrew Inquiry, Spicer claimed that there were no corporate links whatsoever between Sandline and Executive Outcomes—that the two companies were 'arm's length', one subcontracting the other. But Justice Andrew did his own investigations and did not believe him. The corporate profile Sandline provided to the Judge claimed that while Buckingham had 'provided advice' he was not employed by Sandline. However, it said both Sandline and Buckingham's Heritage Oil and Gas had contracts with a UK-registered company, Plaza 107, which provided both of them with representative services in the UK. 'Sandline is one of several overseas companies who enjoy management and support services provided by Plaza 107,' the profile said. 'The owner of Plaza 107 is Michael Grunberg, who is also a director. Mr Grunberg also provided consulting services to client companies and for example assisted Sandline with the drafting and negotiation of the contract with PNG.'

The profile denied that Plaza 107 represented Executive Outcomes or any of its affiliated companies. 'EO is entirely separate from Sandline,

Heritage Oil and Gas and Plaza 107. Further, there are no cross-holdings between Sandline, Heritage Oil and Gas and Plaza 107. In a nutshell, Sandline and Heritage are two distinct clients of Plaza 107 in the UK, and EO is an arm's-length sub-contractor of Sandline.' In fact, the Andrew Inquiry was told, there were two companies going by the name of Executive Outcomes. One was the Pretoria-based company incorporated in South Africa whose principal activity was said to be to provide military training, consultancy and other related services. Its listed directors were Lafras Luitingh and Nico Palm, each one holding fifty per cent of the shares. The other Executive Outcomes was incorporated in England and Wales and its directors were Luther Eeben Barlow and his wife, Susan Barlow. Eeben Barlow held seventy per cent of the shares and Mrs Barlow, thirty per cent.

Justice Andrew concluded that the 'controllers of Sandline International' were 'obviously Mr Buckingham, Mr Grunberg and at least to some extent Mr Spicer'. And he also established a link which seemed to destroy the protestations that Sandline and Executive Outcomes had no corporate connection. 'The Commission inspected documents in Hong Kong including a Hong Kong Bank account in the name of Sandline Holdings,' the Judge reported, 'into which the $US18 million [the first half of the $US36 million contract] was remitted from PNG and received on the 5th February 1997. The signatories to that account are Simon Francis Mann, Lafras Luitingh, Luther Eeben Barlow and Anthony L. R. Buckingham. That would indicate,' the Judge concluded, 'that Mr Luitingh and Mr Barlow, who are the principles of Executive Outcomes, have a direct interest in Sandline Holdings Ltd. It would be an unusual case,' he said, 'if a sub-contractor or contractor somehow had access to one's own bank account and became a signatory to that account. There is a strong inference that Sandline Holdings Limited may be something of a joint venture between the interests of Mr Buckingham and the interests of Mr Barlow and Executive Outcomes. The information provided by Sandline Holdings that they are entirely separate from Executive Outcomes cannot be correct, but the exact nature of their relationship seems clouded behind a web of interlocking companies whose ownership is difficult to trace.'

That web became even more complicated in October 1996, when Branch Energy was taken over by the Canadian-listed company, Diamond Works. After Goulet reported in *Janes Intelligence Review* that Buckingham and the other main players in the Branch Energy group held the majority of the shares in Diamond works, Grunberg put out a statement rejecting the assertion. 'Diamond Works,' he said, 'is a publicly quoted company and the shares are widely held. The owners of Branch Energy are now significant shareholders of Diamond Works but do not hold the majority of the shares.'

He also challenged another claim of Goulet's, that Branch Energy had gone into partnership with members of the Sierra Leone Government to mine diamonds. It was not a partnership, he said, just an agreement on how profits would be shared. 'Thirty per cent of the future profit stream from the Koidu lease granted to Branch Energy is retained by the State and this was a negotiated term as per the original lease application,' Grunberg stated. Justice Andrew found that Buckingham, Grunberg and the others had a keen interest in extending their resource extraction activities beyond Africa. 'The Panguna mine owned by Bougainville Copper Limited is one of the richest copper mines in the world,' he stated in his final report. 'It is apparent that the Sandline interests kept an eye on gaining an interest in the mine.'

In March 1997 as he was preparing the detailed plans for Operation Rausim Kwik, Major Walter Enuma scoured the Internet to find out what he could about Sandline and Executive Outcomes. One article that had wide circulation, from the February 1997 edition of *Harper's* magazine, dealt in some detail with EO's operations, especially in Sierra Leone. Written by contributing editor Elizabeth Rubin, who had visited the Koidu diamond fields, it analysed the success the mercenaries had achieved. 'The South African mercenaries,' she wrote, 'camped on a nearby hilltop overlooking Koidu, were unreservedly hailed by the chiefs, the businessmen and the street people as saviours.' However, Major Enuma probably took more notice of one of Rubin's other paragraphs, drawing conclusions from what she had seen. 'So today, President Kabbah's primary partnership is not with the people who elected him but with a multinational corporation, one that secures his power with force and paves the way for other foreign investment to fill the government coffers. Such monies, however, never seem to trickle down to the benefit of the people, particularly those in the provinces, where basic amenities such as electricity, water, roads and phones barely exist.'

The origins of the Bougainville war—grief over land loss; anger at environmental damage by mining; the misallocation of benefits; intergenerational animosity; government neglect; ethnic hatred; a perceived historical wrong; and social dislocation—have been studied hard in PNG and some of the lessons seem to have been learned, at least by the major resource developers elsewhere in Papua New Guinea, wanting to avoid the mistakes made by CRA. But as 1997 began, Sir Julius Chan's Government seemed to ignore completely all those lessons about how to cope in Melanesia. And, driven by other motives, not the least of which was Chan's own fervent desire to win an election in his own right, chose the folly of hiring these mercenaries specialising in African wars.

Chapter Two

The Bougainville War

*A Background History to the Secession Conflict
(to 1995)*

'The only thing a powerless man can do is commit suicide. That is why,' John Momis told other Bougainvilleans gathered during one of the many failed attempts to find peace, 'we have embarked on a suicidal approach to life.' Momis, the Member for Bougainville and a former Catholic priest, chose an apt metaphor. For almost a decade the people of Bougainville seemed to be on a mission of self-destruction. More than five per cent of the province's population of 160,000 died in that period, either violently or from preventable diseases. And many of those killed in a violent way died at the hands of other Bougainvilleans. Any examination of the Papua New Guinea Government's extraordinary decision to hire mercenaries to try to crush the rebellion on Bougainville must start with Bougainville itself. Why did the conflict, which started out as a factional landowner revolt against mining, develop into an intractable secessionist, then civil, war—a war which everybody, at least up until 1997, seemed powerless to stop?

When Sir Julius Chan became Prime Minister for the second time in 1994, he made negotiating a resolution of the Bougainville problem his number one priority. However, like Rabbie Namaliu and Paias Wingti before him, Chan found that the leader of the revolution, Francis Ona, was absolutely intransigent. Infuriated by Ona's total rejection of his peace initiatives and frustrated by the inability of the PNG Defence Force to gain the ascendancy, Sir Julius became tantalised by Sandline's promise to render Ona's Bougainville Revolutionary Army (BRA) 'militarily ineffective' in time for the 1997 PNG elections. The self-proclaimed President of Bougainville and Supreme Commander of the BRA did not trust Sir Julius nor any other

PNG leader. Ona never deviated from what he saw as his destiny—leading Bougainville back to a pre-contact, self-reliant, subsistence independence free from the contamination of outside influence, no matter what the cost.

'For those who refuse to understand, and for those who came in late,' Ona stated emphatically in July 1996, the eighth year of the secessionist conflict, 'let it be known that there can be no peace before independence. Short of that it remains a war situation until we celebrate military victory.' He was commenting on proposals, supported by the Bougainville Transitional Premier, Theodore Miriung, that Bougainville be granted some special autonomous state within the nation of Papua New Guinea. Ona reiterated the steadfast position he had held since the beginning of the conflict in 1988. He would not attend any talks until the PNG Government capitulated. 'We have business to complete,' Ona said, 'and no time to waste on fruitless negotiations.'

Secession had been on the political agenda of many Bougainvilleans prior to PNG's independence from Australia in 1975 and long before Francis Ona became its champion. Geographically, Bougainville is closer to the Shortland Islands and Choiseul in the Solomon Islands than it is to the rest of PNG. Its incorporation into PNG was the result of the same nineteenth-century colonial map division that has rendered Irian Jaya part of Indonesia. However, the ethnic argument often advanced by the secessionists and their sympathisers that Bougainvilleans are 'physically, culturally and socially' more akin to Solomon Islanders than to other Papua New Guineans is not entirely true and ignores the complexity of Melanesia.

The Bougainvilleans' distinctive very black skin is shared by people in the most western islands of the Solomons group. But further down the Solomons chain, on Guadalcanal and Malaita for instance, and even further down into Vanuatu and New Caledonia, the physical appearance and skin colour of the people is similar to that of those Melanesians living in PNG's Bismarck Archipelago north-west of Bougainville. And some New Irelanders are as dark as Bougainvilleans. Indeed, the argument has been put that the five New Guinea Island provinces—Manus, New Ireland, East and West New Britain and Bougainville—should be grouped together as a federated state. Sir John Kerr, later to become Australia's most controversial Governor General, put that proposition forward in 1965, ten years before PNG's independence, when, as Justice Kerr, he was Director of the Council on New Guinea Affairs. In 1993 when the PNG Parliament was moving to abolish provincial governments, the Premiers of these island provinces discussed seceding as a block from mainland PNG and corresponded with Solomon Islands leaders about the idea.

Prior to outside contact, Bougainville was not a unified political entity. The people were divided into nineteen language groups and a further thirty-five dialects were spoken. Ona had to abandon the name he first chose for his intended republic, Mekamui, because, while it meant 'sacred land' in his Nasioi people's tongue, it was an obscenity in at least one of the other languages, Halia. The indigenous revolutionaries had to revert to the imposed name taken from an eighteenth-century French navigator (Louis de Bougainville). 'Bukas', the name by which the black-skinned Bougainvilleans became known in the rest of PNG during the Australian colonial era, came from the island just to the north of Bougainville, Buka, where about one-quarter of the province's population live. That name (meaning 'What?' in Halia and shouted at Louis de Bougainville's expedition in 1768 and part of a challenge to unwelcome strangers suggesting they were lost) might have been more appropriate. But the people of Buka were the first to split from Ona's proposed Nasioi-led independent Bougainville. Like in the rest of Melanesia, the traditional history of relations between neighbouring language groups was more likely to have been one of hostility than of cooperation.

The first serious attempt to establish an independent Bougainville nation, in the early to mid-1970s, gained impetus from the establishment of the giant open-cut Bougainville Copper Mine in 1972. But, unlike Ona, none of the three most prominent leaders of that movement was from the area most affected by the mine. John Momis was from Buin in South Bougainville, Alexis Sarei from Buka and Leo Hannett from Nissan Island north of Buka. All three had developed their political awareness while training to be Catholic priests. Momis had studied the plight of the landowners and wrote in 1971 that 'it is the tragedy of the Nasioi that the economic benefits [of the mine] are not distributed in the same manner as the social costs'. The independence they declared on 1 September 1975, fifteen days before Papua New Guinea's independence, had significant popular support and was blessed by the Catholic Bishop of Bougainville, Bishop Gregory Singkai. Eleven months later, after extensive negotiations with Prime Minister Michael Somare, they agreed to a union with PNG on the guarantee of provincial government.

Analysing the costs and benefits—two views

The closure of the Panguna copper mine represented a huge economic loss for Papua New Guinea. The Government was a part-owner holding nineteen per cent of the shares in Bougainville Copper Limited (BCL). Up until the mine was closed in May 1989, the company paid more than one billion Australian dollars in tax and dividends to the PNG Government, $33 million to landowners ($28.5 million in compensation and $4.5 million in royalties), and another $83 million in royalties to the Provincial Government. It built two towns, a port and a power station, provided jobs for 3500 people, trained more than 10 000 tradesmen, and provided PNG with forty-five per cent of its exports.

None of those figures impressed the new Panguna Landowners Association, which complained that landowners had received little benefit. What they objected to most was that the company had removed 1.215 billion tonnes of their land and turned 99.4 per cent of it into waste. They blamed the company for the extinction of the flying fox and rejected a study that explained it had been the result of an epidemic introduced from East New Britain. They alleged mining had retarded crop growth, poisoned mango, banana and pawpaw trees, killed off wild pigs and possums, and given fish ulcers. BCL, to their minds, was a scourge on the island: 'Our children are born with so many birth defects', one statement released in 1989 said, 'deformed legs, arms and whole body. We don't remember this happening so often before. So many people become old so quickly and so many die now. Before, the girls would have developed breasts before they began to menstruate, today the girls are very young when they menstruate.'

Significantly, the political leaders of the second secession movement, Francis Ona and Joseph Kabui, were both from the copper mine lease area. Kabui was the elected Premier of Bougainville, heading the Provincial Government, and was from a village that had been relocated to make way for open cut mining. Ona, from a village on a ridge above the pit, had worked as a surveyor at the mine. After an argument with his boss he gave up that job to drive one of BCL's ore dump trucks. He quit altogether in November 1988, furious at the findings of an environmental study by independent New Zealand consultants. The PNG Government had commissioned the study into landowner complaints about pollution. The report was critical of certain company practices but its conclusion that the water in the Jaba River was not toxic angered Ona. He maintained that the landowners knew that all the fish in the river had been killed off by chemical poisoning. And he refused to accept the consultants' conclusion that the fish had deserted the waterway mainly because it was full of sediment and too dirty for them. Ona stormed out of the meeting at which the results were presented. A few days later explosives were stolen from the mine magazine and towards the end of

1988 Ona launched a campaign of sabotage and terror against BCL.

A little over a year before, Ona had become General Secretary of the new Panguna Landowners Association. This had been formed by a group of disaffected younger landowners in 1987 to overthrow the old association executive, which was comprised of older men, representatives of the 850 officially recognised land title holders in the areas leased to BCL. The leases covered the road corridor up from the east coast port of Loloho to the mine in the Crown Prince Range, the mine itself and its tailings dumping area down the Jaba River, which extended to Empress Augusta Bay on the west coast, an area with an indigenous population of some six thousand. Neither Ona nor Kabui were registered title holders. They and all the other non-title holding landowners were classified as beneficiaries. The members of the new Landowners Association believed the old men were being duped or bought off by the company. One of their major grievances, however, was that these officially recognised title holders were not the true traditional owners of the land.

Under the customary law of the Nasioi the land ownership system is matrilineal—the land passes in trust from the mother of the landowning group to the eldest daughter. But when the Australian patrol officers were compiling the list of title holders in the 1960s most of those registered were not the elder sisters who, traditionally and culturally, were supposed to be the caretakers of the land. It was the men the Australians dealt with. For instance, Matthew Kove, Ona's uncle, was on the old executive. He had signed on behalf of his sister who could not write. Kove, who had built the finest house in Ona's village, Guava, was one of the first murdered in the crisis. He was abducted by the BRA in early 1989 and killed. The mine management had refused to deal with the new association and claimed the old executive was the legitimate legal landowner entity. This acrimonious dispute between the 850 'title holders' and the more disgruntled amongst the 5000 plus 'beneficiaries' was a critical element in the build up to the crisis.

Ironically the coming of the mine led to better education for the women, some of whom came to resent the glaring injustice of what was happening, especially in those family groups where the 'title holder' did not share the benefit payments with the 'beneficiaries' as equally as custom required. Ona's first cousin, Perpetua Serero, became Chair of the new Landowners Association. She was one of the most passionate about the destruction caused by open-cut mining. 'The natural state of our land has been exploited and all our resources have been gone forever,' she said a few days after Ona and his followers in the bush started sabotaging the mine in late November

1988. 'The people think this land will never be restored to its natural state. That's why my people are demanding ten billion kina.' Equivalent at the time to $A15 billion, this was the new Panguna Landowner Association's compensation demand, along with half of all profits made by BCL and tighter controls over pollution. 'When the mine started most of my people were ignorant,' Serero said. 'I was a small girl when the company came and I have grown with the company. And I know what's good and what's bad!'

The company, a subsidiary of Conzinc Rio Tinto Australia (CRA), came in the late 1960s, encouraged by the Australian administration (in turn encouraged by the World Bank), which wanted to develop a cash economy for PNG. CRA held the majority ownership, some fifty-three per cent. About twenty-eight per cent was floated and the shares were traded on the Australian Stock Exchange while nineteen per cent was bought by the Australian Government for the future independent State of PNG. This did not mean much to those most affected. The local people vigorously opposed mining from the start. In 1967 one villager said losing land was like taking 'the bones out of a man's legs, the man would not be able to walk'. Speaking in 1989, Bishop Gregory Singkai described the people's regard for their land as equivalent to their life: 'So precious that you can say land is what they live on, live off. They cannot do without it. Not like in any other country where you live on cash.'

Emeritus PNG History Professor Jim Griffin has described the Australian administration's negotiations to acquire the land as 'astonishingly crass'. The people were told that, although their land contained fabulous riches, they did not own the minerals, the administration did. Father Bob Wiley, an American Catholic priest who spent many years in Bougainville, told of Australia's then External Territories Minister, Charles Barnes, flying into the area in the late 1960s: 'He got off and he said, "You get nothing." And he hopped back on the helicopter and was gone. The people just shook their heads. Right from the beginning frustration built.'

The Bougainville people were highly suspicious anyway of the motives of outsiders. J.P. Reynolds wrote in 1970 that the continued opposition to the copper project indicated 'the fear and distrust' many Bougainvilleans had of attempts by the administration and expatriate companies 'to promote economic development which they feel is just another ruse by which the European will exploit the local people and their resources for his own ends'. Cecilia Gemel, another member of the new association's executive, explained why the war had begun: 'We women who have been the backbone of the land, we cried out in the good times, the times of peace, endlessly to CRA to give us the compensation we wanted. But the company would not understand. Our appeals were dashed against rocks. Now it is in the hands of our men.'

The PNG Government did not appreciate how serious the situation really was. In December 1988 then Prime Minister Rabbie Namaliu threatened retribution for those responsible for sabotaging the mine. 'Five arrests have been made,' he told the Parliament. 'The ringleader has also been identified. He is still at large but they are tracking him down with a view to apprehending him.' Ona was still at large three PNG Prime Ministers later. Namaliu had won power in a vote of no confidence against Wingti in mid-1988, promising a new deal for landowners in resource-rich areas. He delivered on that promise in the big resource projects then being negotiated—the Porgera gold mine and the Kutubu oil field, both in the PNG Highlands. But on Bougainville it was all too late. Two chances to redress the Panguna landowners' grievances had been squandered. The first was in 1981 when the Bougainville Agreement with BCL came up for its seven-yearly review. The Government, then led by Julius Chan in his first stint as PM, had been unable to sort out a consistent position and the opportunity lapsed. Seven years later it was a similar story. The Namaliu Government had not even appointed its negotiating team towards the end of 1988 when the destruction began.

Ona found an immediate ally in the mountains to the south of the copper mine, a cult leader, Damien Damen. Damen was an isolationist who vigorously opposed any form of outside authority, be it the National Government in Port Moresby or the Provincial Government in Arawa. He had established his own government, the Fifty-Toea Gavman, and collected that amount per year (equivalent to about seventy-five Australian cents in the 1980s) from his followers. Ona himself became somewhat of a cult figure. He and Serero were both convinced white men constantly lied to Bougainvilleans. Speaking in her village in November 1988, Serero constantly returned to the theme: 'We do not trust any white men.' At one meeting prior to the outbreak of the violence one member of the new Panguna Landowners Association had retorted, 'Logic is a white man's trick,' to an academic who had questioned their reasoning on a particular issue. In a letter dated 10 February 1989 written from his 'Camp Hide Out', Ona told Bougainvilleans to watch out for the lies of the 'white mafia' who ran the world. In another letter in May to the PNG Prime Minister he accused Namaliu of taking 'white mafia's advice' and told him that if Bougainville was not given independence more innocent people would die and he would be 'signing an economic death for your country'.

A serving PNGDF soldier, Lieutenant Sam Kauona, quit the PNG Army to become Military Commander of Ona's BRA. He deserted in early 1989 not long after returning from an Australian Army course in Victoria, specialising in demolitions. Kauona's guerilla forces, which initially numbered fewer than a hundred, operated in small bands and conducted hit and run raids against mine property, commercial facilities closely associated with the mine and government installations such as communications towers. The security forces sent to Bougainville by the National Government found Kauona (who soon adopted the title of General) to be an extremely effective and elusive foe. His guerillas succeeded in shutting down the mine permanently on 15 May 1989.

Kauona's clever tactics included spreading readily believed stories that his rebels had black magic, *puri puri*, working for them. Yauka Liria, a former army intelligence officer posted to Bougainville in 1989, has written extensively of the fear engendered in the troops by this belief. He told of how one platoon, camped for the night on a ridge where they had killed two rebels, released their BRA prisoners before nightfall fearing they would 'use *puri puri* to walk off at night anyway'. Some hours later, 'the night gunners suddenly opened up from two gun positions, claiming dog-like creatures were attempting to crawl' up to them. In the middle of the night, the platoon commander started screaming, setting off the others 'and for some sixty seconds there was wild screaming and shouting from the whole platoon'. The platoon commander explained later he was certain he had been lifted up by some supernatural force, carried outside the perimeter and left rotating in the air.

PNG Government policy during 1989 veered from one extreme to the other. The troops were ordered to flush out the rebels; to pull back; to go on the offensive; to stop; to 'shoot to kill'; and to maintain defensive positions guarding the towns and the mine. Halfway through the year they took delivery of four Iroquois helicopters which the Australian Army did not need any more. Negotiations to acquire the helicopters under the Defence Cooperation Agreement had begun before the Bougainville conflict. But after it started PNG demanded they be handed over to ease the extreme logistical problems its troops were experiencing. Australia's Foreign Minister, Gareth Evans, came up with what Australian journalist, Mary-Louise O'Callaghan, has called 'the lawyers' solution'—a form of words to cover the conditions under which the Iroquois could be used. The PNG politicians agreed that the helicopters would not be used for 'offensive' operations, only for logistics purposes—transport and medical evacuations. But the military commander who ran the war on Bougainville in late 1989 and early 1990, Colonel Leo Nuia, admitted to Deborah Snow on the ABC's Four Corners in 1991 that the Iroquois had been used to fire on villages and dump the bodies of executed rebel suspects at sea.

Attempts to work out a settlement during 1989 were successively frustrated either by the extreme misbehaviour of PNG troops or selective assassinations by the BRA. One man killed by a BRA assassination squad was John Bika, a Minister in the Bougainville Provincial Government who had chaired a committee which toured the province and wrote a comprehensive report proposing an entirely new relationship between Bougainville and PNG that stopped short of secession. Gunmen burst into his house in the middle of the night and shot Bika dead in front of his wife and family. He was to have travelled to Port Moresby the next day to sign a new deal with Namaliu. This would have not only vastly increased the amount of revenue from the mine going to Bougainville but also offered ten per cent ownership of the mine to Bougainvilleans (five per cent to the landowners and five per cent to the Provincial Government). At Bika's funeral Bishop Singkai did not blame the BRA, but simply stated: 'Those who hated him killed him.' Both Sam Kauona and Joseph Kabui later confirmed Bika had been a BRA target.

PNG soldiers on assignment to Bougainville copied a tactic from the police riot squads sent down from the Highlands where they regularly burnt down villages in payback for trouble. Thousands of village homes were set ablaze and it became regular practice during patrols of the mountains of central Bougainville for soldiers to set fire to houses. Yauka Liria said it was totally counterproductive. 'If we can't get them, we'll get their homes was the general feeling... The destruction of homes, accidental or intended, for whatever tactical advantage, brings only complete and unrelenting hatred for the government forces,' he wrote in 1993. 'Every Papua New Guinean knows just how true this is. The village, to a villager, is more than just shelter. It is his livelihood, his heritage, his pride. His village is at the centre of his heart. It has almost spiritual and religious significance in PNG society. You will never convince a Papua New Guinea villager who has sat on a hill and watched his village burn to ashes, that both you and he are on the same side. He will hate you for the rest of his life.'

In 1989 and early 1990 the troops were concentrated in central Bougainville but stories of atrocities spread throughout the province and the BRA gained wide support. By February of 1990 Prime Minister Namaliu was exasperated. Not trusting what he was being told by the military he sent one of his own staff to Bougainville to give him an independent assessment. This man obtained for Namaliu the names and post mortem records of a long list of Bougainvilleans whose broken, mutilated or bullet-riddled bodies had been dumped at the Arawa Hospital morgue by the military. On at least one occasion soldiers dumping off the body bags ordered hospital staff not to conduct post-mortems. Namaliu realised the war was going nowhere and he agreed to a hastily conceived plan for the PNG troops to be pulled out and for an international observer group to witness the BRA voluntarily laying down its arms. Colonel Nuia and General Kauona signed the agreement. A fiasco ensued. The police, fearful they would be slaughtered by the rebels without the protection of the soldiers, fled Bougainville before the PNGDF pulled out. Before they left, they set free all prisoners, including convicted murderers and rapists. Bougainville was abandoned to the BRA. The talks which were supposed to follow never eventuated.

Each side blamed the other and in April the PNG National Security Advisory Council was briefed on how the National Government could apply pressure by imposing a blockade. The brief suggested that 'if discrete economic sanctions are imposed, they be described not as sanctions, but as a withdrawal or suspension of services'. This, it claimed, could be justified publicly by 'the lack of National Government representation in the Province', which meant there was 'no protection or security for assets or services'. The Namaliu Government imposed the blockade. Francis Ona responded on 17 May 1990 with a Unilateral Declaration of Independence for Bougainville. If he could have arranged a referendum then, Ona might well have secured the backing of ninety per cent of the province. But the 'civilian' administration he appointed to run his new country, the Bougainville Interim Government (BIG), had little real power and no control over the young men with the guns, both local BRA fighters and criminal groups. Various prominent Bougainvilleans were appointed Ministers but governance collapsed. Ona himself was exceptionally suspicious. Alleged 'traitors', many of them public servants, were rounded up.

This was one of the more tragic years of the war. Little of the mayhem that followed the UDI on Bougainville has been reported. Every district office was destroyed and community government buildings in more than thirty locations were burnt down. Bougainville had been the best-run province in PNG but its infrastructure was wrecked in those wild destructive sprees. Ona, aloof in the mountains of central Bougainville, was revered by the more fanatical. Niko Numana, a woman who lived in the Siwai district of south-west Bougainville, told the ABC in 1993 of how people in her area in 1990 were forbidden from speaking Ona's name aloud. 'Any civilians who were heard using his name were mistreated by the BRA,' she said. 'Francis never came out openly and talked to the people. He just hid away in his little place up at Panguna.' The island became exceptionally factionalised.

Joe Watawi, who became Chairman of the PNG Government recognised

North-West Bougainville Interim Authority, after chiefs in his area turned against Ona, claimed at a Bougainville leaders meeting in Buka in 1993 that his people would never forgive PNG for 'abandoning' them in 1990. Asked outside the meeting what he meant he replied: 'Because of the experiences the people went through during the time there was no government control in the province, because of that pain. This is why the people will never forgive the National Government for that.' Paul Akoitai, the leader of one group that took up arms against the BRA in 1991, claimed that in the Wakunai area on the north-east coast 'people were dying like frogs on the road'. One of Bougainville's elder statesmen, Sir Paul Lapun, said it was chaos: 'That's the time they should have organised their police force. But instead of that they destroyed everything!' Sir Paul himself became subject to harassment. If anyone deserved respect it should have been Sir Paul. He had been the first to force the Australian administration to recognise landowner rights, winning support in the pre-Independence House of Assembly for the Panguna landowners to be paid five per cent of the mine's royalties.

New Zealand made its first effort to broker a peace in mid-1990 by providing New Zealand warships for talks off the coast of Bougainville. In late July and early August, on board the warship, HMNZS *Endeavour*, a PNG delegation led by 'the father' of PNG, Michael Somare, and including Justice Minister Bernard Narokobi, met with a rebel delegation headed by the former Premier and now Chairman of the BIG, Joseph Kabui. Sitting alongside Kabui was Bishop Gregory Singkai, who had accepted a portfolio in Ona's (on-paper-only) Government. The talks resulted in the Endeavour Accord. But the agreement signed on board the warship never held. It fell apart because neither side honoured it. On the part of PNG, the bureaucrats who were expected to deliver the restoration of services to Bougainville were never convinced they would be safe without the protection of the PNG security forces and so the planned restoration never happened. On the rebel side, Francis Ona had refused to join the talks and repudiated the outcome.

Following the failure of the Endeavour Accord, chiefs in northern Buka decided they had had enough of Ona's style of independence. Widespread destruction of facilities on Buka, including the Hujena High School, had followed the withdrawal of all PNG government authority in March. A number of Buka's leaders had also been arrested, taken to Panguna and interrogated. In September 1990, north Buka chiefs sent a small boat to Nissan Island sixty kilometres north-west of Buka where the PNG security forces had set up a base. They invited the PNGDF back to Buka. Sam Tulo, a former Member for North Bougainville in the PNG Parliament, was instrumental in this move and he arranged for young village men from northern Buka to join with the PNGDF to drive the BRA out. These village militia groups took the name the Buka Liberation Front, and in bloody confrontations over the following months they helped the PNG forces eliminate the BRA from Buka.

The next attempt to establish peace was in early 1991. Joseph Kabui again met with a PNG delegation, this time in the Solomon Islands capital, Honiara. But the Honiara Declaration they signed became a farce. Within hours of the signing, rebel delegates were saying they had not read it properly and did not agree with some clauses. Neither Ona nor Kauona attended, and the following month General Kauona completely disassociated the BRA from what Joseph Kabui had put his name to.

Limited authority

The MV *Sankamap* was trying to dock at the Kieta wharf for the first time since the blockade of Bougainville had been imposed nine months earlier. One lone man on the wharf indicated that the passenger and cargo vessel would not be allowed to berth unless the PNG flag was taken from its mast. The *Sankamap* had belonged to the Bourgainville Provincial Government. But Premier Joseph Kabui had joined the secessionists as Chairman of their Interim Government (the BIG). And so PNG had confiscated the vessel, which had been out of Bougainville at the time of the UDI, and put it to work servicing the province's remote atolls, which remained untouched by the war.

The *Sankamap*, Pidgin for 'sunrise', was so named because Bougainville is the first province in PNG each day to see the sun. On this particular day in February 1991, the sun was only just rising on the rest of PNG as the *Sankamap* nuzzled into the jetty. On board it carried medicines and food, mostly rice, tinned fish and tinned meat. Once that PNG flag came down and the lone BRA commander waved the *Sankamap* in, people saw there were no PNG troops aboard. A large crowd flocked onto the wharf. The boat's visit was a goodwill gesture following the signing of the Honiara Declaration.

The medicines were readily accepted. But there was some uncertainty over the food. Would that be interpreted as the rebels weakening? Proof that they had not become self-sufficient? Kabui, who was on the wharf, decreed that this issue should be decided by consensus. Community leaders, ministers and officials of the BIG and women's group representatives met late that day and most of the night debating whether to accept the food or not. Eventually, all present agreed it should be unloaded and taken to the hospital to be given out to pregnant mothers or women who had just given birth. Unloading began and by late afternoon the last of the rice and tinned food was stacked on the wharf.

A four-wheel drive screeched onto the jetty. The local Kieta BRA Commander, Chris Uma, jumped out, armed and angry. Backed up by young men holding guns, he yelled at Joseph Kabui, 'Put this food back on the boat. We don't accept food from PNG!' Kabui turned to the *Sankamap* captain and shaken, asked if the crew could load the rice and cartons of tinned fish and meat back on board. Laughing, the young BRAs helped throw the food back on the deck. It was clear who was in charge.

The PNGDF, with the help of the Buka Liberation Front, effectively returned Buka to PNG control by the middle of 1991. The Buka Liberation Front set a pattern for other communities in north-west and north-east Bougainville in 1991 and for those in the Siwai district of south-west Bougainville wanting to split from the Nasioi-led revolution in 1992. They established their own local forces to fight the BRA. Resistants, or collectively the Resistance, was the name they adopted. The communities then invited in the government forces who helped arm the Resistants and together they combated the BRA. But in central Bougainville where the memories of 1989–90 were strongest it was a different situation. This was the revolution's heartland and it was also where the rebel militants were generally more disciplined. The spread of PNG's semi-authority faltered.

Suspicion of each other's motives and bluntly ignorant behaviour by elements on both sides sabotaged a number of initiatives to ease the blockade. In early 1992 Prime Minister Namaliu ordered the security forces to allow the Red Cross to visit central Bougainville with medical supplies. The Red Cross chartered a ship, the MV *Cosmaris*. The PNG military was not in favour of the venture. Soldiers inspecting the ship before it left Rabaul refused to allow the Red Cross team to take any food with them. A few days after docking in Kieta, rebels angry with the PNG Government burnt the *Cosmaris*, which sank at its berth. One BRA group wanted to take the crew hostage but when the Australian doctor who led the Red Cross team, Damien Wohlfahrt, said he would not leave the island without them they were allowed to go. All returned safely to PNG via Solomon Islands.

PNG Government policy on Bougainville hardened even further after

Paias Wingti was elected Prime Minister following the PNG elections in mid-1992. Wingti regarded the rebels as simple criminals who needed to be taught a lesson. On one matter there was not much change. Like the Namaliu Government, Wingti's Administration exercised very little control over the military's behaviour. Relations with Solomon Islands plummeted in September when soldiers from the PNGDF's small boats team raided the village of Kamaleai on Alu Island in the Shortlands group. They captured a store owner, Francis Beiaruru, shot his brother-in-law dead, fatally wounded Beiaruru's pregnant wife and put a bullet through the leg of his three-year-old daughter. The military claimed he had been supplying fuel to the BRA and providing the rebels with a radio link. The radio in his store was smashed. PNG troops held Beiaruru captive for several days before dropping him back off in the Solomons. After the Solomon Islands Government raised the matter with the United Nations Security Council, Prime Minister Wingti promised to pull the PNGDF into line. But no substantial charges were ever laid against any soldier over the incident.

Wingti wanted to believe that the BRA was about to collapse and he pushed for the recapture of the Bougainville Copper Mine. At one stage, he made the bold prediction on the Australian Channel Nine 'Business Sunday' program that the mine would be operating again by the end of 1993. The army adopted a new policy of advancing into areas without invitation. Soldiers backed by the Resistance from Rorovana near the port of Loloho retook Arawa, the former provincial capital, in early 1993. The BRA hit back, ambushing a convoy near the overgrown Arawa golf course a few weeks later, killing eight soldiers. Human rights violations also grew. The BIG Health Minister, Ken Savia, who had been arrested during the retaking of Arawa, disappeared. One story, that Savia had been tied to the back of a truck and dragged around a carpark, prompted a question in Parliament from the Member for Central Bougainville, Joseph Egilio to the Defence Minister. Egilio asked for an investigation. The Minister told Egilio to put his question in writing. And it remained on the Parliamentary Questions With Notice Paper unanswered for years and eventually disappeared when the 1992-97 term of Parliament expired. Towards the end of 1993, Amnesty International produced a report providing details of what it claimed were sixty extrajudicial executions carried out by the PNG security forces between 1991 and November 1993.

In April 1994 Australian Labor Party Senator Stephen Loosley led an Australian parliamentary delegation to Bougainville to have a look at the situation. The delegation proposed that PNG set up a royal commission into alleged human rights atrocities but Wingti was not much interested.

Soon after the delegation left to return to Australia, he announced a nine-fold boost in funding for the PNGDF's military operations on Bourgainville. Asked his view of proposals for an amnesty for BRA leaders, Wingti replied: 'I'm not going to entertain that. I think our position is very clear. People who break the laws of our country must face justice.' Peace talks seemed to be out of the question. But behind the scenes Sir Julius Chan, who had been made Foreign Minister in a reshuffle in January 1994, was working on a bold plan to set up a South Pacific Peace Keeping Force. Towards the end of May details filtered out.

Sir Julius had made a series of visits to other island nations in the Pacific and won approval from the King of Tonga and the Prime Ministers of Fiji and Vanuatu that their three countries would contribute troops to a South Pacific Peace Keeping Force. 'Their deployment to Bougainville should be swift, selective and effective,' Chan said, 'in order to allow the people to reach a peaceful solution to the crisis quickly.' But his Prime Minister was not very supportive. During a visit by Fiji's Prime Minister, Sitiveni Rabuka, Wingti said it was just a concept. 'All I can say is that it's not developed to a stage where we can say it's possible. You have to consult with many other countries in the region.' For not the first, nor the last, time PNG Government policy on Bougainville seemed headed in two entirely separate directions at once.

Foreign Minister Chan persisted with his efforts. He devoted a lot of energy to restoring the PNG–Solomon Islands relationship. Sir Julius apologised for the cross-border killing incident at Kamaleai village on Alu Island the previous September. On a trip to Honiara he made a compensation payment to the family of the two people killed by the PNGDF in the raid. The Solomons Government led by Prime Minister Francis Billy-Hilly was also seeking ways it could help resolve the problem in Bougainville. The war was having multiple spill-over effects for the Solomons which had absorbed several thousand refugees. Sir Julius sent senior government officials including the head of his Foreign Affairs Department to Honiara to hold discussions with representatives of the BRA and the BIG, talks that Billy-Hilly himself chaired. By mid-1994 real progress was being made.

However, Prime Minister Wingti favoured a different approach. While the Solomon Islands Prime Minister and the PNG Foreign Minister were working towards peace talks, PNG's PM authorised an assault on the Panguna copper mine. On 16 August 1994 Wingti called a news conference in Port Moresby to announce that Operation High Speed had achieved its objective. 'Today, I'm very pleased to inform the nation,' he said, 'that yesterday night the military moved into Panguna.' Claiming the PNG troops had taken no casualties, Wingti called on the rebels to surrender. 'I think it's a very important event in the history of the crisis because, as you know, the crisis took place because of the mine, the grievances of the landowners and the effect of the mine on the area.' Wingti's euphoria was short-lived. The Major in charge of one of the PNGDF companies was shot dead and the officer in charge of Operation High Speed, Lieutenant Colonel Jerry Singirok, was shot through the wrist.

Suddenly, Paias Wingti was no longer Prime Minister. This had nothing to do with Bougainville. The PNG Supreme Court ruled after months of deliberation that Wingti was really only a caretaker PM. And that he had been just a caretaker since he had secretly resigned one night the previous year (1993). Wingti thought he had been re-elected by the Parliament the next day, just moments after Members were informed of his resignation. This extraordinary device had been aimed at winning himself another eighteen months in power free from challenge, because newly elected PNG Prime Ministers are given immunity from votes of no confidence for one-and-a-half years. However, the Supreme Court ruled that while the secret resignation was valid, Wingti's re-election the next day was not. The spirit of the Constitution, the Court held, had been breached because the Parliamentarians should have had time to make a considered decision. Wingti's majority immediately crumbled. Sir Julius and his Peoples Progress Party (PPP) quit Wingti's Government and Chan announced that, when the Parliament met at the end of August to determine the country's leader, he would contest. Wingti knew he could not win and pulled out. Chan formed a coalition with the opposition Pati Pangu led by Chris Haiveta and won the vote, comfortably defeating the other nominee, Bill Skate.

Sir Julius stated that his top priority was to solve the Bougainville conflict. He immediately took ministerial responsibility for both the Defence Force and the Police saying he intended to make sure PNG's security forces did not wreck his peace initiatives. Just three days later, Sir Julius flew to Honiara for face-to-face talks with the military commander of the BRA, General Sam Kauona. Solomon Islands Prime Minister Billy-Hilly chaired those talks. After two days of hard discussions, Chan and Kauona signed the Honiara Commitments providing for a peace conference to be held in Arawa in October involving people from all over Bougainville. Protection for delegates would be provided by the South Pacific Peace Keeping Force which Sir Julius had been proposing as Foreign Minister. Australia agreed to fund the logistics.

But Sam Kauona soon began to have second thoughts. He claimed that he was not being consulted enough on the make-up of the Peace Keeping

Force and that he did not want any such multinational force to be headed by an Australian. Kauona also demanded to be a signatory to the Status of Elements of the Peace Keeping Force Agreement which was to be signed in Fiji. When told he was being invited along but only as an observer he refused to go to the signing ceremony at the South Pacific Forum headquarters in Suva. Francis Ona sought assurances that the peace keepers would be neutral and would guarantee his safety. The Australian military officer in charge of logistics for the force, Brigadier General Peter Abigail, and the three Colonels from Tonga, Fiji and Vanuatu, who were to be in charge of their men on the ground, flew to Sipuru village in the mountains to give Ona that assurance.

Sir Julius, impatient for success, said he expected to sign an agreement at the end of the week-long conference, an agreement that would mark the end of the Bougainville crisis. He even laid plans to invite regional leaders to witness the historic moment including Australia's Prime Minister Paul Keating. But Francis Ona never turned up. Neither did Sam Kauona nor Joseph Kabui. All that was heard from the three leaders of the rebels was a tape-recorded telephone conversation with Kabui in which he restated their demand that all PNG troops be withdrawn from Bougainville. The South Pacific Peace Keepers packed up and left, wondering what had gone wrong and why they had ever bothered.

Lost opportunities

Standing shoulder to shoulder under a huge malmal tree in the grounds of the forlorn and studentless Arawa High School, the Bougainvillean women's choir sang the lines of the song, 'Island of Sorrow', that one of them, Elizabeth Borein, had written:

> *Bougainville is an island, an island of sorrow.*
> *Bougainville is an island, an island of pain.*

The women and more than a thousand other Bougainvilleans had come to Arawa clutching at the best chance of peace in six years.

> *There are people dying, there are people crying.*
> *Who is responsible?*
> *There's no education, there's no hospital.*
> *Who is responsible?*

Soldiers from Tonga, Fiji and Vanuatu had secured the High School and town guaranteeing the safety of all participants. The peace conference was aimed at getting Bougainvilleans together to discuss an end to the war. But one of the few rebels who did show up, Isadore Lawrence, claimed it was a trick to capture Francis Ona. 'Our leaders will be, you know, killed here,' he said. 'How we believe this is because Papua New Guinea has directed the Peace Keeping Force to work under their own law. And PNG is the overall supervisor. So when that day comes, they'll just put their hands down and let PNG inside.' Isadore claimed nobody from the United Nations had come as the BRA had demanded. When Hiroko Miyamura spoke saying Butros Butros Ghali had sent her from New York to observe, Isadore suggested she was just some Japanese woman the PNG Government found on the streets of Port Moresby.

There are people dying, there are people crying.
Not knowing why.
Bougainville island is an island I love.

The one positive outcome of that Arawa Peace Conference was the emergence of a moderate leader from amongst the previously hard-core BRA Nasioi people. He was Theodore Miriung, a former Acting National Court Judge who had been living in the BRA-controlled North Nasioi area since 1990. Miriung knew well how weary of the war his people were and he had been agonising over the dreadful impact the never-ending crisis was having on the youth of Bougainville. Although warned not to go he decided to attend the conference. And he took considerable personal risks travelling back and forth to see Ona in the mountains during the conference to try to convince him to participate. Failing in that bid, Miriung broke with Ona's policy of refusing to deal with Port Moresby. In the days that followed the indefinite adjournment of the conference, he took his North Nasioi people with him to join the peace process.

Sir Julius was angry that the peace strategy he had worked so hard to put together had failed to produce the stunning result he had banked on. He was particularly bitter about Sam Kauona, whom he had loudly praised as a man of honour when he had signed the Honiara Commitments but who had then refused to attend the agreed October Conference. But Chan continued to work towards a negotiated solution to the Bougainville problem and held a series of discussions with Miriung and other Bougainville leaders. In late November 1994, Chan and Miriung signed what was called the Mirigini Charter. This pledged the 'leaders of the National Government and the people of Bougainville' to continue the peace process, and they committed themselves 'to a new spirit, a new deal for a new Bougainville'. Amongst the measures adopted was the proposed establishment of a legal entity to be called the Bougainville Transitional Government (BTG) which would have an assembly comprising leaders 'nominated by Councils of Chiefs'. Miriung believed he could gradually entice the rebel leaders to join the BTG if it was given the power to negotiate with the National Government on a political settlement to the crisis.

The Transitional Government was sworn in during April 1995 and Assembly members voted for Theodore Miriung to be Bougainville's Premier. Seats in the Assembly covered every part of Bougainville and three were deliberately left vacant for areas solidly under BRA control. The hope was that Francis Ona and Joseph Kabui would take two. A further position in the Assembly was provided for a representative of the BRA, a seat intended for General Sam Kauona. Anthony Regan, a constitutional lawyer who worked very closely with Premier Miriung throughout this period, believed the strategy of using the Transitional Government as the means to bring all Bougainvilleans into the peace process was never well understood nor entirely accepted by the National Government.

'Part of the problem,' he wrote in October 1997, 'was mistrust among many at the national level' of Miriung and some of the other Bougainvillean leaders they saw as being too close to the rebels. 'Indeed, key officers in the PNGDF and the PNG Department of Foreign Affairs and Trade regarded the BTG as a "Trojan horse" for the BRA/BIG.' Regan said Chan lost patience with the BTG when, as time went by, the BRA leaders showed no interest in joining the Transitional Government. 'Miriung was in a difficult position,' Regan explained, 'as he sought to balance the intense pressures generated by being the main moderate leader attempting to bridge not only the deep divisions within Bougainville but also those between Bougainville and the national government.'

Premier Miriung was not a socially graceful man. He was an intellectual who cared little for small talk. He could be rude and abrasive and Sir Julius found him difficult to deal with. On Bougainville, the military regarded Miriung with deep suspicion, believing he was an unreformed secessionist. As 1995 went on, some agreement was achieved on a few matters such as the granting of amnesty to people from both sides who may have committed crimes during the crisis. But progress on the main issue—the political future of Bougainville—was slow. Regan wrote that both sides were reluctant to isolate themselves by agreeing to too much: 'Chan had to deal with not only suspicious National Government Ministers concerned with what was often discussed as the possible "domino effect" of special arrangements for Bougainville but also the many elements of the bureaucracy with their own agendas. Miriung felt constrained from agreeing to too much without assurances that what was agreed would be acceptable to the BRA.'

However, Miriung did manage to convince Sir Julius to allow him to try to arrange talks amongst the Bougainvilleans. A meeting was held in Cairns in September 1995, involving members of the Transitional Government, other prominent Bougainvilleans and representatives of the BIG–BRA based in Bougainville, the Solomon Islands and Australia. Australia met the costs. Ona, once again, did not go. A second meeting was scheduled for Brisbane but Sir Julius refused to allow it to proceed claiming it would not achieve anything. Very reluctantly he finally agreed to allow a second meeting in Cairns in December of 1995, this one co-chaired by representatives of the Secretaries General of the United Nations and the Commonwealth. Kabui and Kauona led the secessionist delegation. The PNG Government had nobody there but Sir Julius was given cassette tapes of what was said. After listening to those tapes over Christmas 1995, Chan became convinced of two things—one, that there was no softening in the rebel position; and, two, that Miriung was not the one who would solve the Bougainville problem for him.

Five years before, in 1990, during the very first attempt to negotiate a settlement on board the New Zealand warship *Endeavour*, James Sinko, then chief of Francis Ona's Supreme Advisory Council, had used a wonderfully descriptive image to explain the relationship, as he saw it, between Bougainville and the rest of PNG: 'Put a possum and a dog together in a cage and you will never get peace!' Bernard Narokobi, PNG's Justice Minister, used a similiarly vivid metaphor when apologising for the human rights abuses perpetrated by the PNG security forces saying that it was never deliberate policy. 'We never once made that decision,' he said and broke into Pidgin: 'Taim dok i-lus long han bilong yu, wanem samting em i-workim, sori tru?' A free English translation might run: 'We are truly sorry but once you let a savage dog free from its leash it's out of your control.'

Shakespeare wrote: 'Cry "Havoc" and let slip the dogs of war.' Frederick Forsyth adapted the phrase as the title to his novel about African mercenaries. Chan would resort to hiring the 'dogs of war' in early 1997. But as 1996 began, he first turned to his new young army commander, Jerry Singirok, whom he had just put in charge of a defence force in considerable disarray.

Chapter Three

An Undisciplined Force

The Nature of the Defence Force that Singirok Came to Command

The defence force that turned against Sir Julius Chan in March of 1997 had been all but written off by some of Chan's closest advisers. They regarded the PNGDF as either useless or ill-disciplined or both. This derogatory opinion was shared by the Australian defence staff at the High Commission in Port Moresby. There was no shortage of evidence to support the contention. Jerry Singirok blamed the Government. 'This Defence Force has a very proud history and we can still uphold that if equipped and funded adequately and given firm government directives,' the Brigadier General told the people of Papua New Guinea on 17 March 1997, when alerting them to the army's revolt against the engagement of the mercenaries. 'The continuous deployment [to Bougainville] of the same members of the Force with diminishing logistical support,' Singirok said, 'has resulted in a drastic drop in morale affecting the standard of discipline and the will to fight.'

That he was leading a thoroughly troubled defence force was news to nobody in PNG. The eight-year-long war had laid cruelly bare the glaring inadequacies and failings of the PNGDF for all to see. Singirok was not wrong about the proud early history though. The Royal Pacific Islands Regiment (PIR), which is the core of the present Defence Force, was formed in the Second World War. Papua New Guineans proved themselves formidable soldiers. The PIR killed 2200 Japanese troops for the loss of only 63 men. Although by war's end the Regiment consisted of four battalions the PNG troops rarely fought as a complete unit even at battalion level. The Australians and Americans quickly came to value the abilities of the Papua New Guineans on reconnaissance and other missions that could best be done by small detachments, and so fragments of the regiment were in action in almost all theatres of the War in New Guinea.

This Melanesian aptitude for operating in small guerilla-like teams is one of the secrets of the BRA's success on Bougainville and it underlay Singirok's own obsession with his controversial Special Forces Unit—the SFU, which, as he wrote soon after becoming Commander, was to be 'based on a five-man patrol' that would be able to 'regroup to full platoon and company [strength] depending on the task'. While recognising this ability to operate at the micro-unit level as a positive attribute of the PNG soldier, Singirok and others in the PNG military were riled by the suggestion, made some time ago in an American document, that in any future wider Pacific conflict the PNGDF's role would be as 'scouts' for the Australians. A quality appreciated from within can seem a slight when seized upon by others. There seemed no limit, however, to the courage displayed by PNG's World War II heroes. By the end of the war, the PIR had won eleven battle honours and twenty-three soldiers had been decorated.

The citations for the medal winners make tingling reading. Distinguished Conduct Medal winner Sergeant John Ehava's citation states that 'at great personal risk' he saved the patrol he was leading when it encountered superior Japanese numbers who were attempting to cross the mouth of the Kumusi River on 8 February 1943. Armed with a Bren gun he 'took up a commanding position ... repulsed the attack and personally killed 30 of the enemy. His outstanding courage and leadership was an inspiration to all.' Corporal Geai, also awarded the Distinguished Conduct Medal, showed 'brilliant leadership' and an 'exceptionally high degree of physical courage' when on 14 August 1945 he extricated his patrol from a carefully set Japanese trap. 'Realising he had been trapped, Corporal Geai called out to his section to take cover and immediately opened fire knocking out a Japanese light-machine gun and capturing it. Intense mortar, rifle and further light-machine gun fire raked the patrol and Corporal Geai was wounded by a machine-gun burst in both the arm and hand. Even whilst injured and with a total disregard of his personal safety, he rushed forward again with his Owen gun, engaging and killing single-handed seven of the enemy troops. At this stage, Corporal Geai was wounded in the leg but despite this additional severe injury, he ... continued to engage the Japanese and draw their fire until he was able to organise and execute the section's withdrawal.' What medal might he have won had he been white?

Disbanded after the War, the PIR was formed again in 1951. The 1st Battalion once more was raised in Port Moresby. The 2nd Battalion, which is based at Wewak on the north coast, was added in 1965 when Australia was worried about the threat to its own safety posed by Indonesia. In the early 1960s Indonesia had taken over Irian Jaya from the Dutch and confronted Malaysia. The PIR then was seen as integral to Australia's defence. 'We saw the PIR as Australia's Ghurkha Unit,' a former PIR Commanding Officer, Lieutenant Colonel Maurie Pears, wrote years later. Australians dominated the officer ranks of the regiment right up until the late 1970s, even after PNG's independence. It was not until May 1971 that the first Papua New Guinean reached the rank of Major. Four years later, that Major, Ted Diro, was a Brigadier General and the first Commander of the PNGDF.

The only PNG officer since Diro to have risen through the senior ranks so fast is Jerry Singirok. Although he spent seven years as a Major, Singirok's astounding rise after that, from Major to Lieutenant Colonel (in December 1993), to Colonel (November 1994), to Brigadier General (November 1995), meant he made the transition from a Battalion Operations Officer to the Commander of the whole Defence Force in less than two years. It helps explain both his popularity with junior ranks and his difficult relations with many officers who regarded themselves his senior, if not his superior. Significantly, the planning and execution of Operation Rausim Kwik, when it came, involved nobody above the rank of Major, apart from the Commander himself.

A law unto themselves

Lawrence Hardie was beaten senseless by PNGDF troops on the main wharf at Lae on Sunday morning, 3 September 1995. Five armed and uniformed soldiers hauled the fifty-six-year-old Australian marine engineer, out of the Sealark Shipping company mini-bus and hit him in the head with rifle butts. When he went down they kicked him. 'It was only when Mr Hardie lay completely still,' a company employee said, 'and stevedores, passengers and crew from overseas vessels saw what was going on' that they stopped. The reason for the beating? The soldiers were not going to get back to Port Moresby as quickly as they expected because the *Sealark*, flagship for the Lae-based shipping company, had hit a log and bent a propeller. The men, who were on their way home from their latest tour of duty on Bougainville were annoyed at the delay.

It is not clear why they took their anger out on Lawrence Hardie. He was on his way to the *Sealark* to fix the propeller. In a letter of complaint the next day to the then Commander of the Force calling for an investigation and disciplinary action, the boss of Sealark Shipping, Hamish

Sharp, described how 'other Defence Force personnel stood by and cheered the five cowardly assailants on'.

Police from the Lae Central Station who were informed about the attack picked Hardie up from a doctor's surgery where he had been taken for treatment and took him back to the wharf to identify his assailants. By then they had been driven off by other soldiers to Igam Barracks in Lae. Sharp told the Commander a 'Sergeant Major who was with the remaining soldiers promised the police that the five culprits would be rounded up and that the PNGDF Military Police would deliver the five cowards to the Lae Police Station ... Of course,' he added, 'this did not happen.'

Before PNG's independence, the Commander of the PIR, an Australian Brigadier, did not answer to the Australian Administrator in Port Moresby. He took his orders from army headquarters in Canberra. This independence of action was shared by neither of the other disciplined forces, the Police or the Prisons Service, who answered to the colonial administration. The Australian Army prided itself on the claim that 'to a notable extent tribal loyalties have been subordinated to esprit de corps'. There were some notable incidents, however, when this 'esprit de corps' spilled over into ill-disciplined clashes with those outside the corps. In 1957, when several soldiers were arrested and charged after a brawl in a Port Moresby settlement, Australian officers allowed the case to be heard at Taurama Barracks. Angered by this intrusion of civil authority, colleagues of the accused staged a riot, chasing the magistrate and lawyers away. And in 1960 there was a minor rebellion in the ranks following attempts to avert a strike over army wages.

There was much debate over what shape the force should take after Independence. Some argued that the PIR should be turned into a paramilitary force and given a police back-up role. Others, including some advisers to the first Chief Minister, Michael Somare, were worried what role an army in an independent PNG might see for itself and they argued for the PIR to be disbanded claiming it cost too much anyway. The contrary argument for a military force with a well-defined role set down in the Constitution won out and the PNGDF, the Papua New Guinea Defence Force, came into being. Australia gave PNG the Australian Navy patrol boats based at Lombrum in the Manus Province, and the sailors became members of the naval element of a unified PNGDF. A small air transport squadron was added. The Constitution which took effect on Independence Day, 16 September 1975, laid down the supremacy of the civilian government.

Section 201 states that the Defence Force is subject to the 'superintendence and control' of the Cabinet through the Defence Minister. But the Minister has no formal power of command within the force.

The cost problem of keeping a military that had become accustomed to Australian conditions was eased, temporarily, by Australia providing a substantial injection of cash. Writing ten years after Independence, an Australian Colonel who had been Chief of Staff of the PNGDF, Colin East, was critical of what he called the 'line of least resistance' taken by Australia. In an article titled 'PNGDF–Colonial Legacy or Independent Force' in the *Pacific Defence Reporter* (1985), East claimed the 'cosmetic surgery' done at the last minute had left PNG with a defence force whose elements were 'meaningful in the framework of the Australian Defence Force of a decade ago' but that as a separate national force the PNGDF was 'militarily unbalanced, expensive and non-viable'.

East's comments still apply. Militarily unbalanced the PNGDF remains. The Defence White Paper presented to the PNG Parliament in the middle of 1996 speaks repeatedly of the need for a 'small, balanced and responsive force'. Small it is at about 4000 personnel. But there has been little progress meeting the other two criteria. Like some other PNG government departments and institutions, the current structure of the PNGDF is virtually what Australia left behind. Despite numerous Cabinet decisions and a number of Defence White Papers, there are aspects of the PNGDF that appear frozen in time–an unfortunate reminder perhaps of Australian bureaucratic and military thinking in the mid-1970s. The shortage of money needed to maintain this colonial-era infrastructure led not to radical restructuring but to dilapidation. The inefficiency of the inappropriately designed, inherited institutions of State in PNG and their seeming inability to deliver desired results provide strong motivation for politicians to look outside the system and outside the country for privatised answers to difficult problems.

The PNGDF has a relatively large headquarters structure designed for an army infantry brigade. Operationally there are three elements to the force–land, sea and air–each divided notionally into combat, support and service arms. The land element is the largest. It has two infantry battalions based on opposite sides of the mainland–at Taurama Barracks on Port Moresby's south-eastern outskirts and at Moem Barracks near Wewak–an engineering battalion comprising both construction and combat engineer companies based at Igam Barracks in Lae, a signals squadron, an explosives ordinance demolition unit, and a preventative medical platoon. It has no tanks or artillery. Since the Bougainville operation began there has been some blurring of divisions between the separate elements and there is now within the land element a small boats team.

The naval element operates a Patrol Boat Squadron of four surveillance vessels (called Tarangau Class in PNG) and a Landing Craft Squadron of two ageing, heavy landing barges. The patrol boats replaced those handed over at Independence and were supplied free in the 1980s by Australia under the Pacific patrol boat program to help Pacific Islands nations with surveillance. At the request of the PNGDF, the four vessels supplied to PNG are fitted with more powerful cannons than those provided to the smaller countries. The main patrol boat base is at Lombrum in the Manus Province just below the equator, while there is a small forward base at Alotau in the Milne Bay Province. The heavy landing craft operate out of a base in Port Moresby harbour.

The air element consists of four UH-1H Iroquois helicopters and an Air Transport Squadron with a fleet of two Spanish CASA CN235 transports, three Israeli short-take-off-and-landing Arava RV201 transport planes and four Nomads. But according to the 1996 Defence White Paper the four Nomads were grounded for technical reasons and were soon to be decommissioned. In mid-1998 few of the other aircraft were operating and some had been cannibalised to keep others serviceable. The Iroquois were donated by Australia under the highly controversial agreement containing conditions for their use. This agreement led to almost perpetual dispute over the operational use of the Iroquois on Bougainville and, until the Sandline affair itself, was the biggest single contributor to souring the Australia–PNG relationship.

The ownership of the even more controversial aircraft that Sandline International arranged for Operation Oyster on Bougainville was still in dispute by mid-1998. These comprised two fixed-wing aircraft brought into PNG by Sandline–a CASA, which was to be fitted with an electronic warfare suite, and a spotter plane; and four Russian-designed helicopters–two Mi-24 helicopter gunships and two large helicopter transports that were being stored at Australia's Tindal Air Force Base in the Northern Territory. Even the model of the transports was in dispute. Sandline had contracted to provide two Mi-17s but a PNG delegation that inspected them at Tindal reported the transport helicopters they saw were an earlier version–Mi-8s.

The permanent assets of the PNGDF are located in twelve sites scattered around Papua New Guinea. Defence headquarters is at Murray Barracks in the heart of Port Moresby. The Defence Department and the Defence Intelligence Branch are also located there. Recruits are trained at Goldie

River north-west of Port Moresby—which is the third military barracks in or around the capital. The Goldie River training depot is also the base of the Special Forces Unit. Officer training is done at the Defence Academy at Igam Barracks in Lae. The 1996 Defence White Paper proposed that all training be moved to Lae and that Goldie River become the base for a new paramilitary battalion whose 'primary task would be that of resource protection'. Although the White Paper called for the raising of this third battalion out of the existing 5200 manpower ceiling there was still no third battalion in 1998.

At Independence the Defence Force numbered 3600, of whom about 500 were Australians. The number of Australian officers fell rapidly but in late 1997 there were still fourteen Australian military personnel working within the PNGDF, half of them involved in training and the rest filling technical and administrative support positions. In 1983 the PNG Government decided to reduce Defence Force numbers to 3050. But numbers never dropped that low and the decision was reversed in 1990 when a target of 5200 was adopted. The 1996 Defence White Paper re-endorsed 5200 as the planned strength of the force but in 1997 numbers stood at just over 4000 with all operational units well under establishment strength. The 1st Infantry Battalion was forty-six per cent below strength, with only 422 troops out of an authorised establishment of 747, while the 2nd was seventeen per cent down with 618 troops. The engineer battalion was 100 short of its establishment of 534. The most seriously deficient operational unit was the air transport squadron. It had only 102 out of 190. Of the 600 positions in the marine element, only 440 were filled.

The 1996 Defence White Paper was very much the work of Brigadier General Singirok. The Australian military expert, Paul Dibb, had been commissioned to write a draft but when the White Paper was eventually tabled little of what Dibb had suggested survived. Several passages reveal an annoyance with Australia. 'Australia's concern for Papua New Guinea's security is comprehensive,' the White Paper says, 'but sometimes allows for patronising overtures to creep in.' It claimed the Australian Defence Cooperation Program was 'out of synchrony' with the PNGDF's needs and that it was time for the Defence Force to develop its own operational doctrine. 'The PNGDF has been conducting operations based on Australian Military doctrines,' it stated. 'It is necessary that the Papua New Guinea Defence Force develops its own doctrine, based on its domestic peculiarities.' One of these peculiarities was Bougainville—which the White Paper said had revealed the need to abandon Australian doctrine.

The 1996 White Paper also criticised PNG's earlier Defence White Paper, tabled in 1988, for having been 'too ambitious and narrowly focused on the modernisation of Defence Force capabilities' and derided its proposals as too 'expensive'. The earlier White Paper had led on to an extravagant wish-list of thirty projects to be implemented over ten years. Only one, the development of the Special Forces Unit, came to fruition. Even what was listed as the top priority in 1991–the acquisition of three forty-five metre patrol boats was still an unachieved objective six years on. The patrol boats were expected to cost K27 million while heavy naval guns to be mounted on them were valued at an extra K42 million. Heavy ground artillery pieces costing K40 million were listed at number ten while down at number fifteen were eight tactical fighter aircraft with a projected price tag of half a billion kina. Papua New Guinea's total 1997 Defence budget was only K93 million, which included a special allocation of K19 million for operations on Bougainville.

The high-cost force Australia had bequeathed to PNG at Independence quickly ran into funding problems. In PNG's first post-Independence financial year, 1975–76, total Defence running costs amounted to about K33 million. Of this, Australia put up K24 million, more than seventy per cent. The Australian money came in two ways–Defence aid worth K16 million and an Australian Defence cash grant of K8 million which allowed the PNG Government to allocate K16.7 million to the PNGDF in its budget. If funding had kept pace with inflation in 1997 those combined figures would have been equivalent to about K140 million. The real PNG Defence budget for 1997, excluding Bougainville operations, was K73.5 million and Australian Defence aid was worth about K12 million. In overall terms that reveals a dramatic real cut in PNG Defence funding.

In the first fourteen years of independence, prior to the Bougainville conflict, Defence spending gradually fell as a proportion of the total PNG budget, inflicting severe problems upon the force. The Defence budget in 1988 was only K35 million. After the troops became engaged on the ground in Bougainville, funding increased but the Government always underestimated what the war cost. Up until 1995, it never even provided a separate line item in the budget for the Bougainville operation. This led to what the Defence White Paper called 'erratic and ad hoc funding'. In 1991, the Defence Force overspent its budget by an astronomical eighty-one per cent, or K41 million. In 1992 actual expenditure exceeded the budget allocation by forty-seven per cent (K26m); in 1993 by forty-two per cent (K23m); and in 1994 it hit a new overspending record eighty-four per cent (K46m).

An investigation ordered by Sir Julius Chan when he was Finance Minister, in September 1993, revealed waste and incompetence, and it raised suspicions of corruption in the way the Defence Department administered the money. In 1992 K800,000 meant for the Bougainville operation was diverted by officials to buy twenty houses in Port Moresby for civilian staff of the department. The report that Sir Julius presented to Cabinet said the department was 'poorly staffed' and had 'no capacity to exercise financial or expenditure control'. There were questions over where some of the money went, especially relating to the Bougainville Risk Allowance, set at K25 per man per day. 'Though there have been an average of about 800 troops actually in the field over the first eight months of the year,' the 1993 report said, 'Defence has claimed risk allowances which equate to 1300 men.' Spending of K5 million could not be accounted for because no records had been kept.

What could be checked revealed that the Defence Force had 'paid exorbitant rates for many goods and services'. Sea charters, which the Defence Force had claimed at more than five times the standard freight rate between Rabaul and Buka, had cost K1.2 million. 'While overexpenditure in such areas as vehicles and travel has occurred,' the report stated, 'Defence has been unable to pay allowances and compensation due to its soldiers in the field ... For 1993 alone Defence still owes its troops allowances of K3.36 million [and] owes compensation for injury or death of K1.48 million.' Those unpaid allowances and constant shortages of food and other basic supplies angered the men on the ground.

PNG's two national daily newspapers regularly feature letters to the editor from the troops on Bougainville. There does not seem to be any PNGDF censorship of soldiers' mail and so the people of PNG get to hear of all sorts of complaints. This includes criticism of officers' tactics and, most often, attacks on the politicians who allegedly never understand nor care about the difficulties of the men sent to fight the war. 'My daily diet is Trukai rice and Besta tinned fish,' the Patriot wrote from Buka. 'This is topped with black coffee, minus sugar at times. Oh! When was the last time I received my risk allowance? Perhaps mum will receive that when I'm boxed home. Hey! Who's complaining? Welcome to the real world of the grunt, the infantry man–the expendable.' He finished the letter: 'To you folk in the rest of this beautiful nation ... please thank God that you're there and not here.'

Another soldier, Concerned Member 2RPIR, Central Bougainville, also complained about the non-payment of risk allowances. 'If the Members of the National Parliament can get their allowances after the parliamentary session, why do they not do the same for us who deserve it more?' He urged politicians and the Defence Department bureaucrats to 'visit us on the front line' to explain where and when the money would be paid. 'Most of my comrades who died had not received their allowances,' he wrote. 'We are just risking our lives on credit. We know we are cheap labourers but our life can not be worked on credit!'

Signing himself Had Enough, another soldier attacked Prime Minister Wingti in March of 1994, claiming security force members were dying from loss of blood when they were shot because there was no money for casualty evacuation. 'Mr Prime Minister, your statement recently stating that troops are patrolling the Panguna mine is false. The truth is I was one of those soldiers given the task of capturing Panguna but my boots and uniform were useless, there was not enough food rations ... and there was no fuel for the chopper to evacuate me when I get shot ... So, Sir, just thought I'd let you know I'm still in Arawa ... waiting for you.'

'Prime Minister, you are welcome to Bougainville, especially in the front line areas,' a group of soldiers writing under the collective pseudonym, State Slaves, wrote in December 1993. They said they were writing to disclose to the general public and to those they called 'the roly-poly men of Waigani' what life was like for the servicemen fighting the war on Bougainville. 'There is inadequate logistic and air support,' they said. 'We are sick of eating one meal per day, sometimes nothing at all or surviving on our own wits ... our field equipment is either torn, damaged or worn out ... If the government can not find a solution to the crisis why not admit it to the world? ... We are human beings and we need to be treated fairly.'

Derogatory comments about officers are regular fare. 'Swallow your pride and admit the truth, General,' one wrote in 1993 when Brigadier General Bob Dademo was Commander. 'Just who are you kidding? Who are you trying to impress?' Brigadier Dademo had been quoted in the newspaper as saying that the Defence Force would be able to manage on the 1994 budget of K54 million it had been given. 'How absurd! This must have been a huge joke the General was making. He is fully aware of the critical situation the Force is currently facing due to poor financial administration.'

Complaining that 'life on the frontline is like living hell', Frustrated of Bougainville claimed soldiers were dying for want of logistic support and the government should admit 'that it has misled our people'. He claimed Government Ministers did not understand 'the military mind'. 'As it is,' he wrote, 'these civilians have no idea about the effects of their decisions on soldiers.' Yet another, Frustrated Serviceman, vented his anger at 'greedy politicians' who had voted themselves an increase in allowances. 'There should be none of these lousy pay rises for politicians,' he said, 'including fancy allowances and other luxuries that invariably go with the job while the soldiers are struggling to eat and have no back-up as they serve this nation more truly and more honestly than any money-grubbing, loud-mouthed politician.'

The second inquiry into the Sandline mercenaries affair headed by Mr Justice Kubulan Los heard numerous examples of the rot in administration that had set in at Defence Force headquarters and which caused much of this frustration to the men in the field. The Defence Secretary (1994-1997), Mr James Melegepa, who had been a former Energy Secretary, gave one instance where he had questioned and stopped a payment approved by the Defence Supply and Tenders Board for generator sets for Bougainville costing three times the market price. Melegepa acknowledged that the Board almost never followed its own tendering rules. Despite regulations requiring public tenders, the Board handled practically every acquisition through Certificates of Inexpediency. Melegepa agreed that the system was abused and that it led to certain suppliers gaining favourable treatment. 'The same suppliers' names kept recurring, yes.'

Melegepa said information on Defence requirements was given to the chosen suppliers by the Logistics Branch headed by the Chief of Logistics, Colonel Alfred Aikung. Questioned at the Los Inquiry, Aikung stoutly defended one company, Pacific Paradise Corporation, which he had ensured won repeated contracts for the supply of food to the PNGDF. The Managing Director of Pacific Paradise, Mr Tom Rangit, admitted to the Inquiry that he was an undischarged bankrupt and that his company kept winning Defence contracts even after being deregistered. Aikung told Justice Los he preferred to deal with Rangit rather than other companies because he knew him. 'I feel comfortable to know ... the people so that I can get stuck into them and Tom Rangit has been coming around and seeing us ... and every time we have problem I call him up and say, "What is going on?"'

Various PNGDF supply officers became very worried about what *was* 'going on' with Rangit's company but Aikung overruled them. Pacific Paradise was often paid up-front but investigations revealed serious shortfalls in supply. The Director of Supply, Lieutenant Colonel John David, noted in January 1997 that the company had been paid almost K2 million in 1996 but that an internal audit revealed K149,000 worth of food had not been delivered. Another Lieutenant Colonel, Daniel Kipo, did his own private investigation and claimed that the situation was even worse. He tallied up alleged discrepancies on K530,000 worth of payments and reported that Pacific Paradise had supplied only K187,000 worth of goods. The Director of Supply ruled that no more orders be placed with Pacific Paradise until it provided the food already paid for.

However, on 27 January 1997 Aikung signed a minute headed 'Clearance of claims for Pacific Paradise Corporation' reversing the Director of Supply's ruling and directing the payment of more money on a further contract. Aikung claimed he had resolved the matter by calling a meeting of David and Rangit. 'I was quite upset also and I called the Director of Supply and Mr Rangit to my office. And we tried to come to some understanding, how we could resolve this ... I really got stuck into Mr Rangit in front of my Director of Supply.' Asked about this, Rangit admitted to the Inquiry there were shortfalls. '[I] did point out that some of the shortfalls were no longer in the market for us to supply and that we would seek a substitute to keep the soldiers going.' After the meeting, Aikung wrote to David: 'As the matter has since been discussed you are to kindly make the payments.'

When Counsel Assisting the Los Inquiry drew Aikung's attention to the other report–Kipo's investigation, titled 'Anomalous Observation Report, Supply of Foodstuffs in 1996'–the Logistics Chief claimed it lacked 'credibility'. Pressed on whether he had read it, he dismissed it as 'just' a report by 'a small boy', and said nobody had appointed Kipo to do any investigation. He admitted the Chairman of the Tenders Board had brought it to his attention claiming it was quite damaging. 'I said, "I will only comment on it if it comes through the Commander. [Otherwise] I will not listen to it. I will not respond to it." ... And to me it was just a back stab in an eye.' Aikung was not asked why he thought Rangit had eyes in the back of his head! Perhaps if Aikung had been fortunate enough himself to have that fabled asset, he would not have accepted Sir Julius Chan's later, disastrous appointment of him as Acting Commander to replace Singirok. As it was, he had to be removed from the job within five days because of the fury of the troops.

Aikung claimed he kept dealing with Pacific Paradise because other companies refused to supply goods to the PNGDF. 'More often they have been closing their doors to us and in my position as Chief of Logistics I had to do everything possible to try and get food for the troops on Bougainville.' The man who had been Chairman of the Defence Tenders Board during most of the dealings with Pacific Paradise, Mr Dennis Apis, tried to defend the Board's use of Certificates of Inexpediency. He told the Los Inquiry that going through normal tendering procedures 'would be too long and it might not meet the requirements of the operational troops at that time ... You have thousands of troops out there who need to be supported at all cost and you have to bend the rules.'

One overseas supplier who did exceptionally well winning contracts via this method from the PNGDF during the early 1990s was the London military equipment provider, J. & S. Franklin (known in the trade as Franklins). Sidney Franklin established a close relationship with a number of PNG Defence Force Commanders—so close with Singirok that he eventually paid £31,000 into a London bank account he helped Singirok open in April 1996. One of the more bewildering aspects of that relationship was that when Singirok was at the front on Bougainville, he shared the average soldier's contempt for the quality of Franklins' equipment. Franklins is a manufacturer of mostly non-lethal military supplies—uniforms, webbing, tents and utensils. It also acts as an agent for companies at the other end of the business—heavy equipment and firepower. Between 1991 and 1994, Franklins was paid almost K12 million by the PNGDF. Its biggest contract year was 1992 when PNG bought K6,392,301 worth of supplies from or through Franklins.

As was the case with Pacific Paradise, the Los Inquiry learned that there was considerable dissatisfaction with Franklins within the PNGDF. In a minute to the Commander (then Brigadier Bob Dademo) that was tendered in evidence and dated 31 January 1994, the then Chairman of the Defence Supply and Tenders Board, Mr Michael Posou, said that the Board had resolved not to buy any more helmets or body armour from Franklins. 'For the last three years,' he wrote, '[the] Defence Force has been purchasing most of their military equipments from J. & S. Franklin Ltd in London. This company has been charging us high prices ... but because of the urgent requirements for the Bougainville Operation we have been keeping on buying from them.' He said some of the equipment did not meet requirements. 'In particular the body armours and helmets supplied by J. & S. Franklin were noted to be not quite safe for the troops on the frontline.' Posou said the Board had discovered that Franklins was buying helmets and body armour from a US company and he accused Franklins of 'double-handed business dealings'.

Despite this resolution not to deal with Franklins, the contracts kept flowing. In 1994, Franklins was paid almost K3 million. Amongst the supplies—more helmets and 6000 camouflage uniforms. Asked at the Los Inquiry what he felt about the quality of Franklins' supplies, ex-Brigadier Singirok described them as 'absolute junk' for which 'exorbitant' prices had been paid. 'I was generally not happy as a field officer about the quality of equipment that we were receiving.' He said the soldiers knew most of it came from Franklins because it bore the company logo. He told the Inquiry of one example, the individual shelter or one-man tent. 'I have slept in it,' Singirok said. 'It cannot withstand torrential rain.' Evidence before the

Inquiry showed Franklins charged $US42 for each shelter whereas a quote from a local PNG company for half that (K25 per unit) had been ignored. Major Walter Enuma, whom Singirok was to task with expelling the mercenaries, also had a poor opinion of Franklins' goods. 'I almost got sunk in a boat off Bougainville,' he told the Los Inquiry. 'I was pretty pissed off, so I asked, "Where did this boat come from?" And they said it was from Franklin.' Enuma said Franklins' webbing fell apart in the tropical conditions. 'I was pretty concerned about it,' he told the Los Inquiry, 'because I was the end user.'

The sense the men had that they had been abandoned on Bougainville contributed to the discipline problem. However, even before the Bougainville crisis blew up, the Defence Force was having significant problems with discipline. Grievances over pay in early 1989 erupted in the capital, Port Moresby. On the night of 7 February that year more than 150 soldiers from the 1st Battalion brushed past their Acting Commander on Taurama Road and ignoring his order to stop they walked, swearing and cursing, the ten kilometres from Taurama Barracks to Defence headquarters, Murray Barracks, to gather support. Once there, they gathered with their 'comrades' at the Kingsbury Club and when officers told them to disperse there was a hail of sticks, stones and bottles. By next morning, the mob had grown. They blocked the main road passing through Murray Barracks, chased off paper boys at the nearby traffic lights and overturned a police vehicle. Then about 400 marched to Parliament tearing off tree branches as clubs and threatening those who got in their way. At the Parliament they smashed windows on the ground floor and car windscreens in the public car park.

The collapse in discipline shocked the Government and led to the establishment of a Defence Board of Inquiry. Three soldiers including a Sergeant were found guilty of mutiny by PNG's National Court and gaoled. Sentencing two of them to nine months hard labour each and the third to four months, Mr Justice Bredmeyer said he had taken into account that the men had 'a real grievance' over pay. It had been thirteen years since the last review of soldier pay levels. A pay rise had been approved based on a complicated formula to redress imbalances but the details were never explained. While most soldiers were to get moderate raises the belief had spread that the increase was to be seventy-two per cent (true for one category alone, Sergeant Major). But some Privates were to get just five per cent. 'There was a delay in paying them,' the Judge said. 'They saw that as a failed promise. The pay rise was much less than they had been led to expect and there seems to have been a lack of communication between the officers and the men as to the details of the pay rise.'

The Board of Inquiry found major problems in the administration of the force but some of its toughest criticism was about the standard of discipline. A 'significant decline' in discipline had occurred, it said, since the PNGDF started to implement the 1983 Cabinet submission reducing its manpower ceiling to 3050. It claimed this had resulted in servicemen being overworked, recreation leave accumulating and low morale. There was 'an apparent inability and/or reluctance by commands at all levels to impose discipline'; officers and soldiers were 'becoming too familiar with each other'; there were 'inconsistencies' in the awarding of punishments; and 'undue delays' in the administration of discipline. The Board also found that a 'significant deterioration' of all aspects of service conditions had adversely affected discipline and there was 'an apparent failure by Defence Force training institutions to instil leadership qualities in the younger generation officers'.

Concern about discipline was nothing new. One year before the pay riot, an extraordinarily public argument was conducted in the pages of the PNG newspapers between the Defence Minister, James Pokasui, and the Defence Force Commander he had just sacked, Brigadier General Tony Huai. Pokasui claimed to the media that morale had slipped during Huai's tenure as head of the PNGDF. Huai countered by saying the problems went back well before his time as Commander. 'We were continuously under-budgeted,' he said. 'Our capital equipment, training and operational programs were always severely affected.' He claimed morale had been in decline since the mid-1970s. 'Gone are the pre-Independence days when we had stacks of personal equipment, stacks of air hours, stacks of land transport,' the ex-Commander complained, 'and we could travel anywhere in the country and spend weeks on patrol. Now we have to live with the reality of the economic situation. This one factor is the cause of morale and discipline problems.'

Terror at the domestic terminal

'The thing that really scared my life, was when that soldier, pointed the gun at me.' Dorothy Jakis, the Air Niugini Traffic Supervisor at Jackson's Airport, was giving evidence at a military court hearing of disciplinary charges against five soldiers who had allegedly terrorised passengers and Air Niugini ground staff at Jackson's on Sunday 13 November 1994. The five, and thirteen other soldiers, all armed, had demanded seats on board Flight PX128 to Lae. The men from the Engineer Battalion based in Lae held only wait-listed tickets and they arrived at the airport half an hour after the Lae flight had closed. But they had been drinking and were angry. They had wound up their tour on Bougainville and had been stranded for three weeks in Port Moresby on their way home to Lae.

'He pointed it at me and said, "Hey! Am I on? Am I on? Are you going to get me on that flight to Lae?" I was too scared to look him in the eye.' Jakis testified that another soldier had pointed a gun at a dispatch officer preventing him from getting the pilot of Flight PX128 to sign the passenger log book before the plane could be allowed to take off. The court heard that some soldiers had rushed out to the tarmac when they heard an aircraft engine start and forced the dispatch officer back into the terminal. However, the noise was from a jet engine on another aircraft being tested. It was about this time, Jakis said, that the glass door to boarding gate three was smashed but she did not see who had done it.

Donald Kaiwi, the Assistant Operations Manager of the company that had the airport security contract, Protect Wormald, told the *Post Courier's* Neville Togarewa the day after the incident that the soldiers' rampage came out of frustration with what they believed was the Government's failure to support them on Bougainville. Kaiwi, who had helped calm the soldiers down, said they told him they had not been paid for a month, they had to cook their own food at Taurama Barracks and there had been no money to send the body of a dead comrade home. 'Many of the soldiers were very drunk,' he said. 'They looked very frustrated, exhausted and depressed.' Nine months later the five soldiers, including a Lieutenant, were found guilty of unlawful assembly, unlawful assault and wilful damage and were sentenced to four months jail. But because they had spent time at a military remand centre they were released within days.

In the early days of the insurgency on Bougainville, there was stark evidence of the extent to which morale and discipline had collapsed. One entire company mutinied. However, it was hushed up at the time and no disciplinary action was taken. Yauka Liria, a former Intelligence Officer, revealed the incident in his book, *Bougainville Campaign Diary*, published in 1993. 'On the eve of a village search near Arawa,' he said, 'the Company got together and told the Company Commander that they would not be involved. Taken completely by surprise, the Commander was dumbfounded. The men told him that they wanted to go home to Wewak the following day, saying they'd had their three months operational duty and "just wanted to go home".

Soldiers had then fired their weapons indiscriminately in the camp to vent their frustrations and to show how serious they were. The Contingent Commander, taking a traditional meal of taro, almost suffered a heart attack when the company boss hurriedly brought him the news ... He simply didn't know how to react.'

Liria told of how the Contingent Commander, a Lieutenant Colonel, headed off in the dark towards the 2nd Battalion's B Company area. 'The soldiers were organised and ready and he played right into their trap. He went to negotiate, to request, to beg! "I'm asking you all to stay on for just another seven days. You must not spoil the Company's three months hard work and good reputation. Will you take part in the operation tomorrow?" The Commander's voice was only disturbed by the pounding of the waves in the dark. "No!" they all chorused. And there was an uneasy long silence. It was dark. The moon had not yet appeared. I could not see the Commander's face, but I felt terribly sorry for him.' The soldiers were granted their wish and were sent home to Wewak.

The slack enforcement of discipline in the PNGDF is sometimes startling, and not only on Bougainville. In early 1993 soldiers burnt down one of Port Moresby's longest established clubs, the Germania Club on one of the city's main thoroughfares, Waigani Drive. It happened in the early hours of Saturday morning, 3 April. On the Friday afternoon five soldiers from the 1st Battalion's Bravo Company, just back from a six-month tour of duty on Bougainville, picked up their field allowances and proceeded to the Nomads Cricket Club next door to the Germania Club to get drunk. By two o'clock the next morning when the club was about to close, they had succeeded. One of them, 'helpless' by that stage according to the army's version of events, was punched. The army news release, signed by the then PNGDF Chief of Staff, Colonel Joe Maras, reported that his comrades came to his aid and a brawl erupted, spilling over into the beer garden of the Germania Club. Police arrived, restored order and told the soldiers to go home to Taurama Barracks.

As the five drunken soldiers staggered back down Waigani Drive, they were approached by a group of men 'alleged to be from a security firm' and another fight broke out during which Private James Adam from the Trobriand Islands in the Milne Bay Province was hit on the head with a sharp object and killed. 'When the sad news reached his comrades at Taurama Barracks,' Colonel Maras said, 'they retaliated by setting the Germania Club on fire.' An internal army report revealed that these 'comrades' had intimidated a corporal into driving them to the Germania in an army vehicle. In front of the club they shouted in Pidgin, 'Kukim Club Germania' ('burn the Germania Club'). It was gutted.

Police rushed to the club for the second time that night only to be pelted with sticks and stones. The Fire Services Director, Oswald Arisa, said one fire engine sent to fight the fire was stopped by soldiers who blocked the road with a vehicle at a roundabout on Waigani Drive. The PNGDF Chief of Staff ended his news release saying an investigation had been initiated 'and those responsible will be disciplined accordingly'.

However, six months later the coroner, David Rea, conducting an inquest into the fire, discovered that no disciplinary action at all had been taken against any of the soldiers involved. Colonel Maras explained this was because the incident happened out of a Defence Force area and so, he claimed, breached the criminal law not the Force's regulations. Maras could not help the court with the names of any soldiers involved. Back in April, shortly after the fire, journalist Neville Togarewa wrote a column for the *Post Courier* on disciplinary problems within the PNGDF and called for a commission of inquiry. He referred to two other incidents in which soldiers had burnt down houses in Port Moresby settlements after brawls and suggested psychiatric counselling be provided because, he said, so many soldiers returning from Bougainville seemed to be suffering from Post Traumatic Stress Disorder.

Togarewa's article prompted an immediate response from the front line in Bougainville. 'I would be one of the few disciplined force members who would fully support what Mr Togarewa wrote,' a soldier who signed himelf Commander Zero, Bravo Company, Bougainville, said in a letter to the editor of the *Post Courier*. 'As you can see most of the casualties suffered by us, the security forces, have been due to carelessness, like not wearing helmets or body armour or by an individual taking off by himself to do laundry or have a wash in a nearby creek.' Commander Zero, however, wanted to defend the name of Bravo Company. He admitted the fire could have been done by 'the boys' but he rejected suggestions Bravo Company was responsible for the two raids on the settlements. 'As a serving member of Bravo Company I can tell you, this is a load of rubbish. We never took part in the Laloki and Vadavada settlement raids. The Laloki settlement raid was done by soldiers from the PNGDF Training Depot at Goldie River.'

Another soldier wrote agreeing with the need for soldiers returning from Bougainville to receive psychiatric counselling. 'I've seen so many of my comrades fighting over very little things either with civilians out in the streets or among themselves in the barracks,' he said. 'Even married soldiers beating up their wives for very little mistakes. Before the Bougainville operation the married soldiers were not like this. They would sit down and talk over the problem with his wife like a good father. But now, it's different altogether.'

Brigadier Singirok was one who tried to introduce counselling for returning soldiers. He said the small size of the army meant the two infantry battalions had to serve constantly rotating tours on Bougainville subjecting them to enormous stress.

Beating defenceless people was a tactic resorted to by soldiers on Bougainville as early as 1989, according to Yauka Liria. 'One way they would vent their anger and frustration,' he wrote in his book, 'was in cowardly attacks on easy catches rather than to face the armed BRA in the field. I remember quite clearly, an officer allowing his men to drag out an innocent villager, in a cordon and search operation near Aropa, and beat him. Blood was oozing from all over the victim's dark face as a group of blood-thirsty soldiers fought each other to have a go at the man ... Unwarranted harassment and beatings of the civilian population were strictly forbidden ... yet it was happening here, in broad daylight, under the very noses of the senior officers in the contingent.'

Liria was escorting the Joint Forces Commander, Colonel Lima Dotaona, at the time and Liria wrote about how Colonel Dotaona ordered the men to stop the beating but was confronted by a junior officer. '"Who said to stop the beating?" An officer, whose men were delivering the beating, advanced toward the Colonel and me, with his M16 levelled at the Joint Forces Commander. The officer repeated himself twice as he closed toward the Colonel, stopping about seven metres short.' Liria says he raised his gun at the officer and was worried that if either fired it would be disastrous. 'For a minute or two, the officer kept his weapon on us, and then he spoke. "Don't say 'Stop the beating', okay?" Me and my men we are the ones who suffer in the bush. We get shot at by these people and we face the hardship and the danger, okay. I don't want people to come here and stop us from doing our work!"'

The Bougainville experience has brutalised many of the men and there are sporadic instances even away from Bougainville of outrageous misbehaviour. Ordinary people going about their everyday work have become victims. On the afternoon of 4 October 1993, for example, residents of Kiunga in the Fly River Province wanting to do their banking at the local PNG Banking Corporation branch found their bank closed. The door to the bank was damaged and the manager, Henry Komberiu, was at the hospital receiving treatment for a badly cut chin and bruises. Soldiers had beaten him up. The trouble started when one soldier from the 1st Battalion stationed at the small border barracks in Kiunga went to the bank and demanded to withdraw money from his account even though he did not have his passbook. Komberiu refused explaining it was against bank policy. The soldier became abusive, kicked the door and stormed out. A short time later, he returned in an army vehicle with a group of other soldiers who helped him beat up the bank manager and a cleaner.

An army that takes industrial action

Papua New Guinea's defences were down in July 1994. Sailors joined the PNGDF's pilots in going on strike. The pilots had been refusing to fly since early July because of money problems but their work boycott had been kept quiet. On 22 July, the sailors went public. At the heavy landing craft base at Port Moresby Harbour they lowered the PNG Maritime Ensign and replaced it with the red and white striped port flag, indicating that operations had been halted.

One Maritime Officer, Major Kim Soso, told Papua New Guinea's National Broadcasting Commission the sailors wanted to do sea operations but the patrol boats badly needed maintenance. He said the maritime element had stopped work indefinitely until the sailors' demands were met. It was not only maintenance they were upset about. There were pay, housing and other claims too.

The PNGDF had been short of cash since well before Bougainville— but by 1994 the force's finances were chaotic. An audit report late in 1993 revealed appalling shortcomings, misuse of money and fraud. The Defence Minister, Paul Tohian, initially denounced the strike as a mutiny and said the punishment for those involved was death. Tohian was not in a strong position to be critical. In 1990, when he was Police Commissioner, he himself had been charged with trying to overthrow the Government after a heavy drinking session at a Defence Force barbecue which became known as the bar-b-coup. All charges against him were eventually withdrawn and he went on to win a seat in Parliament.

Two days after threatening the sailors they could be hanged, Defence Minister Tohian overruled his commander, reinstated two suspended Majors, and promised both to pay outstanding allowances and to provide funds to keep military craft operational. Instead of backing his military chief he said he would order an investigation into the management of the Force. In an editorial the *National* newspaper commented: 'There are very few places on earth where treasonable offences, sedition and even mutinous actions are not treated very seriously. Papua New Guinea is one such place.'

Disrespect for officers and contempt for politicians may be common in all armies but in PNG there is a never-ending stream of examples that have convinced the soldiers that their political masters are corrupt. Asked in Parliament in 1987 about the possibility of a coup, Prime Minister Wingti turned the question back on the Members of Parliament, including his own Cabinet, saying that if they wanted to avoid a coup then they must shun personal enrichment. A coup would only happen in PNG, he said, if people lost faith in their elected leaders. But it was the second Wingti-led Government that in the mid-1990s provided many of the troops with the perfect example to shake their faith. It had to do with a project aimed at solving the PNGDF's by then severe institutional housing problems. The Wingti Government gave a $US55 million contract to the fully owned subsidiary of a big Malaysian construction company, Yeoh Tiong Lay, YTL (PNG) Pty Ltd, in a deal that the Papua New Guinea Ombudsman claimed ignored the law.

The previous Namaliu Government had begun negotiations with the Malaysian Government on what was originally touted as a defence cooperation agreement. When the package was finally put together and agreed to in late 1993, Wingti's Government was in power. The Malaysian Government contributed a grant of $US5 million but the rest of the money, $US50 million, came from a consortium of Malaysian banks. In a major report, the Ombudsman Commission slated Government Ministers and public servants and said the proceedings of the Supply and Tenders Board when considering the project had become 'a farce'. 'No company, other than YTL ... was given any opportunity of bidding,' the report said. 'A certificate of inexpediency was issued in very strange and unsatisfactory circumstances ... normal checks and balances ... were bypassed ... [and] the project was not properly costed', among many other irregularities. The Ombudsman claimed YTL had been granted extremely generous concessions. 'It will pay no income tax, no customs duty, no stamp duty and no sales tax ... Its non-citizen employees will pay no income tax or customs duty.'

'The effect of these concessions,' the report said, 'has been to give this particular company a very, very easy passage into our economy. Suspicion of corruption inevitably arises when these sorts of concessions are made in the course of commercial agreements. The people of PNG deserve much better than this.' The Ombudsman Commission uncovered no evidence of actual corruption but said that did not mean corrupt practices did not occur. 'While our laws for awarding contracts continue to be flouted, and our leaders and their advisers take a complacent attitude to these gross irregularities, corruption will inevitably prosper and there will always be grave suspicion about what has happened. Our government advisers and leaders must both respect and follow our laws—and not try to by-pass them... If the government of the day ignores the laws of the country, then it can hardly expect the ordinary citizens to obey them.' Amongst the rank and file of the Defence Force there was no doubt corruption had been involved—as during the Sandline crisis their chief suspect, Colonel Alfred Aikung, was to learn. Soldiers angry about Aikung's appointment to replace Singirok burnt his vehicle, a Muso which the Malaysians had provided to the Force for the housing project.

There was one earlier occasion when certain members of the PNGDF were ready to take action against the Government if their commander was toppled. It was in 1977, two years after Independence, and the Somare Government reprimanded Brigadier General Ted Diro for holding a clandestine meeting with an Irian Jayan rebel leader. An ex-colonel later told former ABC correspondent, Geoff Heriot, that the 'plan was to blow the Waigani building and take a few of the political leaders, Somare and his advisers, hostage. And then commence some dialogue in order to get the Government to start thinking seriously about their policies and what to do with Indonesia.' It was called Operation Electric Shock and allegedly would have involved soldiers from the 1st Battalion. But Diro was not dismissed and the affair went no further.

As the years went on, the appointment of the Commander of the PNGDF became highly political. Following Diro's retirement to go into politics, the first Chan Government appointed Brigadier Gago Mamae as Commander by-passing Ken Noga who had stood unsuccessfully as a pro-Pangu Somare candidate in the 1977 elections. A year after Somare was returned to power in 1982, he gave the job to Noga and Mamae left the PNGDF to work for Chan. Later Mamae stood unsuccessfully for Chan's PPP. When Paias Wingti defeated Somare in a no-confidence vote in 1985, and Chan became Deputy Prime Minister, Noga was sacked. He was replaced by Tony Huai. Following the 1987 elections, the new Defence Minister, James Pokasui, a former sailor, sacked Huai and installed Brigadier Rochus Lokinap. Huai joined Chan's PPP and stood in the 1992 elections but without success. Lokinap led the force for five years although for six months of that time he was under suspension following the 1989 army pay riot.

During Brigadier Lokinap's time as Commander there was an extraordinary act of defiance of the elected government. The Cabinet decided to shut the airport in the centre of Lae and shift all air traffic movements to Nadzab forty kilometres up the Markham Valley. The Defence Minister had argued that the PNGDF had no money to relocate its Air Transport Squadron to Nadzab but he lost out in the Cabinet debate. So at dawn on 1 June 1988, military aircraft flew sixty fully armed combat soldiers from Port Moresby to Lae. They occupied the strip and, at gunpoint, stopped Civil Aviation authorities from sending in the bulldozers to tear up the runway. Prime Minister Wingti reprimanded the Brigadier General but the troops stayed at the Lae airport and the Defence Force was allowed to keep using Lae until new facilities to accommodate the PNGDF air element were built in Port Moresby from Australian Defence Cooperation aid. A precedent had been set in which the force had dramatically defied civil authority and got its way without repercussions.

Between 1992 and the end of 1995, the PNGDF had four commanders in quick succession. Wingti, back in power in 1992, appointed Brigadier Bob Dademo to replace Lokinap. Dademo, a shy, difficult man, had problems with his senior Colonels from day one. He attempted to neutralise these former rivals by having them posted to jobs outside Murray Barracks. Colonel Leo Nuia, who had been labelled the 'Butcher of Bougainville' by secessionist sympathisers after his admission that his men had dumped the bodies of executed rebel suspects at sea in 1990, was one. The Commander won Cabinet approval to have Nuia posted to Jakarta as Defence Attache. But Nuia refused to go and never did. Three years earlier, in 1989, the Government of Rabbie Namaliu had ordered Nuia to go to Jakarta but he had refused then as well and within months was posted by Brigadier Lokinap to take control of the Bougainville operation. When in charge on Bougainville, both then and in later years, Nuia took initiatives that often contradicted official Government policy. Brigadier Dademo became closely identified with Prime Minister Wingti and with an Australian adviser of Wingti's, Dennis Reinhardt, who had a chequered history in mining in Australia.

When Chan took over in 1994, he immediately replaced Dademo with Huai, whom he had enticed back from a career in private industry. But fifteen months later, Sir Julius asked Brigadier Huai to stand aside in favour of thirty-eight-year-old Jerry Singirok. Singirok had been one of the few soldiers to have won praise from almost all quarters during his first tour of Bougainville in 1989 as Operations Officer. The son of a traditional leader on the still-active volcanic island of Karkar in the Madang Province, Singirok was talented and ambitious. He had enlisted in the PNGDF in 1974 after matriculating from the Sogeri National High School. By 1986 he was a Major and replaced the last Australian to be Operations and Training Officer with the 2nd Battalion. After his stint on Bougainville in 1989, he was selected to do a course in strategic studies at the Australian Command and General Staff College at Queenscliff in Victoria. The Australian Army offered the promising Major Singirok a job as an instructor at the Land Warfare Centre at Canungra in Queensland. For two years there he taught Australian soldiers up to the rank of Lieutenant Colonel in the art of conventional warfare.

In 1993 Singirok was recalled to take over as Operations Officer on Bougainville again. He carried out the job with distinction. In December 1993 he was promoted to Lieutenant Colonel and became Commanding Officer of the 1st Battalion. Back on Bougainville in 1994, he led the Wingti Government ordered occupation of the Panguna mine, Operation High Speed. Singirok was wounded in action. 'I have lost 40 per cent of the functions of my left arm,' Singirok told one of the later Sandline inquiries when asked about this incident. '[The] rebels had killed a senior officer and his batman [but] it was impossible to extract them because of heavy enemy engagement. After all attempts had failed, as the Commanding Officer, it was important for me to go out ... and recover the two bodies. I went with the recovery team on a Hevi Lift helicopter and as we were attempting to land at the airfield where the dead bodies were, whilst still airborne, we were sprayed ... by an automatic weapon from the enemy into the helicopter ... I was shot through my left arm.'

After recovering, he was promoted to Colonel and made Chief of Intelligence. Less than a year later, Sir Julius Chan called Singirok to the Prime Minister's office. He asked the newest and youngest Colonel in the PNGDF how he would go about gaining the military ascendancy on Bougainville. Chan had been in power for fifteen months and progress towards a peaceful solution on Bougainville was eluding him. Increasingly fed up with what he saw as the stalemate on the island he gave Singirok twenty-four hours to prepare a Concept of Operations. 'If I interview somebody and want to appoint him to a position,' Sir Julius told the Los Inquiry, 'I like to get some sort of indication that he will be able to live up to it ... [I wanted] to have someone to help me resolve the Bougainville situation.' Dated 15 November 1995, Singirok's plan proposed a decisive, six-week campaign striking at the BRA stronghold, the Kongara, in Central Bougainville. A particular target was to be the village of Sipuru south of the Panguna mine that Ona used as a base. Amongst the listed aims was to: 'Destroy and kill BRA leaders ... and those who are actively supporting the armed struggle.' Singirok wrote that 'Operational commanders ... must realise the importance of eliminating the BRA to such a level where they are completely demised of the ability and energy and the will to continue armed struggle ... Every member of the Security Force must assist in ... placing the National Government in a favourable position to enable it to control the situation.'

Asked by Singirok's lawyer at the Los Inquiry if it was true that, when presenting this 'Operational Concept' paper to him the next day, Singirok had tempered it with the observation that the military option was 'not the best possible solution' for Bougainville, Sir Julius replied: 'If he did, he would not be speaking out of place because I, too, was looking for a political solution.' Sir Julius convinced his Cabinet it was time to try a new, youthful Commander with operational experience on Bougainville to lead the PNGDF. Extremely popular in the ranks, Singirok had lots of enemies at Murray Barracks. The reaction to Singirok's appointment as Commander was well summed up by the headlines in the PNG *Post Courier* the next day. The larger headline read, 'Singirok As CO–Joy On Bougainville'. A second story was headed, 'Army Chiefs Meet In Anger Over Top Job'. The first story spoke of how some Bougainvilleans, their leaders and many soldiers greeted the news with jubilation. Premier Miriung was reported to have responded by singing a chorus of a hymn, 'his common way of showing happiness'. The other story said a group of Colonels 'older and with longer service than Singirok' had met and were 'disgruntled that Cabinet had ignored them'. The Opposition Leader, Roy Yaki, congratulated the new Commander welcoming what he called the appointment of 'a real soldier' who he believed had 'the total support of the troops'.

In his announcement Prime Minister Chan, said it was time 'for an up-and-coming young officer to inherit the important task of rebuilding the Force'. Asked if Singirok would get the Government support he needed to tackle the PNGDF's many problems, Sir Julius replied: 'We're going to try to give him the capacity to deal with unforseen situations and the sooner we bring the Bougainville situation to a close the better it is for everybody. Yes, we just can't appoint a new man without capacity. We've got to put wings to him.'

Chapter Four

Defence Systems Limited— The Forerunner to Sandline

The First Attempt by British Military Consultants to Win a PNG Government Contract

The Defence Minister in the Chan Government, Mathias Ijape, rightfully claimed credit for initiating the Sandline contract. It was not a deal he was ever ashamed of. Quite the opposite. He boldly boasted to the first of the two Sandline inquiries that if Brigadier Singirok had not aborted Operation Oyster then the rebel leaders—Francis Ona, Joseph Kabui and Sam Kauona— would have been captured and tried in the very courtroom in which he was then giving evidence to Justice Warwick Andrew. 'Commissioner, these Bougainville exercises are very expensive, not only for the Defence Force but for the country as a whole,' he said in evidence on 25 April 1997. 'Every soldier that stays on the island is paid K25 a day and we have about a thousand soldiers on the island ... it is very, very costly. And this thirty-five or thirty-six million that we have proposed for this project I think it is a drop in the ocean because I was confident, Commissioner, I was 101 per cent confident that on D-Day, on the 30th of April, this month, we would have got those people.'

Ijape was sure the Sandline mercenaries would have enabled the Government to seek out and crush 'the head' of the rebel movement. 'Yes, we would have got them and we would have brought them to Waigani [the Port Moresby suburb where the PNG Supreme and National Courts are located] and they would have been through the courts now. And that same 36 million, Commissioner, as I said, is a drop in the ocean as opposed to the benefits of having [opened] the mine, bringing peace to the island [and] bringing services to ... Bougainville.' Ijape said he hoped that the government formed at the then imminent 1997 national elections would honour the contract and get Sandline back to complete the job. 'But if this project does not go ahead after the election, Commissioner, I am telling you this war will be there for another twenty years.' The new Skate Government never followed Ijape's advice. It kept Sandline out and pursued a negotiated settlement. By early 1998, when Ijape, who had lost his seat, was giving evidence to the second Sandline Inquiry, much progress had been made towards peace on Bougainville. Unabashed, Ijape still claimed the credit. 'This peace process in Bougainville would not have happened had Sandline not been engaged,' he claimed to Justice Kublan Los. 'Sandline is the one that forced the BRAs to come to the discussion table ... we brought peace on that island.'

Ijape, a former police prosecutor from PNG's Eastern Highlands who had put himself through law school, left the Parliament a wealthy man. He told the Los Inquiry he owned five coffee plantations. But he strenuously denied that any of his wealth had resulted from secret commissions arising from the Sandline deal. The Los Inquiry did manage to uncover one previously secret Sandline commission–a $US500,000 payment to a former political colleague of Ijape's, Benias Sabumei. Sabumei, also from the Eastern Highlands, had been Defence Minister in the government led by Rabbie Namaliu (1988-92) when Ijape had been Police Minister. The two Ministers, both members of the relatively small, junior coalition partner, the National Party, had been enthusiastic about engaging foreign specialists with a military background to work in PNG from the early 1990s. The first group Police Minister Ijape tried to hire was a British company with ex-Special Air Service (SAS) connections called Defence Systems Limited (DSL) of London. Ijape's initial idea was to get DSL to train an elite squad of PNG police to protect PNG's major mining, oil and gas projects. However, despite Ijape's vigorous efforts, DSL never quite clinched the deal.

Ijape went into Opposition after the 1992 elections. His colleague, Sabumei, lost his seat. DSL remained interested in the possibilities for its line of work in PNG and, according to Sabumei, took him on as a consultant. 'After I left the ministry,' Sabumei told the Los Inquiry, 'I was in contact with DSL and ... through my consulting work ... I unsuccessfully tried to establish the company here in PNG to offer security services to mines and other establishments.' DSL almost pulled off a $US10 million deal to train an anti-terrorist police squad for the Wingti Government. But it did not work out and DSL closed down its Port Moresby office. A few years on, in early 1996, Ijape, back in government as Sir Julius Chan's Defence Minister, wanted to renew his acquaintance with the ex-SAS experts at DSL. 'The Minister asked me whether I had contact with DSL,' Sabumei testified. 'I said, "Yes." I put him onto a contact in London.' It was a contact Ijape knew well, DSL's Chairman, Alistair Morrison, whom he had dealt with extensively when Police Minister. Morrison referred Ijape on to Tim Spicer.

After the Sandline contract was signed a year later, in early 1997, and Papua New Guinea had paid the first half of the contract price, $US18 million, into Sandline's bank account in Hong Kong, Sabumei was paid half a million US dollars. He claimed it was a legitimate 'introduction fee'. The money was transferred out of Hong Kong on 24 February 1997 and deposited on 27 February into an account Sabumei had opened in Queensland with the Charlotte Street, Brisbane, branch of Citibank. Ian Molloy, Counsel Assisting (who filled the role for both the Andrew and Los Inquiries), demanded to know who else had shared the fee. He traced the money trail to PNG. But then it dried up. Sabumei transferred more than $US400,000 (K714,000) into two accounts in PNG much of it then being withdrawn in cash. Sabumei risked contempt of the Los Inquiry by refusing to disclose where the cash went or what it was used for. 'It is my business, Mr Molloy. I will not tell you,' he stonewalled under relentless questioning.

Cash payments

Benias Sabumei spent an uncomfortable few days in the witness box before the second Sandline Inquiry. Some shrewd detective work and helpful connections in Hong Kong and Australia enabled Counsel Assisting the Inquiry, Ian Molloy, to confront Sabumei with a mass of material relating to the $US500,019.39 that Sandline Holdings paid him out of its account number HK 6007 74426 at the Queen's Road East branch of the Hong Kong Bank. Sabumei began by refusing to acknowledge the payment. Then he challenged the authenticity of the information. 'I want to know where Mr Molloy got this,' he complained to Justice Los. 'He may have picked it up in a rubbish bin in Hong Kong. Where did you get this?'

Eventually, he conceded the money had been deposited into an account of his at a branch of Citibank in Brisbane. But he would not disclose what happened to the money once it reached PNG.

'Have a look at this,' Molloy asked producing a cheque book. 'Do you see that the first of those large payments is in respect of Cheque No. 202—K80,000? Can you find the cheque butt for 202? ... If this was a legitimate business expense why would you not fill out the cheque butt so it could be seen who you were paying the money to?'

'I do not have an answer for that,' Sabumei replied.

'Well there is no answer, is there? And then the next one is 207—K115,000, you can check that butt as well and I suggest to you that you have not written the name of the recipient of that money either?'

'I am not going to answer that.'

'And I suggest the same goes for the K69,000—cheque number 214; K50,000—cheque number 216; another K50,000—cheque number 217; and the K60,000—cheque number 225. None of those cheque butts has been filled in. You can check that for yourself and can you tell me why you have not filled those butts in? Got any answer to that?'

'No,' Sabumei replied.

Justice Los reminded Sabumei of his obligation to answer but the former PNG Government Minister refused. He suggested the payment was in part recognition for consultancy work he had done years before for another British company, DSL, but he could offer no convincing explanation as to why Sandline should pay him for that. He claimed Tim Spicer, from Sandline had contacted him after Spicer had arrived in PNG in late 1996. 'I said [to Spicer] I would be looking at half a million at least.' And he maintained Spicer said that amount 'sounds okay'.

Sabumei argued the $US500,000 was 'a legitimate consulting fee that I earned by putting two parties together. That is normal international business. How I pay, who I pay, it is my business Your Honour and I will not tell Mr Molloy or the Inquiry as I believe it is a private business matter and I will not answer any more questions.'

Molloy did not stop. He presented Sabumei with the original cheques, most made out to cash, and forced him to admit he had rung up the bank a day in advance of calling in to pick up the huge cash withdrawals. Molloy asked Sabumei why he had taken out a loan for K10,000 to go on a holiday to his wife's home country, India, in mid-1997 when he apparently had access to hundreds of thousands of kina. Sabumei objected to the question. 'I am suggesting to you,' Molloy continued, 'that you remitted the money in those large amounts back to PNG and then distributed to the person or persons the money was intended for?'

'I refuse to answer that question,' Sabumei replied.

In summing up at the conclusion of formal evidence Molloy described as 'a most unlikely scenario' Sabumei's claim that the half a million US dollars was an introduction fee. 'Sandline, if nothing else, have proved to be astute and tenacious business people,' he said. 'There was plainly no obligation upon them to pay Mr Sabumei anything. It is ludicrous to suggest that

Sandline, through Spicer, have simply acceded to Sabumei's demand for a commission in the circumstances he describes. Mr Sabumei's version of events means that the money was his to use as he wished. However, he has not shown how any part of that money was used for his own benefit. On the contrary, the evidence is that in 1997, whilst the money (or part of it) sat in an interest bearing deposit in Australia, he defaulted in payment of credit card charges in that country. In addition in about July 1997, Mr Sabumei applied to increase an existing personal loan by borrowing a further K10,000 from a PNG bank for the purpose of a holiday in India. This is not the behaviour of a person who has up to $US500,000 in cash at his disposal.'

Counsel Assisting invited the three Commissioners to make a number of findings about the payment. 'The irresistible conclusion, I submit, is that Mr Sabumei was being used as a conduit. The account which he estabished with Citibank in Brisbane was a convenient location for the payment of $US500,000 by Sandline International for the benefit of some other person or persons. The only reasonable conclusion is that this payment was of a corrupt nature. The question is who was intended to benefit from the payment to Mr Sabumei.' Molloy suggested that Ijape and the then Deputy Prime Minister and Minister for Finance, Chris Haiveta, were not above suspicion. Lawyers for both men, Marshall Cooke QC for Ijape, and Stuart Littlemore QC for Haiveta, accused Molloy of being unprofessional and irresponsible. Littlemore urged the Commissioners to 'reject out of hand' what he called Molloy's 'wild and outrageous' suggestions. 'Counsel Assisting wants the Commission to guess as to the facts,' he said. 'No. It is a matter of convincing evidence or nothing.' Sabumei's refusal to answer many of the questions put to him left the issue obscured.

However, DSL's own earlier venture into PNG is worth examining in its own right to gain an understanding of how the whole Sandline deal could have happened. The connection began a full six years before Sabumei received his Sandline 'success fee'. DSL's failure to secure its own paying contract reveals a great deal about ministerial initiatives, PNG's beleaguered disciplined forces and the workings of the apparatus of State in Papua New Guinea.

DSL was formed in Great Britain in 1981 by a team of ex-SAS officers and City of London financiers with the 'objective', its own promotional material claimed, 'of providing credible solutions to the ever-changing and increasingly sophisticated and complex security threats facing governments, multinational corporations and individuals around the world'. DSL's core business, it said, 'is security consultancy and training through the provision of highly qualified specialists with international experience in practical security, law and order and counter-terrorist operations'. And they prided themselves on knowing their business. 'DSL personnel, because of their SAS backgrounds, have taken part in actual operations dealing with international terrorism and heavily armed criminal activity.' Initially part of the British Hambros international banking and financial group, DSL was taken over in 1997 by an American company, Armour Holdings.

Ijape became a great admirer of Alistair Morrison OBE MC, the driving force behind DSL. A former second-in-command of the world-renowned 22 SAS, Morrison had a distinguished military career. Commissioned initially into the Brigade of Guards, he was a regular British army officer for twenty years, undertaking four tours of duty with the SAS. 'He was awarded the Military Cross for operations in the Middle East and the Order of the British Empire for his direct involvement in the hostage rescue operation from the Lufthansa aircraft at Mogadishu in 1977,' the company informed the PNG Government in a profile it provided in 1993. 'The Mogadishu hijack focused the world's attention on such terrorist actions and resulted in many countries reviewing their response and indeed developing their own capability. During his final two years as second-in-command of 22 SAS, Alistair Morrison was instrumental in helping some thirty-two countries develop their counter-terrorist response.'

Morrison took his expertise to the private sector. He founded DSL in 1981 and is still its Chairman. By the early 1990s, DSL had, by its own account, 'become one of the leading UK specialist security companies' providing 'security management services for multinational companies and Governments in most of the high risk areas of the world including Angola, Mozambique, Zaire, Guyana, PNG and Colombia'. DSL's work in Papua New Guinea to that point had been in security consultancy services for mining and oil companies but it was keen to become a contractor to the Government. In Angola, its corporate client was Endima, the Angolan State Diamond Corporation. The DSL Chairman, therefore, got to know well the work of Eeben Barlow and Executive Outcomes, who had turned the Angolan civil war in the government's favour, much to Endima's benefit.

The other director of DSL who Ijape befriended, Noel Philp, also had excellent military credentials and had actually worked in PNG. Just a few years earlier, in 1989, Philp had retired from the New Zealand Army with the rank of Lieutenant Colonel, having commanded the New Zealand Special Air Service for four years. He had served for a total of twenty-two years in both the British and New Zealand armies, spending fourteen of those in either the British or New Zealand SAS. During his tours with Britain's 22 SAS, Noel Philp commanded the counter-terrorist team, was an instructor to the Royal Protection Group, trained South American police forces in diplomatic protection duties and was responsible for raising and training a national counter-terrorist force for an Organisation of African Unity (OAU) conference. And, after leaving the army, he had worked for DSL advising on security at gold and oil projects in PNG and Indonesia.

'PNG's widely publicised security problems and its considerable mineral and petroleum wealth made it an attractive market to DSL,' according to Sinclair Dinnen, a criminologist who worked with PNG's National Research Institute in the early to mid-1990s and is now with the Australian National University. In his doctoral thesis, 'Challenges of Order in a Weak State', Dinnen tracks the various attempts DSL made between 1991 and 1994 to seal up multimillion-dollar security training and consultancy deals with successive governments in PNG. There are some fascinating parallels and obvious points of difference with the later Sandline negotiations. And it could be argued (certainly by those who agree with the right of PNG Ministers to privatise their nation's security protection) that the DSL experience contained lessons as to the importance of keeping Australia ignorant.

The saga began in August 1991, when Ijape as Police Minister met with senior members of the PNG Chamber of Mines and Petroleum, PNG's most powerful industry lobby group. He informed them of his concerns about possible disruption to PNG's major resource projects in the lead-up to the 1992 national elections, then just ten months away. Ijape had an ambitious plan. He wanted to offer the companies greater police protection by building seven new barracks for a total of 270 police in various locations around the country. One of these was to be a base in his own electorate of Goroka for forty policemen. Like the others the new Goroka Barracks would include single and married accommodation, a dining hall, an armoury and a gymnasium. As is often the case with PNG Ministers' initiatives, however, there was a funding problem. But, Ijape informed the Chamber of Mines and Petroleum, if the resource companies would pay for the new police bases, he would arrange for them to claim the costs against tax.

The Chamber was indeed concerned about security. But it was not so certain Ijape's plan provided any answer. Goroka, for instance, was not near any of the major resource projects. Neither were Port Moresby or Lae, sites for two of the other six proposed barracks. The Chamber's response was to set up a security sub-committee which advocated project-specific police units to be located on site and which would remain in existence for the productive life of each project. Up until this time, if there was any major outbreak of trouble at or near these big extractive projects police mobile squads were sent in. The mobile squads had earned a worrying reputation for destroying villages and crops and perpetrating human rights abuses in payback style raids against suspected culprits. The Chamber's counter proposal to Ijape was to offer police the use of existing company accommodation at selected projects. Chamber members would also build additional houses and barracks provided the Police Department obtained the necessary land and government approvals, and provided all associated costs were tax deductable.

Later that month Ijape refined his own proposal. On 23 August 1991 he wrote to the Chamber proposing the establishment 'of a large central base in the Highlands for the new units'. The Chamber countered with a proposed two-phase approach–phase one was for mobile units to be located at the Porgera gold mine (in the Enga Province) and at the Kutubu oil and Hides gas fields (in the Southern Highlands) for twelve to eighteen months while the new units were recruited and trained; while in the second phase those new, trained units would be deployed on site and housed by the companies. The proposed central base, the Chamber suggested, should be deferred until the new system was evaluated.

In a Cabinet Submission dated 22 October 1991, Ijape proposed the creation of a police Rapid Deployment Unit (RDU). His submission claimed this had the support of the Chamber of Mines and Petroleum but there were significant differences between what Ijape wanted and what the companies had agreed to. 'The thrust of Minister Ijape's submission was to start the construction of a large RDU base before the 1992 elections in his own constituency of Goroka in the Eastern Highlands, some considerable distance away from the nearest project site,' Dinnen said. 'The base would eventually accommodate 250 married and 56 single staff and would have offices, training buildings, an armoury, weapons range, school, health centre and recreational facilities.' His RDU was to be well equipped with specialised motor vehicles and both helicopters and fixed-wing aircraft.

The projected cost of all this was put at about K39 million. Ijape advocated that private security companies should be hired to train his RDU police. The Minister 'made no acknowledgment of the Chamber's reservations about mobile squads or their preference for developing a community policing orientation,' Dinnen said. Letters exchanged between Ijape and the President of the Chamber revealed further differences. The Minister stated the RDU would also be required for police duties elsewhere while the Chamber President said members 'were not convinced that the huge expenditures required' were 'justified at this stage'. The Chamber said its proposal of on-site accommodation 'was the most viable alternative' and would cost 'a more realistic' sum of several million kina. Annoyed, Ijape replied on 24 November 1991: 'I further do not agree with your views that 30 million kina is not justified expenditure at this stage ... when would you justify the expenditure? At the time when the mines are up in flames or being disrupted? Unfortunately mine disruption and illegal activities are not timed like other good controlled lawful activities, a point you don't seem to comprehend or appreciate.'

Within two months Ijape had the justification he needed to push his Rapid Deployment Unit concept forward. In January 1992 CRA's mining camp at Mount Kare near the border of the Enga and Southern Highlands Provinces just thirty kilometres from the hugely successful Porgera gold mine was attacked. Mount Kare had been the scene of an extraordinary gold rush in 1988 after one of CRA's camp labourers found a gold nugget in a creek bed. Thousands of Papua New Guineans converged on Mount Kare scooping and gouging an estimated $A100 million worth of alluvial gold out of the muddy creeks running down the slopes below the CRA camp. After most of the easily accessible gold was gone and the rush subsided, CRA entered into an agreement with a landowner company to jointly dredge for what was left of the alluvial gold while continuing hard-rock exploration. But divisions within the landowning groups led to endless conflict. On the night of 9 January, fifteen armed men stormed the Mount Kare alluvial mining operation and put a pistol to the head of the camp manager. 'They stole cash and gold from the safe and ransacked and set fire to part of the camp and some mining equipment,' a CRA news release the next day related.

Perturbed by the raid and worried about disgruntled landowners elsewhere, the Chamber of Mines and Petroleum warned of damage to PNG's investment image. A few days later representatives of the major companies met with senior Ministers at Parliament House. Ijape told the *Post Courier* newspaper the 'signs of Mount Kare snowballing to Porgera are crystal clear. If the Porgera mine goes it will cost the company K2 million a day.' And he repeated his intention to get the Rapid Deployment Unit base built. Prime Minister Namaliu agreed to meet the Chamber's security sub-committee which expressed its concern to him about the slow progress of the official police investigation into the Mount Kare incident.

'Against this highly charged background,' Sinclair Dinnen wrote, 'the NEC [National Executive Council, PNG's Cabinet] approved Minister Ijape's submission on 22 January 1992.' Phase One of the approved proposal provided for accommodating 150 single police at selected project sites, their training and the procurement of specialised equipment prior to the issue of writs for the national election. This 'Phase One' was misleadingly referred to in the Cabinet submission as being the Chamber of Mines and Petroleum's proposal. 'Among other things,' Dinnen argued, 'this sleight of hand illustrates how elements of the "weak state" sought to capture the powerful mining industry in pursuit of their own electoral agenda.' Although the submission had not nominated who would do the training, Cabinet approved giving the work to the company favoured by Ijape, DSL.

Ijape did not win on every point, however. There was debate in Cabinet as to where the Rapid Deployment Unit's permanent base should be. Ijape's suggestion of Goroka was rejected and replaced with Tari in the Southern Highlands, a location far closer to the main resource projects. Phase Two of what the Cabinet approved involved the 'immediate' construction of this permanent base and associated facilities at Tari for 150 police. Phase Three was the doubling of the Tari base's capacity to cater for the full 300-member RDU and work on that was to begin in June. Tax rebates for costs borne by the industry were also approved. Announcing the Cabinet decision, the Acting Prime Minister, Jack Genia, said the 'sole task of the Rapid Deployment Unit will be to provide around-the-clock security for mines and oil fields and gas projects and to effectively deal with any disturbances around these projects rapidly on short notice'.

Ijape wrote to DSL's Chairman, Alistair Morrison, inviting him to PNG and suggesting that subject to contractual negotiations, DSL could start training the RDU in March. Morrison and one of DSL's directors travelled to PNG in February to be met by an enthusiastic but frustrated Ijape. There was no money for his grand plan. His appeal to the giant resource projects for funds had elicited no response despite the tax rebate offer. 'At a specially convened security meeting Minister Ijape expressed the government's intention to involve DSL in the RDU project,' Dinnen said. 'Mr Morrison stated that his company was prepared to fund initial training until the larger project proceeded.' Looking around for funds Ijape turned his attention towards Australian aid. But he was to be disappointed.

Australian opposition

The prison-like concrete walls topped with razor wire that surround the $A20 million Australian High Commission residential compound at Konedobu in Port Moresby bear testimony to Australia's official concern about law and order in Papua New Guinea. So when Australia decided to phase out direct cash support to the PNG budget and gradually switch the $A300 million a year aid grant to 'agreed' programs and projects it was hardly surprising that one of the early targets for assistance would be the Royal Papua New Guinea Constabulary (RPNGC). By early 1992, when Police Minister Mathias Ijape was promoting his Rapid Deployment Unit idea, Australia had already contributed more than $A30 million towards the Police Development Project.

It was, at that time, the largest single project the Australian aid agency, AIDAB (now AusAid) was funding in PNG. Under this program of 'institution building', significant numbers of Australian advisers were attached to the PNG Police Force. Incidentally, this was the opposite of what was happening with the PNG Defence Force. The Australian Army was cutting back its numbers in the PNGDF. The return of Australians to advisory roles in the Police Force was not universally appreciated. At the annual PNG–Australia Ministerial Forum in Madang in early 1992, Ijape told the media, 'We have more than enough advisers in the field now.'

The Police Minister was seeking an extra $A100 million from the Australians for 'infrastructure and capacity building' but he wanted it without the entanglement of having to take any more advisers. Australian ones, anyway! 'From the outset,' Sinclair Dinnen said, 'the proposal to involve Defence Systems Limited met determined resistance from police advisers to the AusAid-funded RPNGC Project and, less consistently, from senior RPNGC officers.' The advisers claimed DSL would both duplicate and interfere with what they were doing.

The PNG Police Force's senior management body–the Police Executive Committee–moved to try to have the Cabinet decision approving DSL's engagement as trainers for the Rapid Deployment Unit overturned. At the request of the Police Commissioner, Ila Geno, senior officers drafted a new Cabinet policy submission paper dealing with RDU funding. This sought Cabinet approval for K770,000 towards the implementation of Phase One of the project (the selection and training of the first RDU members who were to be provided with accommodation at the project sites) and it asked Cabinet to reconsider its decision to engage DSL because of financial constraints and the existing AusAid-funded training assistance.

The draft policy paper raised what the Police Executive Committee believed to be DSL's 'inappropriate' military (as opposed to police) background. It also attempted to point out to Cabinet Ministers that the Police Commissioner had a certain independence, that he had constitutional rights and prerogatives as far as operational and training matters were concerned. '[The] Commissioner feels that just as it is his prerogative under the National Constitution to give members operational direction, it naturally follows that he alone must decide the training necessary as well as the personnel required to give professional effect to such directions.' Standing up to Ministers and pointing out to them the proper legal limits to their powers has become an increasingly risky course of action in PNG since the late 1970s. Not surprisingly, Ijape never presented that draft submission to Cabinet.

Brushing aside the Commissioner's objections, Ijape devoted his energies to finding the money he needed to set up the RDU's central base. 'At a meeting with industry representatives in February, the Minister stressed the importance of getting the RDU operational before the June elections,' Dinnen wrote. 'He warned that a new government might be less committed than his own to improving project security. While the NEC decision appeared to secure the future of the RDU, lack of funds and institutional capacity impeded implementation.' The officer put in charge of the RDU project, Chief Superintendent Geoffrey Vaki, was pressing the Finance Department for cash. But by April none had been released. One Finance official said only K100,000 would be available while another told Vaki he might get K300,000. That was the 'absolute ceiling'. Police estimated K900,000 was the minimum required to make Phase One viable.

By now the elections were fast approaching and Ijape looked elsewhere for the cash. In late April 1992, not much more than a month before voting was to begin, Ijape prepared a new submission for Cabinet. This was for a proposed 'turnkey' project for the Goroka base to be built by Downer Constructions. PNG Ministers love the concept of turnkey projects under which all the costs are borne by the developer until the job is completed. Then, at the handing over of the new building or facility, 'the turning of the key', the Government begins paying back all the capital, interest and other costs. Having no up-front costs is a very attractive proposition to Ministers whose departments are constantly telling them they have no money. Committing the State to huge repayments down the track means the problem of payment is transferred into the future. It need not be an immediate concern at all.

In his new submission Ijape claimed the earlier Cabinet decision (in late January) had instructed the Ministers for Police and Finance 'to report back to the Cabinet on the possible source of funding and conditions of funding arrangements from the Chamber of Mines and Petroleum for the implementation of the RDU base headquarters to be constructed at Goroka'. Dinnen pointed out that the former Cabinet decision 'did not, in fact, contain any such instructions and, moreover, specified Tari as the site of the proposed base!' Ijape explained away the selection of Downer Constructions on the grounds that owing to 'time constraints' it had not been possible to abide by normal government tendering procedures. His submission requested Cabinet to direct the Departments of Finance and Justice to negotiate an appropriate financial package with Downer.

The PNG Cabinet approved this submission on 6 May 1992, despite the fact that the Finance Department (on 22 April) had rejected the consulting engineer's recommendations on the turnkey project. Finance officials considered the financial terms and conditions proposed by Downer to be unacceptable. Nevertheless, Ijape took it upon himself to finalise the financial package and with the elections all but underway he presented another submission to Cabinet proposing the adoption of the turnkey package costing K37,002,630. Under his scheme, Downer would arrange the finance facility and once the base had been completed, the State would assume total liability for repayment. Voting in the PNG elections had already begun when Ijape's Cabinet submission was approved. Prime Minister Namaliu announced the decision on 26 June, just one day before final votes were cast.

Rabbie Namaliu's news release on this announcement caused considerable mirth amongst journalists in PNG at the time. This was not because they found the decision hilarious, although some might have found it so had they known the full background. No, the humour arose because one letter had been dropped from a crucial word throughout the release. The staff member who typed it up and faxed it out to the various news media had probably never encountered the term 'turnkey' before. So from the heading right on through to the last paragraph the release spoke of something quite different. It had the headline: 'Turkey Package'. The first paragraph repeated the mistake: 'Prime Minister Rabbie Namaliu,' it stated, 'today announced that Cabinet had approved a K37 million turkey package for the construction of the infrastructure works and buildings for Phase Two of the Rapid Deployment Unit in Goroka.' For Downer Constructions 'turkey' probably was the most appropriate description. The grand RDU base was never built. DSL, however, did not give up.

When the newly elected Parliament met for the first time on 17 July, Paias Wingti defeated Rabbie Namaliu by one vote and became the new Prime Minister. Wingti's Government announced an immediate freeze on all turnkey projects. Although Ijape's best efforts had gone towards the unrealised Phases Two and Three of the RDU concept, Phase One had already been partly implemented. Police had been sent to the mines and oil fields and they had been accommodated by the companies (at a cost estimated by the resource developers to be K880,000). The Chamber of Mines and Petroleum believed these police had done a reasonable job. But the new Wingti government took an aggressive stance towards the mining industry.

Whereas initially the new Police Minister, Avusi Tanao, was receptive to the industry's security concerns, the more influential Wingti Government Minister for Mining and Petroleum, Masket Iangalio, was scornful. Tanao had, in fact, at first supported the RDU idea and he had re-proposed Ijape's suggestion that Australian aid be used to build the RDU base, admittedly on a more modest scale. He took over another of Ijape's ideas—he wanted the base to be located in his electorate, Kainantu, which is even further away from the major resource projects than Goroka. Iangalio, however, demanded that the fledgling RDU be disbanded. He had been a trenchant critic of the Rapid Deployment Unit while in Opposition, alleging it was nothing more than a multinational protection force.

The Wingti Government hired the controversial Australian mining industry maverick, Bob Needham, to head up the Government's Mineral Resources Development Company and soon the minds of mining executives in PNG were being dominated more by the security of their investments than the security of their property and personnel. With Needham's help Prime Minister Wingti and Iangalio demanded a greater PNG share of the Porgera gold mine, claiming PNG had been misled about how profitable the mine would be. They argued the Government was entitled to increase its shareholding to the thirty per cent allowed for State equity under PNG's mining legislation. Back when the mine agreement was signed, the State had limited its holding to ten per cent. This dispute over the ownership of Porgera developed into a major confrontation and within months nervous investors had deserted PNG resource stocks wiping one billion dollars off their value on the Australian Stock Exchange.

As has become common in PNG following changes of Government, the Police Commissioner was removed and replaced by somebody considered to be more beholden to the incoming administration. Henry Tokam, a former Police Commissioner who had been made head of the prisons service, was chosen to replace Ila Geno in October 1992. DSL made a decision about this time to set up a permanent presence in PNG. The man Alistair Morrison chose as DSL's first PNG country manager was another ex-soldier with a colourful combat background. Major Peter Codyre had spent twelve years as a soldier serving in three different armies. He had seen active service in Northern Ireland and Cyprus with the British Royal Marines, in Rhodesia with the Rhodesian Light Infantry, and in Oman with the Frontier Force of the Sultan's Army. Joining DSL in 1989, he had trained and run a 500-strong guard force for the US Embassy in Zaire. While in Zaire he had also been responsible for the raising and training of guard forces for commercial enterprises.

In his first term as Prime Minister (1985–88), Wingti had never been an advocate of tough law-and-order measures. He had argued that PNG's crime problems were short-term, that they would be overcome as more and more people got jobs, particularly in agriculture. Early in his second term, Wingti's Government was confronted by a surge in crime. While not abandoning his belief that jobs were the eventual answer, Wingti announced drastic measures to curb lawlessness. 'The Wingti Government renounced the RDU concept,' Dinnen says, 'in favour of increased police funding and the enactment of a broad law-and-order legislative package. The latter included the controversial Internal Security Act which was stated to be "an Act to make provision for maintaining the internal security of Papua New Guinea by providing means to combat terrorism and terrorist activities, and for related purposes".' The draft submission to Cabinet recommended that it increase police funding by K36 million. Dinnen said a study of subsequent Cabinet decisions reveals that only about K10 million was ever actually approved.

'As the political climate turned against the RDU,' Dinnen said, 'consideration was being given to the establishment of another special police unit more in tune with the Wingti Government's internal security policy. The proposal that eventuated entailed setting up a Police Tactical Force (PTF) based around a concept developed by [guess who] Defence Systems Limited.' In May 1993 DSL hosted a visit by a senior PNG police delegation to Singapore and Malaysia where they inspected special police tactical units. Upon their return, the delegation proposed PNG establish a unit of its own. In July 1993 Police Commissioner Tokam described the functions of the proposed PNG Police Tactical Force. Its members were to: 'a) provide an armed police Quick Reaction Force to incidents involving dangerous and armed criminals; b) provide armed hostage rescue and assault operations in criminal hostage/barricade situations; c) conduct armed raids on known/ suspected armed criminal locations; d) conduct surveillance operations to gain intelligence; e) provide close protection for VIPs; and f) as directed, enforce the Internal Security Act'.

Police tactical units were to be located in Port Moresby, Lae, Mount Hagen and Rabaul, reporting directly to the Police Commissioner. 'Prime Minister Wingti agreed to proceed with the project at a meeting in the Prime Minister's office on 27 July 1993,' Dinnen said. 'DSL were to consult with the police who were to prepare an NEC submission covering the raising, training and equipping of such a force. The subsequent DSL proposal envisaged a total contract period of 24 months divided into four training stages administered by a team of six DSL instructors'. The cost of the project was estimated at $US10 million.

Convincing the ministers

In crime-burdened Port Moresby the promise of 'close protection for VIPs' might have been enough on its own to win support from Cabinet Ministers for the Police Tactical Force concept. But Defence Systems Limited offered much more. 'The benefit of engaging DSL consultants in the formation and training of PTF-type units,' it argued, 'is that the client is buying the United Kingdom Police/Army model which is a proven, tried and regularly tested set of concepts and responses to violent crime and terrorism.'

Ministers were told that Papua New Guinea's PTF members would be given individual training to gain 'the confidence to take personal risks'; they would become 'highly skilled in weapon handling and marksmanship'; 'skilled in close-quarter battle tactics in the urban environment'; and be self disciplined, alert and adhere to 'proven and practised procedures'. The construction of a Close Quarter Battle House was included in the K10.6 million PTF training price tag. This was needed so PTF members could 'guarantee a head shot at up to ten metres'; develop the capability to make such crack shots 'with the use of a torch'; and learn to 'make split-second shoot/no shoot judgements in low or no light, gas and smoke-filled conditions'.

'In contracting DSL,' the company told PNG Cabinet Ministers, 'the [PNG Police Force] will receive the services of a company with an international reputation for providing solutions to complex security problems.' In a reference undoubtedly directed at the AusAid Police Project and its Australian advisers, DSL said that 'as a contracted company [it] is responsive to the political requirements of PNG and does not try to impose external political influence . . . DSL has an excellent track record of confidentiality and integrity which will be vital in this instance because of the sensitive nature of the task'. And, in a further pitch certain to appeal to Ministers wary of Australia's motives, Defence Systems said, 'DSL has no external motivation to produce a compromised solution.'

Dinnen said Australian Police project officials observed these developments with concern. 'In a document responding to the DSL initiative [dated 9 August 1993] it was claimed that the proposal had 'nothing new to offer'. Phase One of the AusAid Project had already included training in counter-terrorist and armed offender operational skills. The rarity of armed hostage/barricade situations in PNG and the absence of 'terrorism' beyond the Bougainville context were also noted. Questions were raised about the practicality of a small number of 'SAS-trained elite squads' in PNG's difficult geographic terrain. It was also suggested that scarce funds could be better spent on improving the resources and training of existing regular police. These views were circulated and discussed among senior RPNGC officers and several began to express serious reservations about the PTF concept and involvement of DSL.'

One very senior PNG police officer complained off the record to the ABC of the pressure that was coming from the Police Minister and the Minister for Mines and Petroleum. Sinclair Dinnen saw one internal police document referring bitterly to the tendency of politicians to approve costly new proposals without any consideration as to their funding. And in cases where the proposal was implemented, the funds almost invariably were plundered from the already inadequate Police budget: '[We] should learn from past experiences and oppose such proposals,' it said, 'unless Government approves the appropriate funds. We have been forced to implement similar Government decisions within our recurrent budget in such cases as the RDU. The current proposal is just another monster.' Later, the PNGDF was to experience exactly the same problem when funds to pay Sandline were extracted from the recurrent Defence budget.

Influenced no doubt by these rumblings within the Force, Commissioner Tokam had a change of heart and opposed the hiring of DSL. 'In a letter [dated August 18 1992] to the Police Minister,' Dinnen said, 'Commissioner Tokam reiterated many of these points and expressed his "total opposition" to the PTF proposal. On the question of the costs involved, he suggested that any available funds "should be directed towards my grossly under-funded recurrent expenditure requirements, so that the Constabulary can make good some of its current deficiencies, and improve its services to the people".' He asked what would happen after DSL left at the end of their contract. The Commissioner sent a copy of his letter to the Secretary for Finance who replied that the proposal should be dealt with on a government-to-government basis owing to the national significance of internal security. Otherwise, he said, in view of the amount of money involved, the training contract should be dealt with by open tender. He concluded that the

'Minister for Police should be advised to withdraw the DSL submission and be discouraged' from dealing 'with questionable private agencies'.

Police Minister Tanao noted Tokam's 'strong objections', but never addressed them. He told the Commissioner the PTF was part of the government program to combat law and order problems, the Prime Minister was behind it and, anyway, at the meeting in Prime Minister Wingti's office on 27 July Tokam himself had appeared to support the proposal. In early September 1993 the ABC broke the story reporting that PNG was considering the creation of a new 250-member police unit to enforce the Internal Security Act and that DSL was proposing a $US10 million contract to establish and train the new force. 'Papua New Guinea's recently gazetted Internal Security Act has been widely criticised by the Opposition, the Churches and human rights groups,' the report said, 'because its anti-terrorism provisions give the Government much stronger powers to restrict individual freedoms than ever before. Now Mr Wingti's Cabinet has been presented with a submission to create a special Police Tactical Force whose role would include enforcement of the Act.'

DSL's country manager, Peter Codyre, went on the offensive and sought the support of other influential sections of the PNG bureaucracy. He wrote to the Acting Director of the government's Policy Coordination and Monitoring Committee Secretariat promoting the DSL proposal. The Secretariat had been set up by the Wingti Government to vet all Cabinet submissions. Codyre noted the Government's oft-proclaimed concern about lack of discipline and effective leadership in the Police Force. He attributed the 'failure' of the Rapid Deployment Unit to its lack of discipline, the absence of a proper command and control structure, and an inadequate number of officers. He presented the DSL proposal as an appropriate remedy for these problems of discipline and leadership.

Minister Tanao's submission for the creation of the Police Tactical Force was approved by Wingti's Cabinet in November 1993. But there was a catch. While the Cabinet directed the police 'to raise a PTF to be trained by DSL' it also directed that the funding be sourced from internal savings' within the Police budget. There was also an inferred criticism of the effectiveness of the Australian Police Project. The Police Minister was asked to 'review the achievements' of the Australian aid program which was costing $A10 million a year and 'make necessary recommendations'. And in what could be interpreted as annoyance with perceived shortcomings of the AusAid project, Cabinet directed that 'the PNG Police are to regard the move to employ DSL as an indication of Cabinet's determination to reintroduce to the Police Force the essential virtues of discipline and good order'.

The matter was taken up at the PNG-Australia Ministerial Forum in Mount Hagen in December 1993. Police Minister Tanao stated the PNG Government preferred that Australian assistance be directed to PNG's 'priorities and aspirations'. Dinnen says Australian Police Project officials became concerned that the Minister might attempt to divert some of the AusAid Project funds into the DSL-PTF proposal or, alternatively, secure additional Australian funding for this purpose. 'Senior project officials prepared a brief which concluded: "It can be assumed that the Australian authorities would not be prepared to reduce, cancel or otherwise forgo the current AusAid funding earmarked for [this] project in order to fund the DSL proposal in any way whatsoever".'

Tanao was removed from the Police Ministry in a Cabinet reshuffle in January 1994, and Wingti appointed a relative newcomer, Stanley Pil, as Police Minister. At his first news conference Pil called for an immediate increase in Police funding and Commissioner Tokam told assembled journalists his 1994 budget of K79.5 million fell far short of the K97.5 million he needed to maintain its existing operational capacity. In such circumstances there were going to be no 'internal savings' to pay the proposed DSL contract. But Codyre convinced the new Police Minister it should still go ahead. Pil prepared yet another Cabinet submission to secure additional funds for the PTF. Drawn up in early March 1994, this noted there were no internal savings and that funding from Australia was 'unlikely'. That was an understatement. He sought special funding for a reduced PTF–140 not 250 men–but for some reason there had been a cost blow-out. He estimated the creation of the PTF would now cost K22,333,779.

Australian advisers continued their opposition. The project's Special Services Division team leader wrote a letter saying the 'change in doctrine from a "police" bias to a "military" approach' was 'counterproductive' to the progress that he claimed had been achieved during the previous four years helping the Police Special Services Division (SSD). He claimed that attaining the project objective of enhancing the capability of SSD units would be 'significantly more difficult with the introduction of DSL training as they are not required to follow the accepted police doctrine. This will cause confusion in the minds of the RPNGC instructors and members and retard the progress of their development and the achievement of project goals.'

Senior PNG police were in a difficult position. 'While remaining privately sceptical and in many cases directly opposed to the proposal,' Dinnen says, 'senior police had to maintain an outward show of deference to their political masters. Among other things, this reflected the acute institutional insecurity experienced by senior PNG public servants who regularly find themselves subject to purges by new ministers. Indeed, rumours abounded at this time about the imminent removal of Tokam and his deputies.' Jerry Singirok told the Andrew Inquiry some years later of experiencing a similar acute institutional insecurity over Sandline. But back in 1994 the DSL-PTF proposal was about to expire despite the support DSL enjoyed from Prime Minister Wingti and his Police Minister. Events, both political and economic, were moving against this first attempt by PNG to hire private military expertise.

PNG's economic situation became even more precarious as 1994 went on. Masket Iangalio, who had been switched to the Finance Ministry from Mining and Petroleum in the January reshuffle, was forced to introduce a mini-budget in March, drastically cutting back all government spending. And although as late as May he was quoted as guaranteeing funding for the DSL venture, his officials could not find the money. His Secretary for Finance even suggested to the Police Commissioner that the whole PTF idea 'should really be a component of the Australian Technical Assistance project'. DSL tried one last gambit. The company invited Minister Pil and Deputy Police Commissioner Bob Nenta on a tour of DSL projects and facilities in Singapore, Malaysia and the UK towards the end of May. The plan was to finalise contract documents during the trip but the necessary papers were not ready.

Finally, during August 1994, the PNG Supreme Court ruled that Wingti's snap resignation and re-election in 1993 was unconstitutional and that the Parliament would have to vote again on who should be Prime Minister. The numbers deserted Paias Wingti so dramatically that he announced the day of the vote that he would not recontest. Sir Julius Chan had already resigned as his Deputy Prime Minister. Chan stood, winning the vote easily. He formed a coalition with the opposition Pangu Pati. The Government of Sir Julius Chan quickly scrapped the whole Police Tactical Force idea. The informal coalition of concerned senior Papua New Guinea police, cash-strapped PNG Government finance officials, Australian police working on the PNG Police Assistance Project and worried Australian aid officials had kept the private British security consultants at bay. Such was not to happen with Sandline.

Chapter Five

Initial Contact

The Bougainville Situation Deteriorates and Ijape Looks for Help
January–May 1996

In the change of government Mathias Ijape returned to the Ministry. This time he was made Minister for Defence. Whereas the Police Ministers who had followed him had seen the need for SAS-type training for the police to enforce Paias Wingti's draconian Internal Security Act, Ijape still saw a role for a specialised police unit, whatever its name, to guard the nation's wealth earners–the big mining and oil projects. Indeed in June 1995, following an incident in which one disgruntled group of landowners sabotaged the power supply system running from the Hides gas field to the Porgera gold mine, Ijape said he had been instructed by Prime Minister Chan to prepare a submission to reactivate the Rapid Deployment Unit concept. He claimed the cost of establishing the RDU had risen to about K70 million but that was 'nothing compared to revenue earned from these projects'. Little came of it. But Ijape had not forgotten Alistair Morrison. In early 1996 as the peace initiatives on Bougainville that Sir Julius Chan had pursued since taking over as Prime Minister at the end of August 1994 foundered, Ijape felt sure the former second-in-command of the British Army's crack 22 SAS may have had answers for the PNG Defence Force.

In the first week of January 1996 PNG soldiers patrolling the sea border between Papua New Guinea and Solomon Islands intercepted, chased and fired upon delegates from the Bougainville Interim Government (BIG) and Bougainville Revolutionary Army (BRA) returning to Bougainville from the second round of all-Bougainville peace talks in Cairns. Nobody was killed but the Chairman of the BIG, Joseph Kabui, alleged it was a planned ambush by the PNGDF. He said he and his fellow delegates in the boat, including the BRA's Operations Commander, Ishmael Toarama, were lucky to escape death and the incident was further proof the PNG Government could not be trusted. It had broken a guarantee that his team would be allowed safe passage back to Bougainville.

Sir Julius dismissed the claims saying Kabui and his group had themselves to blame. He said the PNG Government had offered the rebel delegates a free helicopter charter home from the Solomon Islands capital, Honiara. That was the way they had come out. They had refused to accept it, had stayed on in Honiara for several weeks holiday and then tried to sneak back across the border without informing PNG. They had been pursued and fired upon, Sir Julius claimed, because they had run into a PNGDF patrol on the lookout for gun smugglers. On 12 January Chan made a one-day trip to Buka announcing that he would not entertain any more peace talks overseas. He insisted that any further talks must be held in PNG.

One rebel source claimed the Kabui delegation had declined the offer of the free helicopter ride back to Bougainville because on the way out the commercial helicopter that had picked them up in the mountains of central Bougainville had been trailed by one of the Australian-donated PNGDF Iroquois helicopters all the way to the border. They were worried the same thing might happen on the way home and that soldiers in the Iroquois might try to strafe them after the civilian helicopter had dropped them off. The BRA went back on the offensive. Within days of the alleged ambush there were rebel raids in south Bougainville leaving several people wounded in the village of Kanauro and at the Piano Care Centre. The government office at Tinputz in the north-east was burnt down and later in the month a young PNGDF officer, Lieutenant Algal Ai, was shot dead in a dawn raid on the Haisi Care Centre in the island's south-west. A second solider was killed on 25 January in a shootout at Piano.

The Bougainville Premier, Theodore Miriung, told the ABC of his frustration with the upsurge in fighting. He claimed the BRA was spreading disinformation. Radio Free Bougainville, he claimed, was quoting support for independence from the representatives of the United Nations and the Commonwealth who had jointly chaired the Cairns talks. 'At no time during the talks did they say that,' he declared. On 1 February 1996 in Honiara the house of the exiled Secretary to the BIG, Martin Miriori, was burnt down. Miriori and his family escaped injury but the fire destroyed the rebels' major Solomon Islands communications base. The BRA alleged the arsonists were in the pay of the PNG Government.

Claims and counter claims of human rights atrocities grew over subsequent weeks. The BRA's Australian-based spokesman, Moses Havini, alleged PNG soldiers and the anti-BRA Resistance massacred civilians in a raid on the village of Simbo in south Bougainville, killing twelve people including an eight-month-old baby. The representative of the Resistance in the PNG-recognised Transitional Government, Sam Akoitai (who became National Minister for Bougainville after the 1997 elections), claimed his Commander at Kunua on the north-west coast was shot dead by a rebel raiding party. He alleged the BRA deliberately targeted civilians including a mentally retarded man and the elderly wife of a north-west Bougainville chief. 'She was shot from the back as she was coming back from the toilet,' Akoitai said. 'The mentally ill man was shot in his house in front of his family.'

PNG's Defence Minister looked outside for help. 'About early February of 1996,' he told the first Sandline inquiry, 'I said [to the Commander] I was aware of a private security company called Defence Systems of London and I had an engagement with them in the last government for them to provide training for the Rapid Deployment Unit of the Police Force. I said that because Australia and New Zealand would not provide the capabilities that the Defence Force want through the normal government process—government-to-government arrangement—I suggested to the Commander and the Secretary of Defence that we should now seriously consider private military personnel in private business to help us.' The Minister, the Commander and the Secretary make up the PNG Defence Council and under Ijape the Defence Council held regular meetings and they often travelled together.

That February they spent five days in Singapore (from the fifth to the tenth). Singapore's Deputy Prime Minister and Minister for Defence had invited Ijape to a military air show. Sidney Franklin, of J. & S. Franklin, met them and arranged much of their itinirary. Franklin was an agent for the Singapore Government and its arms company, Unicorn International Pty Ltd. He organised a tour of Singapore Government military establishments and an inspection of Unicorn's facilities. Franklin was concerned that he seemed to have lost one of his better customers. After being awarded contracts worth almost K12 million in the four years up to 1994, Franklins had not made a single sale to PNG in 1995. Franklin was keen to get to know the newly appointed Commander. According to Singirok, they met in Mr Ijape's hotel suite where, he claimed to the Los Inquiry, Franklin complained about a directive Singirok had issued putting all Defence purchases on hold. Singirok said he had first met Sidney Franklin in 1987 when serving as a Staff Officer at PNGDF Headquarters but had not seen him for nine years. The Defence Secretary, James Melegepa, told Judge Los that following this trip there was an understanding that the PNGDF would purchase small arms and heavy mortar launchers from Unicorn through Franklin.

However, it was military expertise, not just military supplies, that Defence Minister Ijape was looking for. Both Brigadier Singirok and Secretary Melegepa, recall Ijape raising his proposal for the engagement of 'private military personnel in private business' with them in February. Singirok told the Andrew Inquiry the Minister brought the matter up on a number of occasions and told him the group he had in mind 'can enable us to open the Panguna mine'. He claimed that at one meeting in the Minister's office in Parliament House on 22 February Ijape had said to him, 'Bro, you can be a rich man if you engage this group.' He said he was shocked. Ijape vigorously denied he ever said that. Melegepa, who was running late for the Defence Council meeting, arrived after this alleged comment had been made. He said Ijape had made no such suggestion to him. However, he did say Ijape had raised the issue of private military help several times in early 1996 because, he said, the Minister did not think the military approach being taken by the PNGDF was working and that by engaging outsiders PNG could get the mine reopened.

'The Minister's view was that the whole problem started with the mine and it was an economic reason.' Melegapa said that Ijape believed the landowners had not started out with secession in mind and that it was only after Ona had turned to violence by sabotaging the mine that he had taken up the wider secessionist cause. 'So you had to reopen the mine. His words were that "the approach taken at the moment is like looking for a needle in a haystack" ... If you open the mine then it is a strategy to attract the rebels who are still very persistent to come out and basically try to close the mine. That is when you probably will be able to capture them,' Melegepa quoted Ijape as saying. This simplistic strategy ignored all the lessons of 1989–that the Panguna mine was entirely vulnerable to sabotage. The rebels had been able to close the mine by knocking out its power supply and terrorising the workers travelling up and down the indefensible access road. The only time the BRA had moved to Panguna in force was after the PNG soldiers pulled out in 1990.

'About early March,' Ijape told the Andrew Inquiry, 'I contacted Noel Philp and Alistair Morrison of Defence Systems of London ... I had intended initially to visit one of Defence Systems operations in Africa and the Middle East together with the Commander and the Secretary.' Arrangements were put in place for the three members of the PNG Defence Council to visit Singapore, Malaysia, Great Britain, the United States and New Zealand. The excursion to Africa was left open as a possibility. Ijape advised DSL of the intended trip. On 11 March DSL faxed the Commander advising that its

Chairman, Alistair Morrison, would be in Hong Kong 'during your intended visit to London' and suggested a meeting in Hong Kong. The Minister's party set out on their world tour on Wednesday 13 March, just as events on Bougainville took an even nastier turn. The BRA hit right at the heart of PNG Government-controlled territory, Buka Island across Buka Passage from the Bougainville mainland, killing six members of the security forces.

Killed off Matsungan

The BRA's Chief of Operations, Ishmael Toarama, led the raid of retribution himself. Toarama, one of the most feared fighting men on Bougainville, was one of the party on the eventful trip back to Bougainville from the Cairns talks in January. Somebody had seen Ishmael's well-armed 'boys' on their way to Buka in late February. Bougainville's Provincial Police Commander advised residents to 'take extra precautions and stay indoors especially at night'. Police operations had intensified 'due to the reported sightings of armed BRA rebels at the northern tip of Bougainville'.

In a bloody engagement off Matsungan Island west of Buka on Monday 11 March, Toarama's group sunk an eight-metre-long banana boat that had gone searching for them. They killed six of the seven PNG security force members on board. Peter Niesi of the PNG *Post Courier* (who won the Pacific Islands News Association's 1995 Journalist of the Year Award for his comprehensive coverage of Bougainville) interviewed the sole survivor, Police Constable David Bulumaris, the operator of the boat. Niesi reported:

> 'He said that after they had come within a mile of the shoreline, they saw armed rebels running to take up positions onshore. He said there was some hesitation as [they] realised they were vulnerable. He had suggested that they retreat . . . "I was still trying to work that out when my gunner opened up on them [with a Mag58 machine gun mounted on the bow] . . . they retaliated and I think the first hail of shells put us off—injured a number of us. The gunner was the first one to go down which gave us no hope but to retreat." He said that two grenades had been fired at them. The first landed a few metres from the bow. "At that moment, most of us were not really injured seriously but because of the panic, everyone moved from the front to where I was at the back. As I tried to go astern to get out of their firing range, seawater kept

coming into the boat. There was no way I could turn the boat around without exposing us all," he said.

' "Then the second grenade landed on the boat. Many of them were then seriously injured and, by that time, the water in the boat was almost level with the water in the sea . . . most of them also did not have life jackets on (although there were life jackets in the boat) . . . Shortly after we jumped overboard, I heard a boat coming and circling the area," Constable Bulumaris said. "I could tell exactly that was the enemy circling the area and firing at us while we were floating. That's how I got two shots in my back and neck." Constable Bulumaris believes . . . he survived because of his semi-conscious condition which kept him still . . . "I basically kept afloat and let the tide sweep me along until it swept me over the reefs at Tung Island," he said.

Shooting disarmed people in the sea is a tactic both sides used. Peter Niesi's colleague at the *Post Courier,* Bougainvillean journalist Moresi Tua, was similarly left for dead in the early 1990s after being shot in the neck by PNG troops after they had ordered him and others to jump overboard from their banana boat off south-east Bougainville.

The killing of the six security force members caused panic on Buka. The airport was closed down, which ironically delayed a twenty-eight member police mobile squad ordered to fly in from East New Britain to provide greater protection for residents and police families. The Buka District Chiefs met and condemned what they described as 'barbarous, horrendous and senseless' killings. They appealed to the rebel leadership 'to stop the carnage and to come to terms with the people's wish for peace on Bougainville'. Deputy Premier Thomas Anis, who chaired the Buka District Chiefs meeting, said they also called for the remobilisation and re-arming of village homeguards. These homeguards, formerly known as the Buka Liberation Front, had been instrumental in driving the BRA off Buka in 1991. Anis said the chiefs at the meeting wanted the National Government 'to clarify' whether the cease-fire declared in 1994 was still in effect.

Two days after the Matsungan Island incident, on Wednesday 13 March 1996, Defence Minister Ijape announced he was going to ask Cabinet to let the PNG military return to the offensive on Bougainville. He then boarded an international flight with the Commander and the Defence Secretary for their proposed trip to Asia, Europe, Africa, North America and New

Zealand. The Prime Minister, Sir Julius Chan, was furious. The party got as far as Malaysia when they received orders to abandon the journey. In a faxed letter dated 14 March, Sir Julius said he had expressly refused Ijape permission to travel in his ministerial capacity and the Minister would be personally responsible for all costs. Ijape faxed a letter back complaining that he believed he was carrying out the Prime Minister's instructions to explore how he could get assistance from sources other than Australia to help the PNGDF beat the BRA. 'While I understand your zeal to act expeditiously you have apparently misunderstood my position,' Sir Julius replied on 15 March.

'What I require of the Defence Council is carefully prepared plans and estimates of the costs involved in an operation of the type discussed which can be submitted to me for NEC [Cabinet] to consider and approve. You should return forthwith so that we [can] proceed in a proper legal and constitutional manner.' Sir Julius told Ijape that the Defence Council could not 'contemplate the type of arrangements' it appeared it intended 'to negotiate and enter into' during its proposed tour without Cabinet authorisation. The Defence Council members returned to PNG. While they were on their way home, Toarama's raiding party on Buka ambushed and killed four more security force members, one regular policeman and three reservists, at Malasang village just ten kilometres from the town of Buka, the temporary provincial headquarters. All four were Bougainvilleans. In the two months since the BIG-BRA delegation had been fired on, the BRA had killed fourteen soldiers and policemen.

The political reaction in PNG was strong. The Opposition Leader, Roy Yaki, called for a lifting of the cease-fire and demanded that the military be given a 'free hand'. 'Let the military handle the problem of bringing the island under total control,' Yaki stated, 'and we should provide them with a decisive and precise direction with all the appropriate support.' Another Opposition MP, Bernard Narokobi, claimed Chan's Bougainville strategy had failed and he should resign. 'The moral decadence of his government and inconsistencies in allowing his Ministers to rob the people in broad daylight,' Narokobi claimed, 'are all too apparent to the people and I am sure the rebel leadership has seen through Sir Julius.' However, the Members for North and Central Bougainville, Michael Ogio and Joseph Egilio, attacked Narokobi claiming he should not link Bougainville with other political issues. 'The BRA are prepared to fight to their last man and will never voluntarily surrender,' they said in a joint statement. 'Because they have committed so many atrocities they are terrified at being answerable to the law when Bougainville returns to normal. There is heavy support among the Bougainville people,' the two claimed, 'for a military solution to now take precedence over a political solution.'

The PNG Cabinet met on 21 March 1996 and, after listening to a presentation by Brigadier Singirok, approved the lifting of the cease-fire and 'directed the Department of Finance to immediately provide K10 million funding to specifically implement the measures contained in the [Defence Minister's] Submission'. Those K10 million measures were for a military operation to be codenamed Operation High Speed II, aimed at capturing the rebel leadership in central Bougainville. In a nationally broadcast address that night Sir Julius Chan publicly abandoned his Bougainville peace strategy. He told the people of PNG his Cabinet had met that morning and directed that the cease-fire be lifted and that the Defence Force be better equipped to deal with BRA elements 'inside and outside' Papua New Guinea.

'It is time to face the truth that continued talking is not working,' Sir Julius said. He admitted complete frustration with everything he had tried in the previous eighteen months. 'I am now convinced,' he said, 'that we have exhausted all human tolerance. Every time an agreement of any sort was reached, the rebels reneged, defaulted–and continued killing and destroying. There is not one shred of proof, no indication at all, that the rebels are sincere.' He was even giving up on the one major achievement of his Bougainville policy–the creation of the Transitional Government. 'All attempts by the Bougainville Transitional Government itself,' Sir Julius claimed, 'have been abused and compromised, to the extent that its ability to assist with the strength required to resolve this conflict has declined.' He said Cabinet had agreed that Bougainville should come under the general provincial government reforms which meant, in effect, that the Transitional Government would cease to exist.

Sir Julius wound up his national address with a warning to the rebels. 'Whilst I will continue to listen and be receptive to all constructive peace moves, I must also now act decisively. And that is exactly what I am doing. To those criminals who continue to kill, destroy and destabilise the peace longed for by all–let me say just this. Your darkest hour has arrived. Your number has been called and you are now facing the full force of the law.' Delivered in his most solemn tone it was one of Chan's most impressive speeches. But the inadequacies of the forces at his disposal meant that the threat to capture and prosecute the rebel leadership rang hollow. However, the Opposition applauded. 'The time for talking and paying bizarre compliments to the leadership of the BRA and BIG is over,' the Deputy Opposition Leader, Roy Evara, said when welcoming the lifting of the cease-fire and the order to the military to 'flush out' the rebels. 'Peace can not be achieved,' Evara maintained (in a quaint argument about conflict resolution), 'when the enemy does not surrender.'

John Howard had won the Australian elections several weeks earlier, on 2 March 1996. This had raised hopes amongst members of the Chan Government that a Liberal–National coalition in power in Canberra would be more sympathetic to the PNG military's requests for greater practical help on Bougainville. The Keating Government had rejected Defence Minister Ijape's appeals for specialist counter-insurgency training and the provision of sophisticated eavesdropping capabilities to enable the PNG Army to target the rebel leadership in the mountains of central Bougainville. But any heightened expectations of support from the new Howard Government were soon dashed. The first official statement on Bougainville by Australia's new Foreign Minister, Alexander Downer, was not what Ijape wanted to hear. Downer called on both sides to exercise restraint. Issued on the same day as Chan's proclamation of war, Downer's statement said the Howard Government 'would like to see the peace process revived'.

Interviewed by the ABC the day after Chan's national address, the new Australian Defence Minister, Ian McLachlan, acknowledged that PNG had requested logistic support for its planned crackdown on the rebels. But he said that all that Australia would provide were regular supplies of items that could not be used in any offensive way. 'There is in place a supply arrangement now whereby they can get certain non-lethal material and that supply line will continue to operate,' McLachlan said. 'Things that are non-lethal–ration packs, that sort of stuff ... What I'm really saying is that we're not ... going to make any special arrangements.' He said the Australian Government did not see any need to expand its assistance. 'And we're not about to encourage anybody to escalate these problems.' McLachlan's rejection of the high-tech help Ijape wanted was a big disappointment to the PNG Defence Minister.

At the first Sandline inquiry a year later, Ijape said this convinced him he had to go elsewhere. 'Only when Australia and New Zealand did not want to help us with the helicopters and the type of equipment that we wanted, the listening devices and the electronic stuff that I thought was necessary for any operation on the island to fix the problem,' Ijape said, 'when that was not forthcoming, I raised the matter with the General and said we must look elsewhere ... It was soon after the Cairns meeting failed ... there were some soldiers and policemen killed in Buka ... so the Prime Minister said we must mount an operation. And that was the time when I started talking about looking at the possibility of having a private security company assisting us to build our capabilities to go and destroy the BRA headquarters.'

Bullying the Solomons

Papua New Guinea's Defence Minister warned the Solomon Islands Government the PNG military would make life 'hell' for their people along the border if the authorities in Honiara did not cooperate with the PNG military in teaching the BRA a lesson. On 26 March 1996 Mathias Ijape accused Prime Minister Solomon Mamaloni's Government of causing PNG to suffer because of its alleged 'weak attitude' to the BRA. 'The Solomon Islands Government has literally made the people of Papua New Guinea lose hundreds of human lives and K700 million financially while their people continue to be spectators and enjoy [the] good life,' he claimed.

'The Solomon Islands continues to provide shelter for criminals who escape from Bougainville under the disguise of humanitarian reasons. The cease-fire has been lifted and we will expect [an] unprecedented influx of criminals from Bougainville to Solomon Islands. The Solomon Islands must help us track down those criminals hiding in their territory. I am warning Solomon Islands,' Ijape said, 'that if criminals cross the border and want to get refuge in Solomon Islands, the PNGDF will cross their border in hot pursuit and deal with those criminals on Solomon Islands soil . . . I expect nothing less than full co-operation . . . anything less will be treated by [the] PNG Defence Force as [a] slap on PNG's face . . . All that PNG is asking,' he concluded, 'is for Solomon Islands not to let their soil become a criminal hideout . . . If they do we will make it hell for them.'

In Port Moresby, the daily newspaper, the *National*, decried Ijape's statement calling on him to withdraw the threats. 'In this day and age,' the paper's editorial said, 'you cannot go out and threaten a sovereign state as if it were a neighbouring tribe! There are international protocols and conventions to abide by. PNG has itself in the past taken a dim view of countries which acted the bully to smaller nations . . . The national and international support which the Government gained in the last 18 months looks like being lost in just one week,' the paper lamented.

Contacting DSL again, Ijape was informed that it was not in the business of providing helicopter gunships and the sophisticated electronic warfare equipment that the PNG military had been denied by Australia. 'I spoke to Alistair Morrison,' Ijape told the Andrew Inquiry, 'and he put me in touch with Tim Spicer.' The company name Ijape was given was Plaza 107. Tim Spicer told the Inquiry that Morrison was 'a friend' who had rung him while he was visiting Italy in March. Both were ex-Guardsmen. 'It was a very brief conversation,' he said, 'just giving me an outline. It was to do with helicopters. He gave me the Minister for Defence's name and telephone number and suggested that I get in touch.' Spicer rang Ijape when he returned to London and they arranged to meet.

The initial plan was that they meet in Papua New Guinea. But because Brigadier Singirok was going to be away on the date suggested, the venue was altered to Cairns. Ijape wanted all three members of the Defence Council to be present. Singirok claimed he received instructions from the Minister on the Wednesday before Easter to travel to Cairns the next day and spend the Easter weekend at the Cairns Hilton hotel. He was annoyed because he had wanted to spend the Easter break with his family. He told the ABC's 'Four Corners' program more than a year later that he assumed Australian intelligence was monitoring their movements. 'For the Commander and the Secretary for Defence and the Minister for Defence to get visas at short notice to depart to Australia would definitely raise eyebrows at the Australian High Commission,' he said. The men left Port Moresby on three different flights.

On his flight to Cairns Brigadier Singirok made notes in his diary about the matters he would be discussing with the men from London. The notes included things such as electronic warfare systems which would give the PNGDF the capacity to pinpoint BRA targets such as Radio Free Bougainville. The members of the PNG Defence Council met with Tim Spicer and Sandline's ultimate boss, Anthony Buckingham, at the Cairns Hilton on Easter Sunday 7 April 1996 in the hotel's coffee shop. The coffee shop was chosen to minimise the chance of the conversation being bugged. 'Four Corners' claimed the Australian Security Intelligence Service (ASIS) knew of the meeting but took no action to listen in.

Spicer and Buckingham handed out business cards. 'Spicer's simply stated his name and business address, 535 Kings Road, London,' the Judge who headed the first Sandline inquiry, Justice Warwick Andrew, reported. 'Buckingham's card indicated he represented a company, Branch Energy Limited.' The meeting went on for several hours over cups of coffee. 'The conversation was concerned with establishing what Papua New Guinea wanted that Spicer and Buckingham could provide,' the Judge's report said. 'The focus was on Bougainville and the belief, in particular on the part of Mr Ijape and the Commander, that there was a need for sophisticated military equipment including attack helicopters.'

PNG's Defence Secretary remembers Buckingham made mention of mining interests in Africa. Asked at the Inquiry what was said about Buckingham's company, Branch Energy, Melegepa said they had been told it invested world wide. 'When they introduced themselves, they said they are not only in the line of military business but they are also professional businessmen in the mining and petroleum area.' And questioned on whether they had spoken directly about taking a share in the Panguna mine, the Defence Secretary replied that they said they would 'be prepared to look at investments in Papua New Guinea, in mining and petroleum, not specifically the Panguna mine'. Right from the first face-to-face contact with his prospective clients, Buckingham revealed his agenda was broader than simply providing PNG with a mercenaries package. 'From the Sandline side of things,' Justice Andrew concluded, 'the interest in the mine was there from the start and seems to have remained an important consideration.'

The name Executive Outcomes was mentioned. 'We produced a video tape explaining the roles and capabilities of Executive Outcomes,' Spicer told the Andrew Inquiry. 'We explained that Sandline was sort of, effectively a consultancy service and was able to call on a number of, not corporately related, but friendly organisations that we have worked with in the past to assist in a number of different military disciplines. And we explained that whilst we were not one and the same company we were very closely related. We had introduced them to other governments and we were thoroughly satisfied that they were professionally competent and they were a good organisation to be associated with.' One government they had introduced Executive Outcomes to, he said, was the Government of Sierra Leone 'where they provided military assistance ... in terms of training, helicopters and military forces integrated into the armed forces of Sierra Leone'. A rough costing of the Bougainville exercise was put at $US30 million. The Cairns Hilton coffee shop meeting ended with the understanding that Spicer would prepare a written proposal that would be given to Brigadier Singirok on a forthcoming visit he was to make to London.

The Defence Minister returned home from Cairns eager to tell the Prime Minister that he believed he had found the people who could provide the Defence Force with the type of help the Australians had refused to give. He found Sir Julius unenthusiastic. 'I had to report to the Prime Minister on my trip to Cairns and I explained what Plaza 107 would provide to the Government. And the Prime Minister said we just did not have the money ... I said, "You had insisted to have the head destroyed. And as Minister responsible that is what I had researched and I am convinced that these guys would do it with the technology, with us, with the Defence

Force" ... He [Chan] said, "It is interesting but ... there is no money!"'
PNG was at the time in the midst of a major dispute with the World Bank. 'We had the World Bank on my door step,' Chan told the later Los Inquiry, 'and the IMF on my door step and I kept on throwing all these things away until I could resolve this World Bank issue first.'

The central element to the dispute with the World Bank was whether PNG was obeying the terms of the Structural Adjustment Program (SAP) that had been negotiated in 1995 to rescue the country from its 1994 financial crisis when its foreign reserves had been exhausted. A World Bank supervision team had been told to leave PNG in late February. The team leader, Pirouz Hamidian-Rad, had pointed out to the PNG Finance Department more than a dozen areas where the mutually agreed conditions relating to the rescue package were not being adhered to. He claimed the SAP was impacting on the poorest people while the politicians seemed unprepared to share the pain. As well, the cutbacks in spending that were being achieved were not the result of the promised readjustments of the public service but simply because the Government was not spending money on essentials. Public servants were being paid but had nothing to work with. Sir Julius and his Deputy, the Finance Minister, Chris Haiveta, reacted badly when the story about the fracas with Hamidian-Rad's team was broken.

Shoot the messenger

In late February 1996 I pulled over to the kerb along Port Moresby's Sir Hubert Murray Highway to record Question Time off the radio. I was running late for Parliament and had just heard a question mentioning my name.

'I am aware of the ABC Sean Dorney report last night,' Sir Julius Chan was saying in reply, 'which probably captured the limelight of the current election going on in Australia. Both of these reports are totally unfounded. I was said to have cancelled a meeting with the World Bank. I had no request to have any meeting at all with the World Bank. The World Bank people are in the country ... and I think so far discussions ... have been very productive.'

The talks, far from being productive, had broken down irrevocably the previous day, Tuesday 27 February 1996. I had reported that the World Bank team was being thrown out; that the team had told PNG officials the Structural Adjustment Program was seriously off track; and that the Forests Minister had broken undertakings to the Bank by seeking to amend the Forestry Act to give himself unfettered power. The *National* newspaper had followed up the story.

'The ramifications, the damages that have cost this country as if we are just little kids playing with these big people,' Sir Julius went on, 'there seems to be some motive behind some of these people to denigrate and continually besmirch the good work of the Government.' Hamidian-Rad and his team were packing their bags as Sir Julius spoke. The World Bank team leader had been given a letter by PNG's lead negotiator, Morea Vele, saying there was little point in him staying in PNG. 'It has become clear to me that your state of mind and your attitude over the last few days is not conducive to continuing discussions with Government officials on the Terms of Reference of your Supervision Mission on a reasonable and responsible level and manner,' the letter said. Hamidian-Rad said at the airport on his way out he interpreted the letter as 'being told to leave'.

'As Minister responsible,' Finance Minister Haiveta's voice could now be heard on the radio broadcast of Question Time, 'I feel that the credibility of the country and not [just] the Government has once again come under undue fire ... I'd like to refer the authors of these articles to the Privileges Committee. Namely, the ABC Correspondent, Mr Speaker, and the Editor of the *National* newspaper.' The Speaker, Sir Rabbie Namaliu, deliberated but decided such a reference would serve no good purpose as 'it would do more harm to the dignity and the decorum of Parliament' if Members 'were to appear over-sensitive' by reacting to 'every comment and criticism'.

Within a week of returning to Port Moresby from the Defence Council's meeting with Spicer and Buckingham in Cairns, Brigadier Singirok was off on his trip to London via Singapore. He would also go on to the United States, where he wanted to discuss buying armed personnel carriers and ten surplus US Army helicopters. The US Army was offering Iroquois for sale under its Foreign Military Sales program for $US240,000 each. The idea Singirok had was to spend $US2.4 million buying ten helicopters, three of which would be cannibalised for spare parts to keep the rest of the PNGDF's Iroquois fleet operational. In Britain he was to inspect military factories. But first, he wanted to confirm orders he had already placed with Singapore for the purchase of equipment for the impending Operation High Speed II. The Commander asked for a senior Finance Department official to accompany him. Acting Deputy Secretary Vele Iamo was sent along.

A few weeks earlier, on 1 April 1996, just ten days after Cabinet had agreed to release K10 million for the new Bougainville offensive, Singirok had personally approved buying just over K2 million worth of weapons and ammunition from Unicorn International. Included in the purchase were 120 mm mortars. Asked at the Los Inquiry why he had become personally involved in this order, Singirok said he was under a time limitation. 'I had to produce the goods ... Singapore [was] a one-stop port and [because the] relationship had already been established by [the] Minister for Defence from PNG and [the] Minister for Defence in Singapore, the green light was given to us to go ahead at Unicorn ... This was one of those very rare cases that a Commander gets involved.' Asked by Chan's lawyers why he had not obtained any other quotes, Singirok replied that Australia had closed the door on sales of weapons and ammunition to PNG and that, anyway, Australia did not produce 120 mm mortars. 'There were no other suppliers during that time frame ... we were preparing to go on a major offensive, Operation High Speed II.' He also said he was advised by his own munitions specialists that they were given good prices.

Sidney Franklin was on hand to accompany the Commander on his inspections of Unicorn's production run. Franklin was now devoting a lot of time to developing his relationship with the youthful PNG Defence chief. They had met three times in less than three months. After renewing his acquaintance at the Singapore air show in February, the British military supplier had also met Singirok and the other members of the PNG Defence Council in Kuala Lumpur in March when Chan aborted Ijape's world trip. On this latest trip, Singirok spent three days in Singapore and then flew on to London on the same flight as Sidney Franklin and Franklin's wife. They were met in London by Franklin's son, David, and by two representatives of the British Defence Ministry. The Franklins organised the itinerary in Britain for Singirok and Iamo from the Finance Department.

That itinerary did not include the proposed meeting with Tim Spicer. Brigadier Singirok never even told Iamo about Spicer and the indications are that at this stage he regarded Ijape's proposed privatised military help project as an example of ministerial fantasy. The figure of $US30 million that had been mentioned in Cairns was equivalent to almost half the entire PNG Defence budget for 1996. Singirok had been allocated K10 million, or only $US7.6 million, for Operation High Speed II to knock out the rebel headquarters. Given the fight PNG was having with the World Bank and the IMF over its economic recovery program the unbudgeted spending of so much money must have seemed fanciful. Singirok did meet with Spicer but without much enthusiasm. According to the Brigadier's private diary, which was tabled at the Andrew Inquiry, he met Spicer and the owner of Plaza 107, Michael Grunberg, on 18 April in his room at the Royal Horseguards Hotel.

The lawyer representing Ijape at the Andrew Inquiry suggested this had happened because the Commander had failed to keep an appointment at the Kings Road offices of Plaza 107. Iamo was not at the meeting in the hotel room and said he knew nothing about it. Under questioning at the Andrew Inquiry, Singirok complained that Spicer and Grunberg did not treat him with sufficient respect. 'I was a bit amazed,' he said, 'that as the Commander of my country I was not accorded the protocol that was required ... because my itinerary with the British Government previously was all official and this particular meeting took place in my room.' He described it as a 'peculiar arrangement' and said he had expected 'we would go to a board room ... where all the marketing packages will be properly arranged and discussed ... but that never took place'. But he then admitted that it was he who had been avoiding Spicer. 'It was [at] Tim Spicer's insistence that he would meet up with me. In fact I was not keen to even meet with him at that stage but I had to fit him in and he said he must come and see me and it was his idea that he meet me in the hotel room.'

Spicer presented Singirok with a four page document called 'Project Contravene–A Military Support Package for the Government of Papua New Guinea'. The proposal covered two areas–electronic warfare and helicopter support. Under the heading 'Concept' it read: 'There is a military requirement to carry out a specific counter-insurgency operation within a short timeframe. This operation is highly sensitive and needs to be carried out with a precision that will completely disable the enemy command structure with the minimum collateral damage in order to make it acceptable to the Government and people of PNG and to world opinion. To achieve this, the military imperative is the ability to gather high-grade, specific intelligence about the location, capacity and intentions of the enemy force, particularly their C3I assets [command, control, communications, intelligence] and match that intelligence with a strike capability, the key ingredients of which are firepower, mobility, precision, speed [and] surprise.'

The document promised that a 'strategic EW capability' combined with 'both attack and support helicopters can generate a massive increase in Combat Power out of all proportion to the cost'. The electronic warfare (EW) part of the package was to include a fixed-wing aircraft to act as a 'surveillance platform' and a $US4.8 million, fully computerised 'EW suite' to be carried on board, consisting of 'sensors and processors' gathering 'pinpoint intelligence' and having 'VHF, HF, UHF, intercept, DF, voice and statistical analysis capabilities as well as the ability to track beacons [and] transmitters'. There would be eighteen sets of Night Vision Equipment, an on-the-ground computer system 'to process, store and retrieve the operational intelligence gathered and an imagery interpretation and enhancement package'. Eighteen personnel would be provided to operate the surveillance and electronic warfare system. As for the 'Strike Package', that was to comprise two Russian-designed Mi-24 helicopter gunships costing $US8.2 million and two Mi-17 helicopter transports costing $US3 million. Twelve crew, including gunners, were to be provided with the Mi-24s while eighteen, including gunners, would operate the Mi-17s. The Mi-24s would be provided with enough rockets and other firepower to run twenty-five sorties.

Spicer proposed that the 'objective' was to have the full package and all personnel 'in theatre by 15 May, 1996'. That was just over four weeks away. The project document said the timing would be dependent on the date they received a confirmed order 'as we require four clear weeks from receipt of your instruction to proceed and payment of the initial sum'. The total cost of Project Contravene was put at $US32.7 million but 'we are prepared to quote a fixed price of $US30 million, including the provision of all personnel, management support and appropriate training resource for up to one year'. Summing up, the document promised to provide the Government of PNG with 'a surveillance and strike package to enable the Commander to carry out precise effective operations with very little collateral damage, thus satisfying the political imperative'.

Brigadier Singirok told the Andrew Inquiry the elements he wanted were there—surveillance, mobility and firepower—but he regarded the Project Contravene proposal as 'very ambitious'. Defence Minister Ijape quoted him on his return to PNG as saying it 'looked good'. But one not insignificant problem was money. The Brigadier said Spicer and Grunberg wanted to talk to him about how the payments would be arranged but he told them finance was an entirely separate subject. 'Mr Grunberg, as the financial adviser, wanted to discuss issues of funding and sourcing and I said, "I have no guarantee where the funding is going to come from."' As a former Commander in the field on Bougainville, Brigadier Singirok knew what a problem it was to get money out of the PNG Government even when it was budgeted. While he had a senior Finance Department official travelling with him, he kept Grunberg well away from Iamo.

The Acting Deputy Secretary for Finance participated in every other part of the trip. Sidney Franklin and his son, David, took Brigadier Singirok and Iamo on a tour of a number of military manufacturing plants, including the GNK Tank Factory where, according to Singirok's diary, he drove a tank on

Friday 19 April (the day after his hotel room meeting with Spicer). But tanks were not what Singirok had in mind for Bougainville. He told the Andrew Inquiry he was interested in looking at things like troop-carrying vehicles and small combat boats. After visiting Franklin's own factory he jotted in his diary, 'quite impressive'. Asked about this, Singirok told the Inquiry that up until then he had doubted the 'credibility' of Franklin's company because of his experiences with what Franklins had supplied to the troops on Bougainville. Singirok's attitude to Franklin had been transformed. However, when the full extent of their flowering relationship was exposed more than a year later the revelations were to shatter Singirok's own claims to credibility on issues pertaining to corruption.

Sidney Franklin paid Singirok's hotel bill and that of Deputy Finance Secretary Iamo at the Royal Horseguards Hotel, a bill which came to £1662. Iamo told the Andrew Inquiry he did not know who picked up the costs of his accommodation because he had been invited along on the trip by the Commander who was covering the expenses. Singirok admitted to Justice Andrew that Franklin paid the bill but he claimed that he had remitted his unspent travelling allowance when he returned to Port Moresby. He also denied he had received any other benefits from Franklin. It was not true. Franklin helped him set up a Visa Card account at Franklin's bank, the Waterloo Place, Pall Mall, branch of Lloyds. Franklin then paid a total of £30,000 into Singirok's account in three separate transfers over the following ten months–in July and December 1996 and February 1997.

The South Pacific Correspondent for the *Australian*, Mary-Louise O'Callaghan, obtained the bank documents and broke this story in July 1997 after Justice Andrew had presented the report of the first Sandline Inquiry. The second Inquiry headed by Justice Los spent days grilling Singirok about his Lloyds Visa Account. He testified that Franklin insisted on accompanying him to the bank. At first, he claimed that he had opened the account by depositing his travelling allowance. But when asked how that money came to be converted into exactly £1000, he said Franklin had arranged a transfer for that sum and he had given Franklin an equivalent amount in kina and American dollars. Later, Cooke QC, Chan's lawyer, drew Singirok's attention to the fact that the Visa account was opened on 24 April– when he was no longer in London. On that day he was in New Orleans. Singirok's explanation was that the account did not become 'operational' until after he had left London.

He claimed that it was not until May, after he had returned to Port Moresby, that Franklin rang him offering further help. 'Mr Franklin's assistance,' he claimed before Justice Los, 'was related to assisting me and my staff to attend military exhibitions so that it will give us the opportunity to see the type of equipment ... available in the world market ... I said, "It is not possible for me to travel because we ... do not have finance to travel." And he said, "It is not a problem." And that he would help me ... He asked me for my account and I said, "This is the account number." And he credited me.' Singirok claimed he only knew how much was transferred after the end-of-July account statement reached him. Asked what Franklin had said the money could be used for, Singirok replied: 'Well, he said, like I said, "It was for our convenience to travel." And he said that, "The money is yours, you can use it."' Counsel Assisting, Ian Molloy, suggested it was absurd that Franklin would give Singirok money so he could go to exhibitions to look at competitors' products. 'You had better ask him,' Singirok replied.

Molloy tried to get Singirok to admit that the payments were in fact bribes. 'Do you see now that they work? Do you see in hindsight that these were bribes from Mr Franklin to have you cause the Defence Force to enter into deals with Unicorn?' 'No,' Singirok maintained. Singirok used more than £20,000 from the Lloyds Visa Account on personal expenses such as buying tailor-made suits from Singapore and as a part payment to secure a mortgage on a property he and his wife bought in Port Moresby. None of the money was spent on what he claimed Franklin had given it for–travel by PNGDF staff to military exhibitions. A small amount had gone to paying staff accommodation bills during a trip to the Philippines in February 1997. 'When I look back at it now,' Singirok finally admitted to the Los Inquiry, 'I know that I have done something wrong as far as the Leadership Code is concerned.' But he still protested that the payments were not bribes.

Singirok's Visa Account

The Visa Card Account bearing the name, J. Singirok Esq, was opened at the Pall Mall, London, branch of Lloyds Bank on 24 April 1996 courtesy of a transfer of £1000 from another account at the same bank, J. & S. Franklin's. The second deposit, £10,000, also by way of an internal bank transfer from the same Franklins account, was credited to Singirok on 5 July 1996.

Jerry Singirok told the Los Inquiry he learnt how much had been put into his account through 'the mail, or if not, through fax'. On 27 August 1996 he withdrew £6660 and paid that into his account with the Westpac Bank in Port Moresby. 'I think I got a cash advance for some personal use, I cannot recall,' he said. On 16 October 1996 Singirok withdrew £1479. He said he could not recall what he spent this money on either but it was for 'personal' expenses.

On 12 December 1996 Franklin credited another £10,000 to the Visa account. Singirok told the Inquiry he knew nothing about this second lump-sum transfer until he got his statement at the end of December. In January 1997 there were some minor withdrawls. On 5 February 1997, Singirok withdrew £3567 pounds. 'I was preparing to go to the Philippines so I did get some advance,' he said. He used his Visa card during this trip to the Philippines to pay some accommodation bills for his staff. In Singapore he paid £1575 to a tailor, Am Yap, for three tailor-made business suits. On 14 February 1997 the third and final transfer of £10,000 was credited by Franklin to his account. Singirok continued using the account after his dismissal as Commander in March 1997 but told the Los Inquiry he ceased using it in December.

A few weeks before the first major transfer was made in early July 1996, the PNG Defence Department paid Franklin K289,680 (£144,000) out of the special K10 million High Speed II allocation. This payment had nothing to do with High Speed II. It was settlement of a long-outstanding bill dating back to 1994, before Singirok became Commander. Singirok denied knowing anything about this payment and refuted suggestions that Franklin was thanking him for settling the account. He also rejected speculation that the payments were linked to a proposed purchase of patrol boats from Unicorn International in Singapore.

When she broke the story of the 'secret' Visa Account, Mary-Louise O'Callaghan suggested that the money he had received from Franklin could explain Singirok's later aborting of the mercenaries' mission. Singirok denied there was any connection claiming Franklins and Sandline were not in the same league or even the same business. 'There was no conflict of interest,' a statement released at the time through his lawyer argued, 'because Sidney Franklin's firm was not a competitor in the supply of equipment and personnel in the category and scale outlined in the Sandline Contract.'

While Singirok was visiting the United States after leaving London in April 1996, Spicer couriered copies of his Project Contravene document to Defence Minister Ijape in Port Moresby. In the accompanying letter on Plaza 107 letterhead, Spicer described the meeting with Singirok as 'very useful' and he informed Ijape that the PNGDF Commander 'concurs with it'. Recognising that the Defence Minister would have to present the proposal to Cabinet he suggested another selling point—regional clout. He claimed the electronic warfare equipment and the helicopter strike force would make PNG a power to be reckoned with in the South Pacific. '[The] package we have put together for this particular project will not only resolve the specific problem,' he told Ijape, 'but will have considerable impact in enhancing your overall military capability within the region. It will give you the following: 1. A national intelligence capability (internal and external). 2. A powerful strike capability which will act as a deterrent. 3. Massive increase in Combat Power. 4. National control over these assets with "no strings attached".'

While Ijape, fresh from his own sabre rattling with Solomon Islands, may have appreciated the point, he never incorporated Project Contravene into a Cabinet submission, at least not in 1996. He never even bothered to take it to the Prime Minister, Sir Julius Chan. He was still smarting from being turned down after the Cairns trip. 'When the Prime Minister said, "There is no money," and I knew that there was no money, I did not want to bother going back to him because he would just say, "No!".' Sir Julius Chan told the Andrew Inquiry that he had by then rejected other proposals for private military intervention on Bougainville. 'I told the Defence Minister that I have also received a number of proposals [involving] foreign private military companies which I have dismissed out of hand.' Asked why, Sir Julius told Justice Andrew there were several reasons. 'Last year [1996] was a very bad year for this country. We went through some tough economic conditions. I was not ready to entertain any cost to that effect so I completely wiped out any possibility of incurring further cost.'

The Project Contravene idea seemed dead. All those at the PNG end who appeared before the Andrew Inquiry agreed on that. Ijape was no longer prepared to raise it with the Prime Minister; Brigadier Singirok said he had no confidence that the money could be found; and the third member of the PNG Defence Council, James Melegepa, was not even shown the Project Contravene document. Asked about the Commander's attitude after he returned from London, Melegepa said Singirok told him he had met Spicer and that there was a written proposal which he promised to copy to the Secretary, but never did. 'I do not think he took it seriously,' Melegepa said. 'He thought the proposal looked good but he did not think the government would pursue it, I suspect, at that time.' Asked about the Minister's reaction, Melegepa said Ijape had told him the Prime Minister would not agree with it. 'There was not much discussion about that after the Prime Minister's reaction to it was negative,' Melegepa said.

But Spicer was keen to follow up his $US30 million proposal and he started peppering both the Commander and the Defence Minister with telephone calls and faxes. The Brigadier said the calls became a nuisance. 'It even got to the stage where he would ring me and my wife at very odd hours ... and there were certain times that we had to unhook the phone because it was about two or three in the morning, PNG time.' Ijape told Spicer the proposal could not proceed because PNG did not have the funds. Justice Andrew said the faxes at this time were still on Plaza 107 letterhead. 'He addressed Mr Ijape using his Christian name, Mathias. Mr Spicer's approach,' the Judge reported, 'was that of the salesman and Plaza's (and later Sandline's) ongoing interest in mineral resources is apparent.'

On 14 May 1996, a few weeks after the couriered copies of Project Contravene had reached the Minister, Spicer faxed him: 'Dear Mathias, Following our telephone conversation of last Friday, I am writing to you in order to state our present position. We do understand your difficulties; at the same time we are, of course, disappointed that the main contract is not to go ahead in the way we all originally hoped. This disappointment is underlined by the fact that we have positioned men, aircraft and equipment on your behalf but at our expense. Anyway—we do understand and we would like to therefore propose that you immediately go ahead with the airborne electronic intelligence (ELINT) package part of the original proposal. This can be made immediately available at a cost of $US14M. If you can get the above order for $US14M started immediately then we believe that we will be able to match this commitment and help you find the other $US16M. This will then allow the full project to go ahead. These funds could come from private sources and it may be possible to raise them against oil and mineral concessions and production rights.'

That is the way Anthony Buckingham had been able to work in Africa. More proposals on how the operation could be funded were to follow, but for the moment the attention of the Government in Papua New Guinea was being focused towards the PNGDF's own plan to track down and capture the rebel leadership—Operation High Speed II. It was an operation they would mount without any of the sophisticated technology that Brigadier Singirok would have liked to help him pinpoint the rebels. Australia would not help there. On his first visit to PNG as Foreign Minister that same month, in May 1996, Alexander Downer reiterated the point: 'We've made it clear of course in the last few weeks that we won't provide logistic support to the Papua New Guinea Defence Force in the context of Bougainville. I obviously haven't changed that position today—that remains our position,' Downer told the media.

Chapter Six

High Speed II Meets No Mercy

Humiliation for the PNGDF—A Military Fiasco and a Massacre
June-September 1996

The PNG Cabinet decision of 21 March 1996 lifting the eighteen-month-old Bougainville cease-fire specifically authorised the PNG Defence Force to 'deal with BRA elements both inside and outside Papua New Guinea'. In his national address that night, Sir Julius Chan had used the same words 'inside and outside' PNG when issuing his grim warning to the rebels. Just where most effort would be concentrated to deal with the BRA 'outside' PNG was not specified. But speculation arose as to the safety of the rebels' overseas spokesmen, Moses Havini in Sydney and Martin Miriori in Honiara. Miriori, whose home had been fire-bombed in February, was considered at real risk especially when, in April, Defence Minister Ijape demanded Solomon Islands 'repatriate' him to PNG 'or we will get in and get him back ourselves'. The United Nations High Commissioner for Refugees arranged asylum in Holland and, much to Ijape's annoyance, Australia flew an Air Force jet into Honiara on the night of 30 April to whisk him and his family away from perceived danger.

However, the focus of the crackdown on BRA sympathisers outside PNG was stated clearly in the military's Top Secret Operational Plan for High Speed II. Phase One of the PNGDF's plan called for 'sealing off the maritime border' with Solomon Islands 'to commence [in] May and June 1996 and remain in force throughout the operations period'. From early May, soldiers from the PNGDF's small boats teams and Bougainvilleans from the south Bougainville Resistance conducted a series of raids into Solomon Islands targeting known pick-up and drop-off points in the Shortland Islands and Choiseul. They stole two-way radios from stores and mission stations, radios which PNG military intelligence claimed were used by the rebels. They began interrupting regular mission radio schedules.

On Saturday, 1 June a PNGDF patrol boat crossed over into the Solomons. According to the Solomon Islands border police, the Field Force, it fired at a village in north Choiseul. Solomon Islands lodged a diplomatic protest accusing PNG of 'armed harassment' and describing the incursion by the patrol boat as 'an act of aggression'. The Field Force has its own boats supplied under the Australian Pacific Patrol Boat Program so the prospect emerged of a small naval battle in the border corridor, involving vessels donated to both sides by Australia. Sir Julius Chan admitted that the PNG patrol boat had crossed into Solomon Islands territory. 'I know there has been some incursion,' he told ABC radio, 'I know that. But I think it is in some sort of hot pursuit.' The man that the PNG military told him they were pursuing hotly was the BRA's Operations Commander, Ishmael Toarama.

Cross-border incidents continued and by the second week in June, the Solomons claimed there had been eighteen separate border incursions. It said it intended to submit compensation claims for each one. The interdiction and harassment exercise closed the border. The Shortlands-Bougainville route had been interrupted for some time but the one remaining route in and out—from south of Koromira on the south-east coast of Bougainville to Choiseul Bay, where the sick and wounded were dropped off and medicines and other supplies picked up from the Moli Catholic Mission—was shut down too. Life for the ordinary villagers on the Solomons side was disrupted. All primary schools in the Shortlands closed and the Catholic Church shut its girls' vocational school.

On 2 July PNG claimed that its observation post on Tarato Island just inside the PNG border spotted eight armed rebels in a speed boat passing Ovau Island on the Solomons side heading into PNG. Brigadier Singirok himself released the details: 'A helicopter went to investigate. Three rebels on board started firing at the helicopter and the troop occupants fired back. The speed boat turned around to go back to Ovau, to the Solomon Islands Field Force observation post. The helicopter followed and on the way the troops fired. From the reports I have got approximately six people were killed and the speedboat was disabled.' The Commander admitted that this engagement with what he called 'an opportunity target' occurred in Solomons waters but he rejected suggestions that the Iroquois had been used as a gunship. 'The difference with a gunship,' he argued, 'is that they are mounted with air-to-surface missiles or machine-guns, a weapons system that is controlled from the central console, from the cockpit. Our soldiers who fired are just being transported in the helicopter.'

Brigadier Singirok had a warning. 'Unless the Solomon Islands Government comes out quite clearly about what to do with these illegal activities by the rebels we will continue to have violations of this nature.' The Solomon Islands Field Force claimed to have no knowledge of the incident and cast doubts on whether the soldiers on the Iroquois had killed anyone. The Brigadier General had been unusually forthcoming but the motivation seems to have been part of High Speed II's PsyOps, its Psychological Operations. The aim was to spread fear so that the rebels would not try to escape to the Solomons. Singirok told the Andrew Inquiry the PsyOps adopted during High Speed II had been effective. Australia's Shadow Minister for Foreign Affairs, Laurie Brereton, called on the Australian Government to review Australian defence aid to PNG 'to ensure that no direct support, logistic or otherwise, was given to offensive operations on Bougainville'.

Phase One of High Speed II was later to be hailed by the PNG military as the only part of the whole operation that succeeded. 'This phase was successful,' an August report to Chan and Ijape claimed. 'However clashes [between] the high-powered speed boats used by the rebels and the small boats team caused frequent border crossings into Solomon Islands which were a major concern. At the same time the rebels crossed from Solomon Islands into Bougainville which resulted in our military helicopter intercepting and causing injury to the occupants of a boat in Solomon Island waters.' The report, written a month after High Speed II was over, complained that the patrol boats 'were subjected [sic] to breakdown', that 'spare parts problems' had 'forced them to seek shelter during rough weather' and that their surveillance program was 'restricted'. However, despite 'a lack of credible surveillance devices, the sailors did their best,' it said, 'and maintained a tight control on the Papua New Guinea-Solomon Islands border'.

Closing the border

Village people on Choiseul Island identified them. 'They were mostly Bougainvilleans,' the Solomon Islands villagers told their Catholic Bishop. 'But there were "redskins" amongst them.' (Redskins is a term the very dark skinned Bougainvilleans and people from the western Solomons use to describe other Melanesians with lighter, brown not black, skin.) They came ashore at night at the Moli Catholic Mission in Choiseul Bay wearing army fatigues and balaclavas. These armed members of the South Bougainville Resistance, SBIA (taking its name from the South Bougainville Interim Authority, which had turned against the BRA), and their PNG army 'allies' confiscated two radios, one from the health clinic and one from the mission centre. The small outboard-motor-powered runabouts operated by the PNG Army's small boats team picked them up again.

'They've been coming in on their Yamaha Ray boats with high-powered engines,' said Bishop Bernard O'Grady whose diocese covered the Solomons side of the international border, 'coming in at times when they are not expected.' The Moli Mission had been operating for several years as a forwarding base for shipping medical supplies into Bougainville. Bishop O'Grady said the people got to know the BRA rebels fairly well. These latest visitors were not BRA. 'They've also been harassing the people by setting off volleys of shots and forcing the people, who are terribly frightened, to sleep in the bush. I've one of the sisters with me in the room at the moment,' he said over the radio telephone. 'She just came down from Choiseul two days ago and she and others have told me that it's pretty well a nightly affair.' An Australian Sister visiting in the previous month, May, told him a helicopter had been buzzing around parts of the Shortlands.

'My own impression,' Bishop O'Grady went on, 'is that it's being done deliberately to follow up what the PNG Defence Minister [Mathias Ijape] said several months ago—that they would pursue into Solomon Islands waters any Bougainvillean BRA people and make hell for the Solomon Islanders. Well they've certainly achieved that. They're frightening the hell out of the local people.'

The timing of Operation High Speed II hinged on what, by 1996, had become the annual change-over of the PNGDF's two infantry battalions on Bougainville. The Wewak-based 2nd Battalion had been in the province for about ten months when the Cabinet decision was taken in March to, in the words of Defence Minister Ijape, 'destroy the BRA headquarters and where possible arrest [the] key BRA leadership'. The 1st Battalion was not due to begin its tour of duty for another two months. To maximise the number of soldiers that could be mobilised for the operation the decision was taken to leave the 2nd Battalion in place for an extra six weeks and to deploy the fresh troops from the 1st Battalion to conduct a pincer thrust in July into the rebel stronghold, the Kongara—the mountain jungles to the south of the abandoned Panguna mine.

Singirok's diary reveals that in early May he had jotted down an outline for the plan. After utilising the small boats teams to close off the possibility of escape south, there were to be preliminary landings at the old Aropa International Airport south of Kieta and at a number of other locations. The advancing troops were to 'leapfrog into the valley' and launch a 'simultaneous assault' on Sipuru, one of the villages regularly used by Francis Ona for his moveable headquarters. The diary notes also make a reference to mortars. These were to be the new 120 mm mortars purchased from Unicorn in Singapore. Up until this time, the PNGDF had used smaller 81 mm mortars similar to those on regular issue to Australian infantry mortar squads.

As the preparations for the mid-year military operation proceeded, PNG came under greater international scrutiny. In Geneva on 12 April a United Nations Human Rights Commission report criticised both the Government and the military. The author of the report, Wally N'diaye, a UNHRC Special Rapporteur, had visited Bougainville the previous October at PNG's invitation but been frustrated in his attempts to visit BRA-controlled central Bougainville. He said he had asked the Chan Government about specific allegations of human rights violations but there had been no response. 'It has been reported to the Special Rapporteur,' N'diaye said, 'that between the beginning of 1991 and October 1995 at least sixty-four persons were believed to have been extra-judicially executed by the PNGDF, some of them after being beaten or cut with knives. Other victims have been tied to the backs of trucks and dragged along the road before being shot and killed.' The Special Rapporteur recommended that non-governmental human rights and humanitarian organisations should be allowed access to all the population of Bougainville.

However, with High Speed II gathering momentum, the PNG military was imposing greater restrictions on access, not easing them. The soldiers halted all non-military air and shipping services to the province and imposed tight new regulations on movement and trade within Bougainville. When these new measures were reported in the media, Sir Julius declared them illegal and called for the officer responsible to be reprimanded. But most remained in force. The former Bougainville Administrator, Sam Tulo, who was amongst those who had complained to Port Moresby, was picked up at gunpoint and taken away for questioning. He was released unharmed but harassment of others continued. Troops detained overnight the Transitional Government's Peace Coordinator, James Togel. The military imposed limits on the quantity of food or fuel people were allowed to buy in Buka. And at the check-point at Siara on the main island just across Buka Passage anything in excess of the allowed limit was confiscated. A short distance away, soldiers sold the same items back to travellers. A gallon of petrol cost K4.50 on Buka but K11.00 the other side of the check-point.

A second United Nations report dealing with Bougainville was presented to the Human Rights Commission in Geneva on 16 April. This one carried the name of the Secretary General, Boutros Boutros Ghali, and it expressed regret at what it described as the 'recent negative turn of events' on Bougainville. The Secretary General had sent the Director of the UN's East Asia and Pacific Political Division, Francesc Vendrell, to co-chair the second Cairns talks in December. His report spoke positively of the 'momentum towards peace' that had been generated in Cairns but said it 'had been marred by a series of incidents which have cast a cloud over the peace process'. The UN Secretary General said his envoy had been unable to get to Bougainville and he quoted Vendrell's view as being that 'only a resumption of the peace process and patient perseverance in the negotiations can bring to an end the conflict'. On Bougainville itself the BRA captured a large cache of weapons and ammunition when its fighters surrounded a small outpost of soldiers near Koromira and drove them off into the sea.

Papua New Guinea's Police Commissioner, Bob Nenta, was the nominal boss of the whole operation on Bougainville. And over the weekend of 15-16 June a notice in his name was issued warning people in the mountainous Kongara area of central Bougainville south of the mine to flee to government Care Centres. 'There will be a major operation to clean out these criminals who have caused you to suffer,' the notice read, 'and therefore you all must leave your homes quickly.' Nenta's office in Port Moresby at first denied he had signed anything. But later there was an admission that if the warning was to do with an operation on Bougainville then the military were probably using his name 'legitimately'.

A news release a few days later from the Defence Minister confirmed that Operation High Speed II had commenced. But Ijape claimed it was not a declaration of war. 'If it was a war situation,' he said, 'then those pamphlets to warn people to move out of the military danger zone issued by the Police Commissioner could not have been dropped.' No, he claimed, this was an operation geared towards capturing 'the hardcore armed bandits' who had terrorised ninety per cent of the rest of Bougainville. 'There is this ten per cent of the island's area that has [the] BRA's hideout called Kongara and Sipuru that security forces want to visit,' Ijape said. 'I have positioned my men on the ground and we have sealed off the escape routes of these criminals and the operation has commenced.'

That same day, 20 June, Australian Foreign Minister Alexander Downer told the Parliament in Canberra he had seen indications that PNG was planning a military offensive on Bougainville. 'When I was in Papua New Guinea in May,' Downer said, 'I offered Australia's help to try to reinvigorate the peace process, which broke down when the PNG Government formally lifted its cease-fire in March this year ... But I repeat: we do not believe there is a military solution to this problem. Indeed if there is to be an attempt to achieve a military solution, it is my judgment and the judgment of the Government that this will simply exacerbate the situation.' Downer said he had instructed the Australian High Commissioner in Port Moresby, David Irvine, to make representations to the PNG Government expressing the Australian Government's concern.

'I am concerned, we are concerned,' an irritated Sir Julius Chan told journalists in Port Moresby. 'You don't have to get Mr Downer to be concerned about this. We are so concerned we are spending a lot of money there. We are so very concerned about the whole Bougainville situation we brought in the Peace Keeping Force, we allowed meetings to occur outside this country. We made all the necessary [concessions] from amnesty to forgiveness to everything you can think of. We are concerned! So I don't just want anyone to say they are concerned. It is time Australia allowed Papua New Guinea to run our own business. We are a sovereign nation.' Asked if the operation into the Kongara would still go ahead if the estimated 12,000 civilians did not respond and flee, Sir Julius said the aim was minimum loss of life. 'I don't want you to make the comparison of the Americans advising the Japanese to get out when they dropped the Hiroshima bomb at that time. But we are trying to get as much information out to the people as possible to move away from the rebel-held, criminal-infected area. A lot of these people, you have got to realise, are being prevented against their choice from getting out. I think we will help to free them.'

The BRA's Military Commander, General Sam Kauona, said his forces were prepared. 'The morale of the BRA fighters is very, very high and they are excited about it. I hope also,' he said in a statement issued through the rebel information network, 'that this will be the final and deciding game between the PNG Government and its forces and the BRA forces.' Asked to react, Sir Julius said: 'I don't trust him. I simply don't give him any credence at all.' He said nobody should believe a person who had pledged to attend a peace conference during talks hosted by the then Solomon Islands Prime Minister, Francis Billy-Hilly, but who had broken his word and failed to show up. Questioned on how he had reacted to a proposal by the new Solomon Islands Government for a peace plan involving the complete withdrawal of PNG troops from Bougainville, Sir Julius replied: 'Very coldly.'

Bougainville's Transitional Premier, Theodore Miriung, said his administration would not be able to feed the people the PNG military was urging to desert their villages and flee from the mountains of south-central Bougainville. Miriung himself was banned from travelling to the Bougainville mainland from the Transitional Government headquarters on Buka. 'I am told not to visit the districts lest the soldiers of the Defence Force kill me in the event that some of them are killed by the BRA,' he said. 'I was told that by their senior officers. At the same time,' he complained, 'they go out and tell my people that I live in hotels, that I eat good food and I do not do anything to bring about peace. This is a complete lie and I think it is evil.' Premier Miriung's relations with the military were by this stage poisonous. And he was not afraid to speak out about human rights atrocities that came to his attention.

Just a few days after Ijape's announcement that Operation High Speed II had commenced, Miriung revealed on ABC Radio details of the alleged extra-judicial killing of former BRA fighters. 'I was told by Chief Sinato,' he said, 'that there were eight young men killed by the security forces in the north-west area of Bougainville near Kunua. There was some kind of dispute among people at the Care Centre and these eight young men who were reformed BRA were reported to the security force members stationed there by one of their big-men, the chief. Acting on the basis of what he told them the security forces went and the eight young men were killed. The chief, instead of using his traditional authority to deal with the dispute, thought he would get the security force members to settle it for him. And they settled it! In that way.' Brigadier Singirok issued a statement saying he would not tolerate extra-judicial killings and ordered an investigation. Later Sir Julius announced the results. The military claimed the ex-BRA members were being reactivated by Ishmael Toarama and had died in a shoot-out. Reports from the island indicated they had been disarmed the day before they were shot.

About 1000 infantry were to be engaged in Operation High Speed II. With additional police, members of the Resistance and support personnel, the potential government forces totalled more than 2100. However, the main strike force that was to press inland into the Kongara from the beach-head at Aropa in the hope of capturing the rebel leadership was made up of two companies from the 1st Battalion, about 250 men. That amphibious landing was planned for early July and was part of Phase Three. Phase Two involved 'preliminary operations' by the 2nd Battalion during June 1996 'to clear pockets of resistance of rebels in government-controlled areas'. The PNGDF had not been able to acquire any additional helicopters and only two of the Australian-donated Iroquois were still operational. High Speed II started to unravel when, during one of these preliminary operations, one of these two helicopters was knocked out of action.

Rebels at Orami in the mountains seven kilometres south of the mine raked one of the Iroquois with automatic fire on 29 June. It was attempting to resupply troops it had inserted at Orami three days earlier. Twelve rounds hit the control panel on the chopper blade. The Iroquois pilots managed to pull it up and away to the south-west but it needed to be repaired and could no longer take part in the operation. Although the official military report that went to the government claimed this damage was inflicted during Phase Two, Orami could not be described as being a 'pocket' of rebel activity 'in a government-controlled area'. It was right in the middle of the Kongara just ten kilometres from Sipuru. The PNG troops who had been dropped into Orami on 26 June had to fight their way back out of BRA territory on foot. The disabling of one of the two serviceable Iroquois caused severe complications for Phase Three of High Speed II which involved further 'air insertion into selected areas' of the Kongara as well as the Aropa beach landing.

The General speaks

While Operation High Speed II was under way, Brigadier General Jerry Singirok made an official trip to Australia to meet his Australian counterpart, General John Baker. On his return he gave a lengthy interview to Neville Togarewa, the PNG *Post Courier's* most knowledgeable writer on Defence matters. The interview was published on 5 July 1996. Some excerpts:

Q. What is your objective?

A. [The] aim is very simple—to eradicate the sponsors of these criminal acts, within and outside of Bougainville . . . We have specific intelligence on rebel concentrations, so-called strongholds, their communications centres, and the only way to neutralise them is to go on an offensive, which is basically to go out, seek and destroy . . .

Q. Today's reports say the security forces have gained control of Orami and Sipuru and are on the verge of securing Guava and Panguna?

A. Yes, but there's a difference between seizing it and putting it under government control, meaning putting in government services. Panguna is not important. We're not after the mine site. I was the [Battalion] Commander in 1994 and I can tell you it is not difficult to seize and control the mine site. We are concentrating on [the] BRA . . .

Q. The whole question of Australian supply of weapons?

A. The Australian public perception and political view is not to supply us with any arms. We appreciate that . . . I think the perception which has not been corrected in Australia is that Alexander Downer keeps talking about a 'military solution'. We don't have a military solution. I had lunch and dinner with Downer and I explained that we have 'military options'. I stressed that we didn't have a 'military solution'. He went back to Australia and continues to talk about a 'military solution'. It's just not on. The military has a job to do on Bougainville but we don't have a military answer.

Q. There was a newspaper report that you went on a spending spree in Singapore and spent K10 million on arms and other materials.

A. The Government gave us K10 million and we budgeted our spending based on five major functions—operational upkeep, allowances, food, transportation, and weapons and ammunition. Yes, we went to Singapore to buy arms and ammunition. And why not? We are an independent country. Why do I have to go to Australia? I could go anywhere else in the world as Commander to buy any hardware I require. So whether it's Singapore, Malaysia or Russia it doesn't matter. We know the Australian attitude. You can put a big cross on them because they're not going to give it to us.

The move on Aropa went ahead anyway on 8 July. A suppressive barrage preceded the men being sent ashore. Two patrol boats fired their cannons at suspected rebel positions while mortar teams set up on the decks bombarded the shoreline and surrounding hills. A PNGDF landing barge then took the first troops ashore. But the BRA were ready. And the PNG soldiers were soon pinned down. Kauona's forces had added considerably to their weapons arsenal when they recovered the equipment abandoned by the PNGDF contingent they had driven into the sea near Koromira just to the south two months earlier. His men shot dead an army engineer in the early skirmishes. But their major success was hitting the only military helicopter left. The PNGDF's last operational Iroquois was grounded after it 'was shot in the rotor blade'. According to the official report to Sir Julius this elimination of helicopter support shelved any hope of the security forces advancing 'any further than a few kilometres from the coastline'. In fact, the troops did not make much progress beyond the burnt-out remains of the Aropa airport buildings just a few hundred metres from the beach. A second soldier was shot dead on the third night after the landing.

Kauona claimed on 12 July that his rebel forces were inflicting damage on PNG naval craft using old Japanese World War II 70 mm anti-aircraft guns. He also claimed his fighters had driven the PNG troops out of the ruined brick airport terminal back to the beach. The BRA did have one Japanese gun that they had reconditioned so that it could fire off one shot at a time. And they used it very effectively. Kauona claimed his men had recovered documents revealing PNG's battle plan when they recaptured the terminal ruins. He boasted that the PNG soldiers had achieved only one of their four primary objectives. The Commanding Officer of the 1st Battalion, Lieutenant Colonel Seke Berapu, stayed offshore on board one of the patrol boats. And on 15 July, one week after his men hit the beach at Aropa, he ordered an evacuation abandoning the beach-head. It was a humiliating defeat for the PNGDF. Brigadier Singirok relieved Lieutenant Colonel Berapu of his command of the 1st Battalion and demoted him to Major.

Nine days later the 2nd Battalion left the island, ending its fourteen-month tour of duty boarding ships heading home to Wewak. High Speed II had failed. The first military report to Sir Julius Chan summing up the operation, attempted to gloss over the extent of the failure, but in doing so emphasised it. It claimed the rebels were 'on the run' but by the time Sir Julius read it in August, this was obviously far from correct. 'The operation involved seventy per cent of the entire Defence Force on Bougainville,' it said. 'It involved two infantry battalions, a patrol boat squadron of three ships and a small fleet of helicopters.' The report claimed Phase Two, the clearing out of rebel pockets in government-controlled areas, had gone well. The 2nd Regiment, it claimed, had 'successful encounters with the rebels which caused substantial casualties'. But it did not reveal these casualty numbers even to the Prime Minister. 'Number killed–restricted,' is how his briefing read.

Asked at the Andrew Inquiry by counsel representing Sir Julius why he had not provided the Prime Minister with the number of rebels killed, Brigadier Singirok became testy. 'I do not believe that you could equate military success with bodies and that is why at that time it was not important for me as the Commander to provide such statistics ... I thought it would raise unnecessary expectations amongst the politicians ... Unfortunately our politicians seem to relate success with dead bodies.' Six security force members, four soldiers and two policemen, died during Operation High Speed II. The report described Phase Three as 'a major setback' and put the blame on the lack of mobility caused by the two helicopters being rendered useless. It recommended that the 'National Government purchase an appropriate fleet of helicopters'. Asked by Marshall Cooke QC, counsel for Sir Julius, if it wasn't a 'dismal failure', Singirok replied: 'Yes. It goes back to my earlier statement when I said there is no military solution to Bougainville.'

One of the most senior officers at PNGDF headquarters, Colonel Reg Renagi, wrote after attending the High Speed II debriefing session that 'senior staff officers failed to give professional advice' to the Commander. '[The] prevailing tactical situation,' he claimed, 'did not warrant a conventional joint amphibious operation in broad daylight and worse, in full view of the enemy who [was] clearly expecting us and was prepared to stand his ground and fight... He was fully prepared and ready... while we were not.' Colonel Renagi believed the attempt at 'a major strike' against the rebel headquarters 'exposed numerous problems the PNGDF' had always had. He said the 'search and destroy mission in the Kongara Valley' seemed to have no clear objective and was rushed. 'With very limited resources,' he claimed, 'the PNGDF should not have even conducted this very expensive operation... in such a conventional manner to incur great losses in material... [It] was not only unfeasible but uneconomic as well.' The overall outcome: 'a poor plan badly executed resulting in a rout of our own troops once landed ashore'.

The day after the embarrassing abandonment of the Aropa beach-head the facsimile machine in the PNG Prime Minister's office received a call from London. Dated 16 July 1996, the fax that came through was from Timothy Spicer OBE. Spicer had made little progress with the proposed $US30 million Operation Contravene proposal by contacting Singirok and Ijape direct. So he tried Sir Julius. 'Dear Sir,' the fax from Plaza 107 said, 'You may be aware that we have been in discussion with your Minister of Defence. He has asked us to set our position in detail, and to that end I enclose my latest communication with him.' Spicer told Sir Julius that both he and his Chairman/Chief Executive, Tony Buckingham, 'would like to have the opportunity of coming to brief you in person about our abilities and the possibility of helping your government and investing in your country'. He suggested to Sir Julius that they would like to visit PNG between 12 and 18 September. The former Scots Guard Lieutenant Colonel ended his fax: 'I hope that we can come to see you as we feel we really can help.'

The timing of the correspondence was hardly coincidental. Although the retreat from Aropa was not confirmed until a few days after the troops pulled out, the whole High Speed II military operation received wide coverage. BBC radio had taken a keen interest and Moses Havini in Sydney had been issuing daily 'Media Information Updates' which claimed many more killings of PNG troops than ever was the case. These releases were seized upon by many journalists who had only a marginal knowledge of Bougainville and often run without question. By this time, Spicer was keeping a close watch on news out of Bougainville. In an interview with the ABC in April 1997, just before he left PNG, Spicer commented on how his company was following events: 'In our business we keep a fairly good data base of conflicts or potential conflicts and, obviously, Papua New Guinea featured on our data base. You know, we can't monitor the detail of everything all of the time. But once there is an interest then we start to increase our effort at information gathering and completing our data base on a potential client country.' Spicer received no reply to his initial approach to Sir Julius Chan. He followed up with another fax on 21 August. Sir Julius passed this on to his Departmental Secretary, Noel Levi, with the handwritten notation: 'I would NOT be taking this too seriously. Check and ADVISE.'

On Bougainville Premier Miriung was despondent, believing High Speed II had been a massive mistake and a huge setback to his peace efforts. 'One of the effects of Operation High Speed II,' he told the ABC's 'Indian-Pacific' Program in late July, 'is that it has highly psyched up the Bougainville Revolutionary hardliners. Whether or not the BIG-BRA will use that psyche-up of themselves positively or negatively is up to them. But if I were on their side—instead of being a hopeless, middle peacemaker—I would ask the National Government, the security force senior officers and invite them for talks.' Talks were the last thing on the mind of BRA Supreme Commander Francis Ona. He issued a number of proclamations of military victory. On 30 July he declared a counter to Operation High Speed II. He called it Operation No Mercy and announced that BRA units had been directed to wipe out the small encampments of PNG troops that were dotted in various locations around Bougainville. Many of these were located in or next to Care Centres.

The same day that Ona issued his Operation No Mercy directive, Sir Julius Chan was questioned in Parliament in Port Moresby on comments Australia's Foreign Minister had made at the ASEAN Foreign Ministers Meeting in Jakarta suggesting PNG's use of the Iroquois in offensive operations on Bougainville put continued Australian defence aid at risk. 'Now that Mr Downer has seen fit to issue an open threat to PNG,' Sir Julius said, 'I guess it's time for the entire arrangement to be reviewed.' At the PNG end he wanted the review to begin straight away, describing the Defence Cooperation Program (DCP) as a colonial remnant. 'This aid has a two-way benefit,' he told Parliament. 'It is money that goes back to Australia as 'boomerang aid' in the way of wages and salaries paid to Australians and in purchases from Australian companies.' Maybe it should be cancelled, he implied. 'Too heavy a reliance has created a paternalistic Australian mentality,' the Prime Minister said, 'and is a form of post-colonial bondage.'

Sir Julius was also highly critical of what he claimed was Downer's lack of understanding of what Chan believed to be the reality on Bougainville—that most Bougainvilleans had opted for negotiations and it was Ona who was the obstacle to peace. 'I fail to understand how Mr Downer can continue to get it so wrong,' Sir Julius complained. 'I am appalled that some people can be so naive about what is happening on the ground on Bougainville.' Sir Julius also attacked Australia for condoning what he called 'treasonous actions', by allowing Havini and other secessionist supporters to issue anti-PNG propaganda. 'These people are allowed to spread disinformation and to actively campaign against the State of Papua New Guinea,' he claimed to the PNG Parliament. 'Their smear campaign, and their continued distortion of the truth, help to prolong the cycle of civilian killings. I will not sit back while Australia gives the impression it prefers to side with various of our citizens resident there who actively campaign against our territorial integrity.'

It was not a good day all round for Julius Chan or Jerry Singirok that 30 July 1996. It was also the day on which the United States Embassy in Port Moresby informed the PNGDF Commander that his hoped-for purchase of ten second-hand US Army Iroquois for $US2.4 million had been vetoed by Washington. 'In the light of Papua New Guinea's legitimate right to defend its territorial integrity from attack by secessionists on Bougainville,' the State Department advised, 'we have carefully considered the request [by the PNGDF] to acquire excess helicopters. Prime Minister Sir Julius Chan recently enquired about the status of this issue and expressed his position that military assistance to Papua New Guinea not be tied to specific conditions. However,' the note continued, 'the acquisition ... would require that conditions be placed on their use. Further, concerns about the ability to effectively monitor these conditions ... in the field have led us to conclude against proceeding.'

Singirok, Chan and Ijape were all convinced Australia had influenced the American decision. In his written statement to the Andrew Inquiry Ijape stated it as fact: 'The Australian Government ... requested [the] American Government not to allow PNG to purchase second-hand American army helicopters.' Australian officials claim they were told by the US Ambassador that the State Department had made up its own mind on human rights grounds. Brigadier Singirok asked Chan if he could look elsewhere. In a covering letter informing Chan about the US veto he told his Prime Minister he was deeply concerned about the PNGDF's lack of helicopters, adding that this would have 'serious repercussions' for operations on Bougainville. 'I further seek your views for us to go [to] Singapore, Israel or China to seek their assistance.' He suggested that the PNGDF should follow through the

Government's 'look-north policy' because the prospects of significant military help from PNG's 'traditional allies have dwindled in the light of their misconception of our strategies in Bougainville'.

Brigadier Singirok's relations with Australian defence authorities had soured remarkably in the eight months since Sir Julius Chan had chosen him to head the PNG Defence Force. Singirok's view of the DCP was accurately reflected in the derogatory remarks Sir Julius had made to Parliament. One of the major issues of contention concerned maintenance of the Iroquois. Early on in Singirok's command, the Australians decided to pull out the staff they had seconded to the PNGDF's air transport wing. Canberra felt too much money, too many personnel and too much effort was being expended for very little flying time. So the Australians devised a contract that could be put out to private tender for the upkeep of the Iroquois. Responsibility for funding the proposed four-year contract would be gradually transferred to the PNGDF. In the first year seventy-five per cent of the cost would be carried by the DCP and by year four PNG would be paying the lot. But Brigadier Singirok wanted his Air Element to be trained to fix the Iroquois themselves. 'We had to force him kicking and screaming into this commercial support contract,' an Australian official commented later.

There was a company on the other side of the world well versed in 'military assistance packages' that was only too willing to fill in gaps not covered by the Australian DCP and with well-developed plans to provide the PNGDF with alternative helicopters to American Iroquois. And it saw opportunities in PNG beyond pure military help. Two days after Sir Julius had described the DCP in the PNG Parliament as a form of 'post-colonial bondage', Tony Buckingham sent a fax to PNG's Defence Minister. 'Dear Mathias,' it read, 'I know you have been talking to Tim about the PM's view of the military situation and are trying to make an appointment for Tim to brief the PM. Coincidentally, I have today had a meeting with the financial institutions with whom we have invested into Angola, Sierra Leone and other clients. To date these investments total some $US200 million. All of this investment has been into the extraction of mineral resources (oil, copper, diamonds, gold) and all have involved high risk security/military situations,' Buckingham wrote.

'These investments, and the military land, sea and air operations that have gone with them, are, as you know, a matter of public record. In the course of our meeting, and without any prompting from us,' Buckingham told Ijape, 'one of the senior financiers broached the subject to us of PNG. He asked if we were aware of the situation and of the immense economic potential. A discussion followed in which we basically agreed with their assessment. At *no* point in the discussion did we state or hint that we had inside information: your confidentiality stayed strictly intact,' PNG's Defence Minister was assured. 'The point is this,' Buckingham went on, 'the above institutions have large sums of money which they say they are ready to invest in PNG if the government of PNG are interested. A further condition for their involvement would be the provision of our help with the operational security but I do not think that you will have a problem with that!'

Buckingham told Ijape they needed to talk 'as a matter of urgency', since the available funds might be invested elsewhere if the opportunity was not seized, 'and you and I want to see them firmly into the economy and interest of PNG and its present government'. However, Buckingham acknowledged that some mechanism might have to be devised to enable him and these financial institutions to get involved. 'Making these investments will not be straightforward,' he said, 'given the fact that large Western mining interests already hold the key concessions. In order that we can urgently progress this I would like to visit you as soon as possible in Port Moresby. I am ready to travel now—can you please send a fax of invitation for visa purposes for myself, Tim Spicer and Michael Grunberg (passport details attached). I will let you know my flight details. With best regards, A. L. R. Buckingham.'

Two weeks later, Spicer was on the telephone again to Ijape discussing the military situation on Bougainville and ways in which the proposed Project Contravene could be funded. He followed that up with a fax which set out what he called 'our position' in detail. He reminded the PNG Defence Minister that, working to the budget of $US30 million 'you gave us,' he, Spicer, had produced a proposal 'for a quick low-profile solution which would be precise with little collateral damage and the minimum political risk'. However, that had been rejected due to lack of funds. 'We then responded that we might be able to assist with funding and could come to some arrangement regarding part repayment with mineral concessions etc. Coincidentally, our financial associates raised the issue of significant investment in your country.' Spicer then set out Plaza 107's latest proposal.

It was in three parts. First, he suggested a visit to PNG during which he and Buckingham would brief Ijape and the Prime Minister 'on our history, capabilities and structure'. Second, that they assist PNG 'with the resolution of the Bougainville problem in a more modest way, and in any way that your government finds politically acceptable'. This would involve the provision of equipment and specialist operators together with training for PNG personnel at a slimmed down cost of $US3–5 million. And third, there was a proposal to get the Bougainville mine producing. It involved forming 'a joint venture with your government, ourselves and RTZ to reopen and operate the Bougainville mine once recovered. It may be,' Spicer suggested, 'that RTZ may be prepared to fund some of the costs of military operations to recover the mine.' CRA, RTZ's Australian subsidiary, claims it knew nothing of this. 'You are aware of our track record,' Spicer reminded Ijape, 'and the fact that we can provide effective low-key security assistance together with a high level of investment with government in the oil and mineral areas. This can only be healthy for the country concerned.'

Spicer ended his fax to the Defence Minister with a request for an invitation to be extended to visit PNG the following month, September, to discuss the matter in detail. Ijape told the Andrew Inquiry that he had not replied to this fax. He claimed he told Spicer he had no say over the issue of mining licences. 'I said it is not my portfolio–talking about mineral concessions and mineral ownership. I am only interested in the military capabilities and your assistance to the Defence Force in that respect. But if you want to talk about all these things you have to talk to the Minerals and Energy Minister.' A few weeks after getting the fax, Ijape was confronted with another military catastrophe. Twelve members of the security forces were massacred at Kangu Beach in south Bougainville and five others were taken hostage, as they were to remain for a further ten months.

A platoon from D Company of the 1st Battalion, reinforced by a number of Mobile Squad police and supported by a Resistance group, were responsible for guarding Kangu Beach and protecting the Kangu Beach Care Centre. Kangu Beach is the only port (for want of a better term) on the south coast of Bougainville. A road runs from Kangu Beach inland to the only town in south Bougainville, Buin, and so it held strategic value as the main access point to the south of the island. The Japanese had built a small railway from Kangu Beach to Buin during World War II. Several hundred people who had deserted their villages because of the fighting lived in the ramshackle Kangu Beach Care Centre huts. On the afternoon of Sunday 8 September the soldiers and police were caught completely unawares when members of what they thought was their loyal Resistance group turned on them. Combining with the BRA's H Company based at Laguai a few kilometres to the north-east they slaughtered ten PNG soldiers and two policemen. A number of bodies were mutilated, several having their penises severed and shoved into their mouths.

Kangu Beach

Sir Julius Chan's regular Thursday afternoon news conference was unusually sombre. The PNGDF Commander, Brigadier General Singirok, had presented the Prime Minister and the Defence Minister with the Force's internal investigation into the Kangu Beach massacre. 'I take no pleasure in announcing the results,' Sir Julius said. 'The Report's findings are tragic and they reveal a serious breakdown in security, discipline and morale among those security force personnel based at Kangu. They provide an adverse assessment of the Force's chain of command and have highlighted severe difficulties of discipline and unacceptable behaviour among many of those bearing the responsibilities for the conduct of our operations in Bougainville.'

Sir Julius said the report described the massacre as being the result of retaliation 'resulting from anger, hatred and frustration over ill-treatment ... There was evidence of drug abuse among soldiers,' he said, 'and heavy consumption of home-brewed alcohol. The report also alleges that fraternisation between soldiers and local women had caused considerable friction ... The dissatisfaction among Resistance Force members seems to have been the trigger for the whole tragedy,' the PNG Prime Minister said. 'On the day of the massacre many soldiers were drunk or asleep while others were playing volleyball ... Many of their weapons had been carried by Resistance fighters who had later acquired all the weapons,' he said.

'The killing had commenced with the killing of D Company's Officer-in-Charge, Major Panao, as he slept, by a Resistance Force member and was the signal for a general slaughter ... The report says the soldiers had tried to retaliate, but their weapons ... were in the hands of the Resistance fighters who gunned them down. Some bodies of those soldiers slain were later mutilated in a gruesome manner,' Sir Julius said.

Cornelius Tare, the Resistance leader who shot Major Panao and led the massacre, boasted at Laguai village in January 1997 about how many weapons they had captured. 'We took thirty-four guns, a mortar and plenty of ammunition,' he said. 'Twenty-four of those guns were high-powered.' One of Cornelius's 'boys' stood nearby holding a light-machine-gun, one end of the machine-gun belt lodged in the firing chamber the other slung over his shoulder.

A month after the Kangu Beach massacre the PNGDF's own investigation revealed the security forces had brought the uprising on themselves by misbehaviour. Announcing the findings Sir Julius said there had been extreme provocation and a serious breakdown in disciplinary control 'from top to bottom'. But that was not where the Defence Minister had laid the blame initially. Speaking on 10 September when the details of what happened were not known and reinforcements were still trying to reach Kangu Beach overland, Ijape said military intelligence indicated Premier Miriung was responsible for inciting the mass attack. He said the Premier had been placed under surveillance and would not be allowed to leave Buka. 'I will be recommending to the Prime Minister to have him removed as the Premier,' Ijape told journalists. Asked what evidence he had, the Defence Minister offered none, claiming only that there was 'trouble' every time Premier Miriung visited mainland Bougainville.

Speaking from Buka, Miriung said he was mystified at the allegation. 'I know nothing about my being an instigator of what's happened at Kangu Beach,' he said. 'I don't know anything about it.' He said his main point of contact with the BRA had been through Martin Miriori but that had been broken when Miriori left Honiara after being granted asylum in Holland. 'Since then we have lost contact. At the moment we do not know what's happening.' Peter Niesi of the *Post Courier* visited the PNGDF's Tactical Commander on Buka, Lieutenant Colonel Yaura Sasa, to ask him about the surveillance of Premier Miriung. 'There were looks of disbelief on the faces of Lieutenant Colonel Sasa and his senior officers,' Niesi wrote at the time. Sasa told him he had received no such instructions. But the newspaper headlines about Ijape's accusation of Miriung's alleged role in the massacre were pinned up in military camps all around Bougainville.

At that same news conference the PNGDF Commander said the attempt to relieve another seven soldiers cut off on a hill overlooking the sea near Kangu Beach had been hampered by lack of mobility. 'The Government has already been advised of the desperate situation regarding helicopters,' Singirok said. 'And the Minister has assured me steps are being taken now to acquire two helicopters.' Ijape announced that downpayments would be made on two Bell helicopters operated by the PNG Highlands-based company, Hevi Lift. 'There's one already on the island and we have made arrangements with Hevi Lift. It's on hire today. But we are buying it now.' He said a half-a-million-kina deposit had been paid. Ijape visited Brisbane, Australia, later that month for talks with Australia's Defence Minister, Ian McLachlan, but his appeals for the sort of logistical support he believed was needed to help the PNGDF round up the rebel leaders was rejected.

The head of the PNG Prime Minister's Department, Noel Levi, submitted the results of his investigations into Plaza 107 and Tim Spicer to Sir Julius Chan on 19 September. Levi had contacted the British High Commissioner, Brian Lowe, and also utilised one of his own contacts developed when he was PNG's High Commissioner to London. Levi told the Andrew Inquiry Lowe had told him 'something to the effect that I should not touch Plaza 107'. Lowe said that was not quite correct. 'I had a call in either late August or early September from Noel Levi who asked me what I could tell him about a company called Plaza 107 and two British subjects called Tony Buckingham and Tim Spicer,' the British High Commissioner said in an interview in September 1997. 'I suggested he should do his own checks in London as well but that I would ask the Foreign Office. The message back was that these people deal with mercenaries and we don't approve of them.'

Levi's own source in London, a barrister (whose name was given to Justice Andrew but not published), provided the Secretary of the PM's Department with the detail for his memorandum to Sir Julius. Levi told the Prime Minister Plaza 107 was a London-based affiliate of Heritage Oil, a company registered and operating in Sierra Leone, Africa. 'It is part of an international network,' he said, 'which specialises in exporting military equipment together with mercenary soldiers. The network is headed by a former South African military officer by the name of Eeben Barlow who runs the operation under the umbrella of a mining and petroleum company called Heritage Oil. This company has extensive interests in Sierra Leone after they were invited there by the Government to put down the rebel movement in that country. As a mercenary outfit,' Levi wrote, 'Barlow's organisation is regarded as the best in the world. They are professional, efficient and are known for doing their job effectively.'

However, Levi's London contact had sounded a strong warning. 'Their method of operation however leaves very little room for any meaningful dialogue between a host government and the people whom they help to pacify. In another word,' Levi said, 'they are not concerned about the aftermath of their operation and very often have left long-term ill-feeling behind in countries where they have been engaged to put down rebellious opposition to the elected government. Their operation often leaves very little room for dialogue and negotiations. The price a country pays for their services is a substantial up-front cash payment and participation in [its] mining and petroleum industry as well as other investments. The London operation is run by Tim Spicer and Tony Buckingham. Tim Spicer is the military man but according to my contact, he is not highly regarded as a military strategist by his former military colleagues. Tony Buckingham is an economist and is highly regarded as a financing and investment expert.'

Levi provided an assessment: 'Based on the foregoing and my conversation with my contact, I would suggest that the Government should consider this matter carefully with a view to rejecting it. Our aim on Bougainville is not to completely alienate the people and therefore engaging this organisation would be contrary to our long term political and constitutional interest.' Sir Julius read the memorandum the next day, 20 September 1996, and wrote on it one word: 'Reject'.

That might have been the end of the mercenaries deal had it not been for Deputy Prime Minister Chris Haiveta, and for a conversation taking place that very day between a Hong Kong-based investment adviser, Rupert McCowan, and Spicer in London. McCowan worked as an Assistant Director in the Equity Capital Markets Division of Jardine Fleming Securities Limited. Haiveta, as Finance Minister, had appointed the big Hong Kong investment house as joint lead underwriter for the global float of Orogen Minerals Limited. Orogen was the company being set up to take over the PNG Government's oil and mining assets and forty-nine per cent of its shares were to be offered around the world. McCowan had struck up a strong rapport with Haiveta and was organising his participation in the Orogen Roadshow. The Roadshow was to visit Great Britain in October. Spicer found out about this and contacted McCowan.

Justice Andrew wrote in his final report that McCowan 'came to take on the role of intermediary' between the Independent State of Papua New Guinea and the Sandline interests. 'In fact the first reference to the name Sandline appears in Mr McCowan's note of his first conversation with Mr Spicer which occurred on 20 September 1996,' Justice Andrew reported. 'Mr Spicer, on learning of the PNG Roadshow's visit to London, spoke to Mr McCowan and explained to him his dealings with PNG officials to that time. He mentioned their interest in helicopters and explained in some detail the proposal he had prepared. Given the confidential nature of the proposal prepared by Spicer, which expressly recognised in clause 6.1 "that security is vital" it is a little surprising,' the Judge said, 'that he discussed it at all with Mr McCowan. Mr Spicer also mentioned a change from Plaza 107 Limited to a new structure headed by Sandline International. With Mr Haiveta,' Justice Andrew stated, 'the proposal for Project Contravene took on new life.'

Chapter Seven

Orogen Opens the Window

*Haiveta Supports Sandline; Miriung Murdered;
Spicer Visits PNG
October-December 1996*

After spending the first three-quarters of 1996 grappling with the World Bank over the implementation of stringent economic reform measures, Papua New Guinea's Deputy Prime Minister and Minister for Finance, Chris Haiveta, thoroughly enjoyed the Orogen Roadshow. The international financial community was dazzled by the earning potential of Orogen shares and the tough exchanges that had gone on all year with World Bank officials were suddenly supplanted by compliments and good-humoured banter from fund managers keen to subscribe. The underwriters had pitched the price deliberately low because of the uncertainty about PNG's economic performance and the Orogen Minerals prospectus certainly did not understate the problems of investing in PNG. But the earning potential of a share of the Government's stake in already performing mines and oil fields and its rights to future projects was irresistible to those managing big money. The Orogen float was ten times over-subscribed.

Just before he went on the Roadshow, Haiveta had to endure one last humiliating capitulation to the World Bank. Earlier in the year, following the row that led to the World Bank's supervisory team being invited to leave, the Bank had issued PNG with a ninety-day warning of the cancellation of its Structural Adjustment Program and the withdrawal of further aid. Australia had been firmly backing the reform program and refused PNG's request for adjustments in its aid payments to ease the pressure. Then in July, when it seemed that most of the measures the World Bank wanted had been adopted, the Forests Minister, Andrew Baing, amended the Forestry Act to do what PNG had promised it would not do—give Baing control over all appointments to the National Forests Board. When the World Bank complained and demanded that the amended Act be repealed, Haiveta and Sir Julius Chan accused the Bank of interfering with PNG's sovereignty. There were even suggestions that members of the World Bank team be hauled before the PNG legislature on charges of contempt of Parliament.

Sir Julius told journalists at the South Pacific Forum in the Marshall Islands capital, Majuro, in early September that the World Bank could 'go to hell'. Haiveta had then prepared a mini-budget for late September aimed at following that rhetoric through. He outlined a strategy to Parliament that he claimed would steer PNG around the need to rely on the $US158 million in structural adjustment loans that had been stalled for so long. 'Members of Parliament will find that the years 1997 to 1999 will be prosperous,' Haiveta predicted in his mini-budget speech, 'if the Government is able to continue with the policies which it has had the guts to put in place.' His new revenue measures, he claimed, would ensure that even without World Bank support 'Papua New Guinea can stand tall and do it alone'. Amongst the measures were an eleven per cent import duty on rice, a seventy-five per cent increase in petrol excise and personal income tax rises of four per cent across the board.

The reaction from throughout PNG to Haiveta's 'courageous' mini-budget was immediate—and all negative. 'Haiveta's Horror' was how one of the national dailies described it on the front page. Public and private sector unions threatened to strike. The Government's own backbench and Haiveta's own Pangu Pati caucus were deeply disturbed. A national election was just nine months away and their party leader was taxing rice! The man senior PNG Ministers and officials had been describing for months as the villain, World Bank team leader, Pirouz Hamidian-Rad, rang from Washington to express the World Bank's fury. He described the new revenue measures as 'crazy' and was widely reported stating that 'the burden will fall hardest on the poorest forty per cent of Papua New Guineans'. Within hours of delivering his mini-budget speech, Haiveta was having second thoughts. The strategy of standing tall and standing alone had been endorsed by the Prime Minister but Chan was not present when Cabinet approved the revenue-raising measures.

Sir Julius was in New York addressing the United Nations General Assembly. And while, in that address, he attacked the World Bank for dictating to developing countries and claimed PNG would not surrender its sovereignty to international institutions, he sent a message back to his own party that he did not support what Haiveta had done. In one of the shortest news conferences ever held in PNG, the Leader of Government Business,

Andrew Baing, presented journalists with a one-paragraph statement from his party leader saying Sir Julius would 'review' the revenue-raising measures when he returned home. Baing, who as Forests Minister was at the heart of the dispute and seemed to have a lot to answer for, refused to take questions and closed the news conference. Confusion reigned. Then, during Question Time on Friday 27 September, three days after the mini-budget was introduced, Haiveta revealed that the new duties, excises and taxes were no longer government policy. They could be changed and he said Cabinet had directed Baing to write a letter to the World Bank offering to compromise on the Forestry Act.

Haiveta did not remain in Port Moresby to withdraw his mini-budget. He flew out heading for the World Bank's Annual Meeting in Washington where, with some irony, he was to be elected on rotation as one of the two deputy chairmen of proceedings. He carried Baing's letter with him. Sir Julius flew back the other way from America and took over the passage of Haiveta's hastily rewritten revenue package. In explaining the sudden turnaround to Parliament, the Prime Minister said that after several lengthy telephone discussions with Haiveta he had 'quickly and decisively' directed a major rethink. There was not a word in Sir Julius's speech about the World Bank-sponsored structural adjustment loans package. His only reference to the World Bank was to criticise it and he also criticised the Opposition and 'those who are always difficult to please—like journalists who will zero in on the bad news while by-passing anything that is good'. The World Bank won and released the loans in early 1997.

Orogen prospectus

No potential foreign investors thumbing through the Orogen Minerals Limited prospectus could have been fooled into thinking Papua New Guinea was a nice, safe, reliable, friendly place into which to put their money. The sober, honest statements appearing in such sections as 'Risk Factors' were not the stuff of PNG Government media releases or PNG Tourism Authority brochures:

> 'The company and the projects are located in Papua New Guinea, a country which is subject to political, economic and other uncertainties, some of which may not be found in other countries such as Australia, the United Kingdom or the United States. Future government actions concerning the economy or the operation and regulation of nationally important facilities such as mines or oil

> fields could have a significant effect on the company. In 1993 concerns about the State's resources policy were raised as a result of the State seeking to renegotiate its equity participation in Porgera against the wishes of non-State Porgera Joint Venture Participants. This led to the State acquiring a further 15 per cent in Porgera ... In 1995 Papua New Guinea was rated in Category 'D' by the Export Finance Insurance Corporation, the export credit insurance agency of Australia ... the highest risk category.'

The Prospectus was just as brutally frank in another section, 'Social unrest': 'The rapid pace of political and economic change in Papua New Guinea has been associated with tension and conflict at various levels of society. The rapid dislocation of what were culturally and linguistically diverse societies has on some occasions manifested itself in communal violence and criminality.'

Landowner problems were explained: 'Title to land is often unclear and disputes over land ownership are common, especially in the context of resource developments where financial implications may arise due to ... compensation and royalties. Identifying all affected landowners, and structuring compensation arrangements that are both fair and acceptable to all of them, is often extremely difficult ... Intolerance of outsiders, particularly other Papua New Guineans, can result in friction between the project workforce and local people.'

The Prospectus, written before PNG's late September capitulation to the World Bank, went into some detail of the dispute over policy reform and it warned investors that PNG could lose all World Bank support.

From Washington Haiveta went on to join the Orogen Roadshow. By the time the Roadshow team reached London it was clear the float was going to be a huge success. Floating forty-nine per cent of the State's holdings in the Kutubu and Gobe oil fields and the Porgera, Misima and Lihir gold mines had the World Bank's support. The Bank was also negotiating with PNG officials what Papua New Guinea might do with its final share of the proceeds and what conditions might be put on their use. Those proceeds would amount to more than $US50 million after the debts of the State's holding entity, the Mineral Resources Development Company, had been paid off and other expenses met. Haiveta might therefore have been in an understandably buoyant mood when Rupert McCowan took him along the Kings Road, Chelsea, on 11 October 1996 for an appointment at No. 535, the head office of Plaza 107 and, by now, the London office of the British Virgin Islands incorporated company, Sandline International.

Both Tim Spicer and Chris Haiveta told the Andrew Inquiry that McCowan stayed in an outer office. From the notes Justice Andrew saw that McCowan had made during his September conversation with Spicer when the meeting was being arranged, it might have saved a little time if he had sat in. For the first few minutes, according to the versions both Spicer and Haiveta gave to the Andrew Inquiry, they spoke at cross-purposes. 'In fact he was not quite sure why he was coming to see us,' Spicer claimed. 'I think Mr Haiveta thought he was coming to discuss the acquisition of armoured vehicles which I had no knowledge of ... and I explained that that was not the case.' Haiveta said he was carrying a catalogue Brigadier Singirok had given him back in March of proposed military acquisitions. 'My impression was this meeting had to do with the sale of armoured personnel carriers,' Haiveta told the Inquiry. 'The initial couple of minutes was spent trying to understand why [we were meeting]. My misunderstanding ... was based on the catalogue that the Brigadier had left with me.'

Once that was cleared up, they both agreed in evidence before the Andrew Inquiry, Spicer gave the PNG Deputy Prime Minister a copy of the original $US30 million Project Contravene proposal. He explained that he had given it to the Defence Minister in April but that he had received little response and he asked Haiveta if he could 'throw any light on it as to what was happening'. Spicer said Haiveta seemed never to have seen the document before. 'He had a brief scan through it. He said that it looked interesting and that he would take it away and if there was any government interest, I should come to Papua New Guinea to discuss it.' Haiveta gave a similar account. 'Mr Spicer complained to me. He said: "Look, I met with your Minister, your Commander and the Secretary and we have been discussing a project on Bougainville. I have given a proposal to them but despite my numerous phone calls, I have not had any response" ... And I said, "Well, it's not my fault. I do not know these things. If you want to know, the best people will be the army people. So why don't you come across?" And I offered him an invitation to come.'

However, this version that McCowan was left outside in the waiting room reading magazines seems curious in the light of handwritten notes that Justice Andrew inspected on his trip to Hong Kong in May 1997. The Judge acknowledged in his final report assistance he had received from the Hong Kong Independent Commission Against Corruption. He said he had seen notes made by McCowan dated 9 October 1996, two days before this first meeting between Haiveta and Spicer, referring to 'Mr Buckingham, Angola and Sierra Leone and,' the Judge said, 'apparently in the context of the provision of military services, "exchange for concessions".' Justice Andrew said in his 'Report on the Engagement of Sandline International' that he was 'satisfied that it was part of Sandline's agenda to obtain an interest in the Panguna mine'. Those notes that he inspected were made the day after a dinner at which Haiveta had had an opportunity to discuss PNG's military problem on Bougainville with Britain's best-known living soldier, retired General Sir Peter De La Billiere. Sir Peter had been in charge of Britain's forces in the Gulf War where Tim Spicer had been his Military Assistant.

The former General is a non-executive Director of Robert Fleming Holdings, which is associated with Jardine Fleming, and he had been asked, 'at short notice' according to the Jardine Fleming submission to the Andrew Inquiry, to stand in for a colleague to host a formal dinner in London on the night of 8 October for the Orogen Roadshow team. 'Sir Peter had a distinguished military career before retiring in 1991,' Jardine Fleming's submission said, 'and his views on military matters are frequently sought by governments and others, and in the course of the dinner Mr Haiveta raised with him the problems in Bougainville and informally sought his opinion. The following day ... Mr Haiveta made a courtesy visit to Robert Fleming's offices and, while there, he met Sir Peter briefly and he may again have mentioned to Sir Peter the Bougainville problem.'

McCowan had been at that Tuesday night dinner in London too and after leaving Spicer's office on the Friday, Haiveta gave him the Project Contravene document and asked him if he could show a copy to Sir Peter for his comments. Haiveta told the Andrew Inquiry that he had done his own 'research' on Spicer 'to see if he really was capable of providing the advice and the consultancy that the Papua New Guinea Government wanted'. Asked what research he had done, Haiveta replied: 'I asked one of his former bosses ... a retired General in the British Special Air Services who was the Commander of the British contingent in Desert Storm.' And had Sir Peter given him a favourable reference regarding Spicer? 'Yes, he did. And indeed Spicer was his MA or Executive Officer or someone like that during that operation,' Haiveta answered.

However, McCowan recorded a somewhat less glowing appraisal in the private notes he made of the conversation he had with De La Billiere. 'McCowan records that Sir Peter described the proposal on 29th October as a "narrow package" and "quite expensive",' Justice Andrew reported. 'He had earlier described Mr Spicer to Mr McCowan as "very go" and "a salesman".' The British journalist, Andrew Lycett, claimed that following the Gulf War Spicer 'persuaded British Airways to give him, the General and their wives,

Concord tickets to fly to a ticker-tape parade in New York'. Jardine Fleming suspended McCowan during the Andrew Inquiry hearings and in its formal submission sought to distance De La Billiere from Spicer. 'Sir Peter recalls meeting Mr Haiveta on only the two occasions described,' Jardine Fleming told Justice Andrew. 'Although Mr Tim Spicer had been a Ministry of Defence appointed military assistant to Sir Peter during Sir Peter's last year of military service in 1991, Sir Peter had no contact with him during the period which is being considered by the Inquiry.'

Back in Papua New Guinea the Bougainville crisis took yet another tragic turn. While Haiveta was still in Great Britain, in fact the day after his meeting with Spicer, the Transitional Premier of Bougainville, Theodore Miriung, was assassinated. He was shot dead at close range on Saturday night, 12 October 1996, while eating dinner under his wife's house in her village, Kapana, in the Siwai district of south-west Bougainville. She was upstairs. One of his young sons was splattered with his body tissue. An autopsy twenty-four hours later revealed Miriung had been shot in the back. Six wounds on the left side of his back resulted from automatic gunfire and one major wound on the right was from a shotgun blast. That wound to his back on the right was surrounded by eight smaller pellet wounds. Miriung's assassination caused outrage. Brigadier Singirok immediately blamed the BRA and the BRA blamed the army. Sir Julius Chan called the murder of Miriung 'an act of madness–perpetrated by ungodly cowards'. But he did not accuse anyone directly and pledged that the 'Government's full capacity will be used to trace the murderers and bring them to account'.

Partly at the urging of the Minister by then in charge of Bougainville Affairs, Peter Barter, who had come to admire Miriung greatly, Sir Julius asked the Commonwealth Secretary General for help to find somebody to investigate the assassination. Barter was convinced that only a truly independent inquiry would establish the facts and be internationally credible. A retired Sri Lankan judge, Justice Thirunavukkarasu Suntheralingam, was appointed coroner. Justice Suntheralingam was a good choice. He had considerable experience of getting to the truth in tough circumstances. He was Chairman of the Sri Lankan Presidential Commission of Inquiry into Involuntary Removals and Disappearances of Persons from Control in troubled provinces in Sri Lanka. Announcing the coroner's appointment, Sir Julius said the coronial inquest had 'clear and unambiguous aims–to arrive at the full truth behind the murder of Premier Miriung. It is to conduct a full investigation and establish the identity of the persons behind this brutal murder.'

Justice Suntheralingam interviewed seven witnesses who were flown to Port Moresby. An eighth, a Resistance fighter whom he summonsed, was on his way but was prevented by PNG soldiers from boarding the aircraft in Buka. This 'fairly important witness', as the Judge called him, was then put on a helicopter and flown back to the Bougainville mainland. Although he found the PNG Defence Force obstructive Justice Suntheralingam's finding was unequivocal. 'The evidence of the seven witnesses who testified before me,' he stated in his report submitted in early December, 'leads me to the finding that the persons concerned in the wilful murder of Theodore Miriung are members of the Defence Forces stationed in the Tonu Camp and a few Resistance fighters.' He directed the PNG Police CID to continue their investigations and to take steps to arrest all those involved in Miriung's murder. He also recommended to the PNG Government that the entire unit of nineteen soldiers be pulled out of Tonu. The PNGDF was slow to respond to the Government's order to withdraw those men. In mid-1998, eighteen months after Justice Suntheralingam presented his report, the soldiers he named had still not been handed over to the police.

Miriung's assassination

Justice Suntheralingam's Coroner's Report states:

The deceased arrived at his wife's house in Kapana village at about noon, on Friday the 11th October, 1996. At about 1pm the same day one, Sylvester Makau, a Resistance fighter, working with the Defence Forces attached to the Tonu Camp, was heard telling the soldiers in the camp that Miriung had come to Konga by helicopter that day. At that time, Makau and another person attached to that camp and referred to by his initials SK were heard to remark that the deceased will not be returning to Buka but 'will be going down six feet'. In the afternoon of 11.10.96 Makau got himself dropped near the deceased's house. He was armed with a pump action shotgun ... On the next day ... around 12 noon another witness, who had known Makau previously, had seen Makau armed with a gun on the main road ... looking towards the deceased's house.

At about 5pm on 12.10.96, Makau and five soldiers from the Tonu Camp, all dressed in battle gear, left the camp in an ambulance used by the Defence Forces. The ambulance was driven by Makau. The ambulance was seen being driven slowly past the deceased's house towards Konga at about 6pm ... A little later ... the ambulance was seen parked at Konga station. At that

> time there were only four soldiers with the ambulance. They were identified as Yamu, a Corporal from Rabaul, another known as JK from Kerema/Kavieng, another from Kavieng and the fourth from Rabaul. A short while later gun shots were heard from the direction of the deceased's village. Upon hearing the shots, the soldiers got into the ambulance and [it] was driven by Yamu towards Kapana village. At about 7pm ... the ambulance returned to the Camp driven by Makau. He was alone ... A few minutes later the other five soldiers were seen returning to the Camp, on foot.
>
> While the ambulance was parked at Konga, the deceased was gunned down at his home when he was having dinner with the members of his family under the house. Immediately thereafter, two soldiers in battle dress armed with guns were seen moving around the deceased's house ... The same night, 26 spent cartridge shells were recovered from near the body of the deceased by relatives ... and kept under an orange tree. Early next morning David Mikisa, a Resistance Force Commander from Konga called at the deceased's house and took the empty shells away ...
>
> It seems to me clear beyond reasonable doubt that the six persons who left Tonu Camp in the ambulance at about 6pm on 12.10.96 are either principals or accessories in the murder of Miriung.

In the absence of any criminal trial the motivation for the elimination of the Premier remains a matter of speculation. Senior officers had warned Miriung of the danger he was in from the PNGDF rank and file. As detailed earlier, Miriung was banned from leaving Buka in June during the build-up to High Speed II. 'I am told not to visit the districts lest the soldiers of the Defence Force kill me in the event that some of them are killed by the BRA,' he had told the ABC. And he had accused those same officers of spreading lies that he was 'a criminal' and had given money to the BRA. In August Miriung had been prevented from addressing a Women's Peace Conference in Arawa. Armed soldiers had picked him up, taken him away in an armoured vehicle and put him on a helicopter back to Buka. At the time, the PNGDF Chief of Staff, Colonel Jack Tuat, objected to news reports that Miriung was 'sent packing at gunpoint'. 'The Premier was accorded the highest military respect including a salute,' Colonel Tuat claimed, 'and told politely that his movement restrictions were purely for security reasons.'

The eulogy at Miriung's funeral service at the Catholic Cathedral in Port

Moresby was delivered by another Bougainvillean, PNG's Chief Ombudsman, Simon Pentanu. Pentanu said Theodore Miriung was not well understood. 'There were threats to his life and he did not hide this fact,' the Chief Ombudsman told the big crowd packing St Mary's. 'He would say, as indeed he said when I last met him when we had a meal on a beach table outside the Malangan Lodge [in Kavieng, New Ireland] that there were Bougainville-type crises happening all over the world. He used to say that the nature of these sorts of conflicts wherever they were in the world was that they resulted in loss of life to the people who were often needed the most and who had contributed the most in trying to find solutions to those conflicts. Tragically and sadly,' Pentanu said, 'Theodore has fallen victim to his prophesy.' Ijape, who had never retracted his wild allegations that Miriung was to blame for the Kangu Beach massacre, attended the service and laid a wreath on the coffin.

In the weeks before Miriung's assassination there had been a build up in tension on Bougainville. Catholic Bishop Gregory Singkai, who had returned to the island in May after a long absence, died. Singkai had been named in Francis Ona's first BIG Cabinet and had taken part in the 1990 peace talks on board the New Zealand warship *Endeavour* on the rebel side. However, he soon found that Ona's Interim Government ministers had no power. While he was the nominal Education Minister, Singkai had been unable to prevent widespread destruction of Catholic schools including the Rigu High School situated right next to the Bishop's house at Tubiana. Bishop Singkai had moved back to his village at Koromira in central Bougainville and in 1994 made his way south through Solomon Islands to Australia for medical treatment. In 1996 the Pope directed Singkai to return to Bougainville to take care of all the people in his diocese, not just those living under BRA control. Sir Julius Chan agreed to his return to PNG and Singkai was given safe passage to Bougainville. However, he was sick and died of natural causes after being admitted to the Catholic hospital at Vunapope in East New Britain in early September.

The BRA alleged he had been killed by Papua New Guinea. Bishop Singkai's body was taken to mainland Bougainville and into the rebel held Koromira area for burial. Sam Kauona attended the burial service. He recorded a television interview and several nights later on Sunday 22 September EM-TV News broadcast the BRA Military Commander's threat to execute the five hostages taken at Kangu Beach. General Kauona gave a deadline of the end of September for the complete withdrawal of PNG troops from Bougainville. 'This deadline will expire on the 1st of October,' he said. 'We must receive some positive reply to our demands. If we do not, okay, we will kill one of these captured prisoners of war—one will die on that date.' Kauona was speaking in Pidgin and he used the term 'nekim' which strictly translated means 'cut his throat' but it is a common term for kill, no matter how it is done. He said the other four hostages would be killed, one a day after the first, if the PNG troops were not pulled out of Bougainville.

The Catholic Bishops Conference of Papua New Guinea and Solomon Islands desperately appealed to Kauona not to carry through his threat. 'The actions you have threatened are against the law of God,' the Bishops said in a statement, 'against the principles of mankind in general and certainly against the beliefs of the late Bishop Gregory Singkai.' The Australian Catholic Church supported that appeal. The Chairman of the Australian Catholic Social Justice Council, Bishop Kevin Manning, appealed to Kauona to show Christian mercy. 'Using prisoners of armed conflict as hostages and threatening to slit their throats one a day until their unrealistic demands are met take the BRA further into the terrorist sphere,' he said. The details of how the military's own misbehaviour had led to the Kangu Beach massacre were at this stage not yet public. The twelve deaths and the threat to execute the five survivors, one a day from 1 October, led PNG's Governor General, Sir Wiwa Korowi, to call for another military offensive against the BRA.

'Constant and merciless killing of the members of the two armed forces has been a common preying ground for BRA criminal elements,' Sir Wiwa said in his Remembrance Day address on 27 September 1996. 'The nation has witnessed this horror of merciless killings but we have not made up our minds on how to counter it. We have given orders to our forces to move to Bougainville with no precise military objectives to achieve.' The Governor General, dressed in a white ceremonial military uniform himself, claimed the PNGDF was the best army in the South Pacific but it had not been given a fair chance. It was time to abandon what he called 'indecisiveness' and confront the BRA. 'The nation should send a signal now to the BRA,' Korowi said, 'that enough is enough and the full force of the law be thrown at them.' This demand for a new military assault was backed up by Deputy Opposition Leader Roy Evara. In full-page advertisements outlining his solution to Bougainville Evara called for full military operations. 'The Government [must] declare an all-out-war on the rebels,' he said. 'We have to speak the same language that the BRA knows best, that is all-out-war.'

Sam Kauona never carried out his threat to 'nek' the hostages one by one. Actually he never had them under his direct control. The BRA military structure is such that each Company Commander is boss in his area. It more resembles a loose coalition of local warlords with a common final objective than it does a unified revolutionary army. Thomas Tarii, the Commander of H Company at Laguai in south Bougainville, kept the five hostages under his care throughout their ten months in captivity. Tarii received orders from time to time to deliver them to General Kauona in central Bougainville but he never did. In early October the Member for Bougainville, John Momis, made a trip to Laguai and spent an hour and a quarter with the five hostages in their bush prison. That meeting in fact took place on the very day Kauona had threatened to kill the first one of them but Momis was able to report back to their families that the three soldiers and two policemen were alive and under no immediate threat of execution. Kauona claimed Momis had lied and the 'prisoners of war' were with him in central Bougainville. It was not true.

Defence Minister Ijape told the Andrew Inquiry that at about this time he went back to Sir Julius Chan. 'When all these events happened,' he said, 'you can imagine the amount of pressure that was put on me from the Government, from the people and everybody. And I went and saw the Prime Minister and I said, "Look, can we engage Plaza 107? We may be able to get this job done. We may be able to hit the head, strike the head, destroy the head or disturb the head at least. Can we engage them?" And the Prime Minister at that time said, "No".' Towards the end of October, three more soldiers were taken hostage by another BRA group in the north of Bougainville. Sir Julius was rapidly running out of patience with a defence force unable to produce any positive news. In a letter on 31 October he complained angrily to his Defence Minister.

'We have all now realised the fiasco surrounding Operation High Speed II,' he wrote, 'which in the main was the result of lack of proper planning and coordination... With the latest developments and the capture of the three soldiers, it seems the Force is continuing to lose control of what soldiers are doing on the ground. You know very well that the NEC was explicit in its direction with regard to the objectives of Operation High Speed II... To date the Secretary and the Commander have not accounted for how and where the K10 million was expended... Minister,' he chided Ijape, 'the Kangu massacre was clear evidence of the total breakdown in command and control... For some time now I have watched with dismay the adverse reports regarding the management of the Force and the defence organisation at large.'

Brigadier Singirok's problems were not just with his own men. He had numerous detractors outside the force and the reversals on Bougainville gave them ample material with which to denigrate him. Sir Julius Chan's own Chief of Staff, Amos Emos Daniel, was one who had little regard for Singirok. Daniel had been a civilian in the PNG Defence Department and risen to be head of Defence Intelligence before losing his job in early 1996. Daniel is from New Ireland, from Julius Chan's electorate of Namatanai. His brother, Ephraim Apelis, had announced his intention to stand against Sir Julius in the 1997 elections. Chan, in an effort to undermine Apelis's campaign and always on the lookout for astute staff, took Amos Daniel on to head up his personal office. Another influential critic of Singirok and also a New Irelander, was a former PNGDF Commander, Rochus Lokinap. Lokinap had been appointed as a special adviser to the National Security Advisory Council and had an office not far from that of the Chairman of the Council and head of the Prime Minister's Department, Noel Levi. Levi, too, was from New Ireland. Singirok had few friends at court.

Questioned at the Andrew Inquiry about the criticisms contained in Sir Julius Chan's letter of 31 October, Brigadier Singirok claimed the breakdown in discipline on Bougainville stemmed from political neglect. 'The conduct of the men in Bougainville is a direct reflection on the lack of support, lack of direction by our politicians,' he argued, adding that soldiers should not be in charge of Care Centres. 'I told the Minister that neither myself nor any senior officer should be made directly responsible ... for the men who died in Kangu as a result of looking after Care Centres.' He claimed other government agencies should have been given the job. PNG's Foundation for Law, Order and Justice agreed. The Foundation, one of the country's more effective NGOs, ran conflict resolution courses in Bougainville and had first-hand evidence of how ill-suited soldiers were to be refugee camp guardians. None of their training prepared them for it. 'The result is that the soldiers become bogged down in police work,' the Foundation said in late 1996, '[with] games of "cops and robbers" on such matters as home brew and they often finish up acting as prosecutor, judge, jury and punishment team. This leads to friction and anger within the Camp and severely damages their image.'

During the Andrew Inquiry the lawyer representing Sir Julius made much of an independent audit report into the spending of the K10 million allocated for the High Speed II operation. Marshall Cooke QC alleged Brigadier Singirok had spent money meant for the troops on 'luxuries', some for the Commander's official residence, Flag House. Cooke questioned the Brigadier at length on items such as K39,355 for 'curtains and carpets', K10,875 for 'furnishing', and K45,000 for 'cutlery'. Singirok said he and his family had not moved into Flag House until October 1996, three months after Operation High Speed II was over. He claimed the Finance Department never provided the K10 million on time and the Force had to reallocate money from its recurrent spending to fund the operation. He told Cooke 'the politics and the difficulties' of dealing with the Finance Department were well known in the PNG bureaucracy and from the witness box it was impossible for him to explain exactly 'how it was spent'. In late 1996 Sir Julius had himself blamed Defence Secretary James Melegepa, not Singirok, for any misspending. 'The Secretary is the chief Defence accounting officer,' he said in a separate letter to Ijape, 'therefore he has to answer for the mishap.'

Sir Julius's reprimand of Ijape and his criticism of the 'command and control' breakdown in the PNGDF led to an announcement by the Defence Minister in mid-November that Australia would be asked to adjust its much-criticised Defence Cooperation Program. 'We would like our NCOs, our junior officers, senior officers as well, to go through courses,' he said, 'especially on command and control and other management training.' Ijape also revealed that nineteen soldiers, 'bad apples' he called them, had been sacked from the Force for refusing to go to Bougainville. What emerged as well from that news conference was that Brigadier Singirok had purged the senior ranks of the PNGDF to remove redundant officers—a number of whom, he was sure, were undermining him. The Defence Minister revealed K3.5 million had been spent paying off fifty officers including three Brigadier Generals and six full Colonels. The Brigadiers were former Commanders. 'There were so many Colonels who were hanging out at Murray Barracks who had no line positions in the Defence Force,' Ijape said, 'and all they do is get their pay! And these are the guys, I believe, who have been causing some commotions at Headquarters.'

Haiveta had arrived home after the Orogen Roadshow and by early November was helping arrange Tim Spicer's first visit to PNG. The Deputy Prime Minister told the Andrew Inquiry that during his briefing of Sir Julius on the very successful Roadshow he mentioned his meeting with Spicer. 'I did mention to him in passing that I had met with a gentleman in London who had an outstanding proposal with our Government to which there was no response,' Haiveta said. On 15 November a member of Haiveta's staff, Paul Sosori, rang Spicer to formalise the invitation. 'I was away on business in November,' Spicer told the Inquiry, 'when I got a call from my office saying that somebody from the government, I think from the Deputy Prime Minister's Department, had rung to say that the proposal had been considered, was of interest and I should be prepared to travel to Papua New Guinea to discuss it with government officials.'

Spicer faxed Ijape a few days later, this time under the letterhead Sandline International, not Plaza 107, saying, 'I understand you now wish to talk to us again.' He added a note of explanation. 'In case you are wondering—Sandline is the new name of our military consultancy company.' Ijape told

Justice Andrew he was surprised and a little suspicious about the change of name. But with the Deputy Prime Minister now interested his own enthusiasm for hiring private military consultants surged again. The first that Brigadier Singirok knew of Haiveta's involvement was when he was asked to lunch at the Seoul House restaurant in Port Moresby on 27 November. Haiveta was meeting with the heads of PNG's commercial statutory authorities to get estimates from them on the dividends they were likely to pay to the Government in 1997. He had been informed these could be well in excess of what was in his budget forecasts and thought this might be one way he could fund Project Contravene.

Haiveta said he invited Brigadier Singirok so he could tell the Commander about his London meeting with Spicer and let him know he had a copy of the proposal. 'I asked the Brigadier if he had a copy,' the Deputy Prime Minister told Justice Andrew. 'He said he had a copy and I asked what he was doing about it and we talked about Bougainville as a military problem more than anything else... I informed him I was looking at it seriously... He said it was a good proposal.' Singirok's version is that they adjourned to another room in the Seoul House restaurant to talk. 'He raised it with me and [said] he was in London in October and he had met up with Mr Spicer and an ex-British General who recommended and had confidence with Mr Spicer in the package that was being offered.' Singirok claimed he had raised with Haiveta funding difficulties the Force was having on Bougainville. 'He assured me that the cost ... was not important as the country had enough reserves to finance the operations.'

Laguai

The young Bougainvillean parish priest leading the prayers for peace in the south Bougainville BRA village of Laguai has been a relentless campaigner against violence. When the BRA took its first PNGDF hostage early in 1996, Father Peter Pinoko refused to leave Sergeant Petueli Samuel's side and travelled into rebel territory with him to ensure his safety. The BRA who captured Sergeant Samuel were annoyed with the priest, who insisted on staying, especially when reports were broadcast that they had taken Father Peter hostage too. Father Peter later raised hackles on the other side, telling of an indiscriminate mortar bombardment by PNG soldiers based at Buin in December 1996, in which nine village people were killed. A mortar bomb blew their bush church building apart.

'Those who have been killed by that mortar bomb,' he said, 'were my church workers and their small children who were with them.' Asked if there was any explanation for the mortars being fired, Father Peter replied, 'I was in Buin town Care Centre that morning. There wasn't any shoot-out in the Buin town Care Centre or whatever and all of a sudden I could hear mortar bombs being exploded. Some hours later, I was told of the deaths in that village of Malabita. A few days later, I was there. And I confirmed the deaths. It's very true.'

The war in south Bougainville has oscillated from periods of violent confrontation to relative calm, often depending on the calibre of the PNGDF officer in charge at Buin. In 1994–95 when Major Walter Enuma was the unit commander there was a period of remarkable peace. Major Enuma was highly regarded by many in south Bougainville and the rebel groups loosely under the control of the BRA's Southern Region Commander, Paul Bobby, desisted from armed confrontation. Enuma even encouraged independently run conflict resolution courses which were attended by some of his and Bobby's men. But when Enuma was replaced, the new Buin PNGDF Commander tried to ambush and kill Bobby. He escaped and the war in the south blew up again to a new level of intensity.

Tim Spicer flew into Papua New Guinea for the first time on the morning of 3 December 1996. With him was his boss, Tony Buckingham, who was travelling on a Guernsey, Channel Islands, passport. Together they went to the PNG Government offices at Morauta House in the suburb of Waigani looking for Haiveta and Ijape. A Cabinet meeting was in progress and the two visitors were ushered into the reception area outside the Cabinet room where officials wait to be called by their Ministers. The Brigadier was there. He was very surprised to see them. There was an angry verbal altercation. Spicer explained it this way: 'There was one instance where he got upset about something in public. I cannot remember which visit to PNG it was but we had been taken to, I think, where the Cabinet meets and the General was sitting outside and he was concerned that we were there. And for some reason got upset and left.'

'On Tuesday December 3 1996 I was at the [Cabinet] waiting room,' Singirok told the Andrew Inquiry. 'Mr Spicer and Mr Buckingham arrived ... I was quite surprised ... Tony Buckingham and Tim Spicer asked me if they could see the Minister for Defence and the Deputy Prime Minister.' He told them they would have to wait. But he said they became insistent because it was already past 11.30 a.m., the time they said they had been given for their appointment. 'Buckingham ... said words to this effect: "What kind of country is this? You do not keep appointments" ... I said, "We have a very important meeting. It is called a Cabinet NEC meeting. We do not interfere ... " But both gentlemen insisted and by that time I was already upset ... and I told them, "You have no respect ... You are naive about this country. This is not Africa where you manipulate our leaders ... I cannot appear in London at your Cabinet and demand to see your Defence Minister and Deputy Prime Minister." I said, "Who the hell are you! If you want my job you can get it, I am not here." And I stormed out of Morauta House.'

The Commander was no more helpful when they tried to arrange a meeting with him. The Deputy Prime Minister took charge. 'I did see Mr Spicer after his arrangements to see the Commander had failed,' Haiveta said in evidence. 'He came back to me so I then said, "Well if the Commander cannot see you then the [Defence] Secretary should" ... and so the Secretary and Mr Spicer came and met with me ... I told Spicer that although the proposal and the concept was good, it was not good enough for any kind of operation to take place and the government needed much more detail in the form of a consultancy report about what the proposal would entail.' Spicer says the consultancy idea evolved over a number of meetings he had with both Ministers, Haiveta and Ijape. 'What they really wanted was what I would term a military appreciation of the current situation,' he said.

Justice Andrew in his report stated that this series of discussions that Spicer and Buckingham had with the two Ministers and their senior public servants dealt with Project Contravene 'and particularly the mine'. The Ministers decided to engage Sandline to prepare a detailed report to be delivered within a month. Sandline proposed a fee of \$US350,000 at the rate of \$US1165 per hour. Brigadier Singirok said he supported the idea of a consultancy but claimed he was 'amazed' at the hourly rate. He did not have much to do with negotiating the fee. Defence Secretary Melegepa was given that job. Haiveta suggested \$US350,000 was too high. In a fax from London on 7 December Michael Grunberg defended the fee claiming that the 'nature of the project justifies such an hourly rate'; that Spicer was Sandline's top man; and that the fee reflected 'the extent of the work already undertaken on your behalf at no cost'. Two days later Sandline agreed to reduce its charge to \$US250,000 and Melegepa and Spicer signed the consultancy agreement.

PNG agreed to transfer the first \$US150,000 to an account called Sandline Holdings Limited at the Queens Road, Central Hong Kong, branch of the Hong Kong and Shanghai Bank on Tuesday 10 December and the balance to the same account on Monday 6 January, the proposed delivery date for the consultancy report. There was a complication with the transfer of the first instalment and the full consultancy fee was still outstanding four months later, in March 1997, when Brigadier Singirok cancelled the whole Sandline deal. But despite this early premonition of trouble, Spicer set about gathering the information he needed for his military appraisal. 'I spent some time here with the Defence Force,' he told the Andrew Inquiry. 'I obviously made notes, went to briefings, interviewed various people and then conducted a reconnaissance ... I spent two and a half days in Bougainville [accompanied by] the Intelligence Officer of the Special Forces Unit ... and then returned to London to produce the detailed paper.'

He was to base his report on consultations with six people in PNG. Apart from the SFU's Intelligence Officer, Captain Siale Diro, there were two other military men, the SFU's Commanding Officer, Major Gilbert Toropo and Brigadier Singirok; the civilian head of the Defence Department, Melegepa; and the two politicians, Haiveta and Ijape. Sir Julius Chan's office was apparently unaware of the $US250,000 consultancy contract agreed to by Haiveta and the only person in the PNG bureaucracy who had done any checking at all on Sandline's background, Secretary Levi, went on leave on 18 December. He was to be away for the crucial next six weeks. The person who became Acting Secretary of the PM's Department, and therefore also Acting Chairman of the PNG National Security Advisory Council, was the Cabinet Secretary, Peter Eka, who had never seen the September memorandum Levi had written explaining the background to the group Spicer represented.

While Spicer was busily working on his expanded Project Contravene proposal there was a peaceful attempt to secure the release of the five Kangu Beach hostages. It failed. A team of three Parliamentarians, led by Sir Michael Somare and including John Momis and Bernard Narokobi, travelled to Laguai village in south Bougainville to negotiate with the BRA's H Company Commander, Thomas Tarii. Several of those held captive were Sepiks from Somare's and Narokobi's electorates. The two Members of Parliament were allowed to see and talk to the hostages who looked fit but distressed. They each recorded Christmas messages to their families. On his return to Port Moresby Sir Michael said he would be submitting a report to the Speaker of Parliament and be calling on Sir Julius Chan's Government to consider replacing the soldiers in south Bougainville with police. He said he had promised Tarii he would return to Laguai in January when he hoped the five men would be released.

One reason Brigadier Singirok was less than enthusiastic about the Sandline proposal was that he had begun negotiating separately with a supplier in Germany, IBCOL, the International Business Company Limited, to provide the PNGDF with Russian designed transport helicopters built in the former East Germany. He wrote a Defence Capacity Building Program submission in December recommending Mi-17s for the PNGDF, the same helicopter transports that Spicer had recommended in April. The unit price from Germany was K3 million ($US2.2m) each. Sandline's Mi-17s had been priced at $US1.5 million each. Other items on Singirok's list included sophisticated surveillance, thermal imaging and night vision equipment. Asked at the Andrew Inquiry about all this, Singirok claimed it would have been a better deal than Sandline's. 'What Sandline is going to offer us is something that we have no control over. It is just going to appear on our doorsteps ... Take it ... this is yours, use it.' The PNG delegation that visited the Tindal Air Force Base in April 1997 to inspect the Sandline deliveries diverted there reported that the helicopter transports provided were not Mi-17s but a much older model, Mi-8s. Singirok claimed the German deal would have cost K4.5 million per year for five years.

On Christmas Day, Spicer got a call from Buckingham to say that Defence Minister Ijape had been in touch with him and that he should be on standby to go to PNG immediately to present his report. 'I then had to move fairly quickly and finish off the paper which was done on the 27th of December,' Spicer said, 'and I returned to Papua New Guinea on the understanding that we were going to meet with senior government officials and, I believed, possibly the Prime Minister to present the paper some time very quickly after the New Year.' Spicer flew into Port Moresby again on the very last day of 1996. Just how clearly Sandline's main aim was to reopen the Bougainville copper mine was spelt out in this longer, more detailed version of Project Contravene.

Chapter Eight

The Cabinet Decision

*Spicer Convinces Chan; Cabinet Approves the
Mercenaries Deal
1–20 January 1997*

Lieutenant Colonel (Retired) Tim Spicer had spent a total of just ten days in Papua New Guinea when he began writing his one-quarter of a million US Dollar appraisal of how to bring a swift end to the Bougainville war. But that short stay had been long enough for him to detect amongst those he spoke to a deep antipathy towards PNG's former colonial master, Australia. He heard complaints, too, about New Zealand, which while number two in the South Pacific power hierarchy was smaller in both population and geographical size than Papua New Guinea. Spicer's consultancy report picked up these themes and pitched a strong appeal to nationalistic sentiment. 'PNG is potentially one of the world's richest countries per capita,' the new Project Contravene document said in a section devoted to regional attitudes. 'If its mineral wealth ... is fully realised it could give the country the economic power to threaten Australia and dwarf all other economies in the region. If this wealth was combined with a well-trained, effective and combat-experienced military, then the country could become a very significant regional power.'

Spicer advanced an enticing argument to explain why the Bougainville crisis had been so hard to fix, suggesting the existence of a conspiracy to keep PNG weak. 'It is possible, therefore,' he wrote, 'that there is a deliberate policy on the part of Australia and New Zealand to prolong the Bougainville problem, either by omission or commission.' Evidence Spicer provided to support his theory included the 'lack of direct Australian military assistance' on Bougainville; the 'caveat' that prevented the PNGDF from using the Iroquois offensively; the 'lack of political impetus' to assist PNG resolve the issue 'except through negotiations/peaceful means', which Spicer dismissed as 'not practical'; and Australia's allowing the BRA to have 'representative offices in Sydney'. Other examples of complicity in this alleged campaign to 'drain' the economy and slow PNG's economic growth were the 'number of pro-BRA/anti-PNG articles in the Australia/New Zealand press' and the absence of any real pressure on Solomon Islands 'to stop active support for the BRA'.

In summing up Part I of his consultancy report Spicer highlighted what he described as seven 'key points'. The fourth one of these was his anti-PNG conspiracy theory and he informed the PNG Government: 'There may be a wider dimension to the conflict that has not been appreciated hitherto, i.e., not only external support from the Solomon Islands but possibly a prolonging of the conflict as a deliberate policy by Australia/NZ in order to slow down PNG's economic potential.' Point seven of the key points went to the nub of Tony Buckingham's interest in PNG: 'The Panguna mine is central to the resolution of this problem.' Earlier Spicer had succinctly summed up Sandline's assessment of the situation: 'The two key issues are the defeat of the BRA and the re-opening of the mine.'

In Part II–his 'Mission Analysis'–Spicer listed the final task as being: 'Retake and hold [the] Panguna mine–this is the key element to the problem, the cause of it, the symbol of it and probably the end of the conflict.' In attempting to define areas of 'enemy concentrations' he named one as being the Panguna mine area: 'This is the key–it is the location of Francis Ona, close to it is the Radio Free Bougainville transmitter. It is also vital ground as it is the psychological centre of gravity of the campaign as well as the main physical asset.' This was not a very accurate assessment because Ona, like Radio Free Bougainville, had no permanent fixed 'location'. In 1994 Singirok, then commanding the 1st Battalion, had recaptured the mine site in the High Speed I operation. By the time his men got there, Ona was long gone. Nevertheless Spicer stressed that capturing the mine site would be a major strategic victory. His quick reconnaissance trip to Bougainville had given him only a superficial understanding of the complexity of the problem and his military analysis seemed to discount the difficulty of combating determined guerilla warfare in mountains blanketed by tropical jungle.

Spicer described the Bougainville mine as 'the key economic asset for the island (and possibly the whole country)'. It had ceased being much of an economic asset seven years before and even CRA was resigned to the fact that the mine would never reopen unless there was a 'consensus in favour' of that amongst Bougainvilleans. However Spicer's frame of reference was Africa not Melanesia. Assessing the cost of the operation Spicer said Sandline estimated that the 'neutralisation of the BRA and the recapture of the mine' could be done for approximately $US35 million. 'However, subsequent operations to hold the mine to allow the operators to get it working, to mop-up the remains of the BRA and to follow up with civil reconstruction would cost more. These subsequent costs,' he predicted, 'would be paid by the Panguna mine operators and other foreign investors.' Under a section titled 'Political Implications' Spicer stated that amongst the matters the government 'must consider' was: 'Early discussion with Panguna mine owners and other foreign investors.' The Deputy Prime Minister, Chris Haiveta, who was the first to receive Spicer's consultancy report, was to follow up that recommendation with zeal.

But first they had to convince the Prime Minister, Sir Julius Chan, of the need for Project Contravene. The consultancy report addressed in some detail what might attract Sir Julius–how employing Sandline might help him win the 1997 PNG national elections. Sir Julius had promised to solve the Bougainville crisis when he took over as Prime Minister in 1994. He had, he believed, tried almost everything and time was running out. 'If this Government can achieve a significant result before the election in June,' Spicer's report promised, 'it will be able to demonstrate to the people of PNG and the world that it is strong, effective and magnanimous.' Magnanimous! But, he warned, the time frame was tight. 'The kudos in political terms for whichever government resolves the crisis, i.e., defeats the BRA, reopens the Panguna mine and begins the longer term process of reconciliation in Bougainville, is immense,' he predicted. 'There is an imperative on this Government to resolve the crisis before the election in June. Therefore time is of the essence.' Spicer's report resorted to capital letters to make the point: 'IT IS CRITICAL THAT THE WAR COUNCIL MAKE A DECISION AS TO THE MILITARY OPTION THEY WISH TO ADOPT BY NO LATER THAN 12 JANUARY 1997.'

Contravene's four options

Tim Spicer told the PNG Government it had four military options. One was to 'maintain the military status quo and negotiate a political settlement with the BRA'. The problems with this option were almost too terrible to imagine. While it would keep 'Australia plus other regional powers happy', PNG would be negotiating 'from a position of weakness'; it would be 'unpopular' with the military; revenue would be lost because the mine would remain closed; the Government would lose prestige becoming 'known as the government who gave away Bougainville'; and, since negotiations would take time, 'the government would have to face the election and could lose' before any settlement was concluded.

Option two was to spend $US20 million buying transport helicopters, training up the PNGDF for another offensive and revamping the military command structure on Bougainville. The problem with this was that it might 'not succeed at all' due to capability gaps in the PNGDF and it 'would not help win the elections'.

Option three, priced at $US30 million, was to conduct 'high-speed covert' military operations 'to conclude the crisis in the required time frame'. The aim would be to kill or capture the BRA ringleaders. Amongst option three's suggested advantages were that the morale of the armed forces would rise; that the military would be seen as capable of effective action 'thus giving confidence to foreign investors'; and that a 'precise and surgical application of combat power' would not only minimise collateral damage but also discourage 'potential enemies such as Solomon Islands'. As for political impact: 'This will be excellent. It will demonstrate the Government to be effective, tough but clear thinking' and 'it will certainly improve the chances of election victory'.

Finally, option four proposed a $US30 million 'coup de main' operation to seize the Panguna mine without taking on any other BRA targets. 'This option would get straight to the centre of gravity of the problem,' Spicer said. Its advantages included being the 'quickest way' to bring the crisis to a close; it would 'be attractive to mine owners'; it would 'be attractive to the international community'; and it 'would be an outstanding achievement' for PNG's armed forces 'if successful'.

Spicer's recommendation was for a combination of the latter two of the four military options he presented to the PNG Government. He recommended strikes against 'five key' BRA targets and the seizing and holding of the Panguna mine. His named 'targets' included BRA President Francis Ona, Chairman of the rebel Bougainville Interim Government Joseph Kabui, BRA Military Commander Sam Kauona and BRA Operations Commander Ishmael Toarama (however he misspelt three of their four names–Kaburi, Karona and Ismail Toronau). Spicer stated that one of the first tasks of the operation's military commander would be to confirm the locations of these individuals. Once known, their locations would be attacked and destroyed. He said the BRA leaders should be killed or captured with his preference being to 'capture at least one to put on trial'.

Spicer's proposed fire-power hardware and electronic warfare package was similar to the list he had prepared and given to Brigadier Singirok in London in April 1996. He recommended that the PNGDF's Special Forces Unit (SFU) should be taken away from their base at Goldie River Barracks 'and moved to a more suitable isolated location (away from Australian advisers)'. There they would be given a one-month special forces training course followed by a mission preparation package. 'Security will be paramount,' he said urging that the Government's intentions 'must be kept secret' from the enemy, the local population, external governments '(this includes Australian advisers)' and the media. 'It is perfectly possible to effect a military solution within the time frame and with total security by not changing the pattern of activity on Bougainville,' Spicer assured his clients, 'but this would involve using a combination of external forces plus [the] SFU together with high tech air and EW assets.'

Asked at the Andrew Inquiry if his report was advocating the use of Sandline or Executive Outcomes personnel in military operations on the ground on Bougainville, Spicer said that was an issue for the PNG Government to decide. 'We are perfectly prepared to support military operations if that is the decision of the Government. And the way we prefer to do that is to either provide technical support—in other words technicians that the country concerned does not have such as pilots, ground crew, intelligence operators etcetera—but also, if necessary, and if it is the wish of the Government, to provide specialist forces integrated within their own command structure to assist them with operations.' That is how Executive Outcomes had been engaged by the governments of both Angola and Sierra Leone. The 'external forces' mentioned in Project Contravene were ready and available for use by the PNG Government if it wanted them.

Spicer arrived back in PNG on 31 December 1996 and met up with his boss, Tony Buckingham, who had been on a trip to Australia. 'We stayed at the Islander Travelodge,' Spicer said, 'waiting for an appointment to see the appropriate Ministers. I brought ... twelve copies ... and eventually we saw the Deputy Prime Minister into whose custody I gave the reports.' The indication that we were going to see the Prime Minister to present [it to him] ... fell away. I believe he was away over that period.' Sir Julius Chan was out of Port Moresby. He had gone home to his mother's island of Huris in his New Ireland electorate of Namatanai for the New Year. Haiveta told the Andrew Inquiry he gave one of the twelve numbered copies of the top secret Project Contravene document to one of the Prime Minister's personal staff, Hudson Arek, who told him he would arrange for it to be delivered to Huris. Sir Julius said he never saw it. Buckingham and Spicer considered flying to New Ireland on New Year's Day but at 8.30 that morning Ijape rang the hotel to leave a message that the visit 'to see PM in Namatanai ... may not be possible so Mr Tony Buckingham could leave today.' Buckingham left.

Spicer stayed but he had to wait another week for his chance to talk to Sir Julius. 'We were getting concerned,' Spicer told the Andrew Inquiry, 'in that we were going to be invited to perform, participate in this project against the time frame that had been set for us. Each day that a decision was not forthcoming, it could have a sort of incremental knock on effect on the timing, the ability to perform.' While he waited, Spicer learnt a little more about the army Sandline was to work with. The PNGDF was in the headlines regularly in that first week in January. 'Ten Per Cent Of Soldiers Have HIV' one story alleged, quoting an anonymous doctor who claimed adultery was rife in the military barracks because soldiers were absent for long periods serving on Bougainville. Brigadier Singirok publicly dismissed the claims saying AIDS testing confirmed only four HIV cases amongst troops in 1996. Another story on the news was about a hand grenade being hurled at a Military Police vehicle at Defence headquarters, Murray Barracks, in the early hours of New Year's Day. Three soldiers were admitted to hospital.

The PNG Prime Minister flew off to Marshall Islands on 5 January to attend the funeral of the late Marshall Islands President, Amata Kabua, whom Chan admired greatly. Sir Julius had been invited to deliver Kabua's funeral oration. He chartered a Falcon jet from Cairns and asked his Defence Force Commander and Police Commissioner, Bob Nenta, to accompany him on the seven-hour trip. Chan seated the Brigadier opposite him for much of the journey. 'I had very extensive discussions on the general operation of the Defence Force with Mr Singirok,' Sir Julius told the Andrew Inquiry. But he said the Brigadier never raised the Project Contravene document with him. He repeated this evidence at the second inquiry. 'I wanted him to update me on everything that happened in the last 12 months,' Chan told Justice Los. 'You have got to remember, we had no contract with Sandline at that time. We did not have any arrangement with Sandline. But the discussion centred around buying boats from Singapore.'

This was one issue on which the testimony of Chan and Singirok was identical. In this lengthy, face-to-face discussion the Prime Minister and his army chief talked about Bougainville, the Defence White Paper, restructuring the PNGDF and buying patrol boats from Singapore. But the proposed spending of more than $US30 million on attack helicopters and the engagement of Sandline was never broached. According to the Defence Minister he had directed Singirok to give the Prime Minister a thorough briefing on the Project Contravene consultancy report. Ijape claimed the Brigadier told him on his return that he had. 'He did not say anything about the Prime Minister's reactions but he said it was a good briefing,' Ijape told Justice Andrew. All the evidence before both the Andrew and Los Inquiries, however, indicated that at this fairly late stage it was still not Singirok who was advocating the Sandline deal. He travelled for two days cooped up in a small executive jet with the Prime Minister and did not bother to raise it.

On their way home from Marshall Islands on 7 January, Sir Julius dropped into the Solomon Islands capital, Honiara, for talks with his counterpart Prime Minister, Solomon Mamaloni. They discussed the Bougainville war's continuing impact on the Solomons. Chan and Mamaloni never liked each other but this meeting seemed to go well. One suggestion Sir Julius made was an exchange of personnel between the PNGDF and the Solomon Islands Field Force. Another was joint border patrols. 'By having exchanges of personnel manning different posts on the border,' Sir Julius explained, 'in this way, with better communication and with our people, and theirs, on both sides of the border, maybe we could help stop these unnecessary spill-over effects.' The Prime Ministers agreed to put the proposal to their respective forces. They even considered inviting a third party to patrol the sea border. Sir Julius Chan's newly acquired press secretary, a former Australian freelance journalist, Mark Lillyman, who had helped arrange the Chan-Mamaloni meeting, was euphoric about what he claimed was this 'breakthrough' in relations. Lillyman had been into Bougainville with the BRA in the early 1990s and believed his links with the secessionists would enable a peaceful solution to the war to be found. He knew nothing of the looming alternative—the Sandline solution.

While the two Prime Ministers were meeting, PNG's Police Commissioner Nenta received a call from Port Moresby alerting him to an alleged assassination plot. Chan was supposedly going to be killed by a bomb blast on his return to Port Moresby. A subsequent National Intelligence Organisation report claimed the source of the tip-off was an official on the civilian side of PNG Defence Intelligence. One of the men allegedly involved was Leo Nuia, the so-called 'Butcher of Bougainville', whom Singirok had purged from the Defence Force several months earlier. Sir Julius was to claim later that he had been considering recommissioning Nuia and that this bogus assassination 'plot' had in fact been hatched by Singirok to discredit Nuia. Little first-hand evidence was produced to support either theory. But any bomb scare had to be taken seriously. Soldiers retrenched long before Nuia's dismissal had been engaged in an acrimonious dispute with the Government over their retrenchment pay and on at least a couple of occasions in the previous two years grenades had been thrown at Mourata House, the building housing the Prime Minister's Department. A bomb had also blown apart a toilet in the main PNG government office block just before the New Year, a week or so earlier.

It was in this atmosphere of threat and intrigue that Sir Julius arrived home at Port Moresby's Jackson's Airport. The Falcon jet avoided the main terminal and taxied to a secure area. Armed police and soldiers were everywhere and Chan was whisked away under escort. Back at his office in Parliament House, Sir Julius found the Defence Minister and Spicer waiting. Sir Julius shook Spicer's hand but would not agree to an immediate meeting. 'I wanted to introduce Tim Spicer to him so he could explain the project,' Ijape told the Andrew Inquiry. 'But the Prime Minister said it is an unscheduled meeting and that he should stay [outside] and I should meet him. So we had private discussions ... and then he said, "Look, you go and tell Tim Spicer to bring a brief for me—a small brief why this project should go ahead." So me and Tim Spicer went back to my office and we prepared this short memo ... we wanted to see him the same afternoon but it was not possible so we met him the following day.'

That next day, Wednesday 8 January 1997, was the critical day on which Spicer convinced Sir Julius he could defeat the BRA before the elections, using mercenaries supplied by Sandline. The three-page brief Spicer had prepared the previous afternoon was delivered to Chan's office with a covering note from Ijape. A meeting was scheduled for the afternoon. Spicer's brief said Sandline was happy to let the PNGDF take all the credit for any military success. 'Sandline forces could do the whole operation on their own,' Spicer informed Sir Julius, 'but this would be a much more expensive option. On the other hand involvement of PNG forces increases the operational time frame and the security risk. A sensible compromise is to use elements of PNG forces who would remain in isolation for the duration of the operation until phase 4/5.' Phases four and five in Project Contravene were the recapture of the Panguna mine and mopping up the BRA.

'Therefore the Sandline proposal,' Spicer's brief went on, 'is to plan the operation in detail; prepare the SFU for operations; enhance the SFU with 40 Sandline personnel (mostly black skinned); provide electronic intelligence gathering capability; provide Special Forces standard helicopter support, both gunship and troop lift; provide ability to operate at night; procure all necessary equipment; [and] carry out military operations with PNG forces.' After the initial operations the Sandline Special Force personnel would train the PNG SFU up to their level and teach them how to operate the electronic warfare equipment. This additional provision of the forty on-ground combat mercenaries—he called them a forty-man Special Forces (SF) team—was costed at $US4.5 million. Spicer estimated their equipment and similar equipment for the PNGDF's SFU would cost $US900,000 and positioning costs (bringing the men together and flying them from Africa to PNG) would amount to another $US100,000. This boosted the total package to $US38.2 million but it would be provided at a 'fixed price' of $US36.2 million.

The wider agenda for Sandline's boss, Tony Buckingham, was also mentioned. One of the listed benefits for PNG from the engagement of Sandline to plan and help carry out these operations to destroy the BRA and reopen the copper mine was said to be: 'Costs recoverable from mine revenue—NB purchase of mine by Branch Minerals.' Branch Minerals was one of an array of interlocking companies in which Mr Buckingham had interests. Spicer saw a continuing role for Sandline's operatives after the mine was recovered. Under 'Subsequent Operations' he wrote, 'Sandline involvement to be discussed including provision of guards force for [the] mine.' Chan's son, Byron, had set up his own security company, Network International Security Services, and over the following few weeks Singirok became convinced that—following a pattern Executive Outcomes had established with governing elites in Africa—Sandline's connections would go into partnership with Byron Chan to provide security for the reopened Panguna mine. A term of reference to examine the role of Network International Security Services was initially given to the Los Inquiry but it was discarded before the Commission got down to serious business.

Sir Julius Chan's version of the 8 January meeting is that he wanted to know whether Spicer knew what he was talking about. Whether 'he was well-versed with the terrain in Bougainville' and if the specialised equipment could 'focus' on the rebel leaders. He needed an assurance that Sandline could accurately identify and pinpoint the rebel leaders whom he wanted captured alive. But if there were any 'miscalculations' he wanted to know if casualties would be kept within an 'acceptable' range. 'I emphasised that the best victory I wanted in spite of all these gadgets will be one that can be achieved without a shot being fired,' Chan told Justice Andrew. 'My main concern at all times was to contain damage and casualties.' He claimed that at the briefing he rejected 'any suggestions of arming foreign consultants to kill Papua New Guinean citizens'. The Sandline people, he claimed, were to be 'advisers and backroom operators', flying aircraft and doing 'monitoring'. That is not what the contract ended up providing for. It closely followed Spicer's written brief. 'I did not see this contract,' Sir Julius told the Los Inquiry when quizzed on it. 'I did not even see it until the [first] Commission of Inquiry was appointed'.

Spicer said Sir Julius questioned him thoroughly during their 8 January meeting. 'I was asked a number of difficult, searching questions,' he said, 'about what I thought the sort of state of military play was in Bougainville ... What I thought the possibilities [were] of success ... I said that I thought that the military operations in Bougainville are ... complex. I believe I said [they] should only form part of a coordinated policy which should include other elements—political, economic, social ... but the primary purpose of military operations was to enable a government to be able to negotiate from a position of strength which I did not believe at the time existed.' Ijape's recollection was that during Spicer's briefing, Sir Julius raised concerns about how much damage would be inflicted. 'And Tim Spicer said, "It is an operation, it will cause some damage but with the type of equipment we are getting, the damage would be minimal".' Ijape said Sir Julius stressed he wanted the rebel leaders captured not killed. 'Tim said, "Look, in any operation, killing is bound to happen and maybe we may not be able to get them alive." And we appreciated that.'

Before the meeting ended, Chan asked Spicer for another written brief. 'I was also asked for a number of opinions and then I was asked out of the blue to write a short paper amplifying what my views were,' Spicer said. 'It did not go into military detail. It was more aimed at how a military option might fit into any program the government had.' He wrote this second briefing note that evening. Also dated 8 January it began: 'Sir, You asked me to prepare a briefing note about how you could justify the implementation of a military option involving the employment of high tech equipment and outside specialists to support the Forces of PNG in the time frame January to June 1997.' The justification, he argued, was that nine years of failure 'to resolve the crisis by either military means or negotiation' had handed the initiative to the rebels on Bougainville. They had gained international recognition 'as an oppressed minority in a totally unscrupulous' way and, while pretending 'to wish to negotiate', he said, the BRA had 'reverted to military action when it suited them'. It was time to resolve the problem 'once and for all'.

News had come out of Bougainville that the three hostages taken by the BRA in the north in late 1996 had been killed. Spicer used this to illustrate to Sir Julius that these acts of murder 'in cold blood' demonstrated why it was pointless to negotiate. 'The BRA give the administration no alternative but military action,' he claimed. But not just ordinary military action: 'A radical solution is called for that involves precise military action to destroy the leadership of the BRA, fragmenting their organisation with the minimum loss of life on both sides.' The benefits would include reopening the mine and the possibility of 'cost recovery' although the cost was said to be 'insignificant' compared with the losses already suffered and the damage done to PNG's standing 'in the eyes of the world'. Ending his brief, Spicer justified use of the 'military option' before the mid-year poll. 'Is this cynical electioneering? No. It is the administration's duty to solve this problem particularly in view of the murder of the hostages. The administration has one last chance to complete what it set out to do.'

Sir Julius was won over. 'I found him [Spicer] to be a very sensitive and intelligent operator,' Chan told Justice Andrew. He claimed he tried to find out what Brigadier Singirok thought of the proposal. 'I tried to secure [the] former Commander Singirok to also brief me but he was almost constantly absent from the country,' Sir Julius said. 'However, I met Colonel Jack Tuat [PNGDF Chief of Staff] on two occasions.' Defence Minister Ijape claimed Singirok had told him he was 'very impressed' by the Project Contravene proposal. Spicer, too, told the Andrew Inquiry that Singirok had said to him his proposal was 'in line' with the PNGDF's own thinking on what was needed. There were certainly opportunities in the deal for specialist training for the SFU which Singirok was nurturing as his elite force. And he had been wanting helicopters for the PNGDF to use—free of conditions—ever since becoming Commander. He told the Andrew Inquiry he had never raised any objections to the proposal with anyone at this point.

In fact, Singirok had to prepare the Cabinet submission advocating the adoption of Project Contravene. 'On the 14th January, I was sick in bed,' Singirok said, 'when he [Ijape] called me. He said there is an important NEC meeting taking place on the 15th and it was important that I use the consultancy report to prepare, with the Deputy Secretary for the Department of Defence, Stephen Raphael, an NEC submission in favour of approving the Sandline engagement with the Papua New Guinea Government. So, we sat up until all hours that night putting an NEC submission [together] ... Because I am computer literate, Mr Raphael had to wait until I prepared [it] ... and he took the submission to the Minister that evening.' Asked why he had not objected to the task, Singirok claimed he was following political directions. He said he had been told the Prime Minister was now behind the Sandline proposal. 'The political will is to go into Central Bougainville and kick their arse,' he told Justice Andrew, 'so we have to do it.' Had he refused Singirok claimed he would have been sacked.

In the week between Chan's discussion with Spicer and the Cabinet submission being prepared, the Prime Minister held a series of meetings with his Deputy, Finance Minister Haiveta, to make sure the money was available. That week, too, the World Bank released the $US25 million second instalment of its first structural adjustment loan which PNG and the Bank had fought over for more than a year. 'In one meeting with the Secretary for Finance, the Minister for Finance and the Defence Minister, I was assured by the Deputy Prime Minister that finance will come from outside the Budget,' Sir Julius said. Chan claimed he was given confident predictions that dividends from Government corporations would be well over budget and there would be no cuts to funding of Government operations. That turned out to be wrong and Haiveta admitted it was faulty advice when questioned at the Andrew Inquiry. But Sir Julius had his assurance. 'When I was satisfied that finance was available,' he said, 'I then allowed the submission to come before Cabinet.'

Nobody checked any of the prices provided by Sandline in the Project Contravene documents. When asked at the Andrew Inquiry why he had never asked anybody to do that, Defence Minister Ijape claimed it was not his job. 'That is for the Commander and the Secretary to check ... I introduced Plaza 107 to them and I left it to them to negotiate and at that level, at the official level.' He claimed he would have been interfering if he had tried to check out costs. So the Cabinet submission simply rounded off and reproduced the bottom line figure, $US36 million, that Spicer had put in the first brief he had prepared for Sir Julius (Spicer had suggested a fixed price of $US36.2 million). The big ticket items were the two Mi-24 gunships at $US4.1 million each, the two Mi-17 transports at $US1.5 million each, the CASA aerial surveillance platform for $US2.4 million and the on-board Electronic Warfare systems which were priced at $US4.8 million.

Asked at the second inquiry why he had written a contract cost of $US36 million into the Cabinet submission when the document he had worked from, the Project Contravene consultancy report, had listed $US30 million as being the cost of Contravene's options three and four, Singirok said that both Spicer and Ijape had contacted him to say that was the new price tag. '[Ijape] asked me if I had the figure of 36 million and the break down and I said, "Yes ... I got the figures from Mr Spicer." And he said, "You make sure that those figures appear in the NEC submission." ' As Spicer's brief to Sir Julius revealed, the reason for the $US6 million jump was the engagement of Sandline's Special Force of forty 'mostly black-skinned' on-the-ground mercenaries.

What does a good mercenary cost?

Amongst items tendered as evidence to the Andrew Inquiry was a copy of the typical employment contract for the mercenaries Sandline recruited for the operation in Bougainville. Sandline told Justice Andrew 'it would not be ethical' to release any actual contract signed with any individual 'employee'. However, they were 'happy to provide' a proforma contract.

Item three, under 'Terms', was blunt. It read: 'This Agreement will be terminated upon:—your death.' The employment contract spelt out the risks in greater detail under the heading 'Death or Injury'. It provided for one month's salary to be paid to the deceased's estate and continued: 'You accept that the duties that may be requested in terms of this agreement can be extremely dangerous in nature and could even lead to death. You hereby expressly waive your right to claim against the Company, no matter what may happen or what the circumstances are.'

Sandline was fastidious about security. The contract provided for security clearances and Sandline reserved the right to search any employee. Another clause stated: 'The Company retains the right to carry out polygraph (lie detector) tests on an ad-hoc basis in respect of any employee at any time during and for a period of up to three months after the term of their employment.'

The proforma contract had no specific figures in the section on remuneration. But a simple calculation rendered interesting data. The cost of Sandline's Special Forces Team was set at $US4.5 million for three months. It had forty-two members (forty mercenaries plus two doctors), an average of $US35,714 each per month. This was much more than one of the mercenaries who was engaged in the training in Wewak claimed to be getting. The man who was teaching mortar drills to the PNG troops at Moem Barracks in early March told Michael Ashworth from the *Independent* in London he was being paid under $US10,000 a month. And one PNG SFU member complained he found out a Sandline 'corporal' was getting about $US8000 a month.

Insurance must be high in this line of work but nevertheless, given those figures, that average of $US35,714 a month seemed high. Again and again at the Andrew Inquiry Government Ministers and officials admitted nobody on the PNG side ever questioned any of the cost figures supplied by Sandline.

There had never been a Cabinet submission like this one in PNG before and there may never be again. None of the normal rules were followed. It was regarded as so top secret it never even went to the full Cabinet. In PNG there is no inner Cabinet. Every one of the Ministers (twenty-eight is the constitutional limit) is a full Cabinet member. But Sir Julius suggested to the full Cabinet when it met in the NEC room at Morauta House on 15 January 1997 that because of the 'sensitive and classified nature' of a proposal to deal with the Bougainville problem it should be dealt with by the smaller National Security Council (NSC). Haiveta told Justice Andrew that since it was top secret most Ministers 'did not want to be involved for fear of leakages' and readily agreed to delegate. Cabinet then adjourned and those Ministers who were in the Security Council drove to Parliament House to Sir Julius Chan's office.

The NSC meeting began in the Prime Minister's Conference Room at 3.15 p.m. with seven Ministers present. Another two arrived over the following half hour. The nine included the three who knew something already—Chan, Haiveta and Ijape—and of the six others at least one was horrified, Provincial Affairs Minister Peter Barter. Barter was one of the few Ministers who had made a serious attempt to understand the complexity of the Bougainville problem and so was in a better position than most to evaluate the weaknesses of the Sandline solution. The Ministers were not given much time to read the Cabinet submission. In fact, Sir Julius asked for all copies to be handed back to him and no one was allowed to take their copy away after the NSC meeting. The debate became quite heated with Barter at one stage suggesting that if the object was to eliminate or capture Francis Ona and two or three of the other BRA leaders there might be other ways to achieve that, like hiring assassins, which would be cheaper than paying foreign mercenaries $US36 million.

One important NSC member not present was Foreign Minister Kilroy Genia. Genia never found out the full details until much later. This was to prove somewhat confusing and a bit embarrassing because in the weeks after Sandline's engagement was exposed he publicly denied what other members of the NSC, who understood the full extent of Sandline's role, knew to be true—that is, that the mercenaries were to be deployed on the ground in Bougainville. A simple reading of both the Cabinet submission prepared by Brigadier Singirok and the subsequent Cabinet decision gives little indication of this intent. The submission sought approval 'to officially engage Sandline International' and to approve the PNGDF's Special Forces Unit carrying out 'in depth operations in Central Bougainville' where they would 'conduct pre-emptive strikes on selected targets'. Approval was sought 'for foreigners to be engaged in consultancy work including training and technical support'. Sandline's role was described as providing 'a discreet military consultancy service'.

The submission suggested that Sandline's role was not on the ground at all but in the air–to generate 'massive combat power' by combining 'strategic Electronic Warfare' capabilities with an aerial force of both attack and support helicopters. This would give the PNGDF's strike force, the SFU, 'the ability to carry out timely and effective operations against the enemy while at the same time,' it claimed, 'making the operations politically acceptable'. In detailing the Sandline personnel to be employed, Singirok's submission spoke of technical ground staff and computer operators, air crew and 'trainers'. There was no mention of the forty trainers joining the trained on the ground in Bougainville. Indeed the SFU members were said to be 'the actual front liners and the doers'. Singirok's submission advocated that the Cabinet approve $US36 million for Sandline and K6 million ($US4.3m) for the SFU to fulfil its role. Singirok's version of the SFU doing the dirty work and getting the credit differed from Spicer's who didn't mind the SFU taking the credit as long as his men were in the field with them ensuring success.

The NSC agreed to pay Sandline $US36 million, half of it straight away. But Singirok never got his proposed counterpart funding for the SFU. Its estimated expenses of K6 million to join Project Contravene, the NSC decreed, would have to be met from within the PNGDF's existing budget. It was the old story the police and the army knew well–fund any additional expenses you incur from internal savings. Singirok was miffed. Ijape rang him. 'He called me immediately after the submission was approved and I raised one issue with him again, "Where is the money going to come from?" And he told me not to worry about it.' Singirok told the Los Inquiry the counterpart funding was required for 'the movement of the SFU personnel from here to Wewak, communications, mobility, uniforms [and] allowances in general ... [but] the advice from Mr Haiveta was that we were to take ... that money from the Bougainville Recurrent Operation–which was K19 million [for the whole of 1997]. And this is where I felt angry.' The NSC also directed the Finance Minister to waive tender requirements (something it had no power to do under the Public Finances Act for such a large contract) and 'to exempt from tariff the importation of equipment for use in the project and personal effects of consultants'. There was no mention of income tax exemptions although, later, Sandline was to write a complete absolution from paying any tax whatsoever into the contract.

Two days after the NSC meeting, the Cabinet Secretary, Peter Eka, who was also Acting Secretary of the PM's Department in Noel Levi's absence, called a meeting of senior public servants. Present were the Attorney General, Sao Gabi, the Acting Secretary for Finance, James Loko, and the Secretary for Transport and Works, Miria Ume, who was Chairman of the Tenders Board. Eka told them of the Sandline decision and that now it was up to the public service to implement it. He told Gabi to look at the legal and constitutional implications, Loko to find the money and Ume that the matter would not go to the Tenders Board. Asked at the Inquiry if it was unusual that the Government had not examined the legal and constitutional issues before making a decision, Attorney General Gabi replied that it was. But he understood why—this was a special 'security' case. Security and secrecy also meant these top public servants were not allowed to keep copies of either the NSC decision or the Ijape-Singirok submission.

At the meeting Acting Finance Secretary Loko was handed a letter from his Minister, Haiveta. 'You are directed under Section 24 of the Public Finances Management Act,' it read, 'to reallocate the sum of K50 million out of the [1997 budget's] recurrent expenditure for the Bougainville initiative.' K50 million was the kina equivalent of $US36 million. The Acting Finance Secretary, who had been in the job less than a month, did not act on it immediately. 'I was a little concerned that monies were going to be taken out of the recurrent budget,' Loko said, 'because ... I had an agreement with the IMF about maintaining indicative expenditure targets for the quarter to March.' It was also a direction to do what Haiveta had promised Chan would not be done—cutting budgeted spending. The extraordinary convolutions that the PNG Finance Department went through to try to find the money Haiveta wanted were to take up most of the following two weeks but in the end recurrent spending cuts provided the funds. Health, education and other services in PNG were cut to pay Sandline.

Spicer was back in London when he received a telephone call from Ijape telling him his long-proposed military consultancy was on. 'Once we had the indication that there had been approval for our engagement,' Spicer said, 'and we were now working through a contractual process we put in place a number of what I would call prudent preparatory moves ... we started to earmark personnel, find out where we could obtain specific items of equipment. It was a delicate sort of balancing act between committing ourselves commercially to suppliers and others but, at the same time, positioning ourselves so that we could move immediately on the signing of the contract.' Spicer and his Financial Director, Michael Grunberg flew back into Port Moresby on Sunday 19 January. 'We took a draft contract with us and copies of that contract were distributed ... to the Deputy Prime

Minister, the Minister of Defence and the Commander for consideration.'

That same day PNG's founding Prime Minister, Sir Michael Somare, failed in his second bid to secure the release of the five security force members taken hostage after the Kangu Beach massacre. It was Sir Michael's second foray behind rebel lines in a month. But when he arrived at Laguai village in south Bougainville, he discovered he was no longer negotiating with just the local BRA Commander, Thomas Tarii, whose men held the hostages. In two days of talks held in a classroom at the long disused Laguai Primary School, Sir Michael was confronted by a huge negotiating team including representatives of the BRA high command from central Bougainville. Although Commander Tarii had refused to send the hostages to Panguna he was not prepared to set them free. 'The rightful authority to talk about the release of the POWs,' the Minister for Communications in the rebel government, Andrew Miriki, told Somare's delegation, 'is the Bougainville Interim Government and the BRA leaders.' Tarii said Sir Michael had no real power and that if PNG wanted the hostages back Sir Julius Chan should visit Laguai and talk to him.

There was one Minister who travelled to Laguai with Somare. Provincial Affairs Minister Barter joined the delegation but he had no approval from Chan to go nor to represent the Government. Barter had been in the province flying around with the Australian High Commissioner, David Irvine, who was checking on damage done to the atolls to the east of Bougainville which had been hit hard by Cyclone Justin. Barter joined the Somare hostage-release negotiating team in Buka. After the first day of talks at Laguai, he flew back to Buka to make contact with Sir Julius in the hope of getting some authority to negotiate on behalf of the Government. He did not succeed. Barter was the only one on Bougainville who knew what was coming and he had hoped he might be able to get Sir Julius to back away from the Sandline deal if he could help secure the hostages' release. Sir Julius viewed Somare's trip as an election gimmick.

Back in Port Moresby Defence Minister Ijape said the failure of Sir Michael's mission was no surprise. He claimed the rebels could not be trusted and he announced a ban on any further trips to Bougainville by political leaders. The reason he gave was that the situation would become 'chaotic' if the BRA captured PNG politicians and held them hostage. He made no mention of what was the real reason for tightening up access to Bougainville—the previous week's top secret NSC decision to hire Sandline to 'destroy' BRA locations. Spicer and Grunberg were now in town with their draft contract. And the following day, Monday 20 January, Deputy Prime Minister Haiveta set about making sure Sandline got paid. It was a task he took on 'enthusiastically' according to Justice Andrew.

'At the time of the NEC decision there was no draft contract and no instruction was given to the State Solicitor either to draft a contract or to look at any of the legal implications of what had been approved,' the Judge reported. 'Mr Haiveta seems to have simply accepted the Sandline draft contract because he then set about attempting to arrange performance of its terms on behalf of the State.' The Judge was scathing about what happened. 'No-one, on receipt of the Sandline draft contract, seems to have given any thought to having its terms checked. There had still not been any investigation carried out to verify the prices Sandline had attributed to the equipment it was supplying. Under the draft contract the State was to make an immediate payment to Sandline, in Hong Kong, of $US18 million without receiving anything in return, and without any security or guarantee of performance on the part of Sandline ... Mr Haiveta,' Justice Andrew said, 'showed a strong determination to have the first payment to Sandline made in preference to all else.'

Chapter Nine

Signing up Sandline

*Finding the Money; Negotiating from Weakness;
Paying the First $US18 million
20-31 January 1997*

Papua New Guinea's Deputy Prime Minister and Minister for Finance, Chris Haiveta, swung into action. He called a meeting at the central bank, the Bank of Papua New Guinea (BPNG), on 20 January 1997, involving the Governor of the Bank, Koiari Tarata, the Acting Finance Secretary, James Loko, and the Acting Secretary of the Prime Minister's Department, Peter Eka. He told them he wanted Sandline's first payment sorted out fast and left them to work out how. Tarata advised the others there were only two options. 'One was to seek export credit if they wanted to secure this kind of transaction,' he told the Andrew Inquiry, 'because the 1997 budget had already been brought down. And the second option was to cut the budget by the equivalent amount that they were seeking.' The meeting broke up without any decision being made. The hoped-for windfall profits from the statutory corporations that Haiveta had promised Sir Julius Chan would be the eventual source of the money were months away from being paid.

That night, just over twenty-four hours after Spicer and Grunberg returned to PNG with the draft contract, Haiveta called on Jerry Singirok at home. 'This was going on midnight,' Singirok said in evidence. 'He came to my residence ... and he raised the viability of this whole operation, the [chances for] success.' Singirok claimed he had already told Spicer of his worries that the PNGDF would not be able to meet its obligations under Project Contravene because of money shortages. He said he had told Spicer he had 'absolutely no confidence' any 'counterpart funding' to support the SFU would be provided. 'Tim Spicer guaranteed me that he has got direct contact with the Prime Minister and the Deputy Prime Minister to source funding from somewhere.' But Singirok did not take the opportunity during this midnight visit by the Finance Minister to press the issue directly. He said Haiveta stayed at his home until about half-past one in the morning. Asked what he had told Haiveta about the prospects for success, Singirok replied: 'I said, "It will be successful" ... I still wanted the Defence Force to be the major player in this whole activity.' He told the Andrew Inquiry, however, he was worried about 'willpower within a depleted Defence Force'.

Haiveta's favourite financial adviser, Rupert McCowan, had flown into PNG from Hong Kong at his request the previous Saturday, 18 January, just three days after the Cabinet decision and a day before Spicer and Grunberg arrived from London. Haiveta was already working on something else that had been recommended by Spicer in his Project Contravene document—'early' discussions with the majority owners of the Panguna mine 'and other foreign investors'. Haiveta had decided that the PNG Government should buy CRA out of the Bougainville copper mine. 'I invited him [McCowan] to come and act as a financial adviser for the Government and to prepare the preliminary briefing notes that were necessary for me to take to Cabinet to look at the purchase of BCL,' Haiveta told Justice Andrew, 'and that was the reason why he was here at that time.'

McCowan was in Port Moresby for eleven days but it was not just the CRA buy-out he worked on. He played a major role in trying to make sure Sandline received its first $US18 million. Singirok was called to a meeting with finance bureaucrats on 21 January. He claimed he ran into McCowan at the Finance Department. 'I came across a Mr Rupert McCowan of Jardine Fleming,' he said, 'who was also present at the Finance Department at that time when I was called to go and meet up with the Governor of the Bank of Papua New Guinea along with Mr James Loko.' The purpose of the meeting was to explore ways to pay Sandline, and the Acting Finance Secretary wanted to know why the deal cost so much. Loko told the Andrew Inquiry Singirok described the technology as 'state of the art' and told him the package would give the PNGDF the firepower to deal with the BRA. But Loko's main problem was securing the money. 'We were still arguing,' Loko said, 'because the Governor was insisting ... he could not [fund it from his Foreign Reserves] because he needed some form of documentation and that would have delayed the implementation of the project.'

After the meeting ended inconclusively, Loko decided to go to the Islander Hotel to speak to Spicer directly to explain there could be problems. 'I went to talk to him, to tell him that ... the Government ... did not have the funds available. We had to look at various options so [I said], "I am here to talk to you about whether it is possible for the Government to enter into an export credit facility so that payment of the $US36 million would be made over a period of time, preferably two years" ... [Spicer] said that he had suppliers whom he had to pay. Because the suppliers would not provide the equipment without any payment ... he said he could not negotiate with me.' After leaving Spicer, the Acting Finance Secretary wrote a brief for his Minister. He told Haiveta there were implications arising from the fact that the project was unbudgeted. 'These implications include where the funds would be sourced, the immediate effect on ... proposals to negotiate the second loan from the World Bank ... the 1997 budget and other aspects pertaining to accountability and legality.'

Loko was worried about the Public Finances (Management) Act and he told the Inquiry he thought it would 'not be possible at that time for the government to proceed with the agreement'. Haiveta was not to be stopped. On the morning of 23 January he called a meeting in his office at the Finance Department to issue instructions as to how he wanted the payment made. At the meeting were Vele Iamo, the Acting Deputy Secretary of Finance [who had travelled to London in April 1996 with Singirok], and Ila Temu, the Managing Director of the Minerals Resources Development Company (MRDC). MRDC is fully owned by the State and holds the State's fifty-one per cent of the shares in Orogen Minerals which Haiveta (with McCowan's help) had floated so successfully in October. Haiveta told them he needed $US18 million for a 'classified' military project on Bougainville and he asked Temu to transfer that amount from MRDC to the PNG National Intelligence Organisation. Temu saw difficulties but Haiveta insisted the matter be resolved as 'he expected a bank draft that day if possible'.

The name that kept popping up

If we had taken bets in the press box overlooking Courtroom One at the PNG Supreme Court at the beginning of the Andrew Inquiry, as to which foreign national would be most mentioned during proceedings, the shortest odds by far would have been on ex-Lieutenant Colonel Tim Spicer. But a shrewd punter could have made a killing by going for a name that we in the media might not even have listed as a starter.

That name was Rupert McCowan. McCowan, the Eton-educated, Hong Kong-based financial adviser with the international investing house, Jardine Fleming, was mentioned so many times before Justice Andrew's Inquiry that his own company indefinitely suspended him to contain the damage. It was not only we reporters who were not expecting his name to crop up. The National Court transcription team misheard McCowan's name the first time it was mentioned by Spicer and a Mr McCallum was recorded as having been the one who took Haiveta to Sandline's office in London in October 1996.

That was soon corrected because McCowan was mentioned by almost every witness. Many PNG Government and Banking Corporation officials got to know Rupert very well when efforts were made to send the first $US18 million off to Sandline's bank account in Hong Kong. Rupa Mulina, the Managing Director of the PNG Banking Corporation (PNGBC), said McCowan had accompanied Vele Iamo from the Finance Department to the bank on Friday 24 January and was demanding that the Sandline payment be made. He said McCowan did most of the talking. 'He did not quite explain the reason but he just kept wanting us to process the payment that afternoon,' Mulina said. 'We stayed in the bank till about 8.30 that night.'

Brigadier Singirok claimed he met McCowan in Spicer's room at the Islander Hotel the following weekend. '[While] we were discussing where the funding was going to come from, I was quite surprised that Mr Spicer rang Mr Rupert McCowan ... McCowan was booked in a couple of rooms away from Mr Spicer at the Islander Travelodge. So he appeared within two minutes to basically start to talk about where this funding was going to come from.' In later evidence Singirok claimed that at a meeting in the Finance Ministry the following week he questioned McCowan's security standing. 'McCowan told me that he had been asked to be present during the negotiation for this contract ... by the Deputy Prime Minister ... I went to Vele Iamo and asked, "Who is this man?" Mr Iamo said he is so and so, "He arrived from Hong Kong." I said I cannot discuss anything because I doubt he is security cleared.'

Iamo gave evidence that soon after the meeting with Haiveta broke up, he was joined in his office by McCowan who said Haiveta had asked him to assist with the transfer of the money overseas. At a second meeting with Haiveta that afternoon both Iamo and Temu told the Deputy Prime Minister they believed MRDC was not the appropriate company to make the payment. They suggested a better choice might be another fully government-owned company, the North Fly Highway Development Corporation, known in PNG Government circles as Roadco. Roadco had been set up in 1981 to finance the construction of the road linking the Ok Tedi copper mine with its river port on the Fly River. It received an annual levy from Ok Tedi for the use of that road. In 1995 BHP, Ok Tedi's major shareholder, agreed to help bail the Government out of a cash crisis by arranging for Ok Tedi to pay Roadco a lump sum of K76.28 million to cover road usage for the remaining life of the mine. Since then Roadco had been inactive and (although the officials were not aware) it had been deregistered.

The reasoning Iamo and Temu used to convince Haiveta to switch to Roadco was that it would keep the deal secret. All Roadco's directors were Finance Department officials. MRDC's directors on the other hand included private sector representatives who, they argued, might want to know why MRDC was giving $US36 million to the National Intelligence Organisation! That afternoon Haiveta wrote to Roadco's Chairman, James Loko (keeping the matter in-house because Loko was his acting departmental head). 'In order for the Government to implement its plans relating to Bougainville,' the letter said, 'I have decided to nominate Roadco as the vehicle by which the Government's program of implementation will be coordinated and financed. To this effect, I have directed the Bank of PNG to transfer K33.6 million out of the sale proceeds from Orogen Minerals Limited to Roadco's account ... It should be noted,' Haiveta added, 'that Roadco has been nominated because this expenditure has not been budgeted' and so financing it out of the 1997 budget would create 'technical complications' both in implementing the budget and with the IMF and the World Bank.

On 24 January Loko, still unhappy, followed his Minister's instructions and wrote to the Governor of the Bank of PNG instructing him to transfer K33.6 million from the Orogen proceeds to the Government's main account, the Waigani Public Account. He then wrote a minute to his Public Accounts Division directing them to process a cheque for the same amount in favour of Roadco. Logo flagged in that minute the possibility that he was breaking the law. 'I am mindful of the fact that this payment requires the approval of the Supplies and Tenders Board as required under the Public Finances (Management) Act,' he wrote. 'However as the payment is confidential in nature, it is vital that the secrecy of the payment be maintained. As a result of the ministerial directive, I am instructing you to process this payment without the appropriate approval as soon as possible.' Loko told Justice Andrew of his unease. 'We keep on getting directives from Ministers, our Ministers who are our bosses, so when they give a directive, and even if you do not agree with it, you still have to follow that.'

Bank of PNG Governor Tarata saw two problems with Haiveta's 'solution'. While there was sufficient money in the Orogen proceeds suspense account, about K38 million, Tarata believed that by effectively transferring K33.6 million of that to Roadco he could be placed in a position where he could be breaking the law. He was also worried it would annoy the World Bank and the IMF. 'My concern was that we had agreed with international organisations for them to be consulted before [the] Government utilised these Oregon proceeds,' Tarata said. '[And] I sought legal advice as to ... the legal process to follow, because the letter in itself was directing me to perform a function of government which the Central Bank was supposed not to do ... Public funds cannot be held in accounts other than the main Waigani Public Account.' He said he contacted Haiveta and informed him of the legal advice. Nevertheless he instructed his officials to do what the Acting Finance Secretary had requested and transfer the K33.6 million to the Waigani Public Account.

The strategy worried others as well. On 30 January a senior adviser to the Finance Department, Jim Lamont, wrote an internal memorandum warning of problems. Lamont said he shared 'the Governor's concern that the removal of the K34 million of Oregon funds from the Central Bank is a blatant breach of the Minister's written commitments on Orogen to the World Bank and the IMF and if found would lead to an embarrassing blow up with both institutions'. The chief of the World Bank's PNG and Pacific Islands Division, Richard Calkins, was actually visiting PNG at the time and Loko did not want another rupture in relations that had just been patched up. He used the Lamont letter to persuade Haiveta that the Orogen proceeds be transferred back to the suspense account in the Bank of PNG and that the Sandline funding instead come from general cutbacks to government spending. Loko then wrote to the Central Bank Governor on 31 January reversing the payment of K33.6 million from the Orogen float and proposing instead a temporary overdraft facility to fund the project.

The money for Sandline therefore came from cutbacks in all sorts of areas. The Education Department lost K2 million and the Health Department K2.5 million. K2.5 million also was cut from Police funding while the maintenance vote, always a victim in PNG when the Finance Department is searching for savings, was trimmed by K6 million. The largest individual cut, however, was to Defence–K6.7 million. So, whereas Brigadier Singirok had appealed to Cabinet for an additional K6 million to help the PNGDF meet the costs associated with the proposed joint operation on Bougainville, he found instead that his Defence budget was being slashed. It was a double blow. Not only had he been told to find the extra K6 million his forces needed from within the existing budget but also, he was to learn, his already strained budget was being cut by K6.7 million to help pay Sandline. The notice informing the Commander of this cutback in PNGDF funding arrived in his office in early March and it no doubt was one contributing factor to Singirok's decision to revolt against the Sandline deal.

While the Finance Department was in the process of convincing Haiveta to put the Orogen funds back in the Central Bank, the Deputy Prime Minister was still insisting on the immediate transfer of $US18 million to Sandline's account in Hong Kong. On Friday 24 January 1997 the action moved to the head office of the government-owned PNGBC in down-town Port Moresby. Haiveta had an office there. Indeed as Finance Minister he insisted on having an office in all the financial institutions within his portfolio. So he had an office at the PNGBC, one at the Finance Department on the top floor of Vulpindi House at Waigani, one at Parliament, one at the National Provident Fund at Boroko and one in the Bank of PNG in Douglas Street, just across the road from PNGBC headquarters. Spicer said Haiveta told him and Grunberg everything was about to be finalised. 'We believed at one stage on 24 January that the contract was going to be signed on that day,' Spicer said. 'And to that end, Mr Grunberg and I went to the PNGBC.'

But no PNG lawyer had yet had a chance to examine Sandline's draft contract. In fact, it was to be another full week before the contract was signed. Justice Andrew said the lack of a final contract did not seem to concern PNG's Deputy Prime Minister. On that Friday at about 2 p.m., Haiveta rang Acting Deputy Finance Secretary Iamo asking him to bring his boss, Mr Loko, and other 'relevant officers' to the PNGBC to sort out the dispatch to Hong Kong of Sandline's first $US18 million. Iamo rang the accountancy firm, Coopers and Lybrand, to make sure that Roadco's accountant and company secretary, Chris Burt, turned up as well. Burt had Roadco's cheque book and was another who apparently did not realise that the dormant Roadco had been deregistered. PNG's Registrar of Companies had struck the North Fly Highway Development Corporation off its books on 25 September 1995 for failing to submit company returns for seven years. Burt was aware, however, of the Finance Department's intention to reactivate the company.

On 23 January, the day before he was called to bring the Roadco cheque book to the PNGBC, Burt was notified by Iamo that two of Roadco's directors had been changed. One director replaced was Rupa Mulina, who was no longer with the Finance Department. Mulina had been Finance Secretary up until December when Haiveta removed him from that job and made him the new Managing Director of the PNGBC. Like Loko, who had been switched across to the Finance Department from the Internal Revenue Commission to replace him, Mulina was new to his job. Acting on Iamo's advice Burt notified the Company Registrar on 27 January of Roadco's change of directors. And later, when the story came out that the Government had used a deregistered company to channel $US18 million out of the country, Burt fixed it up. He lodged all Roadco's annual returns from 1988 to 1996 and applied to the Company Registrar to have Roadco restored to the Company Register. On 10 March the Registrar ordered a retrospective re-registration validating all of January's extraordinary and, till then, legally questionable transactions.

McCowan travelled to the bank with Iamo on 24 January. An impressively large cast was in attendance but nobody had much success organising an effective transaction. As well as the Minister there was the new Managing Director of the PNGBC, Rupa Mulina, the Chairman of the PNG Investment Corporation, Eno Daera, the Deputy Managing Director of the PNGBC, Aho Baliki, Iamo, McCowan, Burt, Grunberg and Spicer. Loko arrived later. 'During the course of that day, there seemed to be quite a lot of complications as to process and procedure,' Spicer said, 'and we spent most of the day sitting in a waiting room.' The problem was that PNG's foreign exchange laws require documentation to support the transfer of large amounts of money offshore. And nobody could provide any documentation because all that existed were a top secret National Security Council decision and an equally top secret draft contract drawn up by Grunberg.

Burt testified that he went back and forth to the PNGBC three times that afternoon. Finally, at half-past five, he left the Roadco cheque book with Iamo. 'I suggested that I should leave the cheque book in the care of Iamo and if the transaction was processed that evening that I would attend the PNGBC offices on the Monday to countersign the cheque if that was approved by the Managing Director of the PNGBC.' He said his request for supporting documents for Roadco's files was turned down. 'I was advised by Mr Iamo that he was unable to supply those for reasons of national security but that full details and documents would be provided for our files to put the necessary details in the financial statements the following week,' he said. Iamo, a Roadco Director, was to be the other signatory to the cheque. Asked at the Inquiry why there was such an urgency to get Sandline paid, Iamo said he understood there was some time limit on how long the equipment that Sandline had promised to buy for PNG might be available.

McCowan was the most active of all the people on the upper floors of the PNGBC that afternoon and evening. 'Ultimately, it was put to us,' Spicer said, 'that the contract could not be signed that day and that as a sign of good faith, we would be given letters of undertaking that the contract would be signed and a cheque to hold in lieu of a telegraphic transfer.' He said this was Haiveta's idea. McCowan prepared three letters. Loko, as Chairman of Roadco, signed one and attached to his letter a cheque for K24,657,534 'being the kina equivalent of $US18 million ... made payable to Sandline Holdings Limited in respect of equipment supplied to the Independent State of Papua New Guinea, through its wholly owned company ... I confirm the irrevocable instruction to our bankers, PNG Banking Corporation, against return of this cheque to their Head Office at 10.00 a.m. on Monday 27th January 1997, to make payment of $US18 million, at the rate prevailing at that time, to the account designated by Sandline'.

The second letter signed by the Managing Director of the PNGBC was a letter of guarantee that the funds were held at the bank and that the PNG kina equivalent of $US18 million would be transmitted the following Monday 'from the account of Roadco to the account designated by Sandline Holdings Limited' in Hong Kong. Mulina said he was under pressure to sign. 'I had to sign it,' he told Justice Andrew. He said Haiveta had told him the matter was urgent and the payment had to be made that day. 'The reasons he gave ... were that ... the government stood to lose the equipment because there were other buyers.' Mulina was not told what 'the equipment' was. 'I was in the job for only two weeks,' he said, 'and I had no clue what to do.' Asked by Counsel Assisting the Inquiry, Ian Molloy, about his experience in banking, the man who had been PNG's Finance Secretary till the month before was frank. 'Almost nil,' he replied. The final letter was signed by Haiveta and it confirmed PNG Government authorisation for the arrangements and, again, 'irrevocably' guaranteed Sandline payment.

'Everybody was there till 8.30,' the PNGBC's Managing Director said. 'That was the Minister for Finance, myself, my deputy, Mr Iamo, Mr McCowan and acting Secretary for Finance, Mr Loko.' He even kept his secretary back to type the letters McCowan dictated. He also had cross words with McCowan. 'I had quite a bit of argument over the exchange rate, because I was not happy to put in an exchange rate for that day, the day was over.' And he could not understand why McCowan, whom he had dealt with during the Orogen float when Finance Secretary, was involved at all. 'Maybe Mr McCowan from his experience in Hong Kong thought we could do it, because maybe they do it in Hong Kong.' But PNG was not a tax shelter like Hong Kong. 'I think by 8.30, we realised nobody could do anything and the Central Bank was closed,' Mulina said. 'We did not have the foreign currency to process. We did not have any documentation so we just went home.' But not until all those letters were signed and handed over along with the cheque for K24,657,534.

Buying military hardware

To buy the helicopter gunships, helicopter transports, high-explosive rockets, mortar bombs, assault rifles and other military hardware specified in the Project Contravene consultancy report Tim Spicer needed what are known in the arms trade as End User Certificates signed by the PNGDF Commander. He got them on Monday 27 January just before he left PNG to return to London to start placing the orders.

Brigadier Singirok agreed before the Andrew Inquiry that it was highly 'unusual and unorthodox' for him to issue signed End User Certificates to an agent for an arms deal when there was no contract. But, he said, Spicer was insistent, the Cabinet had made the decision and the relevant Ministers were right behind Spicer. 'I think by then it was general knowledge that this contract was going to be signed,' he said.

Spicer said getting the certificates was a priority. 'I had arranged with General Singirok for those to be produced in fairly short order,' he said, 'so that I could take them away with me back to the UK in order that we would be in a position, once we were in funds, to initiate procurement ... They were delivered at the last minute almost as I was on the aeroplane.'

Two of the End User Certificates he carried with him were addressed to Triton Sal, an arms dealer that Spicer told the Inquiry Sandline had used before. One of these EUCs 'authorised and requested' Triton Sal to supply two Mi-24 helicopters; one Mi-17; six rocket launcher pads; 1000 57 mm C-DSKO rockets; 40,000 rounds of 12.7 ball ammunition; 10,000 rounds of 12.7 tracer ammunition; 25,000 12.7 ammunition links; extra rotor blades, mechanical spares and an engine. The second Triton Sal certificate authorised the purchase of ammunition including 750,000 rounds of 7.62 mm bullets; 5000 mortar bombs; 2000 40 mm grenades; flares; and both smoke and fragmentation grenades. Another certificate addressed to Sandline listed another Mi-17 and included 100 AK47 rifles.

Singirok also gave Spicer blank, signed EUCs. Justice Andrew was critical: 'Mr Spicer said in evidence that these certificates are both valuable, and in the wrong hands very valuable, documents ... Again, it is surprising that these End User Certificates should be given to Mr Spicer before the State and Sandline had entered into a contract.'

Mulina said he had spoken to the Bank of PNG Governor, Koiari Tarata, who was 'very reluctant' to allow any foreign transaction based on no documentation. 'On 24 January, the Finance Department drew cheques and paid [them] into Roadco's account,' Tarata said, 'and PNGBC officials came to my officials to clear the amount of funds that were deposited with them because it was a big amount.' The Finance officials also requested clearance for a foreign exchange transaction remittance. 'And our response was that we needed the Banking laws and the Exchange Control laws to be satisfied before we could entertain their request.'

Haiveta claimed the reason he was so keen to get everything processed was that time was slipping by on the schedule Tim Spicer had laid out in the Project Contravene document. 'I told him [Iamo] to do it immediately because even though I did not have a copy of the NEC decision, I had a copy of the consultancy report and the report was quite specific that there was a time frame in which the equipment had to be procured,' Haiveta told Justice Andrew. 'So as far as I was concerned, the equipment list was provided and there was a need to get that equipment into the country ... The time frame was pretty tight ... Because I believed that the project had been delayed from 12th to 24th and we were advised that if it went beyond the 31st then really it was not possible for the project to be undertaken.' He said he saw nothing wrong with signing his letter to Sandline that night. 'They needed a letter of comfort. So, I signed the letter.'

Justice Andrew was unimpressed by Haiveta's explanation. 'Why it was necessary to provide Sandline with any such assurance,' he said, 'when there was no contract in place and none of the terms of a proposed contract had been performed, is unclear.' Later in his report the Judge was even more critical: 'It is difficult to reconcile Mr Haiveta's conduct on 24th January 1997 with any orthodox approach to a commercial transaction,' he said. And as for Haiveta's explanation that Spicer told him of a competing buyer the Judge said if this was Haiveta's true reason for trying to send the money to Hong Kong 'then that indicates commercial naivety on his part. Furthermore, when the payments could not be made ... Mr Haiveta authorised the provision of a kina cheque and letters of guarantee to a supplier who at that stage had no legal rights or obligations to anything.' Spicer's view was that he was the one taking the risk. 'That cheque—well, I viewed it as security ... we were not particularly happy. I mean it was a risk for us because we had been given a kina cheque which is not what we had asked for.'

Ironically it was on that Friday, 24 January, that the PNG chapter of the international anti-corruption group, Transparency International, was launched at the Travelodge just a few hundred metres up the road from where all this top secret business was going on. TI (PNG) adopted a five point action plan to open up government-business relations to greater scrutiny. One of the measures to be taken was a national integrity audit to survey international business attitudes to doing business in PNG to find out how deeply ingrained perceptions of corruption in the country had become. Invited to launch the group, the Acting Chief Justice, Sir Kubulan Los (who later headed the second Sandline inquiry), was full of praise, saying Transparency International (PNG) would help safeguard PNG's national integrity. 'Its establishment was decided locally by Papua New Guineans who felt they had to act now,' Justice Los said, 'to curb dishonest practices in business and government before the situation got out of hand.'

Not surprisingly, Rupert McCowan did not attend the afternoon launch of Transparency International (PNG). He was very busy elsewhere that day and not just at the PNGBC. Earlier on 24 January he had arranged through a Port Moresby-based lawyer, Peter Lowing, to speak with the Managing Director of CRA Minerals (PNG), Moseley Moramoro. Moramoro had received a call telling him that McCowan was acting for Haiveta and wanted to speak to him about CRA's shareholding in Bougainville Copper Limited. He went to Lowing's office. McCowan arrived a few minutes later but before they began discussions two urgent messages were passed on to McCowan. One was that he should get in touch with Haiveta immediately. The second was that he was wanted at the PNGBC. In an interview in late 1997 Moramoro said he never realised at the time that these messages for McCowan were related to a scheme to pay mercenaries to recapture CRA's majority-owned Panguna mine.

McCowan confirmed to Moramoro that he was representing the Deputy Prime Minister and had two reasons for approaching him. One was that Haiveta was interested in reinvesting the money PNG had raised from the Orogen float–and BCL seemed to Haiveta to be a way to go. Secondly, resentment of CRA on Bougainville could present a problem in convincing local landowning Bougainvilleans to allow the mine to reopen–a problem that would be solved if the Government bought CRA out. McCowan asked Moramoro what CRA's view would be to selling its shares to the PNG Government. 'We don't have a position on that,' Moramoro said he replied. 'I would have to consult CRA's head office in Melbourne.' They agreed to meet a few weeks later when McCowan promised to provide something in writing so that CRA could make a formal response.

In another part of town, at Murray Barracks, others were meeting that same Friday on matters relating to Bougainville. The Attorney General, Sao Gabi, and the State Solicitor, Zacchary Gelu, visited the PNGDF

Commander. The principal reason for the meeting was to discuss the coroner's report into the assassination of Theodore Miriung. The Sri Lankan Judge, Justice Suntheralingham, had urged that investigating police be provided with every assistance. But the CID team was getting little cooperation from a Defence Force that had elevated 'protect your own' into the first principle of military behaviour. Gabi handed the Brigadier a copy of the coroner's report. Singirok changed the subject and gave the two lawyers copies of the Sandline draft contract. Under cross-examination, Singirok agreed he had asked the two government lawyers to comment on the contract but he refused to answer any questions about Miriung. 'If I am probed I will leave the courtroom,' he threatened. Gabi testified that he had a quick look at the contract and directed Gelu as State Solicitor to examine it on behalf of the Government.

On Saturday 25 January Grunberg headed home for London. Spicer stayed. '[We] felt that at that stage we had enough commitment from the Government to believe that they were serious,' he said, 'and I made arrangements for three key members of our staff to fly here ... I remained to see those people in and ... I introduced them to the Commander.' One of the new arrivals was South African Brigadier Nick Van den Berg from Executive Outcomes, who was to direct the military operation. Over the weekend of January 25-26 Spicer and Van den Berg met with Singirok in Spicer's hotel room at the Islander to work on the detail of implementing Project Contravene. The Commander told the Andrew Inquiry he raised again his worries about funding. He said he told Spicer the only funds he had were in his recurrent Bougainville vote and spending those on Project Contravene would be at the expense of his own men on the ground. Spicer rang McCowan in his room at the same hotel and McCowan joined them to give reassurance about the project's funding—Sandline's share anyway.

Chris Burt, the Roadco accountant, said he went to the bank three times on the following Monday, 27 January. During the first visit he countersigned Spicer's K24 million Roadco cheque which Iamo had drawn up, signed and dated the 24th. The PNGBC's Executive Manager, Treasury and International, James Forrester, had returned from annual leave that day and his boss, Rupa Mulina, gave him the job of handling the Sandline-Roadco transaction. 'Vele Iamo and the other fellow, Mr McCowan, came in and wanted to know what we required to get this exchange control approval,' Forrester told the Andrew Inquiry. He quoted them central bank regulations. 'It [the transaction] would require invoices, bills of ladings, some sort of evidence of transport of goods ... I thought at that point in time the transaction would go away, to be brutally frank,' he said. 'Because it was quite clear that they had no documentation they were prepared to show me.' Forrester said McCowan was aggressively keen to wrap up the whole transaction. 'He failed to see why I could not just approve the remittance and send it.'

Faced again with a stalemate at the bank, the man from Finance, Vele Iamo, went back to Haiveta to tell him the transaction could not proceed until there was some documentation to back it up. Iamo said he was unaware that a draft contract even existed. Haiveta told him there was one and that he should get a copy from Singirok and get together with a team of officials to finalise it and get it ready for him, Haiveta, to sign. Those on the negotiating team were Iamo, State Solicitor Zacchary Gelu, Defence Secretary Melegepa, and the Commander. Gelu said he had a call from Singirok that Monday to check on whether he had finished analysing the contract because, the Brigadier told him, it was 'urgent'. He said he told Singirok it would take time and at six minutes past four that afternoon, the official knock-off time for the PNG public service, he went home. But the State Solicitor's working day was not done. Iamo called around to his home that evening and picked him up to take him to McCowan's room at the Islander Hotel.

'I drove out to look around for Mr Gelu and when I found him,' Iamo said, 'we had to go to Mr McCowan's room at the Islander because that was where the Minister said that himself, General Singirok and Mr Melegepa were going to join us.' Gelu said that on the way there, Iamo explained to him Haiveta's keen interest in getting a contract in place. '[He] said the Deputy Prime Minister wanted this matter sorted out quickly and that we have to go through the contract tonight and ... get the contract sorted out and get it signed.' They went to McCowan's room on the eighth floor. While they were waiting for Haiveta they rang Grunberg in London from McCowan's room. Gelu said he told Grunberg there were certain clauses he wanted revised. '[We] wanted these clauses sorted out. But because it was early morning in London, we could not proceed. So, we postponed the discussion till the next morning.'

Iamo said that when Haiveta had not turned up at McCowan's room as promised, he rang the Minister to get further instructions. '[He] told us to go down to Mr Singirok, in his office at the Barracks, that would be around 11.30.' They took McCowan with them to discuss the contract with the Brigadier but at Murray Barracks they were informed that at that late hour he was not available. They left a message for Singirok that there would be a contract negotiation committee meeting the next day, Tuesday 28 January, at the Finance Department. 'It is curious that a foreigner, Mr McCowan, who had been engaged for his expertise in commerce and banking,' Justice Andrew said in his final report, 'should become involved in negotiating a military contract involving the State. Mr Haiveta, in his evidence, admitted that it would be wrong to engage Mr McCowan in such contract negotiations. However, that appears to have been exactly what was contemplated and directed by Mr Haiveta himself.'

Iamo and McCowan attempted to get the money transferred again on the Tuesday. To support their application they produced what they called an invoice. But the PNGBC executive was not persuaded. Forrester explained that he told them it was 'not satisfactory'. 'Nor did I think it was sufficient to even submit it to the Central Bank'. But on their instructions he did. It was not cleared. '[That] document which I submitted to the central bank as an invoice was just typewritten, it did not in my opinion represent a proper invoice ... it was a fairly ordinary piece of paper,' Forrester said. The contract negotiating team—Gelu, Iamo, Melegepa and Singirok—met at the Finance Department. Singirok claimed he did not want McCowan involved on grounds of security. McCowan flew back to Hong Kong. Iamo said that it was at this meeting on the 28th that he found out from State Solicitor Gelu that he was not happy with the contract.

As well, Defence Secretary Melegepa had uncovered the Noel Levi memorandum from September which had advised against dealing with the Sandline people because they were tied up with mercenaries. 'That was the first time when we saw ... what Sandline International was about,' Iamo told the Andrew Inquiry, 'at least for me.' The four members of the PNG negotiating team were not in a strong position. They had a draft contract drawn up by Sandline on the basis of a consultancy report Sandline had prepared and a Cabinet submission which had never been vetted by PNG lawyers. In fact, at this stage, the negotiating team leader, State Solicitor Gelu, still did not know there had been a Cabinet decision. They also had a Finance Minister determined to have Sandline's draft contract approved and finalised as quickly as possible. And of the four of them Iamo, at least, knew that if Haiveta had had his way Sandline would have already been paid half the contract price, $US18 million.

From this impossibly weak bargaining position the PNG negotiators set about their task of trying to make the contract more favourable to PNG. The lawyer amongst them, Gelu, had four matters worrying him. 'The first issue was in relation to the length [of the contract] ... I thought three months was too short in view of the amount involved. The second issue that I raised was in relation to the cost of fuel ... The draft agreement ... provided that the State would meet the costs of fuel and other logistics support. I advised that the State should not meet the cost. It should be Sandline. The third issue I raised was in relation to the balance payment of $US18 million. I thought that some conditions must be tied to [this second] $US18 million being paid ... such as, maybe, the success of the whole operation. And the fourth issue that I advised during our meeting was in relation to training. My view was that in view of the new equipment, training must be extended.'

As team leader, the State Solicitor rang Grunberg in London and put him on a conference-call speaker in one of the meeting rooms at the Finance Department. He told Grunberg of his concerns. 'Mr Grunberg replied that the terms and conditions of this draft contract were non-negotiable and that the terms and conditions have been agreed,' Gelu told the Andrew Inquiry. They spoke for about two hours but the PNG team made little headway. An exchange of faxes and telephone calls followed. Iamo said Gelu told Grunberg the team would advise the Government against entering into the contract. '[That] would have been our intention because Mr Grunberg was not prepared to accept any major variation,' Iamo said.

Justice Andrew commented that Grunberg's position was hardly surprising. 'It has to be said that it is an odd approach to attempt to perform a "contract" by paying a substantial part of the contract price, and only then to try to negotiate its terms,' he reported. 'After all, at the time the negotiations were commenced, it was plain that Mr Haiveta, who outwardly represented the State, was committed to performance of the contract. Mr Gelu's threat to Mr Grunberg that he would advise the State against entering into the contract must have seemed quite hollow.'

Brigadier Singirok also raised problems he had with the Mi-17 helicopters. The PNGDF had four Iroquois and was buying two Bell 212 helicopter transports from Hevi-Lift in Mount Hagen. He argued that the Mi-17s should be cut from the contract (even though Mi-17s were on his own list to be bought from Germany). In a faxed letter to Spicer dated 29 January Singirok described the Mi-17s as 'totally unacceptable' for the PNGDF 'in terms of the variations in skills, maintenance and sustainment'. He suggested that to reduce costs 'we make do with the helicopters already in the country for transportation' and that Sandline 'negotiate with Hevi Lift Mount Hagen for the acquisition of the remaining Bell 212s'. He still wanted the Mi-24 attack helicopters describing them as 'important for the operations'.

Spicer, who was on his way back to PNG, having been recalled by Grunberg from an intended holiday in Mauritius with his family, replied from Singapore on 30 January dismissing Singirok's objections. 'We do not believe this matter is an issue.' He said the Mi-17s were just as important as the Mi-24s and he made it plain to the Commander that the interests of the PNGDF were marginal to the achievement of the objective. 'The equipment we are supplying is for our personnel to conduct a specific operation,' Spicer said. Since the Mi-17s were to transport the frontline soldiers around it was the starkest statement yet that Singirok's SFU was not to be, as he had put it in the Cabinet submission, 'the actual front liners and the doers'. Spicer told Singirok the 'availability of the Mi-17s [and the Mi-24s] to PNG Defence Forces after achieving the objectives is a bonus to the State and is not a critical element of our contractual arrangement with you'. He said that it was 'far too late' to begin negotiations on buying the 'unsuitable' Bell 212s.

'Time continues to pass,' he said. 'If we do not have agreement to undertake this contract by tomorrow [Friday], supported by the necessary funds, we will have no option but to disband the manpower team that has been assembled and subsequently re-form the necessary team members, including a raft of specialists for this type of operation if and when the green light is given. Jerry, please urgently reconsider your evaluation and, if you agree with our analysis, advise the contracts team that the question of the Bells can be dropped so that we continue on the already predetermined path.' Singirok dropped the demand. 'I spoke to him [Singirok] on the telephone from Singapore and asked him to explain what this was all about,' Spicer said. 'As far as I can recall he said, "Okay, that issue is dead, I accept your response. But, I do have a concern about the fact that we do not want you to run off after three months leaving us with all this kit without any sort of arrangement for training and further technical support."'

One of the few concessions the negotiating team did win from Grunberg was his agreement to allow the PNGDF Commander to have a say on operational deployment matters. Under the heading 'Responsibilities of [the] Government', Sandline's draft contract would have given its commanders considerable freedom of action. One clause stipulated that the PNG Government recognise 'that the operational deployment of Sandline personnel and equipment is at the sole discretion of the Sandline Force's commanders'. Grunberg agreed to an amended clause in the final version that provided for a joint liaison and planning team. It added that the 'operational deployment of Sandline personnel and equipment is to be jointly determined by the Commander, PNG Defence Forces, and Sandline's Commander'. Apart from that the only change of any note between the draft contract and what Haiveta did sign was in the name of the operation. Project Contravene became Project Oyster.

Negotiating PNG-Government style

It was not until the meeting of the negotiating team on 29 January 1997, two weeks after the Papua New Guinea Cabinet decided to hire Sandline, that two of the four members of the team learnt that a Cabinet decision had even been made. State Solicitor Gelu claimed he advised the others that he would not be willing to clear the contract until he had seen a copy of the Cabinet decision.

Defence Secretary Melegepa advised him there was such a decision. And so Vele Iamo, the Acting Deputy Secretary for Finance, and Gelu went to see the Cabinet Secretary and Acting Head of the Prime Minister's Department, Peter Eka. Eka showed them a signed copy of the NEC–NSC decision. But there were conditions. They were allowed to 'sight the decision only and not to take notes'. It is sometimes tough being a government-appointed negotiator in PNG.

At the Andrew Inquiry Iamo agreed when Counsel Assisting, Ian Molloy, suggested that the process had gone in the reverse order to what should normally happen. 'From what you have told us so far,' he said to Iamo, 'on the Friday you and the others were trying to send money out of the country and then the following week, on the Monday or the Tuesday, you were trying to negotiate the terms of the contract, is that right? Then, on or about the Wednesday, you were inspecting the NEC decision?' The Acting Assistant Finance Secretary shrugged and replied, 'Yes.'

PNG's Public Finances (Management) Act clearly states that the Finance Minister can waive calling tenders for 'individual transactions' worth up to half a million kina if 'in his discretion' he 'considers that there is an emergency or it is not expedient or proper to call public tenders'. However, this discretionary power does not extend to transactions worth more than half a million kina. Another section of the Act allows for Ministers to sign contracts worth up to K5 million but anything beyond that needs the signature of the head of State, the Governor General. Under examination at the Andrew Inquiry State Solicitor Gelu revealed that he, the Government's chief legal adviser on contracts, had a novel interpretation of these sections of the Act. He told the Inquiry that after he saw the Cabinet decision authorising Finance Minister Haiveta to waive tenders he had no qualms about advising how, in his view, this could be done.

The K50 million (the kina equivalent of $US36 million) could, he claimed, be carved up into 100 separate parcels of K500,000 each and then Haiveta could sign a Certificate of Inexpediency for 100 waivers! The Finance official dealing with the matter, Vele Iamo, said he 'found it a bit strange' but 'we had to try and use the existing legislation to work within'. Justice Andrew described it as an 'extraordinary device'. In his final report he raised as one of the matters which should 'be of concern to the State' that there seemed 'to be a general acceptance at the political level and amongst public servants that some requirements of the law, for example, the requirements of the Public Finances (Management) Act, can be waived'. Gelu defended his interpretation of the Act claiming that the Sandline project was 'classified as top secret'. And he referred to Section 51 of the Constitution which deals with Freedom of Information.

Counsel Assisting, Ian Molloy, could hardly believe what he was hearing. He read from Section 51 saying it provided 'that every citizen has the right of reasonable access to official documents, subject only to the need for such secrecy as is reasonably justified in a democratic society in respect of certain matters including national security'. He suggested to Gelu that this Constitutional provision simply meant certain documents of an official nature were not available to the public and all other documents were. 'That is correct,' the State Solicitor replied. 'Tender documents are public documents. They may become public if it is put to tender.' Gelu also complained that he was in a difficult position because PNG had no laws covering projects involving national security and defence.

But whereas he saw no legal impediment to the signing of the contract, Gelu and the rest of the negotiating team felt PNG was not being treated fairly for the K50 million it was about to pay Sandline. Iamo was given the job of writing a brief for the Acting Secretary for Finance which all of them would sign. They had made little progress with Grunberg. The brief provided some background on Sandline quoting from Levi's assessment including his reference to Sandline's negotiating techniques, a description they had found accurate. 'Their operation,' Levi had written four months earlier, 'often leaves very little room for dialogue and negotiations.' The brief also raised the helicopter sustainment question; suggested PNG should not have to foot the bill for Sandline's fuel; argued that a three-month contract was too short and the price justified twelve months; and proposed toughening up conditions for the payment of the second $US18 million.

'In view of the foregoing,' the brief concluded, 'we are not convinced in the advisability for the execution of the contract without at least some attempt at your level to secure ... concessions on the concerns raised. Having given our views and concerns, we recommend that this proposed arrangement as per NEC Decision No. 1/97 is not implementable unless and until these concerns are addressed substantially.' Iamo and Defence Secretary Melegepa took the brief out to Haiveta's home at about 9.30 on the night of 30 January. But all four 'negotiators' knew there was no stopping the political determination to engage Sandline. Haiveta listened to what they had to say and wrote a few comments in the margin of the briefing paper. '1. Waiver in place,' he wrote. And '2. Second payment condition training for 9 months. Escrow.' At the Inquiry Haiveta claimed he intended to withhold the second payment 'until negotiations on training were satisfactorily settled'. Iamo had taken the tender waiver document relating to the fifty parcels of K500,000 each with him and Haiveta signed that on the spot.

'What the Minister said,' Iamo told Justice Andrew, 'was [that] the Cabinet decision has been made and therefore it is Government policy. And we had to implement it.' The whole briefing took half an hour. 'When he signed the waiver, we knew that that was the end of it, at least from my experience.' Brigadier Singirok, who was one of the four signatories, claimed the Government did not want to listen to expert advice from its own people. At his news conference on 17 March, after staging his revolt against the deal, Singirok was to say: 'Even at the 13th hour, Departmental Heads with me went back and we said, "This whole thing is wrong." We argued but we were told, "You have no choice. You've got to do it." ' At the Andrew Inquiry Haiveta was questioned on his reaction to what was contained in the brief. He said it was not addressed to him but to his Acting Secretary, James Loko. Loko was on compassionate leave on the 30th and 31st, attending to customary obligations associated with his mother-in-law's funeral. Justice Andrew said the contents of the brief 'should have rung alarm bells for anyone who was looking out for the interests of the State'. But Haiveta seemed 'to have brushed it aside'.

Asked if he was concerned about the newly rediscovered research that Levi had done into Sandline's background, Haiveta replied: 'Well, this is background information after the event to me.' He said the Cabinet had made a decision. 'And for me at that stage the important thing was the contractual obligations that we had ... for me that was more important.' On that night, 30 January, there was no contract in place. But Haiveta signed it the next day, 31 January, with his only substantive concern, the length of the contract, unaltered at three months. 'The evidence plainly indicates,' Justice Andrew found, 'that Mr Haiveta was not much concerned with the matters raised in that letter. He listened to what was said but seemed to be more concerned with signing a certificate purporting to waive the requirements of the Public Finances (Management) Act. Mr Haiveta did not pass the letter on to any other person.'

On 31 January, everything fell into place for Sandline. Both the State Solicitor and the Commander had given clearances for the final contract. In a letter to Iamo dated 30 January Brigadier Singirok said: 'In reference to the draft review, you are aware of the same issues we have raised with Sandline representatives, but they are obviously not prepared to negotiate nor accommodate. Otherwise for those issues, the Secretary for Defence and the Commander are happy with the contents of the proposed Contract. Please facilitate signing arrangements for the Deputy Prime Minister on behalf of the Independent State of Papua New Guinea.' Singirok claimed before Justice Andrew that he had been pressured into signing this clearance but the judge found otherwise. A clearance from the Commander was necessary for the contract to be signed and the Judge rejected Singirok's contention that he was fearful of losing his job. He said Singirok was not a man lacking courage. Singirok argued before the second Inquiry that he would have achieved nothing by resigning.

Another vital document facilitating the deal had also been signed by 31 January. PNG's Internal Revenue Commission (IRC) had issued a tax clearance certificate. The Acting Head of Customs, David Sode, who signed the clearance refused to answer most questions put to him at the Andrew Inquiry on the grounds that he was sworn to secrecy on taxation matters. But one letter tendered as evidence revealed less reverence for other aspects of PNG's tax laws. 'I refer to your telephone call to my office,' Sode wrote to the Acting Finance Secretary, 'and the subsequent meeting I had with the Defence Force Commander as a direct result and that I believe involved a highly confidential state secret for which the IRC was to assist with the importation of military equipment. I stand ready to assist the cause,' Sode wrote. Molloy suggested to Sode that the tax clearance he issued had no supporting documentation. 'I cannot comment on that,' Sode replied. He claimed privilege to the next question and when Molloy suggested he had not followed usual procedures he replied: 'I refuse to answer that.'

Spicer returned to PNG on the overnight flight from Singapore arriving early on the morning of that Friday 31 January. He carried copies of the final contract which Grunberg had faxed to him from London. He told the Andrew Inquiry he spent 'another lengthy day in the PNGBC'. He took Nick Van den Berg with him and there they met Iamo. 'We arrived at ten o'clock in the morning and then again there was a period of waiting and hanging about while things seemed to go on behind the scenes,' he said. 'Eventually I was told that there were a number of hiccups with regard to foreign exchange clearance.' At about half-past three in the afternoon Haiveta arrived. 'He went behind closed doors with personnel at the PNGBC and people from his Ministry and eventually, I think, at about four o'clock I was told to come into the Director's office of the PNGBC where I met the Deputy Prime Minister and the contract was subsequently signed.' Haiveta signed on behalf of the State, his signature witnessed by Iamo. Spicer signed for Sandline witnessed by Van den Berg.

Haiveta once again played an active part in the bank transactions making sure that this time the payment did go through to Hong Kong. He left his office at the PNGBC and went across Douglas Street to his office next to the Governor's office in the Bank of PNG. Jim Forrester at the PNGBC had Spicer and Iamo knocking on his door again. They told him that if he submitted the application for foreign exchange approval to the Central Bank again it would be approved. Forrester wrote another letter, attached to it a letter from State Solicitor Gelu and sent somebody across the road to the central bank and up to the Governor's office. At about 6.30 p.m. a fax came back from the Bank of PNG. 'It gave what I called qualified approval,' Forrester said. 'They put the onus back on the PNG Banking Corporation to sight all documents required, to provide a copy of the customs clearance documentation and the copy of Mr James Loko's instructions to the State Solicitor—all to be provided to the Central Bank by 31 March 1997.'

Forrester said he told Spicer he could not proceed on that basis. Spicer called the Bank of PNG. 'He spoke to whoever he was speaking [to] and the next minute he just handed me the phone and said, "The Managing Director wants to speak to you" ... [After] a slight delay ... he came to the phone.' Forrester said he told Mulina he did not like the onus being put back on the PNGBC to present extensive documentation at a later date. He felt he could not guarantee the Bank of PNG anything 'given the type of transaction we were looking at [and] the parties involved'. Mulina told the Andrew Inquiry he was at the Bank of PNG but he never spoke to Spicer on the phone. He said Haiveta was in the room where the telephone was and it may have been the Minister who spoke to Spicer before he was asked to speak to Forrester. 'As the boss of the bank I said, "Go ahead and do it, I will take responsibility."' Mulina said he had seen the contract by then and felt comfortable there was sufficient documentation. He put the time of the phone call at about seven o'clock.

'He [Forrester] still was not happy. At 7.30 that night he still was not satisfied,' Mulina told Justice Andrew. Asked why with his limited experience in banking he had not taken Forrester's advice, Mulina said: 'Because at some stage in the transaction I had to make a decision as to what was important for the State. I mean I assumed that the State was doing the right thing.' Justice Andrew was highly critical of Haiveta's role. 'Overall, the Commission concludes that Mr Haiveta placed a great deal of pressure upon public servants and bank officers, either directly or indirectly, to achieve his purposes.' The $US18 million went off to Hong Kong that night. 'It was a fairly exasperating day,' Spicer commented.

Forrester wrote a diary note the following Monday, 3 February, detailing his concerns about the whole affair. 'Over the past week it has become obvious,' he wrote, 'that despite the initial attempts at deception and lying by Messrs McCowan, Jardine Fleming Securities Ltd, Hong Kong, and Vele Iamo, Under Secretary Department of Finance, that a number of prominent individuals from the Deputy Prime Minister down including [the] Governor of BPNG were aware of and advocated processing of the transaction.' Asked at the Andrew Inquiry if there was any actual lying, Forrester replied: 'McCowan said, "It involved goods and freight ... That makes up the 18 million."' Further on in his note, Forrester commented: 'The lack of ethics, pushiness and general overbearingness of McCowan and the unnamed party who appeared to be connected with the recipient of the funds had to be seen to be believed. Their approach was disgusting and I have no doubt that they would have cajoled, coerced and generally deceived all parties to this transaction.' The unnamed party was, of course, Tim Spicer OBE.

Chapter Ten

Implementation and Exposure

The Mercenaries Arrive; BCL's Share Price Surges; The Story Breaks
1–24 February 1997

February 1997 began with a public statement by Sir Julius Chan that was so cleverly written it was widely misinterpreted. Dated Sunday 2 February it was titled 'PM Calls on BRA to Enter into the Spirit of Democratisation'. Chan complained that what he alleged was 'the current buildup in Tinputz [north-east Bougainville] of armed rebels from Wakunai [central-east] and Torokina [central-west], was 'torpedoing peace initiatives' in other areas. 'In fact, moves like this could well derail our efforts to further democratise Government restoration efforts.' The statement went on to claim that both the National and Bougainville Transitional Governments had made 'real headway in the past few months with the majority of Bougainvilleans supporting the new "grass roots" approach'. Sir Julius called for 'everyone' to 'come on board'. The grass roots approach reference was to a peace strategy that the Provincial Affairs Minister, Peter Barter, and the BTG had been working on, which involved amongst other things a return to respect for traditional leadership through recognising local councils of chiefs.

But it was the next few sentences that encouraged the misleading headlines. 'In line with the changing agenda,' Sir Julius's statement said, 'I believe it is time for a complete review and overhaul of our efforts to date on the crisis. We will be looking at why previous peace efforts such as the Arawa Peace Conference, the Mirigini Charter, the Cairns Peace Talks and others, all failed. The Government will consider changes to enable our "grass roots" strategy to take hold. If that means a complete revamp or a deleting of tired formulas then we will commit ourselves to a reinvigoration of the process. We may well have to come up with a completely new direction regarding the BRA's continued reluctance to follow up their promises,' the PNG PM's news release said.

Many observers (including the ABC's PNG correspondent), knowing nothing of the Sandline contract, wrongly interpreted this statement as reflecting a softening, not a hardening, of the official PNG Government position. Similarly, the BRA–BIG spokesman in Australia, Moses Havini, welcomed what he called 'Prime Minister Chan's new look' for 1997 and commended Sir Julius for his 'fresh start'. Havini wondered, however, if it was just 'another election ploy'. Within Australian Government circles the Chan statement also created false expectations that this might be the beginning of a new peace initiative. What was happening on the ground in PNG went undetected for several weeks. In those first few days of February arrangements were being made to smooth the entry into PNG of Sandline's Special Force of mercenaries and the remaining members of what Spicer had called his CATT–his sixteen-member Command, Administration and Training Team.

Brigadier Singirok sent a list of forty-four names (forty-one South African nationals and three Ethiopians) to PNG's Secretary for Foreign Affairs, Veali Vagi, with a note describing them as 'Republic of South Africa and British army personnel being engaged by the PNG Defence Force for specialist training with our Special Forces Unit'. He asked that they be issued with multiple entry visas since it was 'anticipated' they would 'be involved with our Forces over the next six months'. Simon Namis from the PNG Foreign Affairs Department's Security and Intelligence Branch was given the job of ensuring they entered PNG without impediment. On 4 February he wrote to the Officer in Charge of Customs at Jackson's Airport informing him of the 'imminent arrival of a contingent of Defence personnel'. This was 'a very high level security operation' he said, which involved 'transportation of sophisticated equipment and materials' and 'it would be appreciated if the usual checks be either waivered or kept to a minimum to avoid tampering with the equipment'.

Foreign Secretary Vagi was far more oblique when he wrote his covering letter to airlines absolving the mercenaries of any need for formal visa stamps in their passports. 'To Whom It May Concern' was the heading. Foreign Secretary Vagi confirmed the impending arrival of what he called 'a delegation from South Africa and Ethiopia for official business in Papua New Guinea as indicated on the attached list of names'. Describing those on the list as being members of 'a very high level delegation visiting Papua New Guinea' he explained they would have no visas because PNG had 'no Representative office' in their 'country of origin'. His office had made arrangements so visas would 'be issued upon arrival'. The letter authorised their entry and sought cooperation 'to assist the delegation to travel to Papua New Guinea unhindered'. The Special Force mercenaries arrived over an eight-day period between 7 and 15 February. Most were relocated within days of arriving to Wewak on PNG's north coast.

Inserting mercenaries

The 'mostly black-skinned' mercenary force flew into Port Moresby on five separate Air Niugini flights over eight days starting with Flight PX 393 out of Singapore on 7 February 1997. At a quarter-past six on that Friday morning, ten men hired by Executive Outcomes for their expertise in counter-guerilla warfare in Africa and led by a South African, Q.J.I. Cronje, became the first mercenaries ever to fly into the South Pacific on contracts approved by a legitimate Government. Of the six other South Africans on board one had the surprising name, for a mercenary, of Bambi. This was the flight that brought in the three Ethiopians in the Sandline Special Force, one a doctor.

The next morning at six-thirty another ten, all South Africans, arrived on PX 020 from Hong Kong led by a Mr Van Rooyen. Johnny Maass, an experienced EO operative who was to take charge of the specialist training in Wewak arrived on Sunday 9 February. He travelled with nine colleagues on another Air Niugini flight from Singapore. The remaining fourteen arrived in two groups of seven on Friday 14 February from Singapore and on 15 February from Hong Kong.

The thirty who arrived on the first three flights were accommodated at the Airways Motel on a hill overlooking the Port Moresby airport. But they did not spend long in the PNG capital. On Monday night 10 February they were ferried to Wewak on the north coast of the PNG mainland on a chartered Air Sofia Antonov AN-12 transport which Sandline had hired to bring some of the newly acquired weaponry and 'army kit' to PNG. At Wewak they moved into Moem Barracks, home base of the PNGDF's 2nd Battalion. Members of Singirok's prized SFU flew with them. As Spicer had recommended, the SFU were 'moved to a more suitable isolated location (away from Australian advisers).' Some of their intense 'mission preparation training' was to take place at a former agricultural research station at Urimo, inland from Wewak.

Wewak residents commented later on the unusual midnight flights. Air Niugini is the only airline in PNG using jet aircraft on passenger runs and it rarely operates after dark. The Antonov AN-12 was mistakenly believed to be a chartered Air Niugini Fokker F-28 by some who heard the jets roar. But a few Wewak civilians were aware something was up. PNGDF supply officers had been scouring the town buying new furniture and fridges. Many suppliers in PNG are reluctant to deal with the PNGDF because of past bad debts. But these supply officers were cocky. They had guaranteed funding. And when they ordered the bedding they asked for thirty-six four-inch mattresses, four of them double. Asked why four-inch instead of the PNGDF's usual two-inch, one replied, 'Well, you know what expatriates are like!'

Brigadier Singirok seized the opportunity to outfit his elite SFU with the latest jungle camouflage fighting wear including American combat boots regarded as the best available. Michael Grunberg faxed Tim Spicer on 10 February:

> 'Please could you advise the Commander that the additional costs incurred to-date for which reimbursement required and for items quoted as requested are: Already Incurred–Two internal return flights from Port Moresby to Wewak on 10 February 1997 with chartered AN-12 aircraft, including all incidentals–$US39,000. Awaiting Approval–Camo uniforms (300 sets) and jungle boots (100 pair), inc shipping by air to Port Moresby–$US43,000. The order is required quickly as we have secured these prices by way of consolidating our original order ... Note: sizes required with confirmation of order ... Funds for the above can be lodged at our local bank account (in kina if this is necessary).'

The order went through. But Singirok's concern at what Sandline's presence in PNG might mean for his position and authority was growing. On 6 February Singirok received from the Cabinet Secretary, Peter Eka, a letter the Brigadier found disturbing. Eka had written it on 20 January when still Acting Secretary of the PM's Department and therefore Acting Chairman of the National Security Advisory Council. It referred to the SFU which Eka called the PNGDF's Rapid Reaction Force. Dated the Monday following Cabinet's decision to hire Sandline, Eka's letter informed Singirok of a new Prime Ministerial 'direction'. Firstly, Chan wanted the Commander to know he appreciated the 'protection' he had been given on his return from Honiara in early January, when his life had been threatened. But, now 'aware' that the 'PNGDF Rapid Reaction Force' existed, Sir Julius had 'directed' that it be 'formalised, strengthened and commanded by Police. For administrative convenience,' Mr Eka told the Commander, 'he [Chan] suggested that it be brought under the Department of Prime Minister.'

The letter went on to refer to a previous government decision to establish 'a Protective Security Unit' within the PM's Department 'to respond to threats against VIPs'. Eka said he intended to put the matter on the National Security and Advisory Council agenda and he informed Singirok that he had written 'to the Attorney General seeking his advice on the legal and/or constitutional implications (if any)' and to the Police Commissioner requesting his comments. Singirok had invested a lot of time, effort and Defence money in creating his Special Forces Unit and he had hand picked the officers to lead it. Australian military staff referred to the SFU disparagingly as Singirok's 'praetorian guard'. When he raised the unit in early 1996 Singirok laid down the selection criteria. He wanted volunteers from the army's 'warrior wing' who were single, had a good discipline record, were under twenty-four and who could pass the entry Physical Training test, which included '12 laps of the swimming pool, 52 push-ups in two minutes, 62 sit-ups in two minutes' and a '5 km run in 21 minutes'.

The SFU was Singirok's pride and joy. It was his PNG version of the SAS and he had plans for it to be gradually developed into 'a formidable Special Forces Unit' of 222 men by the year 2000. By February 1997, in existence for barely a year, the SFU numbered only forty-five. Singirok told the Andrew Inquiry he was alarmed by this letter from Eka. 'In that letter I was directed ... [to] relinquish all command and control of the Special Forces Unit [and] to transfer it to the Prime Minister's Department for the convenience of the Prime Minister,' he claimed. 'I thought the whole idea was unconstitutional.' Singirok alleged that Chan wanted to amalgamate the SFU with Sandline's mercenaries and police units to create what Singirok called a 'palace guard' which would provide 'personal protection to the politicians whilst rendering the legitimate Defence Force unoperational'. He claimed this had happened in Africa. 'The Defence Force has the constitutional obligation to defend the country,' he told the Andrew Inquiry, 'not to provide a particular military entity for the Prime Minister.'

Whatever his private misgivings, Singirok went ahead on 12 February and issued the formal military document authorising detailed planning for Operation Oyster. Called the Superior Commander's Intention, it stated that the National Government was 'keen to get into the heart of central Bougainville in the Kongara and Panguna' areas with the 'sole aim' of knocking out the BRA stronghold, including 'the elimination of the political leaders', and assessing 'the viability of reopening the mine at Panguna'. Project

Oyster was described as 'a concept of operations' that would include 'high tech, mobility and firepower with a ready reaction unit' that would 'clear and destroy in depth strategic targets'. According to the document, the Chan-Haiveta Government's intention was to 'kill or capture Joseph Kabui, Francis Ona, Sam Kauona and key BRA and BIG members'; to 'destroy all BIG and BRA communications'; to 'destroy any other rebel targets'; and to 'interdict into Solomon Islands on orders' from above. Oyster was to involve a '120-man strike team' supported by 'helicopters and gunships'.

While the detailed planning for all this was being undertaken, Chris Haiveta and Rupert McCowan were plunging ahead with Haiveta's other plan—to buy CRA out of Bougainville Copper Limited. McCowan kept the PNG Government's prospective future partners informed. Having returned to Hong Kong in late January, McCowan made contact with Sandline's head office in London. In a fax in early February under the subject heading 'BCL' he informed Grunberg that: 'As discussed I am attaching a note on the BCL project in advance of our meetings next week. Please could you copy the note to Tony and Tim. I have sent the same note to Chris Haiveta. We look forward to seeing you in Hong Kong. Regards, Rupert McCowan.' Justice Andrew said the references were 'obviously to Tony Buckingham and Tim Spicer'. Accompanying the covering note was a three-page briefing paper on BCL prepared by Jardine Fleming and dated 5 February.

'The briefing paper sets out BCL's history,' Justice Andrew reported, 'and deals with subjects under headings such as the Resource, the Shareholding, Current Capitalisation, the Proposal (namely the "return" of the mine to the PNG Government by an offer for all the shares in BCL or by acquiring the mining assets). The briefing also mentions a first meeting with Moseley Moramoro who is said to have confirmed that "CRA would consider seriously an offer made for its stake". The other subjects dealt with include Consideration and Next Steps including: "Confirm that adequate funding is available for the project (bring in partner if appropriate)."' Justice Andrew also examined a fax bearing the same date, 5 February, from McCowan to Haiveta which said: 'Regarding the BCL project I am attaching a note which we have prepared by way of briefing for our meetings next week. Tony and Michael have confirmed that they will come to HK on 13th-15th Feb so I am attaching a draft itinerary for your own travel.'

Haiveta, accompanied by Defence Minister Ijape, made the trip to Hong Kong. Their route took them via Cairns. Spicer travelled on the same Port Moresby to Cairns flight. Haiveta's bookings had been done by Jardine Fleming and he and Spicer overnighted on 12 February at the Radisson Plaza hotel. There was no booking for Ijape and so he stayed at the Cairns

Hilton but all three dined together that night. Ijape told the Andrew Inquiry his participation in the trip was a 'last minute' decision and he claimed he went with Haiveta because neither of his two senior Defence advisers were available. 'The Deputy Prime Minister wanted the Commander or the Secretary to accompany him for this trip but because the Secretary was out of the country and the Commander was going to the Philippines ... he asked me if I could accompany him ... I organised the trip myself.' He also said he paid for it himself. Ijape had not claimed reimbursement at the time of the Andrew Inquiry although he said he should have because he had been on 'official' government business.

Haiveta told Justice Andrew his trip was to discuss the CRA buyout strategy with McCowan and Jardine's 'equities and mergers people'. He denied he had any intention of meeting Buckingham or Grunberg. He wanted Ijape with him, he said, to handle any security questions. Haiveta claimed BCL had caused PNG too much pain. 'We have been suffering for a mine that does not belong to Papua New Guineans,' he said, 'and I wanted Mathias to come along ... [to answer] any questions ... [from] Jardines that the buyout was part of the overall strategy. We wanted at the end of the day to buy CRA's interest out and to offer a fair amount of shares [to landowners], partly as compensation and partly to make up for the losses the people have suffered over the years.' Both Haiveta and Ijape professed to be surprised to see Spicer on board the Cairns flight. 'I was not expecting him but he was there,' Haiveta maintained. But Spicer told the Inquiry he knew Haiveta was going to Hong Kong. 'It might have been easier for me to travel with them [on my way back to London] but,' he claimed, 'there was no specific plan to go to Hong Kong.'

On 13 February they all travelled to Hong Kong on the same aircraft. Nicos Violaris, a businessman with close political connections to Sir Julius Chan, was a passenger too. Violaris was a major behind-the-scenes figure in Chan's Peoples Progress Party. The Andrew Inquiry attempted to summons Violaris to appear as a witness but he disappeared from Port Moresby during the hearings and could not be located. Although Violaris's name was mentioned various times in evidence, Justice Andrew made no findings as to what role, if any, he might have played. Strangely, even though Violaris had not made himself available during the public hearings he was one of the first people to gain access to the Andrew Report after the Judge presented copies to the Government at the end of May. The then Acting Prime Minister, John Giheno, suspended the Secretary of the PM's Department, Noel Levi, and ordered an inquiry into how Violaris had obtained one of the few restricted copies that were under Levi's care. But Chan resumed office, lifted the suspension and put Levi in charge of investigating himself. Few were surprised at Levi's lack of success in identifying the source of the leak.

Violaris, a naturalised PNG citizen, did a similar disappearing act during the much longer Los Inquiry. He was the subject of one entire term of reference given to the second inquiry but happened to be unavailable and out of PNG every time the Los Commission sat–that amounted to more than sixty days over more than half a year. The reference asked the Inquiry to determine if any business relationship existed between Chan and Violaris in January and February 1997. Evidence was presented that Chan had sold his interests in a small faltering jewellery company, PNG Gold and Jewellery, to Violaris. 'The business was not doing well,' Chan told the Inquiry. 'I wanted to get out of it and Mr Violaris together with another person wanted to buy into it and then resell it and I was prepared to sell the whole business ... It was the biggest flop I have ever been in [in] business.' Sir Julius had also transferred to Violaris the shares he held in trust for the PPP's business arm, Kalang Pty Ltd, in November 1996. Kalang owned a block of land at Waigani which the Party hoped to develop as government office accommodation with the Australian property developer, Warren Anderson. But the project never got beyond the planning stage.

Haiveta, Ijape, Spicer and Violaris arrived in Hong Kong at about seven o'clock in the evening of 13 February. Violaris, according to what is on the public record, then evaporates from the story. The other three gave wildly conflicting accounts about what happened once they had all booked into the Peninsula Hotel after waiting in line for a taxi at Hong Kong airport. According to Ijape, whose evidence Justice Andrew found the most credible, the three of them had dinner with McCowan, Buckingham and Grunberg. The two men from London had arrived the day before and also booked into the Peninsula. Spicer claimed he remembered having a meal with Haiveta– but it was not dinner, rather lunch the next day with Buckingham and Grunberg but not Ijape. Haiveta's version was that he and Spicer had lunch alone on Friday 14 February. He claimed he saw Buckingham and Grunberg only in passing in the hotel foyer. As for the Thursday night dinner, he had turned down McCowan's invitation to eat with him because he was angry Rupert had not picked him up at the airport. All three denied there was any discussion at all about business interests associated with Sandline becoming part owners of BCL.

Justice Andrew found this impossible to believe. 'The evidence shows that a plan existed,' the Judge said in his report, 'for Mr Haiveta on behalf of the State to meet with the Sandline interests in Hong Kong between 13th and 15th February 1997. I find that the evidence of Mr Spicer and Mr Haiveta that the various persons were coincidentally in Hong Kong staying in the same hotel is untrue. The intermediary once again was Rupert McCowan. The purpose of the meeting was to discuss the acquisition of CRA's shares in Bougainville Copper Limited. It seems likely that discussion included the prospect of Sandline or a company associated with its principals obtaining an interest in the mine and Sandline providing on-going security services at the mine.' Justice Andrew said these were the very matters Buckingham and Spicer had raised in various faxes to Ijape in 1996. 'It also seems likely,' he found, 'that consideration was being given to the same interests providing finance for the CRA buyout. This was plainly a matter that needed to be addressed if the proposal was to go anywhere.'

The Hong Kong mystery meal

One matter that Molloy, Counsel Assisting the Andrew Inquiry, had difficulty pinning down during the hearings was just who dined together in the restaurant at the plush Peninsula Hotel in Hong Kong in mid-February 1997. Even the time of the meal—whether it was dinner on Thursday night 13 February or lunch the next day—remained a mystery.

Tim Spicer was first to give evidence. He said he was travelling to Hong Kong to meet Sandline's Chairman, Tony Buckingham, and Financial Controller, Michael Grunberg. He said the three of them had lunch with PNG's Deputy PM, Chris Haiveta, on 14 February. 'We were going to have an update and a discussion [about Project Oyster] which we had over lunch.' He said he understood Haiveta had travelled to Hong Kong on both government and personal business. Asked if he knew what the personal business was he said he believed Haiveta was buying hairdressing equipment for his wife. 'What about Ijape?' Molloy asked. 'He said he was accompanying Mr Haiveta to assist him in whatever he was going to do.' Molloy was curious. 'What? Buy hairdressing equipment?' 'No,' Spicer smiled, 'with his government business.'

In his evidence Haiveta stated he had gone to Hong Kong to continue discussions with Jardine Fleming on his plan for PNG to buy CRA out of Bougainville Copper but that Sandline was not involved. Haiveta agreed he had lunch with Spicer but strenuously denied eating with either Buckingham or Grunberg. Molloy wanted to know about the Thursday night. 'This is not a very long time ago so you would have a good memory of what happened?' 'Yes.' 'So, I would suggest that you and Ijape, Spicer, Buckingham, McCowan and Grunberg all dined together the night you arrived in Hong Kong?' 'No,' Haiveta replied, 'I was upset with Mr McCowan.'

Haiveta said he saw Buckingham in the hotel foyer the next day and said, 'Hello.' But that was all. Ijape's recollection was quite different. In his sworn statement, the Defence Minister said he had gone to Hong Kong with Haiveta 'just in case' he was needed. He said they arrived the Peninsula on Thursday night and 'had dinner with Spicer, Buckingham, Rupert and Grunberg'. Molloy pressed Ijape. 'Now are you quite clear that you had dinner with them that night?' 'That is right.' Molloy went through the names. 'Yes ... Yes ... Yes,' Ijape said. 'So, any suggestion that Mr Haiveta did not go to have dinner with you and those gentlemen that night would be wrong?' 'He was there,' Ijape answered.

Marshall Cooke QC, representing Haiveta and Ijape, tried to get the versions back in alignment by asking Ijape if Haiveta had been upset with McCowan about having to wait for a taxi at the airport. 'So the Deputy Prime Minister was pretty annoyed?' 'Yes, he was annoyed.' 'Now, can you recall whether the Deputy Prime Minister remained with the parties throughout the whole of the dinner or whether he left early or what?' 'No, he was there at the dinner,' Ijape said emphatically. Justice Andrew found Ijape's evidence 'clear and fairly convincing'. The other two? Untruthful.

Haiveta had tidied up his version of what happened by the time he came to give evidence to the second inquiry. Again he denied that there was any plan for him to meet with Buckingham and Grunberg in Hong Kong. But this time he admitted he had seen them on the night of 13 February in the hotel bar. 'I was pre-booked by Jardines to stay at the Mandarin,' he claimed before Justice Los. 'But I was not picked up by Mr McCowan. I ended up going with Mr Spicer together with Mr Ijape to stay at the Peninsula ... I checked in and went up to the room and Spicer then called me and asked me to join him for a few drinks. I was pretty pissed off with McCowan because he had arranged and organised to meet me and he did not turn up so, before I went down, McCowan called and I said I did not want to talk to him, I would see him tomorrow.' But, he said, McCowan turned up. 'When I went down, I saw all of them there so I still was not too happy about what had happened and from there after the drinks, they wanted to have dinner, I did not stay long. I went back up.' But Haiveta's claim that his meeting with Buckingham and Grunberg was simply coincidental remained at odds with the evidence contained in the McCowan documents Justice Andrew studied in Hong Kong.

On the following day, Friday 14 February, the day Haiveta had his formal meeting with Jardine Fleming in Hong Kong, there was a big jump in trading of Bougainville Copper Limited shares on the Australian Stock Exchange. BCL's share price ended the previous day at forty-three cents. After 156,706 shares changed hands the stock rose to sixty-two cents, a jump in price of forty-four per cent. The following Monday 486,000 BCL shares were traded and the price remained around the sixty-cent mark. The Stock Exchange became suspicious. In an inquiry to BCL on Monday afternoon 17 February, Tim Jess, the ASX Companies Officer, noted the price increase. 'One of the principal objectives of the listing rules,' he wrote, 'is to secure immediate release of information that might reasonably be expected to have a material effect on market activity in, and prices of, quoted securities.' In the 'absence of the release to the market of information which justifies the price fluctuation' he put three questions to BCL:

> 1. *Are any matters of importance concerning the company about to be announced to shareholders and the market? If so, can an announcement be made immediately?*
> 2. *Is the company aware of information... which, if... generally available... might reasonably be regarded as an explanation for the recent trading... If not, is the company able to offer any explanation for the information of shareholders and the market?*
> 3. *Can the company confirm to ASX that it is in compliance with the listing rules'.*

Jess even suggested BCL might want to suspend trading. 'If the information requested is information required to be disclosed under listing rule 3.1 your obligation is to disclose the information immediately ... You may wish to arrange a trading halt of not more than 24 hours.' BCL's majority shareholder, CRA, had no ready explanation. In Port Moresby, Moseley Moramoro had still not heard back from McCowan. On the Friday (14 February, the day BCL's price surged), Moramoro had tried to find out what had happened to the formal PNG Government approach that McCowan had promised him would be coming when they had met three weeks earlier. The lawyer who had facilitated the first meeting informed him McCowan was back in Hong Kong and Haiveta was with him.

One significant BCL shareholder which came under Haiveta's portfolio responsibilities had made a decision on the very day the Finance Minister flew to Hong Kong to sell more than one million BCL shares. PNG's Public Officers Superannuation Fund (POSF) held 2,561,500 shares in BCL. On Thursday 13 February the POSF Board resolved to sell half of its shareholding. The Chairman of the POSF, Acting Secretary for Finance James Loko, told the Los Inquiry that the direction to sell had come from Haiveta. On the same day, 13 February, Loko had been ordered by Haiveta to send him a brief on BCL and its share price. Loko told the Andrew Inquiry he had received a telephone call from his Minister in Hong Kong. 'Well, he said, "Look, get me a run down on Bougainville Copper Limited, the shares, the status as it is now" ... I instructed one of the officers to prepare a brief to send to him.' Loko said that until the phone call he had not been aware Haiveta was even in Hong Kong nor was he aware of the CRA buyout proposal. Asked if it was unusual for a head of department not to be aware that his Minister was travelling overseas on official business, Loko replied: 'Not in Papua New Guinea!'

Loko said he had 'no idea' what Haiveta was doing in Hong Kong. 'He simply asked for a brief on BCL.' The Acting Finance Secretary said he did not find out about the Haiveta strategy to take over the company until the Minister told him about it in late February, about the time it became public knowledge. Haiveta agreed before the Andrew Inquiry that he had not told his Department about the Hong Kong trip. 'I left without telling them but when I got there, I did ring them up to give me the information that I needed in order to talk to Jardines. I did speak to Mr Loko ... it was either Thursday [night] or Friday ... I have got his home phone number ... I asked him to just give me a brief from the Department's point of view on BCL ... especially on the valuation ... they had a brief prepared and faxed across to me.' Haiveta said that after reading the brief he shredded it in his hotel room. 'Because we had already been speaking to CRA or BCL, I thought the information that we had ought to have been kept confidential and that was only for my eyes. I read it and I destroyed it.'

The brief told Haiveta that the 'current market price' of BCL's shares bore no relation to what it would be if the mine were expected to come back into production and 'values in the range of $A2 to $A4 per share could be expected.' Although the POSF Board had resolved to sell, none of its shares were traded on either the Friday or the following Monday, 17 February. Public servants in PNG do not move that fast. By the Monday morning, Haiveta had returned to Port Moresby and, according to the then Acting General Manager of the POSF, Joseph Wingia, the Minister called him up asking for the name of the POSF's share brokers. 'I told him that we used various brokers from time to time and some of those brokers were HTM, Wilson Hambros and ABS White ... He said we should consider selling the shares in Bougainville ... He mentioned that the share prices were going to drop so we should consider selling.'

That Monday afternoon, Wingia and the POSF Managing Director, Ereman Ragi, went to see Haiveta at his office in the National Provident Fund building at Boroko. They took two documents with them—a submission to the POSF Board to approve the sale of 1,280,750 shares in BCL at a price range of 60 cents to 70 cents per share; and a ministerial submission recommending approval of the sale. Haiveta wrote at the top of the first page 'Approved'. The POSF had bought into BCL at $A1.40 and the submission calculated the loss on the shares at $A1,024,600 if they were sold at 60 cents. Asked at the Los Inquiry if he knew about proposals to reopen the mine, Ragi said he couldn't speak for the other directors but he 'definitely' was not aware of any such a plan. Had he been, he said, he would have had serious reservations about the proposal to sell.

Haiveta told the Los Inquiry that his strategy was to flood the market by getting the POSF to unload more than a million shares. 'I thought that if they did that ... the share prices would go down [and] it would, in the national interest, offer the government a leeway that it needed to negotiate a lower price [with CRA].' He claimed the POSF members would have been compensated later. Asked if he felt any conflict between the interests of the State and those of the members of the POSF, Haiveta replied, 'The 'State's interests always come first.' Asked why he wanted the stockbrokers' names, Haiveta replied that he wanted to find out who was buying the shares in the trading that was forcing the price up. POSF Chairman Loko, who scuttled the sale by telling the POSF management to put the whole matter 'on hold', claimed he was worried by Haiveta's tactics, whatever they were. 'I was also concerned that the Australian Securities Commission would find out some time later that the shares were sold for the purpose of reducing the share value of BCL shares on the stock exchange,' Loko told the Los Inquiry.

In his report on the first Sandline inquiry, Justice Andrew could find no evidence that any Papua New Guinean was behind the buying of BCL shares on 14 or 17 February 1997. However, he described Haiveta's claim that he shredded the Finance Department brief in his hotel room in Hong Kong as 'not particularly satisfactory ... overall his description of how he dealt with it, and why, leaves a good deal of doubt'. The Judge suspected somebody at those meetings in Hong Kong was involved. 'At the time of these dealings in Bougainville Copper shares,' he said in his report, 'the State's engagement of Sandline had not been exposed ... No reason, other than knowledge of the State's plan to recapture the Panguna mine, has been suggested for the demand for BCL shares. There were relatively few people who knew about Project Contravene, and amongst those who knew fewer still who would have had the financial resources to buy large parcels of shares. In these circumstances it stretches credibility to think that the demand for shares on the 14th and 17th February was unconnected with the meetings in Hong Kong.' But the Judge said there was 'insufficient evidence' for him to state positively who it was.

Molloy, who was Counsel Assisting at both inquires, said in his summing up to the second inquiry that he believed the extra evidence presented before Justice Los and his fellow Commissioners 'arguably implicates Mr Haiveta' in the share dealings and he suggested that this left it open to the Inquiry to determine 'that Mr Haiveta stood to gain directly or indirectly from dealings in BCL shares in mid-February 1997'. And he said the Inquiry may conclude 'that Mr Haiveta intended to speculate on the price of BCL shares rising, armed with insider knowledge he had concerning Operation Oyster'. Haiveta's lawyer at the Los Inquiry, Stuart Littlemore, dismissed this suggestion as 'totally wrongheaded'.

Ijape discovered that his trip to Hong Kong had been unnecessary. He spent all Friday waiting in his room at the Peninsula Hotel for a call from Haiveta. 'I had never visited Hong Kong before so I just stayed there ... I waited in the room hoping that he will call me and that I would attend those meetings that he was attending,' Ijape told the Andrew Inquiry. 'I never attended any meetings ... it was a rush trip. You know, I should not have gone.' Ijape said he knew the Deputy Prime Minister was with McCowan talking about Bougainville Copper but he knew little of the detail. Haiveta returned to the hotel late on the Friday night. Asked what Haiveta told him about what had gone on, Ijape replied: 'He never said anything about it–he never told me.' Molloy was intrigued. 'Did you not ask what had been discussed? What had been reached? What conclusions had been drawn?' When Ijape replied he had not bothered to find out, Molloy persisted.

'But Mr Ijape, you travelled on short notice from Port Moresby to Cairns, is that right?' 'That is right.' 'And from Cairns to Hong Kong?' 'Yes.' 'And you had stayed in Hong Kong overnight on the 13th and Mr Haiveta asked you to wait at the hotel in case you were needed?' 'That is right.' 'And you did not hear anything from him all day?' 'That is right.' 'And he did not return until sometime in the night?' 'Yes.' 'And when he finally did arrive, all he told you was, "It is a good meeting"?' 'That is right.' 'You did not ask him anything else?' 'No.' 'Did you complain that you had been left there waiting the whole day?' 'I did not complain, no.' 'You were not a bit curious about what might have gone on?' 'Well, my purpose there was security. So I thought my involvement with Rupert and whoever he was talking to was not warranted.' Summing up towards the end of the Andrew Inquiry Molloy suggested Ijape's evidence on the Thursday night dinner should be preferred to either Haiveta's or Spicer's because the dinner, he said, was obviously 'the highlight' of Ijape's trip.

Justice Andrew was extremely critical of Haiveta as a witness. 'The Commission has had the benefit of inspecting certain of Mr McCowan's documents,' he reported. Notes describing the nature and contents of these documents had been provided to Haiveta's counsel who had not sought to have him recalled to give evidence. 'The documents ... indicate that there was indeed a planned meeting in Hong Kong between 13th and 15th February 1997 involving Mr Haiveta and the Sandline interests,' Justice Andrew found. '[The] documents, together with the ... conflicting evidence, and the Commission's assessment of Mr Haiveta as a witness, lead the Commission to the conclusion that Mr Haiveta's evidence concerning his contact with Sandline interests in Hong Kong is untrue ... The Commission gained a clear impression that Mr Haiveta was seeking to conceal what truly happened ... Suspicion,' the Judge wrote, 'hangs over Mr Haiveta in respect of a number of matters.'

At the later Los Inquiry, Molloy tabled documents revealing how, on that Friday, 14 February 1997, Tony Buckingham withdrew $US500,000 in cash from Sandline Holdings' Hong Kong Bank account. Reminding Haiveta of Spicer's evidence to the Andrew Inquiry that they—Haiveta, Spicer and Buckingham—had eaten lunch together at the Peninsula Hotel that day, Molloy suggested that the money had been paid to him. 'No,' Haiveta replied. 'Have you any idea why Mr Buckingham would be withdrawing $500,000 in cash from that account?' 'No idea.' Littlemore, for Haiveta, objected. He claimed Molloy's line of questioning was not backed up by any evidence and that what he had suggested could result in sensational news reports which might lead the public to believe Haiveta had received the money. Molloy asked the question in a more neutral way and was given the same answer: 'No.' In summing up Molloy submitted that Haiveta had given 'false evidence on a number of occasions' and that it was 'open to the Commission to conclude that on all the evidence this money was ... paid to Mr Haiveta'. Littlemore countered this in his final submissions claiming it was an 'outrageous and unjustifiable contention'.

The secret commission on the Sandline deal that was unveiled at the Los Inquiry–the $US500,000 that was paid to Ijape's former political colleague, Benias Sabumei–was transferred out of the Sandline Holdings Hong Kong Bank account ten days after Buckingham's cash withdrawal. 'It is significant,' Molloy said in his summation, 'that the entries in Mr Sabumei's diary (on the page dated 18th February 1997) coincide with the hotel name, fax number and room number where Mr Ijape was staying in Hong Kong. It seems that some attempt has been made to cross out the name of the hotel where it appears in the diary. There appears also to have been an attempt to disguise the prefix of the fax number of the hotel. The same page includes a reference to US dollars ... If the Commission concludes that Mr Sabumei was a conduit for a corrupt payment from Sandline then it could be justified to suspect that Mr Ijape was a recipient (and intended by Sandline to be a recipient) in whole or in part of the money paid by Sandline International to Sabumei's Citibank account.' Cooke QC, for Ijape, vigorously rejected this interpretation.

Haiveta and Ijape left Hong Kong on Saturday 15 February 1997 and returned to Port Moresby via Singapore. Brigadier Singirok was passing through Singapore on his way to the Philippines on a trip sanctioned by the PNG Government to establish a military relationship with the Philippines army. He personally wanted to visit the southern Philippines to learn how the Philippines military had handled the insurgency in Mindinao. 'When I arrived in Singapore,' Singirok told the first inquiry, 'the Embassy staff and the Air Niugini General Manager were there to receive me.' They advised him that his Minister, Ijape, was at the airport transiting from Hong Kong, waiting to board the return Air Niugini flight to Port Moresby. 'And it was only then and there I realised that the Minister had gone to Hong Kong,' Singirok said. Singirok was to be absent from PNG for twelve days. He did not return until 27 February, by which time the story of the Sandline mercenaries being recruited by PNG had well and truly broken.

Amongst the 'Responsibilities of the State' that Haiveta had agreed to in the Sandline contract was one requiring the PNG Government to ensure that information relating to Operation Oyster was restricted. 'Appropriate steps will be taken,' the contract stipulated, 'to prevent press reporting, both nationally and internationally, or any form of security breach or passage of information which may potentially threaten operational effectiveness and/or risk the lives of the persons involved.' For most of the first three weeks after the contract was signed–which meant five weeks after the Cabinet decision– that contractual obligation had been met. It was a remarkable feat. Little remains secret for long in PNG. However, by the middle of February, the

Australians were starting to realise something was going on. The Air Sofia Antonov AN-12 had been joined at Jackson's Airport by another Air Sofia transport, a much bigger Antonov AN-124 which flew in at night with a mass of cargo it unloaded to be stored in the PNGDF's hangars at Kiki Barracks on the opposite side of the runway to the commercial terminals.

Australia's Foreign Minister, Alexander Downer, was about to visit. He was to fly into Port Moresby overnight on an Australian Air Force VIP jet arriving in the early hours of Wednesday 19 February. On the Tuesday Downer was given a briefing in his Parliament House office in Canberra on what Australian intelligence had been able to learn about Project Oyster and the involvement of Sandline International. That night, before heading out of Canberra for PNG, Downer learnt even more at a private dinner. Downer arrived at Jackson's Airport at about two o'clock on the Wednesday morning and his RAAF VIP jet parked on the same apron as the two Antonovs. 'He pulled up alongside the big one,' one eyewitness said. 'The Russian crew walked right past. And people in the terminal were saying, "The Russians are here."' This was Downer's second visit to PNG as Foreign Minister. The first, in May of 1996, had been strained. No Minister had met him on his arrival, just the Governor of Port Moresby, Bill Skate. This time (aside from his accidental reception by the Air Sofia crew) a veneer of cordiality masked the real tension beneath.

By this stage, too, PNG's Provincial Affairs Minister, Peter Barter, was frantically trying to keep alive the peace strategy he had developed with the Bougainville Transitional Government. It suited the purposes of the contrary Project Oyster for him to appear to be succeeding. Chan had already sponsored a constitutional amendment through the Parliament (which is no mean achievement in PNG where two-thirds of the MPs have to agree to it twice) extending the life of the Bougainville Transitional Government past the looming elections and on to the end of 1997. And on the eve of Downer's arrival, Barter won Cabinet endorsement for what appeared to be a dramatic policy shift—allowing the Red Cross to take Australian aid across the blockade into BRA-controlled areas on Bougainville. 'This project,' Barter told the ABC, as Downer was getting ready to fly to PNG, 'is $A4 million for saucepans, shovels, blankets and basic equipment to enable people to return to their villages and restart their lives. It's not only for areas controlled by the Government. In fact in the letter we've written we want the Red Cross to concentrate on making sure that the BRA share this,' Barter said. 'We don't want to set any rules and conditions for the Red Cross.'

The Australian High Commissioner's residence on Touaguba Hill has magnificent views of Port Moresby harbour and the sea and islands beyond.

With that outlook as a backdrop, Downer's official day that Wednesday began with a one-and-a-half-hour briefing. By now the Australians had been able to piece together a bit more of the Sandline puzzle. But despite the huge number of personnel engaged in doing nothing else but keeping the Australian Government informed about what goes on in PNG (and despite the sophistication of Australia's eavesdropping capabilities) there were still significant pieces of information missing. Downer called on the PNG Foreign Minister, Kilroy Genia, at 10 a.m. and then met Haiveta and the National Planning Minister, Moi Avei, at the Deputy Prime Minister's office at Vulpindi House. But he did not raise Australia's concerns with any of them. He saved that for what was supposed to have been just a 'courtesy call' on the Prime Minister, Sir Julius Chan. A courtesy call followed by a genial lunch at Parliament House.

'Sir Julius spent a cordial two hours over lunch with Mr Downer,' the PNG Prime Minister's media statement released that afternoon claimed, 'where they discussed a wide range of issues of mutual interest to both countries ... In welcoming the Australian Foreign Minister, Sir Julius reaffirmed his Government's view that relations between Papua New Guinea and Australia are warm, close, constructive and growing.' He also expressed pleasure that Downer had recognised 'the progress PNG has made in bringing about peace'. The statement contained a number of directly attributable quotes. 'I am encouraged that through regular interpersonal visits like this,' Sir Julius said, 'our leaders can continue to enhance mutual and deeper understanding of each other's concerns and thereby deal immediately with the difficulties. I must express to the Foreign Minister my pleasure at this latest meeting and call upon him to feel comfortable and secure in the knowledge that he can bring up any issue no matter how controversial so that it can be resolved with as little fuss as possible.'

That reference to the sensational nature of the private discussions held when Sir Julius and Downer had met, alone, behind closed doors in the PNG Prime Minister's office was lost on most of the media covering the visit. 'We had just a "four eyes"—me and Chan,' Downer revealed some months later. 'I told him how totally opposed to the concept of bringing mercenaries into the South Pacific Australia was. He told me they were just going to do training. I said even for training we were opposed. But if they were going to be used on Bougainville we would be particularly outraged. Our view was that it would only worsen matters and turn the people of Bougainville even more against the PNG Government. We were very much opposed to the whole precedent being set.' After the one-on-one meeting, Downer rang Australia's Prime Minister, John Howard, from one of the balconies outside the PNG Parliament on a mobile phone. He told Howard what Chan had told him. Prime Minister Howard rang Sir Julius. 'I advised Mr Howard,' Sir Julius told the Los Inquiry, 'that we had the contract with Sandline consultants and that we were bringing military equipment into Papua New Guinea. I was surprised the Australian Government seemed not to have known of the exercise.'

Downer held a news conference late on the Wednesday afternoon during which, he claimed later, he was deliberately careful in choosing his words. He officially announced the $A4 million aid to the Red Cross that Barter had spoken about, saying he hoped it would help bring about peace. 'We see the developments at the moment in Bougainville as being favourable,' he claimed. 'We've been very pleased with the extension of the mandate of the Bougainville Transitional Government and also with the Prime Minister's 2nd of February statement on a comprehensive review of the policy towards Bougainville. We want the momentum to be maintained. We'd obviously be concerned,' he went on, 'if any party took action which undermined these favourable developments and we'd like to see all parties involved playing a constructive role. That includes a view we have which is that the taking of hostages and the killing of people is clearly completely unacceptable and in the context of those comments I would call on the BRA to release the hostages who are currently held.'

Also that day, Wednesday 19 February, the Australians decided to bring more international pressure on the Chan Government. Australia's High Commissioner, David Irvine, invited the British and New Zealand High Commissioners and the American Ambassador to his residence for a confidential briefing. Irvine told them what Australia had been able to uncover about Sandline and the arms shipments. They had photos of ammunition boxes and crates of AK47s being unloaded. But they were still not sure how many mercenaries had arrived and where they were training. 'David Irvine told us what they knew about the mercenaries,' one diplomat confided later. 'The Aussies were caught napping. Prior to Downer's visit they hadn't known very much.' That evening at a reception at the High Commissioner's residence, Downer sought out the South Pacific correspondent for the *Australian* newspaper, Mary-Louise O'Callaghan. She already had some facts. O'Callaghan had been tipped off by others and was following up her own leads. Downer wanted the story printed and directed Foreign Affairs to confirm her information and help her with elaboration.

Missing the scoop

I was battling a malaria attack when I was comprehensively scooped by a very fine journalist on my own patch. Without doubt it was the story of the decade in Papua New Guinea. Mary-Louise O'Callaghan, who is based in Honiara, beat me to the mercenaries story. I have had malaria a dozen times but if you hit it with quinine early enough it is just debilitating not life-threatening. The quinine as much as the malaria makes you feel lousy and, I can testify, together they ruin one's judgment.

When Alexander Downer arrived in PNG on 19 February I just wanted him to go home. I struggled around, ill and sweating, filming his visits to PNG Ministers and covering his news conferences. I never went to the official reception held in his honour at the High Commissioner's residence. Instead, after sending off my radio and television stories to the ABC in Australia, I collapsed into bed.

On the Thursday morning, I dragged myself to the airport to catch Downer for a 'door-stop' interview. But that was to get a comment from him on something happening elsewhere in the world to be slotted into somebody else's story on the ABC TV News that night. During the day I received a tip-off call that should have sent my blood racing. 'Was I aware,' my contact asked, 'that an Air Sofia transport jet had brought Russian-made helicopter gunships into PNG and they were now hidden in the PNG Defence Force hangar?' I had seen an Air Sofia jet next to Downer's RAAF plane. Wearily, I checked out the gunships angle but mentally dismissed the story when told, 'Not gunships, Sean, but lots of other stuff!' Malaria does funny things to the blood. I realised my blunder when the phone rang at home on Saturday morning after the *Weekend Australian* hit lawns around Australia.

On Thursday 20 February, while Downer visited Mount Hagen and the Lihir gold mine in Chan's electorate of Namatanai, Australian diplomatic, intelligence and defence staff continued their furious efforts to learn more about the Sandline deal. At his regular weekly news conference, Sir Julius gave little away despite pointed questions from Mary-Louise O'Callaghan about the possibility of a new offensive on Bougainville before the elections. 'There won't be a big sort of declaration of a war,' he said, 'but we must never rule out the necessity of capturing some of these criminals that... have done a lot of the atrocities and a lot of the killings.' The previous July, in one of his more dismissive statements about Australia, Sir Julius had claimed to be 'appalled' by Downer's 'naivety'. But at this news conference he credited the Australian Foreign Minister with being a quick learner. Asked if there was too much ignorance about PNG at the Australian political level, Sir Julius replied: 'Oh, no! If Alexander Downer represents Australia then he's certainly not ignorant. He seems to know everything that is going on here!'

Speaking on his departure from PNG after his three-day visit on Friday afternoon, 21 February, Downer urged the Chan Government not to change direction with its Bougainville policy. The change had been made more than a month earlier at the NSC meeting in mid-January. But to those unaware of what was going on Downer was speaking in riddles. After congratulating Chan's Government on its initiatives to advance peace by extending the term of the BTG and recognising councils of elders, Downer urged the steady approach. 'It will take time and it requires patience and it requires wisdom to pursue this course that has been set by the Papua New Guinea Government,' he said, 'and not a sudden change of course. And, secondly, it may be that if the present course is pursued then later in the year or sometime early next year it will be possible to put together some sort of talks which Australia would be happy to assist with.' Such a time scale, however, was worthless to a Prime Minister with an election four months away.

The next morning, Saturday 22 February, Mary-Louise O'Callaghan broke the Sandline story in the *Weekend Australian*. Under a front-page lead headline 'PNG Hires Mercenaries To Blast Rebels' she reported in remarkably accurate detail the plan to wipe out the Bougainville rebel leaders. Downer was quoted 'on his departure from PNG' as warning the Chan Government 'not to be tempted by "quick fixes" which would undermine progress made towards peace on Bougainville. "My view is that assaults on hardline rebels and any reversion to military solutions is simply going to be unsuccessful," Mr Downer said. "If that were to happen it would put the peace process back very substantially."' One of the few factual errors in O'Callaghan's scoop concerned the number of mercenaries. Her story claimed that between '135 and 150 foreign mercenaries' were to take part in the operation. The Sandline contract provided for a total 'foreign' Sandline Strike Force of half that number, some of whom were still to arrive with the helicopters.

Under the contract Sandline's '16 man Command, Admin and Training Team (CATT)' was to be deployed within the first week of February 'to establish home bases at Jackson's Airport and the Jungle Training Centre at Wewak'. Over the following ten days further 'Special Forces personnel' would be flown in. These included the forty on-the-ground mercenaries (who were to be 'mostly black-skinned' according to the Spicer brief, although that detail was not in the contract). Finally, there would be aircrew and engineers, intelligence and equipment operatives, mission operators, ground technicians and medical personnel. 'This force will absorb the CATT as part of its numbers,' the contract said, 'bringing the total Strike Force head count to 70.' While the *Weekend Australian* story revealed one half of the contract's aim—to eliminate rebel leaders—it was not until later that the second half became public. 'This Strike Force,' the contract stated, 'shall be responsible for achieving the primary objective.' That primary objective was not only to render the BRA 'militarily ineffective' but also to repossess the copper mine.

One of the first to condemn the Chan Government's now public plan to hire foreigners to hit rebel leaders was Port Moresby's Governor, Bill Skate. Decrying it as an 'act of madness', Skate claimed the move was 'a direct threat' to democracy. 'This decision is an insult and an attack on the PNG Defence Force,' he said. 'For years, the Prime Minister has said Bougainville is an internal problem and that the Government doesn't need foreign assistance to solve this crisis. Now we discover he has engaged a private army of foreign war veterans to execute a surgical strike targeting hard-line rebels!' Bougainville's Transitional Premier, Gerard Sinato, was shocked. Sinato (who had replaced the assassinated Theodore Miriung) said he had not been consulted and the BTG was totally opposed to hiring mercenaries. Premier Sinato feared 'bad repercussions'. The Catholic Bishop responsible for Bougainville said there had already been 'far too much illegal and cruel behaviour'. Archbishop Karl Hesse believed it would worsen the conflict. 'I beg the Government not to be misled into thinking this would be a legitimate or sensible response to the tragedy of Bougainville.'

The Opposition in Australia was quick to comment. Shadow Foreign Minister Laurie Brereton called on the Howard Government to warn PNG against further military action on Bougainville and to express Australian 'abhorrence' at the use of mercenaries. 'Australia requires from Mr Downer an absolute guarantee,' Brereton said, 'that not one dollar of Australia's bilateral aid to PNG is going, directly or indirectly, to the hiring of a crew of Rambo-like assassins.' If such a guarantee could not be given, he said, Australia should threaten to cut its aid. PNG's Opposition was more ambivalent. Opposition Leader Roy Yaki called the move 'desperate'. But he did not reject it. 'If these mercenaries are here for training purposes,' Yaki said, 'then I support the engagement in principle. Our policemen and women and army personnel must be given high class training and modern resources to discharge their roles efficiently and effectively ... What the army needs is less conflicting signals from the Government. They need clear directives with sufficient logistics to accomplish a mission.'

The following Monday morning, 24 February, Downer went on ABC Radio's 'AM' saying Australia would do 'everything possible' to stop PNG using mercenaries to kill secessionist leaders. The Australian Foreign Minister said Australia regarded the proposed operation as 'absolutely disastrous' and he warned it would do great damage to PNG internationally. He said he had spoken directly to Sir Julius Chan about it when he was in Port Moresby the previous week and told him of Australia's 'profound concern'. But, he said, Chan had told him the mercenaries were only in PNG to train the PNGDF. Asked if Australia might suspend its $A300 million a year aid program, Downer said the aid treaty did not expire until the year 2000. Although he did not say it during the interview, Downer was already considering how Australia could bring additional pressure to bear. He believed the final resort might have to be invoking the termination clause in the aid treaty which provided for six months notice by either side.

Sir Julius Chan was stung by the criticism from Australia. And like leaders elsewhere before him he attacked the messenger. In a four-page media release he claimed the *Weekend Australian* report was 'premature and hypocritical', 'inaccurate and sensationalist' and a 'beat-up'. In the light of all the detail to emerge at the first Sandline inquiry, O'Callaghan's story was incredibly accurate, while Chan's release was packed with misleading and untrue statements. He described the Sandline deal as 'a training operation' covered by the Defence White Paper approved in July 1996. 'These training options were canvassed in that paper,' Sir Julius claimed, 'options that were reached with international advice from both Australia and other countries.' That was rubbish. The Defence White Paper never envisaged anything like what was contained in the Sandline contract. 'Now that we have put those plans into action,' Chan's statement went on, 'Papua New Guinea is being accused of hiring mercenaries, not trainers but mercenaries, by the media of a country which endorsed the strategy in the first place.' The truth was that, far from backing the White Paper, Australia had sneered at it.

Years of frustration that had been building on both sides of the complex PNG–Australia relationship erupted with Sir Julius being the immediate, but short-term, beneficiary. There was a surge of support from within Papua New Guinea for Chan's hiring of Sandline. Until Singirok acted to abort the Sandline deal less than one month later, the PNG Prime Minister was carried along on a wave of popularity. Simply, he was seen to have made a bold decision to bring in mercenaries to fix a problem that Australia had refused to help with. And what many in PNG regarded as Australia's hectoring drove local sympathy Chan's way. Singirok was later to label Chan, Haiveta and Ijape the villains. In the interim, Australia fitted the role.

Chapter Eleven

Papua New Guinea Defiant

Australia–PNG Relations Worsen; The Training in Wewak; CRA Buyout Becomes Policy
Late February–Early March 1997

The souring of relations between Australia and Papua New Guinea was made all the more bitter by Australia's belief that it was being regularly and systematically lied to by the PNG Government. On the other side PNG objected to what it regarded as Australia's paternalistic, scolding tone. In a statement issued on 24 February, two days after the story broke, PNG's Foreign Minister, Kilroy Genia–who had not attended the crucial 15 January National Security Council meeting–denied that PNG planned 'to hire foreign mercenaries to eliminate rebel leaders' on Bougainville. 'I want to categorically make it clear that as a member of the National Executive Council,' he said, 'I am not aware of any such decision by this Government.' Indeed, Foreign Minister Genia may not have been aware. But hiring mercenaries was certainly the intent of the contract Deputy Prime Minister Haiveta had signed. And the 12 February edict from the PNGDF Commander was very clear. It stated that the Government's intention was to 'kill or capture Joseph Kabui, Francis Ona, Sam Kauona and key BRA and BIG members'.

While it might sound implausible that PNG's Foreign Minister–the man supposedly presenting PNG's case to the world–could be unaware of what Operation Oyster involved, such things are not unusual in the Land of the Unexpected. Even Haiveta told the Andrew Inquiry he did not see the final Cabinet decision until the crisis was fully blown. 'I never saw a copy of the actual NSC-NEC decision until Tuesday, March 25th, on the floor of Parliament before I got up to debate this issue on nationwide TV,' Haiveta testified. 'Just the Prime Minister and [Cabinet] Secretary Eka had copies.'

And Chan told the Los Inquiry he never saw the contract Haiveta signed until he was given a copy at the Andrew Inquiry. Foreign Minister Genia's lack of knowledge did not deter him, however, from accusing others of getting it wrong. 'The way in which the media, especially in Australia, have beaten up a poorly researched story,' he claimed, 'reflects their ignorance and lack of understanding of what this Government is doing in Bougainville.' It appears that the small circle of those who did understand what the PNG Government was doing did not include Foreign Minister Genia. He went on to defend the hiring of foreign 'trainers' to teach the PNGDF things Australia had refused to teach them.

'I want to say that Cabinet's decision to allow foreign personnel into Papua New Guinea was made for the sake of building the capacities of our Defence Force by training our people to respond more effectively in crisis situations,' he said. 'It must be made clear that we have approached many of our good friends to assist Papua New Guinea through Defence Cooperation but their responses have not been positive. As an independent sovereign country Papua New Guinea has to make decisions and act in the best interests of the country and our people, whether or not others choose to help.' PNG's Foreign Minister was also annoyed by the wider Australian reaction. 'I am extremely disappointed that Australians, especially the Federal Opposition,' he said, 'have called for a review of the aid they provide to Papua New Guinea including aid to Bougainville under the Restoration Program.' In Canberra Genia's statement was scoffed at.

The initial reaction of the newspapers in PNG to the mercenaries story was disbelief. The *Post Courier* called for 'a full and complete explanation' from the Prime Minister. 'The allegation that the Government has hired a group of foreign mercenaries to kill Bougainvillean rebel leaders,' it said in an editorial on 24 February, 'contradicts everything the Government has been saying about wanting a peaceful solution.' The *Post Courier* claimed that the decision, 'if true', would not solve the problem, only harden the rebels' resolve. The *National* preferred the 'trainers not mercenaries' explanation. It suggested Australia's 'excited' reaction was based on fear of losing influence. 'PNG defence advisers have always felt that under the Defence Cooperation deal, Australia was keeping PNG at a certain level of disability,' the *National* editorial said on 25 February. And it defended PNG's right to go elsewhere for hardware and expertise. 'We stand to be corrected,' the editorial concluded, 'but we cannot see a sane PNG Government sanction any mercenary operation on Bougainville.'

While Foreign Minister Genia's statement seemed based on genuine ignorance, the first public statement on the issue by PNG's Defence Minister,

Mathias Ijape, was deliberately untruthful. Ijape had been with Tim Spicer when he wrote the briefing note for Chan detailing the proposed deployment on Bougainville of Sandline's Special Force of forty mercenaries—the cost of which was approved in the NSC decision and covered by the increase in the Sandline contract price from $US30 million to $US36 million. But Ijape's statement of 25 February flatly denied this. 'The Sandline International men will not be sent to the front line on Bougainville but will remain as consultants and trainers,' Ijape claimed. He repeated the 'Australia is to blame' argument. 'Sandline International is giving training to our soldiers more superior than what we have received elsewhere. It is real hard core military stuff, something they have been lacking for a very long time.' Ijape said neither Australia nor New Zealand should complain because both had rejected his approaches to them to provide the PNGDF with the capabilities needed to defeat the BRA.

New Zealand did complain. On the same day that Ijape issued his statement, New Zealand's Prime Minister, Jim Bolger, sent a strongly worded letter to Sir Julius urging a review of the decision to 'employ mercenaries to kill Bougainville rebel leaders'. Prime Minister Bolger said New Zealand did not view the use of 'internationally known mercenaries' as a welcome development in the South Pacific. A few days later Great Britain added its concern. 'In his media release on 24 February,' the British High Commission said in a statement, 'the Prime Minister mentioned an assertion in Sandline International's company brief that they will only undertake projects "acceptable to key western governments such as USA and UK". This is not the case. The British Government has no connection with Sandline International. We do not offer any advice on whether operations in which they are considering involvement are acceptable to the UK or other western governments ... We believe that the use of mercenaries or "consultants" on Bougainville would be counter-productive and would only serve to prolong the conflict.'

Confiscated tapes

The soldiers at the Sir Maori Kiki Air Transport Squadron base on the military side of the Port Moresby airport were getting angrier. They had already surrounded our vehicle preventing us from leaving. It was Monday 24 February 1997 and I was attempting to compile my first television news story on the Sandline mercenaries affair. My cameraman, Frank Mills, and I had driven into the base unhindered. I had even managed to tape a 'piece to camera' standing in front of the squadron base sign explaining how the Antonov transports chartered by Sandline had unloaded significant amounts of weaponry, some of which had been shifted to Wewak.

Unknown to me the Sir Maori Kiki base had also become the hub of the Port Moresby end of Operation Oyster. The PNGDF's Special Forces Unit had set up an office there. Our presence was regarded with great suspicion. The first soldier who approached demanded to know if we had permission. I said I had been trying to contact the Commander all day. Others gathered quickly and the atmosphere sweltered with intimidation. I asked to be allowed to contact the Commander's office but when I went with two soldiers to try to make a call, an officer ordered me out of the base office.

Returning under escort to our station wagon I found that Frank—worried that his camera might be smashed—had extracted the video tape and handed it over. The soldiers also demanded the audio tape out of my recorder. Compliance was the only sensible course. The confiscated video tape contained shots of the Prime Minister, Sir Julius Chan, arriving earlier that day at the official opening of Port Moresby's newest radio station. 'Mercenaries! Is that what you in the Australian media are calling them?' had been Sir Julius's dismissive reply to my attempt at an interview as he and his entourage swept past.

Having surrendered the tapes I feigned anger, masking my apprehension. 'You either arrest us or let us go,' I said. 'We have work to do.' I jumped into the vehicle and started it up even though we were still surrounded. There were some angry shouts and one or two soldiers thumped on the roof. But we edged back out of trouble and drove away—unfortunately without any video evidence of our encounter for the ABC TV News that night.

One letter leaked to the press in those first few days after the Sandline contract was exposed was the one Chris Haiveta had written to his Acting Finance Secretary and the Chairman of Roadco, James Loko, on 23 January, nominating Roadco as the 'vehicle' by which the Government would finance the Sandline deal. That was the letter in which Haiveta informed Loko that he had 'directed the Bank of PNG to transfer K33.6 million out of the sale proceeds from Orogen Minerals Limited to Roadco's account'. Although this direction was withdrawn (on advice from the Finance Department and the Central Bank Governor) and Sandline's money was plundered instead from departmental budgets, the publication of the letter caused embarrassment because of Government promises to the World Bank and the IMF that no Orogen proceeds would be used to fund spending in 1997. Haiveta attacked the *Post Courier* accusing it of 'shoddy reporting' which he claimed had 'the potential to damage Papua New Guinea's international reputation'. PNG's politicians need little help from anyone else doing that.

The management of Orogen Minerals called a special news conference to distance the newly floated company from the mercenary operation. 'The objective of the float was not in any way linked to raising money for Bougainville operations,' Orogen's Managing Director, Charles Lepani, told the media. 'Our concern is to protect the company's reputation, its image. Any decision relating to how the Government spends its share of the proceeds from partly privatising its mining and oil interests is rightly a decision of the constitutionally appointed government. Orogen has nothing to do with that. Whether we like it or not,' Lepani went on, 'the State is the custodian of the interests of Papua New Guinea and the use of these funds is rightly in their domain. We feel that it is regrettable and unwarranted, the nuances and implications that Orogen was involved in the recent revelations, true or not, of hiring mercenaries through the use of Orogen funds from the float. Orogen had no control over the use of these funds once they were handed over to the State.' Orogen's price fell fifteen cents on the Australian Stock Exchange.

Sir Julius agreed to explain the hiring of Sandline in an interview recorded for the ABC's '7.30 Report' on Tuesday 25 February. He acknowledged that Sandline's 'consultants' training the Special Forces Unit at Wewak would go to Bougainville but he claimed they would be going with the men they were training. 'They'll be on the backroom or upstairs type of arrangement, guiding the operations,' he said. And asked if the task of the men they were training was to target the rebel leaders, he agreed.

> *Yeah. It's to get the criminals. The criminals are now not the same criminals as we have been used to in days past when we were dealing with bows and arrows. We're talking about M16s and modern rifles and grenades. And as you know from the recent killings at Kangu Beach a lot of ammunition and a lot of guns have been taken. And we know there have been illegal movements of arms into Bougainville and they're now in the rebels' hands. I can not continually subject my Security Force to just open slather by these criminals. Therefore, we really have to build them up, psych them up for a confrontation they've never experienced before.*

While admitting that the Sandline 'trainers' would be armed and on the ground with the SFU, advising them in operations, Sir Julius still baulked at the term 'mercenaries'.

> *I suppose if you stretch it to the limit, yes. But we are not fools. We are a government. No government will allow its citizens to be killed by foreigners. You'd have to be fools to do that. Mine is a responsible government. In the last eighteen months, you look at all the series of overtures and proposals that I've given to the rebels. I have to say that I am disappointed that they have not accepted one of them although they seemed to pretend that they would. The Australian public continues to entertain all these foolhardy statements from them, and harbours all these criminals who continue to propagandise through the Australian media to get [their message] all around the world. But the fact of the matter is that my Government has done everything that is humanly possible to get them to the table. And I have to tell you after all these months and very hard work we have not got these rebels to the round table.*

The PNG Prime Minister conceded that the involvement of Sandline could destroy any effort to win peace.

> *Yes, that is a possibility. But which government that has the responsibility would not act in the way I am acting at the moment? As we prepare for peace and round tables we must also build up the capacity of our people to be able to stand up to the challenges that may arise. You look at the Israelis and Palestine! What did they do? They just kept shooting. And as they keep shooting each other they talk about peace. And they finally, somehow, got there. I would be very surprised if the Australians didn't hold a stick to back them up if necessary if peace talks fail.*

Asked how confident he was that Sandline would succeed, Sir Julius replied there was no guarantee. 'But if their past experience is a guide they have been successful in other parts of the world. The greatest guarantee that I would get is that my Defence Force people will no longer be sitting ducks. They'll be able to look after themselves out in the field and really deal with the situations as they arise. They'll be dealing with the criminals.' Did he feel Australia had let him down?

> Yes, I think the Australians have let us down. I just can't imagine why the Australians are not coming spontaneously to help us to bring all of this to a conclusion. They handed over an independent, united Papua New Guinea including Bougainville. There are skirmishes in Bougainville. I'm really surprised. We don't want the Australians to fight this thing for us—we just simply want logistic support so that our military can carry this exercise right through. I think we've got to forget we're dealing with some nice guys out there. These nice guys have been knocking at our policeman, they've been knocking innocent civilians, they've been killing the Defence Force. They're criminals. They're murderers.

Asked if Sandline would be allowed to invest in mining in PNG as its boss, Tony Buckingham, had in Africa, Sir Julius said that was not part of the existing contract. 'But if they want to get themselves involved in mining, if some of their connections want to, they are most welcome to buy shares.' He suggested whimsically that they might find Orogen a less risky investment than Bougainville Copper Limited.

Sir Julius's lengthy exposition of his case did not sway anybody in Canberra. 'Australia Rejects Sir Julius's Denial—Situation Serious: Howard' was the headline carried over an AAP report in one of the PNG dailies the next day. It referred to comments the Australian Prime Minister had made to Liberal and National Members at a regular coalition parties meeting. 'He [Howard] said it's obviously a very serious situation, (and) that he became aware last week that a mercenary strike against Bougainville rebels was planned,' a coalition spokesman quoted Howard as having said. 'He said this was the first incursion of mercenaries in this part of the world and that it would be a very regrettable development.' The report went on to say Howard had told the coalition meeting that Australia had played no role in drawing up PNG's Defence White Paper. Further reports out of Canberra referred to a bipartisan motion being drafted by Ian Sinclair (National Party) and Laurie Brereton (Labor) urging the Australian Government to advise PNG that the use of mercenaries on Bougainville would 'prejudice our bilateral relationship including the Defence Cooperation Program'.

On Wednesday 26 February Australia's Foreign Minister, Alexander Downer, called the PNG High Commissioner in Canberra, Brigadier General Ken Noga, to his office. 'I called in Ken Noga on the 26th and expressed our concerns and sought reassurance that these mercenaries would not be used on Bougainville,' Downer said when recalling the affair some months later. Noga had served as the PNGDF Commander in the 1980s and immediately before his posting to Canberra had been head of the PNG equivalent of ASIO, the NIO, the National Intelligence Organisation. However, Downer was left with the impression that Noga had not been fully informed about the Sandline contract. Downer demanded answers from the PNG High Commissioner. 'The set of questions the Foreign Minister has posed to the Chan Government,' the ABC's Graeme Dobell reported from the Canberra Press Gallery, 'are described as part of a measured but firm approach from Australia. And Mr Downer signalled that the answers from Port Moresby will have consequences for future Australian policy.'

'Measured but firm' is not the way anybody in Papua New Guinea was interpreting the Australian approach. The PNG Opposition closed ranks with the Chan Government. 'The Australian Government has gone too far in its criticisms of a decision made by a government of an independent state,' the PNG Opposition Leader, Roy Yaki, said. 'I am amazed and taken aback to learn that politicians from both sides of the Australian Parliament have jointly lashed out at the PNG Government for the engagement of Sandline.' While he said he might not agree with the way a 'private' army had been hired, Australian politicians had no right to make threats. Yaki said the Howard Government's attitude that it could pressure PNG through aid money was interference. It encroached on PNG's sovereign rights. Another Opposition frontbencher, the Member for Wewak, Bernard Narokobi, who had made his name prior to politics as a human rights lawyer, claimed Australia continued to treat PNG 'like its colony' which was 'totally unacceptable'. Narokobi said the reaction made it 'sound like' Australia supported the BRA rebels.

PNG's Defence Minister returned to the attack accusing the Australian Government of having 'a short memory'. He said he could not understand why Australia was so upset at PNG buying military hardware such as helicopters and engaging military consultants for 'special forces' training when his requests to the Australian Defence Minister, Ian McLachlan, for 'high tech equipment and capabilities' and specialised counter-insurgency training under the Defence Cooperation Program had been rejected. 'The Australians refused to help us because they feel ... their people will not welcome such moves. We understand the wishes of the Australian people and their Government's responses,' he said. 'Just what do you expect me as Minister for Defence to do under the circumstances? Just sit down and expect miracles to happen and continue to receive dead soldiers' bodies from Bougainville?' His own answer was that you hire people like Sandline. 'The decision has been made to engage Sandline International,' he said, 'and no one will change the decision.'

Downer's office told the Canberra Press Gallery that Australia would be seeking to exert even more pressure on PNG by urging other 'major players' in the region, especially aid donors, to express their concerns. On the Wednesday afternoon, 26 February, two American jet fighters made a surprise visit to Port Moresby landing with little warning and rolling up to the PNGDF's Air Transport Squadron hangars. Inside the main hangar was Sandline's CASA aircraft–its electronic surveillance platform. The sudden arrival of the two US Air Force F-16 Falcons generated enormous suspicion. The American Embassy claimed there was an innocent explanation. It said the two jets were on their way from an exercise near Geelong, in the Australian state of Victoria, back to their base in Japan when one lost power, so they sought permission to land in Port Moresby. Senior PNG security officials were not convinced, believing this visit by USAF jet fighters was a not too subtle application of the pressure that Canberra had been urging its friends to exert.

One country that did not need any encouragement to complain was Solomon Islands. On 27 February the Solomons' Acting Prime Minister, Francis Saemala, condemned 'in the strongest terms' any intention to deploy mercenaries anywhere in the South Pacific. 'Any involvement of foreign mercenaries in the Bougainville conflict,' he predicted, 'will have far-reaching destabilising effects on Solomon Islands and the rest of the Pacific.' Saemala said every time PNG stepped up military activity on Bougainville there was a surge in cross-border violations. The first such incident for 1997 had already happened. On 16 February, he claimed, 'armed PNG nationals indiscriminately shot at a Police Field Force post and residents of Yariki village in the Shortlands'. Saemala said PNG had refused to consider a United Nations Peacekeeping Force on Bougainville yet it was going off-shore to engage mercenaries. He strongly urged Chan's Government to reconsider, saying he feared mercenaries would only worsen the crisis.

The case that the PNG Government was attempting to put, that Sandline was simply providing trainers and consultants, was undermined when news came from North Queensland that Sandline had contacted the Cairns and Townsville hospitals seeking arrangements for the treatment of its expected casualties. The Queensland Health Department's District Manager stated that nobody would be turned away, that in principle any wounded people would be treated on humanitarian grounds. Queensland's Health Minister, Mike Horan, stated that while the hospitals would treat the critically injured the State Government would bill PNG. The Queensland Premier, Rob

Borbidge, was not so accommodating. Borbidge said any decision to let injured mercenaries into Australia was a Federal Government matter but his view was that Queensland hospitals were for Queenslanders. 'Queensland taxpayers should not be in the business of subsidising other people's wars,' he said. Sandline was not expecting free hospital care. It had the money and was willing to pay for quality treatment.

PNG's Defence Minister told ABC Radio's 'The World Today' that while he knew nothing of the approach that Sandline had made to the hospitals in Queensland it was not something that bothered him. 'We are aware of their involvement in Africa,' Ijape said. 'They have briefed us that in Angola and Sierra Leone they were actually used. Here, we have said, "You will not be used." That is very clear.' But if they were not going to be used on Bougainville why would they be seeking quotes from Queensland hospitals on the cost of emergency operations? 'Well, I mean, as advisers they would be behind the scenes as the Prime Minister said, or at the top of the scenes. So in the course of their advisory role or engagement they could be hurt. And they are probably getting themselves prepared.' Ijape repeated that Sandline was involved because Australia and New Zealand had turned him down. 'I cannot say whether Sandline is giving us the right equipment or the right training. But from what I hear from Wewak the boys are saying this is something they have never got before. So I can assume we have made the right decision. But time will tell.'

SFU boycotts training

The Sandline 'trainers' discovered on Tuesday 25 February that PNG troops have a keen sense, unusual in most armies, of industrial democracy. That morning at Moem Barracks the instructors found they had no one to train. The PNG Special Forces Unit members stayed in their barracks, refusing to come out and claiming they would boycott any further 'sub-standard' training.

The strike caused alarm at PNGDF headquarters and a military flight headed to Wewak. 'When we heard that the troops were refusing to go on training,' Major Gilbert Toropo, Commander of the SFU said, 'myself, Lieutenant Colonel Salamas and Nick Van den Berg went to talk to the troops. Nick Van den Berg went to talk to his men. We went to talk to ours [to ask them] not to rebel against the training.' Major Toropo said his men had passed rigorous selection trials and were the elite of the PNGDF. One of his section leaders, Sergeant Francis Jakis had told him the men objected to being taught 'basic stuff' suitable for raw recruits.

'We almost ended up in a fight with the Sandline personnel,' Sergeant Jakis said. The training had been going for two weeks and his men were dismissive of the fitness level of these Africans they would be fighting alongside. The SFU expected its men to be able to run five kilometres in eighteen minutes. 'I honestly believe that the Sandline troops training with us were totally unfit,' Jakis said. 'When we arrived in Wewak, the first day, we got into full physical training . . . when we started running our boys were fit because we were already psyched up so we would leave them behind—a big gap.'

'On the morning of the 25th,' Sergeant Jakis said, 'myself and two African Sergeants came down from the mess . . . it was roll call time [but] there were no troops around. I was told by Captain Renagi to go up to the Barracks and tell [our boys] to come down. When I approached them they told me, "Only if the training program is amended will we come down and listen." All of them started shouting.' Captain Renagi explained the problem to the head of the Sandline training team, Colonel Johnny Maass. Following Brigadier Van den Berg's visit the training moved inland to the old Agricultural Research Station at Urimo where drills began in intensive counter-insurgency warfare with live ammunition.

There were two other points of contention. One was pay. The SFU troops were angry when they read in the PNG papers what the mercenaries might be getting. 'Morale was still low,' Sergeant Jakis claimed, 'because [our allowance] . . . was only K25 [a day]. The African blacks were getting $US11,000 tax free and the African whites $US20,000 [per month].' The other issue was the ambivalent attitude the SFU had towards training with the Resistance. Ten Bougainvilleans were in training. The PNG soldiers had fresh memories of Kangu Beach where the Resistance turned on and massacred an army unit. Sergeant Jakis claimed a Sandline Major told him the Bougainvilleans would be 'sorted out' after the operation. 'They had a motto,' Jakis said, 'Leave No Trace.'

The Australian and New Zealand Defence Ministers met in Canberra on Friday 28 February. They were in no doubt that Ijape and the PNG Government had made the wrong decision and should reverse it immediately. The two Defence Ministers issued a communique describing the mercenaries as unwelcome. 'We see it as absolutely unacceptable that there should be contracted mercenary forces in the South Pacific,' New Zealand's Defence Minister, Paul East, told a joint news conference. 'To the best of my knowledge this is the first time we have seen a development of this nature in the South Pacific. We don't want to see it take place and we certainly don't want to see it lend any encouragement to anybody else in that regard.' His Australian counterpart, Ian McLachlan, said Australia would look at all avenues to influence PNG, including financial and defence cooperation. 'It's a very, very bad innovation that somebody has seen fit to bring mercenaries to this part of the world,' McLachlan said, 'and we will be doing everything we can to make sure they go away.'

In the midst of all the controversy and adding to the confusion, Papua New Guinea's Provincial Affairs Minister, Peter Barter, announced that he had presented Prime Minister Chan with a draft copy of his proposed PNG Government Peace Strategy for Bougainville. Barter had been developing the peace strategy with the Bougainville Transitional Government for some time. It was a strategy that took no account whatsoever of the NSC decision of mid January. In fact it stated as its basic assumption that all the arguments supporting that decision were wrong. 'The peace strategy assumes that a military solution of the conflict is not possible,' Barter said. 'In the past we have tended to try to impose peace from Waigani. This new peace strategy to a large extent depends on the willingness of all the people on Bougainville to firstly be at peace with themselves, their families, villages and communities and ultimately the entire Province.' In an effort to provide Sir Julius Chan with a possible escape route from the Sandline deal Barter claimed the Prime Minister had 'approved the strategy in principle'.

Barter's announcement was misinterpreted by some in the Australian media as evidence that Chan had backed down. It was, of course, nothing of the sort. Barter's statement quoted Sir Julius as saying the resolution of the conflict 'should be based on initiatives developed by Bougainvilleans themselves'. But that quote was twenty-two months old. It dated back to when the BTG was formed in April 1995. Chan had long since been frustrated with the slow progress the BTG had made. And with an election just four months away he had lost patience completely with Francis Ona, believing he would never negotiate. Barter was working to a different time frame. 'Once the peace strategy is in place,' Barter said, 'I do not imagine it will miraculously bring about peace overnight. It may take many years for peace and normalcy to be restored but at least we now have a plan. The hiccups that have occurred and will continue to occur will not permit us to deviate from our objective, total peace.' Over in Wewak the men were training for a quite different objective.

This first week after the Sandline deal was exposed, was also a time of considerable activity aimed at achieving Haiveta's other aim—the buyout of

CRA's shares in Bougainville Copper. On Monday 24 February the PNG Government received McCowan's proposal relating to Jardine Fleming's involvement as financial adviser in the takeover. McCowan and his associates at Jardine Fleming gave the task the title Project Valentine, taking the name from St Valentine's Day, the day Haiveta met with them in Hong Kong. It was neither a wise nor a sensitive choice. One of the most celebrated atrocities of the Bougainville War was known as the St Valentine's Day Massacre. On 14 February 1990 PNG soldiers dumped the bodies of a number of executed rebel suspects into the sea beyond the reefs off Aropa from one of the Australian-donated Iroquois. Haiveta considered the name inappropriate and by the time he brought the matter to Cabinet in March, Project Valentine had become Project Beacon.

McCowan's letter offered Jardine Fleming's services as 'financial adviser to the Government on an exclusive basis in connection with the acquisition by the Government of shares in Bougainville Copper Limited ... whether by private agreement or general offer'. He proposed that Jardine Fleming's fee be structured in three ways. First, for any shares the Government bought from CRA it would pay Jardine Fleming '1.25 per cent of the number of such shares multiplied by the average of the [BCL] share price over the three-month period' prior to 24 February. Second, for any shares 'acquired by the Government from any shareholders other than CRA Limited and not by way of a general offer', Jardine Fleming would get 1.25 per cent of the gross price paid. And third, if the Government made a general offer to shareholders to acquire BCL shares Jardine Fleming was to get a fee, additional to the 1.25 per cent, 'of 0.25 per cent of the total market capitalisation ... at the highest offer price per share offered'.

The letter was referred to the Finance Department's Economic Policy Adviser, Jim Lamont, who recommended 'outright' rejection of McCowan's proposed fee. 'Jardine has structured the transaction,' he said, in a strictly confidential 'personally transmit by hand only' letter to Acting Secretary Loko 'as though it involved major work assisting in decision making and ultimate implementation of a hostile takeover bid for a very large corporation. Thus their commissions are set at 1.25 per cent under one option and 1.5 per cent under another.' Lamont figured Jardines would get $A3.5 million—equivalent, he said, to 2000-plus working days assuming 'a very generous' daily allowance of $A1500 for each Jardine professional. 'In my view this is outrageous for what (apart from the legals) is a quite simple and straightforward transaction, which boils down to little more than haggling the price and under some circumstances it might be possible to conclude negotiation elements in a day or two's work.'

Lamont had met with McCowan at Loko's request and he had not been overly impressed. 'The State has several people on its payroll with more experience negotiating with mining and petroleum companies than young Rupert McCowan,' Lamont wrote. 'If the Government is not confident to use its own people there [is] no shortage of very senior external Investment Bankers, Mining Consultants etc well known to the State who could be contracted on a daily basis to take on the task. If it is considered necessary to have the full backing of an international merchant banking house then further competition should be added to the current single bid to significantly bring down the fee.' Haiveta rejected this advice that PNG should seek competitive bids. He did write back to McCowan suggesting payment be calculated on a 'time and attendance' basis. But McCowan's subsequent letter, dated 10 March, retained the percentage formula fee tied to the share price.

While Lamont was concerned about the size of Jardines fee, he was perhaps more worried about whether the PNG Government would be able to finance the CRA buyout. He warned Loko of further conflict with the IMF and the World Bank. '[The] project will run contrary to the spirit of the [Structural Adjustment Program] even in the difficult and unlikely event that it can be structured in a way so as to not breach the strict letter of the law with regard to SAP conditionality.' He could not see how the cost could be covered by 'orthodox' budget financing. 'This would increase budget expenditures by around K100 million so breaching IMF expenditure targets. Assuming the resulting deficit were domestically financed it would breach net domestic financing targets (which are already under great stress from the Bougainville initiative transaction) ... If the resulting deficit were externally financed it would significantly breach the ceiling for external commercial borrowing ... Orthodox budgeting techniques appear out of the question if continuation of SAP is desired.'

The IMF's First Deputy Managing Director, Stanley Fischer, who was visiting Canberra in that final week of February 1997, told the ABC's Anne Barker that the IMF was keeping a watch on developments. Project Beacon was not yet public knowledge but the cost of hiring Sandline was very much in the news. Fischer said the IMF–World Bank aid package was designed to achieve economic goals in PNG and the package might have to be reviewed if there was any interference with the agreed budget spending projections and associated borrowings aimed at achieving those goals. 'If the Budget doesn't match that then we're going to have to ask whether all that package is consistent with the goals that we had agreed with them [PNG] to pursue,' Fischer said. 'So ... I don't know what will happen, I don't know what the dimensions of this problem will be, but it could happen.'

Although the $US18 million needed to pay the first half of the Sandline contract had been taken from the first-quarter allocations of government departments, Haiveta was looking for ways by which the money could be made to appear recoverable. He also had the second $US18 million payment to worry about. It was almost due. Under the contract, the second half was to be paid within thirty days of the deployment of Sandline's Command, Administration and Training Team which had arrived in early February. Haiveta's idea was that the whole $US36 million should be treated as an interest-free loan from the State to Roadco. In late February, he rang up Roadco's company secretary, Christopher Burt, the accountant from Coopers and Lybrand who was a co-signatory to the Roadco account. 'He rang me at home,' Burt told the Andrew Inquiry. 'I believe it was the last week of February. He requested I draft a loan agreement ... between the Independent State of PNG and North Fly Highway Development Company. And that the purpose for the loan, to be stated in the loan agreement, was for the company to acquire a majority share-holding in Bougainville Copper Limited.'

Burt was uneasy. 'I did suggest to him that it would be more appropriate for his legal advisers to draft that document because, being a firm of accountants, we are not in the habit of drafting legal documents. But he was very insistent ... He did not give us a time frame but he did make it fairly clear that he wanted it as soon as possible ... I made notes on rough paper whilst I was on the telephone with him and wrote up a file note of that conversation when I got to the office the following day.' Burt drafted the loan document and sent it off the following Monday, 3 March, to Haiveta's home fax number (Haiveta had requested that it be sent to him at home). 'Under the covering fax to the Deputy Prime Minister,' Burt told the Inquiry, 'we recommended strongly that he take his own legal advice both from the State's point of view and also from the company's point of view.' Burt also sent a copy to Vele Iamo at the Finance Department.

'The Roadco loan agreement, in its final form,' Justice Andrew said, 'stated that the State had advanced to Roadco a sum of $US36 million by way of loan. The agreement provided: "... the sum of $US36,000,000 will be treated as an interest-free loan from the Lender in order for the Borrower to eventually acquire shares in the Company (defined as Bougainville Copper Limited) once the Panguna mine is restarted. In exchange thereof, the Borrower [Roadco] will act as the vehicle by which the Lender [the PNG Government] will coordinate and/or finance its Bougainville initiatives. All expenditure incurred under this agreement will be treated as sunk costs in the books of account of the Borrower and will have the first charge on all proceeds from the Panguna mine ..." The agreement provided that the loan was repayable on demand provided that no demand would be made, and no interest would be charged, "before the first anniversary of the reopening of the copper mine" at Panguna.' So the Sandline payment was supposed to be a 'sunk cost'. Sunk it was for sure!

Burt's evidence that he, an accountant, drafted the loan agreement in early March at Haiveta's request contradicted sworn evidence given earlier during the Andrew Inquiry by PNG's State Solicitor, Zacchary Gelu. Gelu had told Justice Andrew under oath that he, the Government's most senior contracts lawyer, had approved the loan agreement more than a month before that, on 31 January, at the same time he approved the Sandline contract. Gelu was adamant when he first appeared before the Inquiry that he had been given a copy of the loan agreement to study by Iamo from the Finance Department on 29 January. 'I was asked to peruse a draft contract which had been prepared by Finance,' he said. 'And on the 31st, I gave my clearance to that particular loan agreement ... I gave legal clearance to it.' He produced a signed clearance letter dated 31 January. Questioned about it, Gelu swore that he had studied the agreement 'thoroughly' in late January.

But after Burt's evidence, Gelu was recalled to appear before Justice Andrew. This second time he brought a prepared statement admitting that he had backdated the 31 January letter. He had not signed it, he said, until 4 March. 'The reason for backdating the letter,' he told the Inquiry, 'was based on instructions ... to ensure consistency between the Sandline agreement and the proposed loan agreement.' PNG's State Solicitor said he made no changes to the Burt draft, simply attaching a covering sheet bearing his office letterhead. Asked if he agreed that his previous evidence had been wrong, Gelu prevaricated. 'I recollect that I did not mention anything in relation to perusing any loan agreement.' Pressed by Counsel Assisting, Ian Molloy, Gelu admitted that he had not cleared any loan agreement in late January, that he had not seen it until more than a month later, that he had then cleared it on 4 March and that he had backdated his clearance letter. Asked why he had not told the truth the first time, the State Solicitor replied: 'I am not sure whether the questions were put to me, I am not sure.'

During his summing up at the end of the formal hearings of the Andrew Inquiry, Molloy drew the Judge's attention to 'disturbing' irregularities including this backdating of government documents. He said the public servants around Haiveta seemed very willing to bend the rules to help him achieve his objectives. 'In fact, it is fair to say some of them were over zealous,' Molloy said, 'and we have the evidence of Mr Gelu and Mr Iamo of their backdating documents which they thought in some way was necessary for getting the NEC approval that was required... And I need hardly remind you, Mr Commissioner, that initially Mr Gelu did say that he had inspected the Roadco loan agreement in draft in late January 1997, but then later... admitted that he had not seen that document until March.' In his final report Justice Andrew referred to this as a matter which should 'be of concern' to the State. 'There seems to be a general acceptance at the political level and amongst public servants that some requirements of the law,' he said, 'can be waived, and documents backdated.' However, Justice Andrew made no reference at all to perjury by one of the Government's top lawyers, the State Solicitor.

Secret agent Bozo

I had early warning that the military were not happy with Sandline but, like Tim Spicer, misread the signals. Chris Haiveta rang me on Wednesday 5 March 1997, telling me that if I could get to Wewak the next morning I would be taken to see Sandline training the SFU. That night, Spicer issued the same invitation when he came to the ABC office to join a live discussion on 'privatising war' on ABC TV's 'Lateline'.

Getting to the airport early, I booked myself on a commercial flight to Wewak but it would not have me there until midday. So I dashed around to the Air Transport Squadron because Haiveta and his party were supposed to be leaving for Wewak on a PNGDF CASA at 7 a.m. But nobody at the Defence base wanted to know. The pilots were nowhere to be seen, one was playing golf. Haiveta turned up on time. So did Spicer. Two hours later, there was still no sign of the CASA being readied. Haiveta called us all together to say he had arranged for some to hitch a lift to Wewak on a private medivac flight. That aircraft developed engine trouble, was delayed twice and, finally, postponed till the next day. Haiveta and Spicer made it on a separate flight. I contacted them in Wewak and they assured me we should still come.

I flew to Wewak with a British journalist, Michael Ashworth. Haiveta and Spicer had left and all the soldiers we met treated us with derision. We were told to go to the Windjammer Hotel and wait. From the hotel we rang Spicer who said one of his men would make contact about midday. We waited. Shortly after noon, the big, wooden doors at the Windjammer that keep everything out including the light were pushed open. We rose expectantly. But in walked... Bozo the Clown! A white man it was, dressed in a clown's costume—tiny hat, big red false nose, make-up, huge baggy trousers and enormous, bright red clown shoes.

It was surreal. Was Sandline's chief Wewak operative in disguise? We wondered if PNG had made a huge blunder and spent $US36 million not on world-class mercenaries but on an international circus act? Had those top secret Air Sofia transports brought in a big-top and a trapeze instead of high-tech hardware? And what use those shoes in the jungle? Bozo had no answers. He gave us scarcely a glance as he plodded through the Windjammer foyer on his way to a Coca Cola promotion.

Another call to Port Moresby led to a message for us to get out to the gate at Moem Barracks. We did. But nobody from the PNGDF would let us in. Finally, after two enraging hours, we were threatened with arrest by Military Police. Just before he left PNG, I asked Spicer if he had any inkling that the PNGDF was dissatisfied with Sandline. 'I recall the day very well when we were going to Wewak and there was a muddle, to say the least,' he replied. 'But I didn't feel there was anything sinister or unhelpful about it. And the fact that you went there subsequently and didn't get in was good security rather than anything else.'

Sir Julius Chan gave evidence that the BCL buyout was raised with him for the first time in late February. 'On the 26th February,' he claimed, 'the Deputy Prime Minister, Mr Rupert McCowan (Jardine), Mr James Loko and Mr Zacchary Gelu discussed possible purchase of BCL shares [with me]. This was announced as recommended by the Deputy Prime Minister because of suspected leakage already to the media. I also asked the Deputy Prime Minister to submit a loan agreement to Cabinet to spell out methods of payment for this contract.' Haiveta claimed this meeting with Chan happened about a month earlier, in late January. But in his written submission to the second inquiry Chan stood by his recollection of the date on which he learnt about what he called this 'Finance Department' initiative. If he did find out about it as late as 26 February Sir Julius embraced the idea with uncharacteristic haste. Just three days later, on Saturday 1 March, following another story in the *Weekend Australian*, he confirmed that buying out CRA was government policy. Chan announced that the proposed takeover of BCL and the hiring of Sandline were part of 'a significant and radical initiative' aimed at resolving the long-running Bougainville problem.

'The original claims and dispute regarding this mine are at the heart of the Bougainville crisis,' Sir Julius said in the press statement he released at Haiveta's urging, 'and are critical to a fair and lasting solution. These are the root causes of our internal battles and the reason for the loss of so many lives.' Yet, once again misreading the antipathy of many of the landowners to any resumption of mining, he claimed the proposed new ownership structure and benefits package would take the landowners 'into account' and allow the mine to reopen. 'A successful venture will speed up restoration and bring enhanced prosperity to Bougainville which is in dire need of a heavy injection of funds.' The PNG Prime Minister was annoyed the timing of the announcement was not of his choosing. 'Press speculation together with leaks,' he said, 'have unfortunately forced the Government to make this announcement prematurely.' The dual strategy—hiring Sandline and buying out CRA—were, he claimed, part of 'a dynamic' plan. 'No demands or speculation or external pressure will deter us from our goal.'

The PNG Cabinet endorsed the strategy the following Wednesday 5 March. Cabinet members were told that the 'classified operation', Project Oyster, was being 'well' implemented. 'It is envisaged that a continuous pursuit of military pressure on the rebels will force them to re-negotiate ... as their main source of support will have been impaired through military operations at a minimum cost.' According to Haiveta's submission these 'mimimum cost' operations would 'provide the desired result to bring back normalcy to Bougainville and hence the reopening of the Panguna mine.' He gave the rationale for the buyout. 'CRA ... may not be too keen to re-enter Bougainville,' he claimed, 'and coupled with potentially excessive demands that they may place upon the State as a condition of their re-entry, plus the high likelihood of their non-acceptance by Bougainvilleans, a strategy will need to be in place ... [to] deal with CRA prior to any reopening of the mine.' The State already owned 19.06 per cent of BCL. Buying CRA's shares would give it 72.66 per cent.

The submission argued that by taking control the Government could 'approach the issue of reopening the Panguna mine with sensitivity, due consideration, caution and care'. It even suggested complete nationalisation. 'Once BCL is fully nationalised as a 100 per cent State-owned company,' the NEC submission said, 'the State can then deal directly with the Bougainvilleans on the most amicable terms acceptable to all key stakeholders concerned prior to any reopening.' Although it was not spelt out in this Cabinet submission one 'key stakeholder', the Secretary of the 'new' Panguna Landowners Association, Francis Ona, was to be excluded from the process. Ona would not be amongst those treated with 'sensitivity, due consideration, caution and care'. Under the other strand of the Chan–Haiveta Government's new 'dynamic and comprehensive' Bougainville initiatives, Ona, by the end of April 1997, was to be either dead—killed by the combined Sandline–SFU strike force—or captured and imprisoned.

The Cabinet submission failed to explain how the PNG Government was going to pay for CRA's 53.6 per cent of BCL's 401 million shares although it did put a 'current market capitalisation' on the company (based on its then share price of fifty-six cents) of $A230 million. Buying CRA out at that market price would cost $A123 million. Just under three weeks earlier, before the flurry of share trading on the day Haiveta met McCowan in Hong Kong, BCL's market capitalisation had been only $A172 million. At that price CRA's shares were worth $A92 million. In an interview with the ABC on 4 March, the day before Cabinet met, Haiveta estimated the range the Government might consider. 'Well, at fair market value it's 53.6 per cent of the total capitalisation of BCL,' he said. 'We could be talking about between 50 and 200 million.' Asked about that sudden St Valentine's Day surge in BCL's price, Haiveta said it could have resulted from a leak. 'But as an interested stakeholder who wanted to acquire more shares,' he said, 'we were very concerned that the escalation could put it out of the Government's reach.'

PNG's Finance Minister denied he had cut a deal with Sandline's other interests over future ownership. 'It will definitely not be part of any deal as has been insinuated,' Haiveta maintained. 'Sandline is not part of the deal. This is a stand alone commercial deal. We will, of course, go to the market. It will be up to the Government to look at the options I will be putting to the National Executive Council tomorrow to see whether they want to go by way of a trade sale or they want to go by way of an international placement offer.' However, the Cabinet submission never did address this crucial question. The issue of how PNG would raise the money to acquire CRA's shares was to be left till later, depending on advice from Jardine Fleming. While Haiveta left open the question of just where the money would come from, he was able to report to Cabinet that Jardine Fleming's fee would be 'equivalent to the costs incurred in the Orogen float'. Cabinet Members were not informed of Lamont's opinion that such a fee was 'outrageous'.

CRA's media spokesman in Melbourne, Ian Head, said the company had still had no official approach from the PNG Government. But, following Chan's announcement it was expecting one. The then boss of CRA in PNG, Moseley Moramoro, who had received the unofficial approach from McCowan in late January had by this time put the entire matter in the hands of head office. 'When Melbourne rang me on that Saturday morning telling me the *Weekend Australian* had a front page story on PNG using mercenaries on Bougainville, I thought, "Ah! That's what it's all about." It clicked. I rang Peter Lowing [the lawyer who had arranged the meeting with McCowan] and said, "I think we've been had! This is now out of my hands. Any further discussions will have to be conducted between one of our people in Melbourne and Jardine Fleming in Hong Kong." Any further decisions would be up to them.'

Justice Andrew reported that during his inspection of a number of McCowan's documents in Hong Kong he found numerous drafts of a letter from Jardine Fleming to CRA dated 27 February. 'The letter, which post-dates the first media reports of PNG's engagement of Sandline, denies that Jardine Fleming had any involvement in negotiations with Sandline or with the transfer of the Sandline payment from PNG. So far as Rupert McCowan is concerned these denials are false,' the Judge said. 'The existence of the draft letters however does support CRA's statement that they were not aware, at least from any meetings concerning the purchase of their shares in BCL, that the State had engaged mercenaries to recapture the mine.'

Brigadier Singirok returned to PNG from his two-week trip to the Philippines on 27 February, five days after the Sandline mercenary story broke. He claimed at the Andrew Inquiry it was during this trip that his opposition to Sandline hardened and became a resolve to get rid of them: 'I decided to abort this operation.' Singirok was annoyed that Spicer had more access to PNG's political leaders than he did. 'I quote an incident when he turned up at Jackson's airbase and directed a PNGDF CASA to [fly]... the Deputy Prime Minister to Wewak without my approval.' Singirok cited this as just one example of how Spicer had issued orders relating to PNGDF resources outside the proper framework of command and control. 'Mr Spicer, in conversation with some officers, stated quite openly that he was a strategic adviser to the Prime Minister,' Singirok complained, 'which leaves me completely out of the equation on these command and control arrangements.' He claimed Spicer was bypassing him and issuing commands after discussing things with the politicians.

His relations with Ijape, never excellent, plunged to new depths. 'I think the Minister was under extreme pressure,' Singirok replied when asked about their relationship in the wake of the public exposure of the Sandline operation. 'When I came back [from the Philippines], I was not able to see the Minister. On 5 March, when I contacted him by phone at his Parliament office, I was quite surprised and quite shocked when he said words to this effect, "You and the Secretary were looking for fat Asian ladies to massage you. I want you to explain your trip." And I was extremely disappointed when he used such language towards me as the Commander of this country.' The day after Singirok's return home, 28 February, there is a reference in his diary indicating that he was hatching a plan to terminate the Sandline deal. It was a discussion with someone he codenamed Flash Gordon. Singirok was later to claim Flash Gordon was the PNGDF's Catholic chaplain, a Bougainvillean, Father Rossi. Asked by Marshall Cooke QC if this was the date that his 'crisis of conscience' brought him down in favour of action, Singirok replied: 'Yes.'

Cooke demanded to know why Singirok used code names in his diary. His chaplain was allegedly 'Flash Gordon' and, according to Singirok, his wife, Weni, was 'Stone'. Outside the Inquiry Singirok said 'Stone' was a reference to the fact that Weni was a rock supporting him. But Molloy cast doubt upon this. He claimed there were instances in the diary where 'Weni' and 'Stone' appeared on the same line. And in another place there was a reference to 'Another day with Stone'. Molloy questioned Singirok at the second inquiry as to why he would write that when he had lived with his wife for many years. He stood by what he said about 'Stone' being Weni.

The diary became a real headache for Singirok before both inquiries. In his written submission to the Andrew Inquiry he had included photocopies of diary entries to back his claims as to the dates on which certain events occurred. The Commission requested that he produce the complete diary which he agreed to do, provided he could blank out references that he claimed were of a personal or family nature. However, Cooke seized on perceived inconsistencies and grilled Singirok for days, regularly ridiculing him. Singirok complained that his diary was never intended to be a comprehensive record. It was just for his personal use. But the diary provides important detail on the first two weeks in March leading up to the Brigadier's move against the mercenaries.

Chapter Twelve

Undetected Manoeuvres

*The Project Oyster Planning Goes Ahead; Singirok
Chooses His Man; Howard Meets Chan;
Preparations for Rausim Kwik
1–16 March 1997*

Sandline had plans to manipulate the media. Its psychological warfare operations included spreading fear amongst the population of central and south Bougainville. The idea was to scare the people so that they would either flee from intended target areas or be too terrified to provide assistance and support to BRA leaders on the move. 'I would not want to necessarily give away details of plans that may still be valid in the future for the PNGDF,' Tim Spicer said in an interview just before he left PNG in April. 'But I think people should understand that just having firepower doesn't mean you are going to use it. It means you are able to use it. And you can use it selectively or not at all depending on how you wish to deploy those assets.' He referred specifically to the Mi-24 helicopter gunships and the rockets they would carry. 'Sometimes it's enough to have them and to threaten to use them without actually using them.' Amongst the 'guidelines' in the Project Oyster planning document prepared by Nick Van den Berg was a plan 'to concentrate the main effort where it will create the biggest visual impact.'

But in the first few days of March—when D-Day for Project Oyster (the day the SFU, mercenaries and helicopter gunships would be deployed to Bougainville) was still a month off—it was BRA propaganda that inadvertently spread the most terror. Moses Havini, the Australian-based rebel spokesman, issued a release on 1 March claiming Sandline had brought in four times as many mercenaries as was in fact the case. 'BRA Intelligence intercepted six call signs they calculate to entail five to six companies of mercenaries,' Havini claimed. The alleged numbers in each group ranged from twenty to forty.

'If the above numbers are correct,' Havini's statement quoted BRA General Sam Kauona as claiming from his command post on Bougainville, 'then we are talking in terms of about 170 mercenaries.' Some news reports quoting Havini placed them all on Bougainville already. Agence France Press (AFP) put the number even higher. The newsagency's Auckland correspondent, Mike Field, quoted 'previous BRA intelligence' as saying there were '40 white and 150 black mercenaries, mostly combat veterans from South Africa'.

One Australian journalist, Lindsay Murdoch, flew to Gizo in Solomon Islands and his reports in the Melbourne *Age* not only had the operation well under way but, according to his BRA sources, the rebels had won the early exchanges. 'A rebel intelligence officer said guerrilla forces had attacked a mercenary base in southern Bougainville,' Murdoch reported. 'The officer said villagers saw three foreigners leading an eight-strong patrol from the eastern coast town of Arawa yesterday towards the centre of the island.' Murdoch quoted Kauona as alleging the mercenaries 'were ready to use outlawed weapons, including chemical and nerve agents'. In a feature titled 'As Helicopters Swoop, Tactics Share the Air' Murdoch wrote of helicopters swooping 'low over the mountains' and he relayed rebel reports from Bougainville of 'the arrival of new PNG forces, who this time have heavily armed strangers amongst them'. According to the *Age*, Francis Ona, the 'reclusive, sword-wielding President', told his BRA fighters to 'shoot on sight anybody without a clearance who enters the areas they control'.

This alarmed AusAid. The Australian aid agency pulled all its workers, involved in restoration projects, out of the province. The Australian High Commission in Port Moresby advised all thirteen Australian citizens known to be on Bougainville to leave. The High Commission said Ona's threat 'to shoot on sight' foreigners who did not have a BRA clearance had to be taken seriously. In Australia the Bougainville rebel support group understood the damage such negative publicity could do. They issued a statement in Ona's name denying he ever made such a threat and describing Australian aid workers as 'honoured guests'. Spicer also decided it was time for media management. He granted three 'exclusive' interviews on that Sunday, 1 March. 'We have several clear rules,' he told the ABC. 'One is that any of our people who work for a government are subordinate to the command structure of that government's military forces. We are not a separate force.' And he rejected the mercenary tag. 'We are not coup makers,' he said. 'We are not government breakers.'

Moses Havini kept churning out BRA propaganda, some of it closer to the mark than his claim that mercenaries had landed on Bougainville. On the ABC he said he believed that Sandline and Executive Outcomes must be after part-ownership of the copper mine. 'Just to come and kill for a fee would not have been sufficient for these mad killers.' Mad killers was not a description Spicer fancied. Cool and confident during his interview in Port Moresby, Spicer dismissed the claims that he had upwards of 200 African troops in PNG. He confirmed there were forty men he described as 'competent operators and technical experts' in Wewak. Spicer had a fading black eye—his tame explanation for it being that it happened before he left England, at home with his children. Over in the East Sepik province villagers in the area near the 2nd Battalion's jungle training ground were warned to stay clear. Defence personnel told them a training exercise involving live ammunition and new weapons would run throughout March. The airspace over the old Urimo agricultural research station was declared a no-fly zone.

Sir Michael Somare, whose East Sepik Regional electorate included the Urimo camp, entered the debate, opposing any use of 'East Sepik soil' to train 'private assassins and mercenaries to go to Bougainville and kill my people'. Somare, who was planning another bid to become Prime Minister after the mid-year elections, called for the immediate cancellation of what he called 'this hideous contra scheme'. He wanted all 'unacceptable foreigners' involved to be deported and permanently blacklisted from PNG. 'Shame, shame, shame,' he said in a news statement also signed by seven other members of his National Alliance, 'and resign en masse as your Government is no good for Papua New Guinea. Get out and stay out!' Prime Minister Chan replied calling Somare 'a disgraced ex-Statesman'. 'I must reiterate,' Sir Julius said, 'that Sandline will not be—must I repeat this for Sir Michael personally?—that Sandline will not be involved in a frontline capacity.' The Project Oyster planning document then in preparation listed its force strength for Bougainville as including Sandline's forty on-the-ground troops.

In Australia John Howard appeared on Channel 10's 'Meet the Press'. And while he reiterated his warnings to PNG he acknowledged the limits to what Australia could do. 'It's not the sort of issue where one should make over-the-shoulder comments on the run,' he said. 'You are dealing with a very sensitive area of international relations and something that is right on our doorstep and something that the rest of the world sees Australia as having a particular responsibility for. You're also dealing with an independent country and you have the sensitivity of a former colonial power telling a former colony what it thinks it ought to be.' But Howard said he had told Sir Julius PNG's reputation could be damaged. 'It really is against that country's medium- and long-term interests to use mercenaries to wipe out the BRA. The only way you can solve that problem is by genuine negotiation,' he claimed. 'We've put that to the Prime Minister of PNG repeatedly. We'll continue to do a number of things to try and bring home to the PNG Government the folly of the course on which we believe that Government has now embarked.'

Planning For April Fools' Day

Any reading of the Project Oyster planning document prepared by Brigadier Nick Van den Berg and dated 13 March 1997 puts the complete lie to the constant PNG Government claims that Sandline personnel would not have been involved in a frontline capacity. Marked 'Secret' the document stated the 'mission' as being to 'neutralise the BRA (active opposition) on Bougainville by 30 April 1997 through equipping, training and deploying the SFU and attached elements'. These 'attached elements' included sixty Sandline personnel—forty in the Sandline Special Force plus twenty others, including those needed to fly and maintain the helicopter gunships and transports and operate the sophisticated electronic warfare package.

Brigadier Van den Berg listed the 'Task Force Composition' as:

Land— SFU: 45;
Sandline: 40 + 20;
RF [Resistance Force]: 3 + 7;
Mortar Platoon (minus): 20;
Support Elements: 20;
Security Platoon: 20 + 29.
Air— 2 x Mi-24;
2 x Mi-17;
1 x Cessna 337;
1 x CASA 212 (EW);
1 x CASA 235.
Maritime— 1 x Landing Craft Heavy (possibly 2);
2 x Fast Patrol Boats.

D-Day was to be April Fools' Day, 1 April. The two Mi-24 helicopter gunships and the two Mi-17 helicopter transports were to arrive in Wewak on 17 March. For the following eleven days (D-16 to D-6) there was to be 'pilot refresher training and ground training'. The movement from the 'Concentration Area (Wewak) to Assembly Area (Loloho)' was to take three days from D-1. The advance party moving with the helicopters would include Sandline's 'Tactical Commander'.

Casualties were expected. 'Due to the fact that Sandline employ two

> medical doctors and several operational medical orderlies, medical aid will be presented not only to Sandline personnel, but also to PNGDF soldiers. The casualty evacuation system is included in the Medical Support Plan.' Under the heading 'Handling of KIA' [killed in action], the document stated: 'Own forces will be evacuated to Port Moresby as soon as possible. Sandline personnel from there according to company policy and international rules and regulations with regard to transporting bodies across international borders.'

The Australian Senate passed a motion moved by Greens Senator, Dee Margetts, calling for a comprehensive review of all Australian aid to Papua New Guinea 'including defence cooperation'. The Senate noted with 'grave concern' reports that the PNG Government had 'contracted a force of mercenaries to undertake covert military operations' on Bougainville. PNG's former Foreign Secretary, Gabriel Dusava, who had resigned to contest the elections, accused Australia of interference. Dusava said his experience as head of PNG Foreign Affairs had taught him that even the most important national security issues could not be kept confidential because of eavesdropping by Australian spy agencies. 'Prime Minister John Howard and Alexander Downer have recently made it plain,' he claimed, 'that there is a continuing attitude in Australia that whatever initiative PNG tries for its own national good, Australia is justified in directing the course as well as the result of that initiative.' Others agreed. A former captain and later coach of the PNG national rugby league team, the Kumuls, John Wagambi, said the reaction from Australia made him furious. 'Australia should back right off.'

Sir Julius made a similar point to Queensland's Opposition Leader, Peter Beattie, who happened to be visiting Port Moresby. 'I reiterated that Papua New Guinea would not entertain diplomatic exchanges through the media,' Chan said after their meeting. PNG's Opposition Leader, Roy Yaki, accused Australia of being patronising. 'Whilst I do not support the manner and style in which the services of the mercenaries were engaged by Prime Minister Chan,' Yaki said, 'the intensive lobby against this particular issue by the Australian Government and governments of neighbouring states is alarming, and to a large extent, quite unacceptable.' He was suspicious of Australia's motives. 'In one sense, the recent chorus of disapproval over a legitimate decision of a legitimate government,' PNG's Opposition Leader said, 'demonstrates the Australian Government's hidden agenda to continue its influence on certain activities and issues in PNG by way of remote control of the actions of any PNG Government which have an impact on Australia's security.'

Alexander Downer was by this time devoting his full attention to the rapidly developing crisis in relations with PNG. He cancelled a planned trip to Mauritius for the launch of a new trade bloc, the fourteen-nation Indian Ocean Rim Association for Regional Cooperation. Graeme Dobell reported from Canberra that Cabinet's National Security Committee met to discuss PNG's use of mercenaries and the implications for Australian aid policy and defence cooperation. Prime Minister Howard chaired the two-hour meeting which studied intelligence assessments and discussed Australia's options if PNG rejected Canberra's concerns. All aid to Bougainville was suspended. AusAid's Assistant Director for PNG, Murray Proctor, described it as 'one of those unfortunate outcomes of the mercenary issue coming to light'. Proctor told the ABC it was a pity. 'We were making significant progress in rehabilitation projects. The fact that all those will now really go on hold is certainly something that I would imagine would worry the Papua New Guinea Government.'

PNG was getting terrible press in Australia. But one commentator was even more critical of the Howard Government. 'Hell, the sage tells us, has no fury like a woman scorned,' the Australian Defence Association Director, Michael O'Connor, wrote in the *Australian*. 'But if we are to make any sense of the Federal Government's incredible overreaction to Papua New Guinea's mercenary adventure, a pretty close second must be the rage of an ignored surrogate parent.' O'Connor, who had once served in the Pacific Islands Regiment, argued that one reason for PNG's desperate gamble had been overlooked. 'Australia's recent contribution,' he wrote, 'seems to have been to insist that there can be no military solution to the Bougainville problem, seemingly ignoring the reality that Port Moresby has been seeking a political solution for years. What Canberra seems to forget is that it takes two parties to achieve a political solution and the rebels, now largely immune from military pressure but also isolated from the bulk of Bougainville's population, have shown no interest in a compromise of any kind.'

While Chan undoubtedly won some support at home by turning the mercenary issue into one of national sovereignty he still had his local critics. The PNG Trade Union Congress claimed the military advisers were 'nothing but mercenaries' and accused Chan of setting a very dangerous precedent because future governments might use the decision to justify calling in mercenaries to stay in power while those outside government might do so to stage a coup. 'The Government's decision to hire mercenaries ... is repugnant and an outright affront to the democratic cause and internal stability,' the PNGTUC claimed. However, the trade union body was not so damning about the proposed buyout of CRA's majority share in the copper mine. 'The announcement', it said, 'should be welcomed but only on the basis that the landowners and people of Bougainville participate fully in its equity and operations as a means of settlement of the Bougainville conflict. We urge the Government to pursue this option with all honesty.'

The Bougainville Transitional Government also welcomed the decision to take over BCL. 'Premier Gerard Sinato has described the move as an important first step towards positively dealing with the Panguna mine issue,' a release from his office in Buka said. But Sinato had some reservations. He urged Chan not to think he could deal with the mine in isolation from political issues. And the Premier was disturbed that the first he learnt about the plan was from the media. 'It is important that the National Government discusses its initiatives with the BTG at the negotiation table as early as possible,' he said, 'to avoid the people misunderstanding the National Government's good intention to re-open the mine.' Francis Ona's attitude towards mining received a good airing that week on ABC TV's 'Foreign Correspondent'. An independent filmmaker, Wayne Coles-Janess, had trekked into the mountains in January and his interview with Ona was broadcast on the night of Tuesday 4 March.

'We truly believe that all of Bougainville is under the threat of destruction by these foreign mining companies,' Ona said. He repeated his long-held belief that PNG planned to open another four Panguna sized open-cut mines as soon as it reclaimed control of the province. Although the whole island of Bougainville is highly prospective there has been a moratorium on exploration outside the Panguna lease since the early 1970s. Despite this Ona claimed 'to know' that aerial surveys had confirmed and quantified massive copper reserves and five mines would be brought into production quickly if he made any compromise. 'We have decided that our economy will be based on agriculture,' he said. Coles-Janess asked Ona if he would accept short-term autonomy provided it led to a referendum on independence? 'It's not accepted,' he replied, 'because I do not trust Papua New Guinea and its army.' Asked what the future was for Bougainvilleans who wanted to remain part of PNG, Ona replied: 'Well, if they want to be part of Papua New Guinea they've got a place to go. And that is back to PNG.'

The Member for Wewak, Bernard Narokobi, claimed the Government lacked 'moral decency' to be thinking of spending more than $A100 million 'on buying a closed mine' while people were dying from lack of medical services. He said church-run health services were closing due to shortages of government funds. All over PNG health services were in chaos because the changes to the provincial government system had delegated responsibility for funding health workers to the provinces. PNG's Church Medical Council said only seven of nineteen provincial governments had provided any money. The Catholic Bishops Conference urged BCL shareholders not to sell to the Government. The Conference Chairman, the Bishop of Alotau, Bishop Desmond Moore, questioned why the Government wanted to buy the dormant mine instead of helping to fund Peter Barter's peace strategy. Bishop Moore also called on the Government to speed up investigations into the assassination of Theodore Miriung to show it was serious about protecting the rights of the people.

From Sydney Moses Havini continued to issue releases detailing the (as yet non-existent) advance of the mercenaries across Bougainville. 'Foreign mercenaries have begun their offensive in the Papua New Guinea Province of Bougainville,' AFP reported on 4 March, 'launching a mortar attack and taking up positions near a huge copper mine.' The newsagency quoted Havini as claiming 'a troop of mercenary-led soldiers also moved in from south-west Bougainville and took up positions at the village of Sikoreva, near the enormous Panguna copper and gold mine'. While none of this had happened, the BRA releases found a ready and gullible audience amongst generally ill-informed Australian and New Zealand journalists suddenly given the task of covering the unfamiliar 'mercenaries for Bougainville' story.

The Solomon Islands Prime Minister, Solomon Mamaloni, threw the international media a handy and lurid South Seas quote. Responding to a PNG security brief leaked by Sir Julius Chan's Media Director, Mark Lillyman, claiming the Solomons had paid for arms that went to the BRA in 1996, Mamaloni attacked the Chan Government's deal with Sandline. 'It is a dangerous precedent which will destabilise the peace and harmony within the Forum countries,' he said, 'and throw everyone back into the former cannibalism days.' He said the Solomons was following through its threat to take the matter to the International Court of Justice. The Solomons would forward its case to Geneva before the end of March. PNG's Foreign Minister, Kilroy Genia, responded, accusing the Solomon Islands Government of taking 'mercenary delight in facilitating access to Bougainville by journalists and the BRA elements' and thereby ignoring PNG's immigration laws and sovereignty.

Two legal cases challenging the constitutionality of the mercenaries deal were launched in PNG. The first was initiated by the principal of a Port Moresby-based law firm and aspiring politician, Rimbink Pato. Pato was attempting to revive the once formidable United Party (most remembered in PNG for having opposed independence). Pato's case named Sir Julius

Chan and Chris Haiveta as the first and second defendants and claimed the Sandline contract was illegal because the funding was not provided for in the 1997 budget. He also claimed they had conspired to raise an unauthorised force. The second challenge was filed the following week by the Individual and Community Rights Advocacy Forum (ICRAF), one of PNG's more vigorous NGOs. ICRAF filed two separate applications in the Supreme Court. The first sought enforcement of the rights of Bougainvilleans and others who had suffered as a result of the alleged 'unconstitutional and unlawful war' waged since 1988. The second was a special reference for an opinion on whether Sandline could be classified as an unauthorised force.

Brigadier Singirok told the Andrew Inquiry that during this first week in March—he put the date variously as the 4th, 6th or 7th—Spicer had told him that because of all the publicity, Project Oyster had lost the element of surprise and the strategy needed to be reviewed. 'The whole emphasis would be the mine,' Singirok claimed. 'Spicer ... told me to drop all other operational plans and go straight to the Panguna mine with a battalion size group.' Singirok had already made up his mind to get rid of Sandline. This, he said, reinforced his decision. He had asked Cabinet for K6 million to fund the 45-member SFU's involvement in Project Oyster. That had been rejected. So he knew who would have to meet the costs of mobilising an entire 500-member battalion—the PNGDF. This was the week that Singirok's office was informed that K6.7 million of his already strained Defence budget had been withdrawn to help pay the first half of the Sandline contract. Singirok told the Inquiry that he told his Acting Chief of Operations, Colonel Walter Salamas, on 3 March that Project Oyster 'was not going to work'.

Singirok's diary reveals that all through this week he began informing those officers he trusted most that he might move against the mercenaries. Salamas was not one of them. The Acting Chief of Operations was kept in the dark until very late in the planning. On 2 March there is a diary entry: 'Confided in ... Gilbert.' Major Gilbert Toropo was Commander of the Special Forces Unit. On 3 March: 'Break-up of Sandline ... Confided with CO 1RPIR.' That was Lieutenant Colonel Tokam Kanene, Commander of the 1st Battalion based at Taurama Barracks. On 4 March: 'Gilbert came in to see me.' On 5 March: 'Confided with CO 2RPIR.' The Commander of the 2nd Battalion which was based in Wewak was Lieutenant Colonel Michael Tamalanga. Like Kenene, Tamalanga had been promoted to command his battalion by Singirok. '[By] the first week of March,' Singirok told the Andrew Inquiry, 'senior officers were quite anxious to know my official view of Sandline ... I directed [Tamalanga] to come down to Moresby.' Singirok told the Inquiry he informed Tamalanga he was cancelling Project Oyster.

On 6 March there is a diary entry detailing a lunch at a Port Moresby Chinese restaurant with the Police Commissioner and the Defence Secretary: 'Confided with Bob Nenta, Secretary Melegepa at the Golden Bowl.' Brigadier Singirok said he never went into the details of what he had in mind but his concerns with Sandline and its proposed strike on Bougainville were discussed. 'I made reference to the fact that we have a serious problem and if they were smart enough at that time they would have seen what I was getting at,' he told Justice Andrew. Diary entry, 7 March: 'Reviewed my statement to the nation ... Discussed threat. Salamas confided with me after meeting with Tim, Nick and Salamas.' Asked what 'threat' he was referring to, Singirok said the word was Spicer's. 'As I said ... by 6 and 7 of March, Tim Spicer had insisted that we reassess the threat and the fact that instead of going straight to Kongara we should now redo our operational plan to go into Panguna ... Salamas by then was also concerned because ... he was becoming worried about the consequences.'

On Saturday 8 March Singirok chose the man he wanted to command Operation Rausim Kwik, Major Walter Enuma. His diary note of 8 March reads: 'Worked on the speech the whole day. Spoke to Ops Officer for Rausim Kwik. Felt honoured.' He told the Andrew Inquiry 'felt honoured' were the words Enuma had used about being appointed to carry out the task. Enuma, highly regarded as one of the bravest and most capable officers in the PNGDF, with a distinguished record on Bougainville, had been seconded to the PNG Electoral Commission in late 1996 to help with arrangements for security for the 1997 national elections. 'I was busy making tours of the country and doing these surveys,' Enuma said in an interview recorded in late 1997, 'until one Friday afternoon, I got a message from the Military Adviser to the Commander that the General wanted to see me quietly in his house that weekend. So I drove up to Murray Barracks, left my car in the Officers Mess and went around the back and eventually got to his house on the top of the hill. I wasn't sure why he called me up.'

Enuma said that as he approached the house he was wondering whether he was about to be reprimanded. For what he was not sure. 'I was thinking it may be about something he was not happy with or perhaps he wanted a briefing on the election plans. But because I was told to go there quietly I expected there might be something.' Singirok told him he was disturbed about the engagement of Sandline and was worried the hiring of mercenaries would undermine PNG's national integrity. 'He told me it was his moral duty as Commander of the Force to be entrusted with the security of the whole country. This was one of those "quick-fix" deals. So I told him I would have a look at the orders. We went down and I read the brief that he had prepared. I had heard about the mercenaries so I told him, "I'll accept the job but I will need time to do my research and put the plans in place". He asked me to take two weeks special leave from the Electoral Commission.' Enuma left the Commander's residence. 'I had a bit of soul searching to do because what he basically told me to do was rebel against the government.'

Major Enuma decides

Sweating, Walter Enuma powered his way up the dauntingly steep hill from Ela Beach to the Port Moresby Travelodge. This day in early March 1997 the infantry Major had more to think about than just staying fit. He had just come away from a secret meeting with his Defence Force Commander, Brigadier General Jerry Singirok, who had asked him to take command of the operation to deport the mercenaries, Operation Rausim Kwik. 'Even before this whole operation, I was preparing,' he told me in September 1997. 'I had a feeling that I'd be involved in something big. So from early January, I'd got into exercise. I was doing runs up and down that Travelodge hill every morning doing my sprints and getting prepared. By that stage I was pretty fit. So in that regard I was ready. The boss had something for me to do.'

He was still wrestling with the decision. Singirok had told him there was corruption in the $US36 million Sandline deal. 'I had been doing these security surveys of the country for the Electoral Commission, looking at economic disparities, politics and we had covered things such as politically motivated criminals, white collar crime and corruption. So I was pretty well bottled up on all this wheeling and dealing that was going on. And I was pretty pissed off! I was determined to ensure that this particular election was a fair one. And that we could get the people to choose their leaders without fear or favour or influence in either monetary terms or by force.'

But this was not an easy decision for Enuma. 'I went for my normal run at Ela Beach. And after I did my sprint, I was sweating up at the Travelodge and I thought, "There's a church here, at the back somewhere. I think I'll sit down there and just reflect. And ask the Big Man if he wants me to do this job." So I walked across to St John's Anglican church. There was this memorial plaque outside. I just stood there and read it. It said: "In grateful memory of those who gave their lives in the defence of this country." I said to myself, "How appropriate." So I walked in and sat down. I didn't pray so much as questioned my conscience. "Do you really want me to do this job? Is it for me? Is it meant?" Because it was going to have a profound effect on the whole country. It means mutiny, a rebellion against the government of the day.'

His reflections took some minutes. 'I cooled down, walked out, came down to Ela Beach. I didn't go for my normal swim. Just got in the car and drove. And as I was driving home I said, "Yeah, I've got to do this job." '

Singirok's plot to undo the Sandline deal was a tightly kept secret. The PNG Government knew nothing about it. Neither did Australia. Foreign Minister Downer admitted later that all the advice he had been given was that Singirok was heavily committed to the mercenary operation. Indeed, on the weekend that Singirok chose Enuma as the man to expel the mercenaries, Australia set up a secret meeting between John Howard and Sir Julius Chan in a desperate effort to persuade Chan of the folly of PNG's proposed joint military action with Sandline. The meeting took place on Sunday 9 March at the Australian Prime Minister's official Sydney residence, Kirribilli House. On the Friday Downer had finally received a reply to his questions regarding Sandline. PNG's Foreign Minister, Kilroy Genia, claimed yet again the 'consultants' were trainers. 'I want to categorically deny that we have engaged Sandline International as mercenaries to eliminate our own people,' he said in a statement. 'We are a responsible Government and will not in any way engage these consultants on the ground in Bougainville.'

Genia said he had spoken to Downer by phone 'and we are both satisfied'. Downer was not satisfied. He knew Genia was either lying or unaware that Sandline's men would go to Bougainville. The statement fooled some however and reports in the Australian media spoke of PNG 'softening' its stand because Sandline would be 'quarantined' to mainland PNG. But Downer was not looking for another public brawl hoping for better news from the Kirribilli House meeting. Australia's Shadow Foreign Minister, Laurie Brereton, was calling on Downer to give PNG the six months notice of cancellation of aid required under the aid treaty. 'I think at this delicate time,' Downer was quoted as saying, 'it is important we keep our options open and continue to work quietly behind the scenes.' In his statement, Genia claimed no Australian money had gone to pay Sandline. 'The aid money is specifically tied to programs,' he said, 'and the other component that goes to budget support is also used for specific projects including restoration programs on Bougainville.' That also was not strictly correct. The budget support grants go straight into the PNG Public Account and so 7.5 per cent of Sandline's payment came from Australian taxpayers.

Howard had a four-hour meeting with Sir Julius over lunch at Kirribilli House. News of the secret meeting between the Prime Ministers came out that afternoon. Howard told Sydney radio station 2UE the following morning that Sir Julius had told him he had 'a very big problem' and that their lengthy discussions had 'canvassed' many things. 'We think any reasonable alternative to mercenaries is to be preferred,' he said. Sir Julius was not available for immediate comment but a spokesman said Howard's term 'reasonable alternatives' summed up what was discussed. As the Australians found out a few days later, Chan did not consider any of the alternatives 'reasonable'. What Howard offered were changes to the Defence Cooperation Program including improved training for the PNGDF and extra non-military aid for Bougainville. Despite being accused of it by some of the BRA's more fanatical supporters, Howard never offered to put Australian troops onto the island nor to provide PNG with Sandline-equivalent electronic warfare equipment. Australia also refused to buy PNG out of the Sandline contract.

Sir Julius revealed at the Andrew Inquiry that he had invited Tim Spicer to brief him prior to this meeting with John Howard. He said he had given Spicer a desk in the Office of the Prime Minister on the top floor of the PNG Parliament building. 'I gave him a desk when he came so that he could prepare this brief for me before I went down to Australia.' Singirok was to claim later that this desk that Spicer was given to use whenever he was in Chan's office was proof that Spicer had become Chan's chief military adviser, further marginalising Singirok as Commander of the PNGDF. Another 'adviser' to Sir Julius, his Media Director, Mark Lillyman, told the media on the Monday following the Kirribilli House meeting how PNG could knock down the price it would have to pay for CRA's shares in the copper mine. CRA would be billed for the war! Although the PNG Government had always held one-fifth of the shares and been represented on the BCL board, Lillyman claimed the Government would argue that the war was the fault of Rio Tinto and so any purchase price would have to take into account the costs run up by PNG since the insurrection began.

As the Australians waited for Chan's considered response to the offers made by Howard in Sydney, preparations went ahead in PNG for two quite different military operations. One, Rausim Kwik, was to cancel the other, Project Oyster. On Monday 10 March Major Enuma presented his 'concept of operations' for Rausim Kwik to Singirok. On that day the PNGDF Commander also sent a draft of a speech he had prepared for the Special Forces Unit to the SFU's second-in-command, Captain Bola Renagi. Captain Renagi was in charge of the men being trained in Wewak and he was directed to read this speech to them when Rausim Kwik began. Sandline's 'trainers' continued their training oblivious to what was coming. The only journalist allowed to observe the training that week, Michael Ashworth of the London *Independent*, wrote that it was relentless. 'The day starts at 5.30 a.m. with an hour of Battle PT. From 8 a.m. to 5 p.m. the platoon is taught the theory and practice of immediate action drills. There is night training most nights. This arduous schedule is followed six days a week, with Sunday the only rest day.'

Misinformation abounded. An AAP story written out of Sydney claimed there were 'four Australians amongst the 125 mercenaries' in Papua New Guinea. There were no Australians. And there were not 125 mercenaries. However, the source for this 'scoop' claimed there were and that he, an ex-Vietnam veteran who had also fought for the Rhodesian Army, was one of the four Australians. Not only that, he was the brains behind the whole scheme. 'One is the architect of the plan under which the PNG Prime Minister, Sir Julius Chan, awarded a contract to Sandline International,' AAP reported. The story also quoted this supposed 'architect' of the deal on the make and numbers of helicopters Sandline was taking to Bougainville for the strike against the rebels. 'He said PNG was in the process of buying 10 to 12 Puma helicopter gunships and troop carriers.' It was utter rot.

One of the two legal challenges to the Sandline contract went before the courts on Wednesday 12 March. The PNG Government applied to include the Director General of the National Intelligence Organisation as a party to the case brought by lawyer, Rimbink Pato. The tactic was to prevent government officers sworn to secrecy from providing documents. 'The NIO has applied to be joined as a party,' Chris Haiveta explained, 'in order to suppress information on the ground that the documents are privileged... and it is necessary to protect the State's interest in protecting security over the right to freedom of information.' Later, in his submission to the Andrew Inquiry, Haiveta claimed PNG's Constitution was too liberal. 'I have always held the firm view that the interests of the Independent and Sovereign State of Papua New Guinea are not afforded proper protection in the Constitution as [are] the rights and freedoms of individuals. No law exists to give authorities the right to properly control insurgencies in this country or even keep State secrets secret.'

At his regular Thursday afternoon news conference, on 13 March, Sir Julius Chan gave Australia a blunt message—you might not like what we are doing but we are going to do it anyway. It was his first public statement since meeting with Howard at Kirribilli House. 'As it stands at the moment we have a contract,' Sir Julius said. 'Not only have we a contract, we've paid for the contract. And not only that, they're on the ground and they're performing according to the conditions of our contract.' He complained about Australian news coverage. 'It's time that people offshore realise that we are an independent, elected government of an independent country. We can not be expected to be perfect. There will be times when the elected government of a country must decide for itself what to do. But every time we want to do something somebody just seems to be smacking me all the time. I mean, I'm not right all the time. But I have a responsibility and I have to decide at some very crucial times what is best for Papua New Guinea.'

Asked to elaborate on the details of what Sandline was contracted to do, Sir Julius became testy. 'I don't think you should treat Papua New Guinea as a little child that has to open up its cards all the time. No nation, however small or powerful, will ever reveal all the secrets about their security matters. But, having said that, we are more open than others okay? All I can tell you is that there are forty consultants, instructors, military experts. They are on the ground engaging our people in a very massive exercise at the moment.' Sir Julius confirmed that Sandline's advisers would go to Bougainville with the troops they were training to prove Sandline's confidence in its product. 'Yes. I mean, the Government would be very foolish not to extend that commitment of confidence.' Sir Julius was scathing about the restrictions Australia had put on the use of the Iroquois. 'We'll give them to the media for sightseeing,' he said to a burst of laughter. 'They're basically, really useless. It's just like putting a piece of cake in front of you and tying your hands. We might ask Australia to sell them to help us finance this project.'

The Australian Government seemed taken aback. Interviewed on ABC Radio, Downer repeated his mantra that Australia did not believe there was a military solution, there had to be a negotiated solution. But he added: 'You have to understand that Papua New Guinea is not a colony of Australia. Papua New Guinea is an independent country and at the end of the day they can make their own decisions.' Howard's office released a statement saying he would wait to see the text of Chan's statements before commenting. Labor's Shadow Foreign Minister described it as a 'massive rebuff'. 'Real action, not just more words, is required from the Howard Government,' Brereton said. 'Driven by his own domestic political agenda the PNG Prime Minister has now thumbed his nose not only at the Howard Government but also at Australian taxpayers who through our $A320 million annual aid to PNG will indirectly help pay the wages of these freelance killers.' He suggested PNG's aid be cut by the cost of the Sandline contract, $US36 million.

Almost raided

The French newsagency, AFP, reported in April 1997 that Sandline's boss, Tim Spicer, had been my house guest. He never was. AFP apologised. The man who had been my house guest, British freelance journalist Michael Ashworth (who wrote for the *Independent*), was regarded by those plotting Operation Rausim Kwik as Sandline's media spy. And they had plans to call on our home on the night of Sunday, 16 March to take him away. Not aware of this I had helped Michael catch a flight to Australia that Sunday afternoon.

What gave rise to the AFP report was evidence given to the Andrew Inquiry by Brigadier Jerry Singirok. He claimed Spicer had told him Sandline had set aside $US240,000 for public relations and would engage an international journalist 'to give positive reporting' to capture worldwide attention. 'From our intelligence sources,' Singirok said, 'I am aware of Mr Mike Ashworth, ex-SAS, Kenyan, British subject, served with Tony Buckingham and a very close friend of Mr Tim Spicer. He came in here as a journalist from London . . . Ashworth was closely associated with a lot of foreign correspondents. In particular, he was a house guest to Mr Sean Dorney from the ABC . . . We were hoping to also detain him.'

Mike Ashworth was a British paratrooper for nine years but never made it into the SAS, being eliminated at the last test in the jungles of Brunei. He left the British Army and took up journalism. Having been born in Kenya he took particular interest in Executive Outcomes and was planning a book. When news of EO's Bougainville involvement broke he decided to visit PNG and have a look. Although the London *Independent* ran his articles he was not on staff and paid his own way. Michael had not been in journalism long and was finding freelancing a financial struggle. I first met him when I tried to report on Sandline's training in Wewak. But the PNGDF denied us access. Ashworth extended his stay to go back to Wewak but was running out of money. He asked me about backpackers' accommodation so I invited him home. Ashworth was sympathetic to Sandline but not uncritical. And he was no expert media manipulator.

On his way back to England he wanted to pass through Sydney to get Moses Havini's side of the story. I took him to the airport on Sunday, 16 March to catch the early afternoon flight but he had no Australian visa. We spent three hours in the Qantas Airport Manager's office and the Australian Immigration authorities in Canberra eventually issued papers to allow him to spend two days in transit in Sydney. He flew out for Cairns.

When I told Walter Enuma all this in September he laughed. 'I'm glad you did that part of the job for me because I was really wondering how I was going to sort this guy out.' He laughed again. 'I was so concerned about that guy, about any leak whatsoever. I was really concerned about that journalist. How was I going to deal with him? But when I learnt late that day he was out of the country, I focussed on getting Spicer and his associates.' Major Enuma grinned. 'So thank you.'

Australia had successfully recruited its traditional allies–New Zealand, the United Kingdom and the United States–to join it in condemning the hiring of the Sandline mercenaries. It found Indonesia less willing to decry the actions of the PNG Government. Radio Australia reported on 15 March that Indonesia's Foreign Minister, Ali Alatas, had declined to join Australia in condemning PNG's plan to use mercenaries against separatist rebels on Bougainville. Interviewed in Perth, Alatas said he had discussed the issue with his Australian counterpart. He said Downer had explained Australia's opposition. 'As far as Indonesia is concerned our basic position is that developments in Bougainville are essentially the internal affair of Papua New Guinea. And we have a very firm policy not to interfere in the internal affairs of others.' Alatas did not mention it but Executive Outcomes had helped Indonesia a year earlier to rescue European hostages held in the mountains of Irian Jaya by the Irian Jayan rebel movement, the Organisi Papua Merdeka (OPM).

Walter Enuma did his own research into the background of these mercenaries from South Africa and their English connections. 'I used the Internet. I read various articles on Sandline and Executive Outcomes getting to know their modus operandi in various parts of Africa. And I got to know about the various operations that they had been involved in including how they had obtained mining concessions from African Governments.' He formulated his plans and selected the men he wanted to help him. 'It took me one whole week of planning. I did my appreciation, went through an elimination process. I knew this would cause ramifications, after effects,' he said. 'And that it was going to take more than just a military operation. It would go beyond the military and into politics. We were taking on the "big guys". I was apprehensive about the follow-up action, about what would happen. So I looked at not only the military operation but the possibility of disruptions to our intentions and planned for that too.'

As the fateful weekend approached, the man who had driven the Sandline deal through, PNG Deputy Prime Minister Haiveta, flew to Australia. 'On the Friday,' Haiveta told the Andrew Inquiry, 'I travelled down to Brisbane for my niece's wedding. Whilst there, Minister Downer's office called my office to see if we could meet.' They had dinner together at Brisbane's Heritage Hotel on the evening of Sunday 16 March. 'Minister Downer said that they had a whole package to offer if we got rid of the mercenaries. We talked about the border and Downer offered to send ships out to patrol the border between PNG and the Solomons and they would get the Solomons to sign the border treaty.' When this was put to him some months later, Downer said the claim that he had offered Australian Navy ships to patrol the PNG-SI border was 'a gross overstatement'. Haiveta told Justice Andrew he explained that 'the essence of the Sandline project' was to enhance PNG's capabilities so that it would be better placed to negotiate peace. 'Minister Downer made a commitment to bring the BRA out to the negotiating table.'

Haiveta said he was surprised at how rapidly Downer had agreed that Australia needed to play a much more active role in encouraging the rebels to deal with PNG. 'Downer said that whilst in the past Australia had facilitated the Cairns talks and other peace initiatives, they were now prepared to initiate and mediate.' The dinner finished at about 11.30 p.m. 'That night, after the dinner,' Haiveta said, 'I rang Singirok to get his views [on what Downer was offering] ... but his wife answered the phone and said that he was out.' There was a good reason why the Brigadier did not want to speak to the Deputy Prime Minister. His revolt against the Sandline deal was already four hours old. 'I called Mr Ijape and Spicer but both were also out,' Haiveta said. Spicer was under arrest and locked up in a landing barge at sea off Port Moresby.

Haiveta did manage to get through to one person in Port Moresby late that Sunday night, Sir Julius Chan. 'The Prime Minister advised that I should tell the Australians to come to PNG but that they should have something new to offer.' It was a little too late for that. Events had overtaken both governments. But not one of the four politicians—not Sir Julius in Port Moresby, not John Howard in Canberra, nor Chris Haiveta or Alexander Downer in Brisbane—learnt what had happened at Murray Barracks that evening until the following day, St Patricks Day, Monday 17 March 1997.

Chapter Thirteen

D-Day for Rausim Kwik

*Enuma Captures the Mercenaries; Singirok Calls
for Chan's Resignation; Chan Sacks Singirok
16–17 March 1997*

'There were sounds of weapons being cocked,' the PNGDF's Acting Chief of Operations, Lieutenant Colonel Walter Salamas, told the Los Inquiry. 'It appeared they were struggling in the Commander's office.' Salamas should have known what was going on. But he did not. He was the only one to have been given a written copy of the orders for Operation Rausim Kwik. They had been in his in-tray since late on Friday afternoon, 14 March. But he had not read them. So Salamas was as shocked as Sandline's Command and Control Group at what was happening in Brigadier General Singirok's office between 7.30 and 8.00 on the night of Sunday 16 March. Singirok had checked with him that afternoon, making sure arrangements were in place for Tim Spicer, Nick Van den Berg and Karl Deats, Sandline's Intelligence Officer, to attend the operational planning meeting he had asked Salamas to schedule for 7.30 that night.

Spicer, for one, was keen for the meeting to proceed. 'We were concerned that we were contractually obliged to assist and we were not really getting the decisions that we were expecting to get. And the purpose of this conference,' he told the earlier Andrew Inquiry, 'was to discuss the whole issue as to what was going to happen ... I believe that it was to the point where we could have presented the Commander with what we felt was a very detailed plan.' The plan had been drafted by Van den Berg. 'I did not actually read the plan myself,' Spicer said, 'because I was due to hear it presented to the Commander on the evening of 16 March.' The plan was never presented. Action superseded presentation. 'I met them at the steps going up to the Commander's office,' Salamas said. Van den Berg and Deats arrived first. 'I was ordered to stay outside. I was not allowed to go into the Commander's office so I stayed out on the verandah.'

Lieutenant Colonel Salamas was the most senior PNG officer there. But it was the Operations Officer for Rausim Kwik, Major Walter Enuma, who was in charge. Soon after Van den Berg and Deats were taken away, Spicer arrived. He suspected nothing. Salamas met him, too, at the steps. 'He walked in. And when he walked in he was also arrested. This time, there was a much bigger sound. I only presume that Tim Spicer had put up a bit of resistance,' Salamas said. 'There were troops, they were pre-positioned around regular buildings at Murray Barracks headquarters. They all came out of their pre-positions followed by vehicles. The armoured vehicle came in.' All these troops were heavily armed. The Acting Chief of Operations was still bewildered. 'There were troops walking around with weapons which is something completely out of normal in headquarters.' Salamas watched as Spicer was also taken away. 'They were marched away at gun point as if they were war prisoners.'

Each one of the five men chosen to assist Major Enuma in this opening phase of Rausim Kwik—the arrest of Sandline's Command and Control Group—had signed their names to an oath of secrecy in front of their Commander, Brigadier Singirok, that afternoon. The five, two Captains, Belden Namah and Ben Sesinu, two Lieutenants, Nick Henry and Augustine Amba, and a Defence Intelligence Sergeant Chris Mora, had received orders to be at the Commander's office on the afternoon of Sunday 16 March 1997. They had been handed their already prepared secrecy oaths soon after being ushered into his office on the upper floor of the two-storey PNGDF headquarters building, which stands partly shaded by huge African rain trees on the rise above the main parade ground. 'The reason the former Commander gave why he had selected us,' Captain Sesinu told the Los Inquiry, 'was because we were his cadets back in the Defence Academy in Lae.' They were issued with 9 mm pistols and M-16 carbines.

'He just gave us a brief that Tim Spicer and two of his other officers were going to arrive at his office and that we were going to arrest them and all the details would be given to us by the Operations Officer.' Captain Sesinu said Brigadier Singirok told them then that the Operations Officer for Rausim Kwik would be Major Enuma. Spicer and the other two were to be separated, kept from communicating with each other and deported from Papua New Guinea. 'The former Commander told us that we would mention to the three that we had arrested the Commander and he had been put away. And we were arresting the three of them because we did not like Sandline here training the PNG Defence Force. He told us that he did not want the Sandline officials to know that he had planned their arrest.' When Singirok had finished he called in Enuma and left him with the junior officers to give them their detailed instructions. 'Major Enuma told us that we would kick off Operation Rausim Kwik at 7.30 p.m. when Tim Spicer and his two officers arrived,' Captain Sesinu said.

Singirok said he knew that the first question that Spicer would ask was, 'Where is the Commander?' He was not going to be there and he wanted Spicer confused and off-balance. 'It was the obvious question. So on the day of Tim Spicer's detention he was to be informed that I was not in the office. I was at home or arrested or something. Tell Tim Spicer that I was not available.' Enuma used the term 'officers coup' when he arrested, first, Van den Berg and Deats, and then, a few minutes later, Spicer. 'That's how the operation started off,' Enuma said when recalling the night in an interview in late 1997. 'When I opened the meeting, it went something like this: "Welcome to the Land of the Unexpected. This is an officers coup. Hands up! Freeze!" They sort of looked at me and said, "We want to talk to the General." "Sorry, the General is not here." "But I saw Walter Salamas down there below." "He's just been isolated." That's how it all started.'

The junior officers had remained in hiding until Enuma gave them a prearranged signal. 'Actually the signal,' Sesinu told the Los Inquiry, 'was that when they walked in Major Enuma would say, "I will get the Commander, he is in the toilet." And when he goes to knock on the door that is when the other officers who were in the toilet were to come out.' Captain Sesinu, who had been wounded on Bougainville before being assigned to Defence Intelligence, said Enuma told Van den Berg and Deats that Singirok had been arrested. 'They did not want to believe us. They wanted to know whose orders are those and we had to force them down on the floor and search them.' Their shoes and belts were removed. It was a similar procedure when Spicer arrived fresh from a meeting with the Prime Minister, Sir Julius Chan. 'He also looked as if he was shocked and asked who gave us the orders to do that. He put up a bit more resistance than the other two. That is when I remember a louvre blade in the office being broken and it did make some noise,' Sesinu said. Spicer claimed that during the scuffle he was able to hide a small pocket knife inside his body, up his anus.

Most of the other soldiers who participated that night also had learnt only a few hours earlier that Brigadier Singirok was aborting the Sandline deal. The Intelligence Officer for the Special Forces Unit, Captain Siale Diro, said he was briefed by the Commander of the SFU, Major Gilbert Toropo, at four o'clock that afternoon. 'We were at our company headquarters at Goldie Barracks and some of my troops were present, those who were here in Moresby. I cannot recall exactly what he said but the gist of the orders was to arrest the Sandline personnel on Sunday evening, approximately two hours later.' Captain Diro said he took up a position in the car park and monitored events. Two of his SFU intelligence officers were to accompany Spicer to the PNGDF's landing craft base on Port Moresby harbour while a third was to go with Van den Berg and Deats to Taurama Barracks. 'After Mr Spicer had been escorted off to his area of containment, I then went to the residence in East Boroko where Mr Spicer had been staying along with the other three and checked their apartment.' Sandline's Logistics Officer had already been arrested there and taken to Taurama Barracks.

The SFU Commander, Major Toropo, was available if needed. 'I was along the corridor towards the western end of the building,' he told the Los Inquiry. 'I really did not have any role. Our role was to have three of our SFU members escort the Sandline personnel to their detention areas.' He said that from where he was he heard Major Enuma issue the order, 'Take them out.' 'That is when I saw different soldiers with three of my men come to pick [up] the Sandline personnel.' There was a minor mix-up. Van den Berg was taken to the landing craft base as well as Spicer. But he was then taken off to Taurama Barracks while Spicer was put on board the heavy landing craft, the HMPNGS *Buna*, which left the harbour. Spicer told the London *Telegraph* many months later that it took him two nautical miles out to sea. 'My mind was racing with all kinds of scenarios: perhaps they were simply trying to test us.' Spicer was held in isolation on the *Buna* for more than thirty-six hours.

Captain Diro's other task that night was to ensure that the Sandline administration staff and air crew who were living at Kiki Barracks at the airport were kept under surveillance. They were as yet unaware of what had happened to their bosses and did not find out until the next morning. Diro, who had been involved longer than most with the Sandline people, said he was in shock. In December Diro had gone to Bougainville with Spicer on Spicer's first reconnaissance mission. As the SFU's Intelligence Officer he had provided much of the background Spicer had used in his consultancy report. And following Deats' arrival he had worked closely with Sandline's Intelligence Officer on what they would be doing in Operation Oyster. Asked at the Los Inquiry why the events of 16 March had shocked him he replied: 'We were heading in one direction, a thousand miles an hour. Then to automatically, or within the space of a couple of hours, head off on a different tangent at the same speed is quite an experience.' Enuma was pleased with his first night's work. 'Certainly it was a success for us.'

Varying accounts were given to the Los Inquiry as to the role of Singirok's

Aide-de-Camp, Captain John Keleto. Lieutenant Colonel Salamas and Captain Sesinu swore that he was involved and had been the one who had shown the Sandline people through to Singirok's office. Others said he had not been briefed although they did see the light on in his office. Captain Keleto's own version was that he had been arranging matters for the coming week and had become scared when he heard all the commotion. He said that after things quietened down he slipped out of his office and went up to the Commander's residence, Flagstaff House. Singirok was having dinner at the time and came to the door in casual clothes. Captain Keleto said he reported the goings on down below and how it appeared some people had been arrested in the Commander's office. Asked what Singirok had said, Keleto replied, 'He said, "Just ignore that and go home."' Singirok's diary for 16 March records that phase one of the operation was successful 'except that Nick was placed on the LCH with Tim'. Then there is a note: 'Rang Flash and Stone.'

Choosing the name and the date

Sir Kubulan Los's Inquiry wasted days trying to get to the bottom of the mystery as to why Jerry Singirok had added the digit three to the name of his operation to expel the mercenaries. His operational orders were titled Rausim Kwik Three. The Brisbane lawyers representing Sir Julius Chan, Marshall Cooke QC and his Junior, Mal Varitimos, seemed obsessed with the question. They demanded to know from witness after witness if they were aware of any orders for Rausim Kwik One. They were a mite confused because they made a great fuss about another set of orders titled Rausim Quick Two (note the English spelling) which appeared in early April 1997, post-dating Rausim Kwik Three. These Rausim Quick Two orders—never implemented—certainly favoured their case, suggesting an even more dramatic political role for the PNG military.

But Major Walter Enuma had a very simple explanation for Rausim Kwik Three when I spoke to him in September 1997. He said there had been two earlier operations with a similar name—not in 1997 but almost two decades before any foreigners from Africa became a concern to the PNG military. 'Jerry and I were Platoon Commanders in Operations Rausim Kwik One and Two. They were on the PNG-Indonesian border in 1978-79 when we had problems with the OPM and the Indonesians were bombing the border. Jerry got the name from those operations when we were trying to get rid of those guys. I think he wanted to get rid of these guys quickly too.'

Singirok told the Los Inquiry that what determined his choice of Sunday 16 March as the day on which he would move against Sandline (and Monday 17 March as the day that he would move against Chan) was the timing of the arrival of the Mi-24 helicopter gunships and their destructive rockets. 'I want to tell the Commission the reason why I selected 17 March. Because within the next twenty-four or forty-eight hours the Antonov would arrive with all the hardware, with all the helicopters, with all the bombs. It had no relationship with political activities,' Singirok claimed. 'I know that I was gambling with my D-Day. If that Antonov had arrived with all the hardware and if I wanted to deport the Sandline people, it would then have been absolutely impossible. There would have been bloodshed.'

At about 6 a.m. on Monday 17 March Singirok drove to the home of PNG Police Commissioner Bob Nenta. The two men held each other in high regard and were friends. Both had been appointed head of their respective forces by Sir Julius Chan, and Singirok believed he had been influential in Nenta's elevation to Police Commissioner in April 1996. Nenta greeted Singirok as he emerged from his vehicle and, he told the Los Inquiry, the Brigadier began by asking him for a favour. 'Not realising the seriousness of it, I said, "Yes, sure." That was as he was entering the gates. So I said, "Yes, sure. Let us go and sit down." So we sat down and as he began to explain it really shocked me.' Nenta's version of this meeting was challenged by Singirok's lawyer. In any event Singirok left Nenta's house definite he had won the Police Commissioner's support. And that belief was reinforced later when Nenta turned up at Defence headquarters. 'I told him I will give it serious thought on the way to work,' Nenta said, 'and then he invited me for another meeting that was set down for half-past eight at Murray Barracks.'

In Singirok's orders for Operation Rausim Kwik he wrote that his 'greatest gamble' was the Police Force. The orders noted that 'the Commissary has been briefed on the circumstances surrounding the whole crisis and will be briefed along with senior PNGDF officers on D-Day to get them either on our side or be neutral all the way'. According to Nenta, what Singirok told him under his house early that morning was roughly similar to what was contained in his later address to his officers, his parade address to the rank and file and his Address to the Nation on the 'Roger Hau'ofa Talkback Show' on Radio Kalang. Namely: that the Sandline contract was corrupt;

that if Operation Oyster went ahead there would be heavy loss of life and massive destruction on Bougainville; that he would be demanding the resignation of the Prime Minister, the Deputy Prime Minister and the Minister for Defence; that he would be asking the Governor General and the Chief Justice to appoint a caretaker government; and that he would demand the establishment of a commission of inquiry into the Sandline deal.

Once back home, Singirok called up his Military Assistant, Lieutenant Colonel Joseph Fabila, and told him to deliver an envelope to the Governor General, Sir Wiwa Korowi, at Government House. 'It was about 7.30 in the morning,' Fabila told the Los Inquiry. 'I went up to Flagstaff House and the Commander instructed me ... [to] inform the Governor General that he was going to ask the Prime Minister, the Deputy and the Minister for Defence to step down ... by way of an announcement on the radio at about 10 o'clock.' Fabila said that at Government House he was asked to wait. When eventually shown in, he handed over the envelope to the Governor General and delivered his message. 'He was obviously shocked,' Fabila said. 'He stared at me for a good one or two minutes and asked me to say it again. I repeated the message.' Fabila said Sir Wiwa seemed uncomfortable and asked him to take a seat while he thought about it. After a few minutes the Governor General picked up the phone. 'I heard him asking for the Chief Justice. I heard them praying. He said, "Let us pray to God."'

The Commander's Military Assistant said that Sir Wiwa spent about ten to fifteen minutes on the phone speaking to the Chief Justice, Sir Arnold Amet. He had noticed there were two separate documents stapled together in the envelope that Sir Wiwa had opened. One was a copy of a letter from Singirok to Sir Julius Chan and the other a copy of the Brigadier's Address to the Nation. 'After speaking with the Chief Justice,' Fabila said, 'he told me to get in contact with the Commander and he asked if I could get the Commander to come and see him right away ... I rang ... and at that stage he was addressing the troops on parade at Murray Barracks. I spoke to Lieutenant Colonel Walter Salamas who was probably holding onto the Commander's mobile phone at that time and I ... asked him to relay the message to the Commander that when he was finished addressing the troops to come and see the Governor General.'

Police Commissioner Nenta had headed off for work not long after Singirok had left his house. Soon after getting to Police Headquarters, he contacted his Chief of Operations, Deputy Police Commissioner Ludwig Kembu, and asked Kembu to accompany him to Murray Barracks. Their recollections differ on exactly what was said. Kembu's version is that he initially thought they were going to Defence headquarters to be given a full rundown on the impending strike against the rebels on Bougainville because he had received a preliminary brief on Operation Oyster the previous Friday. But he became concerned when Nenta explained what Singirok had told him. 'I asked the Police Commissioner if it was some sort of a coup. He said, "Something along that line."' Deputy Commissioner Kembu also maintained that Nenta had raised the names of the Governor General and the Chief Justice and mentioned a possible connection with the, by then, well-publicised, multi-denominational religious crusade, Brukim Skru (Pidgin for 'bend the knee' or 'kneel').

Brukim Skru had been launched in late 1996 as a campaign urging Christians throughout Papua New Guinea to pray for the election of honest, incorruptible leaders in PNG's 1997 national elections. It had the support of most of the major churches. The PNG media had given extensive coverage to various Brukim Skru activities including how Sir Wiwa had 'wept for the nation' at the prayer campaign launch. Sir Arnold Amet's strong religious convictions were very well known. And Singirok's own embrace of religion was no secret. He had formed a prayer group in the PNGDF known as the Military Christian Fellowship. Much was made after the Sandline crisis of an alleged born-again-Christian conspiracy involving Singirok, Sir Wiwa and Sir Arnold to bring down the Chan Government. Singirok's diary had various references to consultations with 'GG' in February and early March. Chan's counsel, Marshall Cooke, repeatedly tried to get Singirok to admit that this 'GG' could be nobody else but Sir Wiwa Korowi. Singirok rejected that but never gave a satisfactory explanation as to who this 'GG' was.

Sir Wiwa adamantly denied he was behind any move to have Chan resign. And when Kembu's comments to the Los Inquiry about his discussion with Police Commissioner Nenta that morning were reported in the newspapers in PNG in November 1997, the Governor General issued a news release claiming that any allegations that he had prior knowledge of Operation Rausim Kwik were completely baseless. Chan became convinced after the event that Korowi had been involved. He told Justice Los that the Governor General had demanded a briefing about the Sandline contract in late February, which he provided. 'After my initial conversation with the Governor General about the Sandline contract,' he said, 'Sir Wiwa telephoned me about every second day, then almost every day until March 17 1997. He expressed concern about what was happening around the country and the people's perception of the contract.'

However, even if the 'GG' reference in Singirok's diary was to discussions Singirok may have had with Sir Wiwa before 17 March there was little the

Governor General could do in any practical way to help Singirok achieve his objectives. Under the PNG Constitution the Governor General is completely powerless. Equally, Singirok's call 'for the Governor General and the Chief Justice to appoint a caretaker Government or a Transitional Ruling Council to ensure the continued running of the country's affairs' reveals such a poor grasp of the Constitution that it is unbelievable that this advice could have come from Sir Arnold Amet.

Commissioner Nenta and Deputy Commissioner Kembu arrived at Murray Barracks in separate vehicles shortly before 8.30 a.m. They went up to Singirok's office where, according to Kembu, the Commander greeted them on the verandah with a smile and said, 'Welcome to the club!' They went inside. 'Singirok started by saying that the Prime Minister, Sir Julius Chan, was corrupt,' Kembu told the Los Inquiry. Singirok told them he had cancelled all dealings with Sandline. 'The Commissioner asked him if the Government would be dissolved and the Brigadier said it would be ... by the Governor General that day and a Caretaker Government put in place ... I was a bit surprised. But as soon as he said that the Commissioner made a comment that he would support him.' Nenta told the Inquiry his memory was that Singirok had asked for a police mobile squad to assist with the deportation of Sandline personnel. 'I told Ludwig to take note of it.' Asked why if he did not support Singirok he had not told him so, Nenta claimed he felt intimidated because there were so many soldiers around.

At 9.00 a.m. they left the Commander's office and walked along the open passageways to the PNGDF headquarters conference room in the adjoining building where about forty officers from all the military units in the PNG capital were assembled. Singirok invited Nenta and Kembu to take seats in the front row. During his address Singirok told his officers that his move against Sandline and the Chan Government had the support of the Police. Asked if he had said anything to refute this statement Nenta said he had not. 'He did not allow anybody [to speak]. He went straight to the address and then dismissed the conference.' Singirok next went to address a major parade to tell his soldiers about Operation Rausim Kwik. Simultaneous parades were happening at other Defence establishments in Lae and Manus and on Bougainville. The Commanding Officers in all three places had received copies of the address with instructions to read it to the men precisely at 9.30 a.m.

Nenta and Kembu separated. The Commissioner went back to Police headquarters in the harbourside suburb of Konedobu to organise a meeting with headquarters staff while the Deputy Commissioner went to the main Port Moresby police station at Boroko to alert the city's Police Chief,

Assistant Commissioner Sam Inguba. 'I informed him of the happenings up at the army barracks,' Kembu said, 'and I told them [Inguba and his senior officers] that we were expecting something serious.' Kembu and Inguba discussed Singirok's request for a mobile squad but decided against sending one to Murray Barracks where it might no longer be under police control. Kembu returned to Police HQ and joined the conference of the force's most senior officers which Nenta had called. Both men agree that at this meeting the Police Commissioner came out against any police involvement in Operation Rausim Kwik. Singirok's office called requesting Nenta to join him at Government House. Nenta said he tried, once, to get through to Singirok on his mobile phone. 'My position was that we were not taking part ... by then it was very difficult for me to get back to the Commander because he was moving around a lot,' Nenta told the Los Inquiry.

The place Singirok moved to after calling on the Governor General was the studios of Radio Kalang in the National Broadcasting Corporation (NBC) premises at Five Mile along the Sir Hubert Murray Highway. Radio Kalang is a commercial FM service that broadcasts to most PNG cities and towns. Kalang's most popular program is the daily 'Roger Hau'ofa Talkback Show'. Hau'ofa is a household name in PNG. He is a very experienced broadcaster who presents and produces an open-ended, informal, lively and often news-breaking program featuring guests he lines up himself, sometimes on the run. Hau'ofa said he received a call at about 9.30 a.m. asking if Brigadier Singirok could come on. 'I agreed and suggested that Mr Singirok could drop in at any time between ten and twelve o'clock.' Hau'ofa was used to such short notice and equally used to being disappointed when those who promised to come never turned up. 'Towards eleven o'clock, I had given up hope and came to the conclusion that the Commander would not come on. However, at about five past eleven Mr Singirok arrived in the studio with his personal bodyguards.'

A truckload of heavily armed troops accompanied Singirok. Some took up positions outside the NBC building. The NBC Chairman, Renagi Lohia, who had been Sir Julius Chan's political Chief of Staff prior to his appointment as head of the national broadcaster, claimed he was advised not to leave the office because his vehicle was guarded by armed soldiers. 'I felt that the NBC was being seized by the Commander and his soldiers,' Lohia told the Prime Minister in an abject letter of explanation the following day. But the military did not take over the station. What their presence did ensure, however, was that nobody put Singirok off the air during the full hour he was on–first while delivering his Address to the Nation and then while answering questions from Hau'ofa and talkback callers. 'I was under the impression that Mr Singirok was going to answer questions from listeners and to help put an end to a lot of controversy surrounding the Bougainville issue,' Hau'ofa said. But instead Singirok told the nation the Defence Force was revolting against what he called the 'corrupt' Sandline deal.

Singirok began by saying he had kept quiet and followed orders but he could remain silent no longer. The engagement of Sandline, he claimed, had 'brought into question the credibility of the PNG Defence Force' and [his] own 'professionalism', which the Government had 'greatly undermined'. He accused Chan, Haiveta and Ijape of making 'false and misleading statements' about the contract and he gave them forty-eight hours to resign. He told his audience he had 'cancelled all further activities' involving the PNGDF and Sandline. He claimed the proposed military operation on Bougainville would 'be counterproductive' because the arsenal to be used was 'totally destructive against human lives' and 'the environment' and was 'not relative to the threat on the ground'. Singirok claimed that, if the contract had been allowed to continue, people 'not only on Bougainville' but 'throughout PNG' would have turned against both the Government and the Defence Force because they had used 'foreigners' for a 'terrible cause'. Foreigners, he said, who had 'no value or appreciation of our culture and background'.

The Brigadier told his listeners most of the equipment being supplied by Sandline was 'ex-Soviet stock' from Eastern Bloc nations which was 'either obsolete' or in poor demand. He alleged corruption, claiming Sandline had bought these items 'for very little' and sold them to PNG 'for exorbitant prices allowing the potential for sizeable percentage for commissions'. He claimed the Government's motive in using Sandline was 'to open up the Panguna mine at the expense of more lives'. But it would not work. The Government, he claimed, was concentrating on an economic goal and had not considered 'the long-term implications of reopening the mine if the conflict which stemmed from the people's protest over the mine' was not resolved amicably. He had stopped the operation 'rather than allow our politicians to sell this country to foreigners for economic gain' at a human cost. And he appealed for support. 'I am now also calling for those individuals and organisations who have been unjustly treated by this Government to come forward openly and expose the actions of dishonest leaders so we can retain our country's integrity and name.'

Singirok's appeal touched a chord. Amongst the many calls of support was one from a woman, Jessie, who claimed Singirok was guided by God. 'My heart just rejoices,' she said in an emotional outburst. 'I am a mother and I have seen what's going on. I stood helpless and I have been asking if there would be a real Papua New Guinean who would stand up, who would rise up and tell the truth ... I just wanted my children to have their birthright of the wealth of this nation ... as I see it slipping though the fingers of PNG, I waited and cried for some real PNG [person] to rise up ... My heart rejoices in the Lord for a man such as him to rise up and take this kind of stand, to have the guts. It must be God that has given him this boldness to do it ... Mr Singirok ... God bless you so much. May the Lord be your canopy of protection.' 'Bless you too, sister,' Singirok replied. 'God is good. For us Christians a lot of people have laughed at Brukim Skru, but if there's any effect, I'm feeling it in my office and in my house. Keep praying.' Enuma was worried when he heard what Singirok was saying on the radio. He told the Los Inquiry he was concerned Singirok would be 'sacked straight away, jeopardising the mission and [increasing] the possibility of bloodshed and civil war'. Enuma went to the NBC to reason with 'his boss'. But Singirok's gamble to get the public mobilised was to produce results over the following few days.

Broadcasting highs and lows

The National Broadcasting Corporation's Radio Kalang had the biggest scoop in Papua New Guinea's post-Independence journalism. The man who was leading the armed forces in a revolt against the Government over its decision to hire mercenaries went to Radio Kalang's studios to announce it. The Roger Hau'ofa program that Monday was riveting radio. I had raced over to Government House because I had been told there was a coup underway and Brigadier Singirok and the Police Commissioner were visiting the Governor General calling on him to sack the Chan Government.

I was not allowed in. But while waiting outside the gates, I saw a truckload of heavily armed soldiers drive up and be waved through. Soon afterwards, one of the Government House security officials beckoned me over and suggested I should switch on my car radio. I did. I scrambled to record what I was hearing. Jerry Singirok was calling on the Prime Minister to resign, accusing the Government of corruption over the Sandline deal. I hurtled back to the office taping the broadcast as I went and put the story to air in Australia live on 'The World Today'.

However the NBC, which generally has had a fine record of defending its independence from government interference, went strangely quiet. This was all the more remarkable considering that one of its own programs had broken this dramatic story. I was so busy myself covering the rapidly developing events and churning out items for ABC Radio, ABC TV and Radio Australia that I heard little further of what was being broadcast locally. But others told me later of the NBC's failure.

One listener using the pen-name Deeply Disappointed wrote to the *Post Courier* about how, having heard other reports, he/she had waited for confirmation on the 6.00 p.m. NBC News. 'I was stunned, astonished or whatever ... that the "Voice" had nothing to say regarding the issue. Again I listened to [the] 7.00 p.m. newscast, but there was utter silence. Then we were told that the evening's "Current Issues" program had been cancelled. No explanations given.' The letter concluded: 'PNG was betrayed on Monday night—not by General Singirok who acted on behalf of his soldiers and the nation but by the "Voice of the Nation" which was trusted by Papua New Guineans to act on their behalf.'

The letter Singirok sent to Sir Julius that morning was much shorter than his lengthy national address. It contained no demand for Chan to resign. Nor did it call for a commission of inquiry into the Sandline deal. It simply informed the Prime Minister that Singirok, as Commander of the PNGDF, had cancelled Operation Oyster 'as of midnight last night'. He listed eight reasons, the last being: 'It is obvious that the Government's motive is to open the mine and it cares less about its people.' He claimed that the Operation Oyster option was 'disastrous' and that by engaging Sandline the Government had 'mortgaged the island of Bougainville and other resource-rich areas to foreigners'. But the letter had not been brought to the attention of the Prime Minister before Singirok began his broadcast on the Roger Hau'ofa program. Sir Julius claimed to the Los Inquiry that he found out about the counter operation, Rausim Kwik, from Radio Kalang. He had a phone call from a former Parliamentarian, Gabriel Ramoi, advising him to listen to the radio. 'I heard him [Singirok] making very adverse comments about myself and the Government and the engagement of Sandline. I was very perplexed,' Chan said. 'He had never expressed any concern to me about the contract. ... I was shocked and felt completely deceived.'

Incredibly, over in the East Sepik Province on the opposite side of the PNG mainland, the majority of the Sandline mercenaries were still training with the Special Forces Unit even while Singirok was speaking. Radio Kalang's FM signal did not reach to the bush training camp at Urimo, inland from Wewak. And Sandline's 'consultants' had received no word from their people in Port Moresby. The SFU's Intelligence Officer, Captain Diro, had been monitoring the Sandline personnel living at Kiki Barracks throughout the night. He was satisfied they were unaware of the detention of Spicer and the others. 'So on the Monday morning, I waited for their administrative officers to come down to our operational headquarters at the Air Transport Squadron,' he said. 'When they walked in I informed them of what had happened. I formally arrested them and then took them down to Taurama Barracks to join the three who were already there.' The remaining ground crew were to be kept at Kiki Barracks. 'We advised them that they were not to panic, nothing was going to happen to them, they were safe,' Diro said. 'They were simply to follow instructions.' Enuma told the Los Inquiry these men were directed to stop work as the contract was going to be reviewed.

It was not until 1.30 p.m. that most of the people training at Urimo found out that Operation Oyster was off, according to SFU Sergeant Francis Jakis. He said the news was conveyed to them by Lieutenant Colonel Michael Tamalanga, who drove out from Wewak that morning. 'Moem Barracks to Urimo, it is quite a distance,' he said. 'It is around five hours drive. So, in the morning, we were doing normal training and when the Commanding Officer of 2nd Battalion arrived, we were having lunch. Captain Renagi, the Acting CO of the SFU, came over and said the CO would talk to us at 1.30. So at 1.30 we all gathered together and the Lieutenant Colonel read us the news that the training was to cease immediately.' Sergeant Jakis claimed there was no great consternation. Nobody was formally arrested. 'There was a troop carrier for each section so we all loaded our belongings, mixed PNG-African, and we drove from Urimo down to Moem Barracks. The soldiers were sent to their barracks line and for us, the Sergeants, with those Africans, we went to the Sergeants mess, put our luggage away and had a few beers.'

In Port Moresby Brigadier Singirok's next appointment was with the media. He held a news conference at 1.45 p.m. More foreign diplomats were present than journalists and Singirok assured them that expatriates were safe. The only 'foreigners' who would have to go home, he said, were the mercenaries. He denied he was staging a coup and said no members of the Government were under arrest. He ended the conference expressing relief that he had gotten 'off his chest' something that had 'been bugging [him] for two months'. In Canberra Shadow Foreign Minister Laurie Brereton 'expressed grave concern for Australia's 10,000 expatriates' in PNG and called for the suspension of defence aid. 'Today we believe it absolutely imperative that the Defence Cooperation Program which has Australian military advisers working alongside the PNG Defence Force be suspended and suspended forthwith,' Brereton said. 'And we believe that those military advisers should report immediately to the Australian High Commission in

Port Moresby.' He need not have worried. They had little else to do. Singirok had forbidden them from entering Murray Barracks.

In his original Rausim Kwik orders Brigadier Singirok made specific mention of these Australians on attachment to the PNGDF. Explaining to the Los Inquiry why restrictions on entry to the barracks had been ruthlessly enforced, Singirok said he wanted to minimise complications. 'That was why I specifically made instructions to keep those people out,' he said, 'I did not want them to get involved in an issue that is more national.' There was another consideration. 'It is now common knowledge that the ADF Third Brigade is on short notice to move to Papua New Guinea,' the Rausim Kwik operation orders said, noting that the Townsville-based brigade had been activated during the first Fiji coup in 1987 in an operation called Morris Dance. Singirok's orders also warned of possible intervention involving New Zealand and the USA. He suggested that their motive would be to rescue their citizens 'especially [as] there is a major military exercise in Australia ... involving 30,000 troops.' To avoid such intervention the orders stressed: 'The key to the success of the operation is orderliness and discipline and conduct that represents nationalism and pride for our sovereignty.'

That afternoon, the two Ministers who had been most involved with Sandline, Deputy Prime Minister Haiveta and Defence Minister Ijape, both flew back into the PNG capital—Haiveta from Australia and Ijape from his electorate, Goroka, in the Eastern Highlands. According to evidence given to the Los Inquiry by the Communications Officer for the Special Forces Unit, Lieutenant Michael David, Haiveta turned up at the Sandline house in East Boroko at about 4.30 p.m. Lieutenant David was there as the SFU's Duty Officer overseeing the changing of the guard on the residence. 'When I went to the door, the Honourable Chris Haiveta was [there] ... accompanied by [Minister for State] Sir Pita Lus and an escort car. Chris Haiveta asked me whether I knew where Tim Spicer was and I said at that moment I did not know.' David claimed that an expatriate with Haiveta then made a call on a mobile phone. The expatriate was Nicos Violaris, the businessman with close personal and political links to Chan. After hanging up Violaris told David he would have to accompany them to see the Prime Minister. 'I said I would not know where Tim Spicer was so it was a waste of time taking me to see the PM,' David said.

Haiveta told the Los Inquiry that after getting back from Brisbane he had gone to see Sir Julius Chan. Both of them were anxious to talk to Spicer and find out where he was. 'We tried to ring him and could not get through so he [Chan] asked me to see if I could go to where he was living to check whether he was all right or not. I mean, it is a crisis situation,' Haiveta said.

'Whoever was there just hopped in the car and we went along. And when we were there we were stopped by armed soldiers and told that he was all right, he was under house arrest and there was nothing to worry about. We did not go in. We were turned away and [so] then turned back.'

Ijape had more success getting cooperation from the military officer he went to see shortly after he arrived from Goroka. Captain Chris Siroi who worked as a Defence Force travel officer was from the same village in the Eastern Highlands as Ijape. It was about five o'clock in the afternoon, Siroi told the Los Inquiry, when Ijape's First Secretary picked him up at a bus stop near the Air Transport Squadron. 'The Minister, his First Secretary and myself, we jumped into the Secretary's vehicle and we drove straight to Parliament House. And while we were driving he asked me, "Have you people gone crazy?" And I said, "Are you talking about me or Singirok?" And he said, "I am talking about Singirok." And I said, "You promoted him and appointed him as Commander so there is no need for you to ask these questions to me. You should ask him."' Captain Siroi spent the next few days working and living out of Ijape's room at the Islander Hotel. But he, too, was unable to trace the whereabouts of Spicer.

Some sections of the media were alerted to a possible news conference with the Governor General at 3.15 p.m. But it never happened. By midafternoon, Police Commissioner Nenta had been to see both Sir Julius Chan to pledge police loyalty to the Government and to Sir Wiwa Korowi to tell him the Police Force disassociated itself from Singirok's Operation Rausim Kwik. Nenta told the Los Inquiry the Governor General had told him that in his earlier meeting with the Brigadier, Singirok had claimed to have police support. But disassociation was one thing, taking on the troops another. 'The situation was such that the soldiers were fully armed with military weapons,' Nenta said. 'And all I told my men was to avoid casualties, just avoid getting into physical confrontation with them.' Asked what measures he was prepared to take to help reassert government authority the Police Commissioner said there were a few ideas floated but his men were comprehensively outgunned. 'If the whole military was involved I would not have had the capacity ... it would have been impossible in my view.'

In the public domain the impression still was that Singirok and Nenta were acting together. The Member for Bougainville, John Momis, praised both men. 'The army boss and his police counterpart need to be highly commended for their very brave stand against their political masters,' Momis said. 'The Prime Minister and his Defence Minister have been burying their heads in the sand in believing that they have the total respect of the security forces. How naive could they be to even dare to assume that paying a handful of foreign mercenaries $US36 million to train our soldiers would boost the morale of the security forces when those soldiers, who still in the end have to put their lives on the line, will not see a toea [cent] out of those millions?' Momis, who had headed the Constitutional Planning Committee and is often referred to as the 'father of the PNG Constitution', claimed Singirok's actions were justified. 'I only wish that he had come out a lot earlier,' Momis said. 'But still, the Prime Minister must know that our people's allegiance to the Constitution does not always mean allegiance to individuals.'

Sir Julius Chan, understandably, did not agree. As night fell, he conducted a news conference at his Parliament House office. It was not held in the usual venue because Ministers were gathering there for an emergency Cabinet meeting. It took place on a lounge suite in the Prime Minister's reception area with a crowd of senior public servants looking on. 'I will make sure the Constitution prevails,' Sir Julius said, professing that Singirok's actions had taken him by surprise. 'I'm sure that he's created such havoc right throughout the nation.' Chan was also concerned about the economic impact. PNG related stocks had lost eight per cent of their value during the afternoon's trading on the Australian Stock Exchange. Sir Julius said Cabinet was about to meet to discuss Singirok's fate. 'You can't give an ultimatum to the elected government. He is wrong. He's free to disagree but he's not free to disobey the direction of the Cabinet.' The Police Association President, Superintendent Aloysius Aviaisa, spoke up. 'Sir, I'm here to present the Association's view,' he said. 'It's 100 per cent support for you and the Cabinet. Democracy will be maintained.' Bob Nenta was also there. Asked whether he had initially supported Singirok he parried the question: 'You never heard it from me.'

The Cabinet then met and sacked Brigadier Singirok as Defence Force Commander. It replaced him with an Acting Commander, Colonel Alfred Aikung. It was a curious and provocative choice. Never before had anyone from the relatively small naval element of the Defence Force been made Commander. And many in the force, especially those who had served on Bougainville, held Aikung in disdain. They held him responsible, as Chief of Logistics, for the appalling shortages of food and other supplies they had regularly endured. Unlike Singirok, Aikung had never been under fire on Bougainville. He was disparagingly referred to as a 'commander of desks not of men'. A ship's engineer by training he had never even captained a vessel. There was also a widespread belief that Colonel Aikung had benefited from the Defence Force Institutional Housing Project which had been funded partly by Malaysian aid but mostly through loans from Malaysian banks. Aikung had given himself twenty-four-hour use of a vehicle the Malaysians had provided for the project. Just a few nights later angry soldiers were to torch it. Explaining to the Los Inquiry why he had taken possession of the vehicle, Colonel Aikung claimed the 'project management' felt he needed it as Chairman of the Housing Project Committee so that he could 'drive freely' around Port Moresby to inspect the housing sites.

Aikung had never expected to head the force. 'I was quite surprised,' he told Justice Los. 'I was in my house and Captain Ron Hosea drove up and told me that I needed to go to Parliament House. The Prime Minister was there, so were all his Ministers [and] he had a media release advising the media what he had done.' But Acting Commander Aikung's appointment was not to be straightforward. A platoon of soldiers had been dispatched to Government House earlier in the day and were refusing to allow the Cabinet Secretary, Peter Eka, though the gates to get the Governor General's signature on the instruments dismissing Singirok. 'The Prime Minister asked myself, the Police Commissioner and the Deputy Police Commissioner to go and assist the NEC Secretary,' Colonel Aikung said. 'So we proceeded to Government House but at the entrance the duty policeman advised us that he was under instructions to tell us that we will get shot at if we go beyond that point.' They withdrew several hundred metres and Commissioner Nenta used his mobile phone to tell the Prime Minister they had a problem.

For a while there was a confused stand-off. Then the officer in charge of the soldiers at Government House, Lieutenant John Weraura, sought further instructions. A Defence Intelligence Captain, Paul Kaliop, told the Los Inquiry he was in the Force Operations Centre at Murray Barracks that night. 'Lieutenant Weraura just walked in, in full combat gear, and announced to Major Toropo that whilst he, this young officer, was up at the Governor General's residence the Prime Minister had called him several times [ordering him] to allow Government officials to go through, but this young officer did not do that. And because the Prime Minister kept on calling him he had come all the way back to Murray Barracks to find out whether to let these people in or not.' Major Enuma went to consult with Singirok at Flagstaff House. Captain Kaliop, who had been excluded from Operation Rausim Kwik, told the Los Inquiry that the Chief of Staff, Colonel Jack Tuat, and Lieutenant Colonel Salamas directed him to go and tell the soldiers to let the Cabinet Secretary through. 'I told them I did not have a weapon and men at my disposal and after much discussion we aborted the idea. It was too dangerous.'

Major Enuma told Justice Los he was surprised to learn there were soldiers guarding Government House—that had not been part of his planning. Singirok had ordered them there. 'So, I went to the General to find out what was happening ... I was concerned about the troops at Government

House. That is why I went to the General ... and the General told me, "You go there and allow access, allow those people access to the Governor General" ... so I went there personally to allow that access and to apologise to the Commissioner and the Secretary.' At his news conference Brigadier Singirok had said he expected to be sacked and would accept it. Enuma went with Major Toropo to Government House. Toropo told the Los Inquiry they saw the Governor General's Secretary and told him Eka and his party would be allowed in. Deputy Police Commissioner Kembu said that after waiting out on the road for forty-five minutes they proceeded up the driveway to Government House. Kembu said he did not know who had ordered the soldiers to let them through but he presumed it had come 'from higher up'.

At the top of the driveway they met Major Enuma who was in full battle gear. Kembu claimed they had a confrontation. But from Kembu's evidence it is clear that Enuma was not obstructing them, rather letting them know that Operation Rausim Kwik would continue no matter what happened to Singirok. 'It is okay for you to go and see the GG,' Kembu quoted Enuma as having said. 'Sandline is now the sideline.' The party proceeded to the Governor General's house where Eka had an audience with Sir Wiwa Korowi who signed the papers dismissing Singirok. Enuma was determined to ensure that the mercenaries were not only sidelined but also expelled–deported from Papua New Guinea. 'I looked at all the options and to ensure that my operation was absolutely successful we had to maintain our aim,' Enuma said when reflecting some months later on how he had felt that night. 'Maintenance of aim–that's one of the principles of war. I had to maintain my aim. My aim was to get rid of Sandline at the earliest opportunity irrespective of what the Government said because we had already rebelled. Whether the General was removed or not–that made no impact on my operation.'

Chapter Fourteen

Days of Havoc

The Troops Rally Around Singirok; Public Demonstrations Turn Nasty; Mercenaries Deported; Spicer Charged
18–22 March 1997

Soon after being sworn in as Acting Commander at about 1.00 a.m. on Tuesday 18 March, Colonel Alfred Aikung returned to Sir Julius Chan's office in Parliament House to celebrate his unexpected promotion. He gave verbal orders cancelling Operation Rausim Kwik. 'It was early in the morning,' he told the Los Inquiry. 'I directed the Acting Chief of Operations, Lieutenant Colonel Salamas, to advise the Defence Force that the operations had to cease forthwith.' Salamas's 'priority' signal to all units read:

> '1. As of 18 March 1997 Operation Order Rausim Kwik 03-97 is now cancelled and made null and void. All troops to revert back to normal.
> 2. Troops engaged in this operation will return all stores and equipment including weapons to Q stores.
> 3. This is the directive of the Acting Commander PNG Defence Force.'

Singirok's supporters were to argue later that this signal was defective, that it needed to come from Aikung himself because Lieutenant Salamas had no authority to overturn an operational order signed by a Commander.

Singirok claimed to the Los Inquiry that he never saw any written order terminating Rausim Kwik. Major Enuma knew about it. 'Walter Salamas sent a signal throughout the whole country as Chief of Operations saying Operation Rausim Kwik was to be aborted,' Enuma recalled. 'And the prisoners had to be released immediately. We had prisoners in Wewak, at

Taurama, at Kiki Barracks at the airport. Guys were all over the place. The whole Force was involved. So I sent a signal the next day to counter Salamas's signal: "Nobody is to release any prisoners."' With Singirok's removal Major Enuma assumed what one junior colleague was to call 'directive control'. 'When the General was sacked, when he got the order on Tuesday, the General simply walked home,' Enuma said. 'I was left in charge of all these guys with so many orders coming in. I just told them, "I'm sorry, I cannot release these guys. Do you know what you're talking about? The men have rebelled." There would have been bloodshed if we'd let these guys go.'

Brigadier Singirok received the written notification of his dismissal at noon. He knew it was coming, of course, and had called a morning parade at which he urged the soldiers at Murray Barracks to act with restraint and within the law. He told them he would accept his dismissal without reservation and that they should respect the office of the Commander and give his replacement their support. Colonel Aikung got very little of either, respect or support. 'On the morning of the 18th,' Aikung said, 'I went to the office and I advised General Singirok. I told him of the changes and he told me, "Yes, it was coming" ... [We] had a short briefing and I said, "I need to take over properly from you." And he advised me that he would do it sometime later and he left and I took over the office.' Singirok left for Flagstaff House which then became the effective nerve centre for Operation Rausim Kwik. Colonel Aikung told the Los Inquiry his first job was to see what he could do to get the Sandline personnel released.

'From that day on, from when the Commander was sacked,' Enuma said, 'my battle was with the Government. I was actually taking the Government by the horns. It was either the whole or nothing. The Government had the resources to stop me. But I had the initiative on my side to get these guys out. My basic aim was to get the Sandline guys out.' Sir Julius Chan thought he had won already. That Tuesday morning he told Mark Stewart, a journalist with the New Zealand *Evening Standard*, that he had 'neutralised' Singirok. Stewart had worked for Chan as his Media Director in 1994–95. 'It was almost what you would classify as a "military coup",' Stewart quoted Chan as telling him. 'Singirok has been sacked by the Cabinet. I think he went out of his mind a little bit.' The *Evening Standard* report also quoted Chan as saying Singirok would be arrested that day and charged for illegally mobilising his men. 'He took over the Governor General's residence and the NBC. It was in the style of a coup but he did not have his men behind him,' Chan claimed confidently.

At Murray Barracks, where many troops had gathered, soldiers were telling the media a different story. 'Any move the Commander does from today onwards I am with him with all my troops now surrounding me,' one junior officer told the television cameras. 'Gentlemen, are you going to stay with me and support the Commander?' Loud cheering was the answer. 'We just can't back down now,' another soldier said. 'He has already done it, you know. It has happened and there's no turning back and whatever happens to the Commander we're all at the back of him.' Some were very angry. 'If the Government can pay $US36 million to Sandline International,' one asked, 'why can't they pay our allowance that is due to us? How about our food in the mess? Since the weekend we haven't had anything.' Crowds had also begun to gather outside Defence headquarters. The police had already flown one mobile squad down to Port Moresby from the Highlands to back up those in the city who had been on alert from the previous day.

The sacked Commander made a final call to his Minister. Captain Chris Siroi, the Transport Officer from Mathias Ijape's village who had by this time moved into Ijape's room at the Islander Hotel, told the Los Inquiry Singirok rang the room at 9.20 a.m. He claimed Singirok told Ijape he was sorry. '[After] he apologised, the Minister said, "We were having lunch together on Friday, why did you not tell me?" Then he said, "The Secretary, James Melegepa, was having lunch with [you] ... on Saturday ... why did you not tell him of [your problems] ... with the contract?"' In a media release Ijape referred to this conversation. 'I spoke to Singirok,' he said, 'and he has assured me that he will accept the Government's decision and will cooperate with the incoming Commander which is a sign of [a] mature and good citizen.' In his own media statement, Singirok said he had been sacked for speaking out. He accepted his dismissal but was still demanding a full inquiry into the Sandline deal which, he claimed, had 'mortgaged the country to foreigners at the expense of its citizens'.

Captain Siroi made an effort on his Minister's behalf to break up the Rausim Kwik leadership clique. He contacted the SFU Commander, Major Toropo, a Southern Highlander who had an office near his at the Air Transport Squadron. 'I rang Toropo ... and told him that the NEC had made a decision. "All the Ministers and even Opposition Parliamentarians know you are the OC, SFU, and they are very well aware that you are actively supporting Jerry Singirok. So since he has been sacked I would suggest to you that you stop supporting Mr Singirok." That was on the 18th, I rang him about 11 o'clock ... I was with the Minister and three other officers ... black-listed by people who were loyal to Singirok.' Siroi said he told Toropo he could arrange a meeting with Ijape but Toropo never took up the offer. Captain Siroi said he learnt later that soldiers loyal to Singirok had threatened to kill him. 'They could not lay their hands on me,' he claimed, 'so they went into my house at Murray Barracks, House No. 140. They destroyed my personal effects worth of K5000.'

'Terminator' controls the gate

Wearing a pink T-shirt, jungle camouflage trousers, dark glasses and brandishing a pistol, Corporal Alan Nangurumo, code-named 'Terminator', quickly became one of the enduring images of Operation Rausim Kwik. Corporal Alan, as he is known, was in charge of gate security at Murray Barracks. Pictures of him 'controlling' officers at the Hohola gate flashed around the world. After one altercation, Alan spoke to Mark Corcoran of ABC TV's 'Foreign Correspondent'. 'They are officers of this place but we don't know what they are up to.' 'You have doubts about their loyalty?' 'That's right. That's right, exactly. That's what it is.' 'And what do you do with people who you think may not be loyal?' Corcoran asked. A second soldier manning the gate replied, 'We have to teach them a lesson.'

The original Rausim Kwik orders anticipated divisions within the Force. A number of Colonels who had been made redundant by Singirok were singled out as potential enemies, 'mainly the senior officers who had been retrenched or are awaiting court decisions based on their appeals,' the orders said. 'They may want to conduct counter operations. They are to be restricted from entering [Murray Barracks] . . . and surveillance is to be conducted on their movements and their residences.'

'When I went out,' Major Enuma said, 'I told Alan and the guys to control the gate. No civilian was to come inside.' Enuma was concerned any disruptions outside would be a distraction. 'In the meantime, I've got prisoners here, there, everywhere. I couldn't get myself tangled up with these little things that were going on. I had things to look out for. I told the guys, "No soldiers are to go out on the street. No civilian is to come inside the camp. If they want to do their protest let them do it outside. We must not be involved. We must be focused on our primary mission which is to get rid of Sandline." So those boys on the gate they did a tremendous job.'

There was a 'suspects' list. Captain Paul Kaliop from Defence Intelligence found he was on it. 'I asked one of the soldiers, "Why am I being singled out?" And he said, "Oh, we have got a list of names of some officers that are not allowed to go out of the barracks . . . you are one of them."' As the days went by he was warned by fellow officers to stay well inside. 'They said, "Just stay where you are and do not try to go out the gate, these guys are after you."'

On that Tuesday morning students at the University of PNG began a boycott of classes in support of Singirok's demands. Bomb hoaxes closed government offices. By noon, a significant crowd of civilians had gathered outside Murray Barracks blocking the roads. The General Secretary of one of PNG's most radical non-government organisations, Melanesian Solidarity (MelSol), Peti Lafanama, was one of the protest leaders. Enuma said he was surprised at the public support. 'I'm a military man and I don't have a lot of connections. A lot of people including Sir Julius say there was a plot by his political enemies and that we were used. I can tell you I was taken completely by surprise by the amount of public reaction. I had never known Peti Lafanama or Jonathan Oata (another NGO leader). I'd never heard of these guys. I was just a soldier who had done my time in Bougainville. I was given a task to do and I looked at the best possible way to do it as speedily as possible,' he said. 'And I was completely taken aback by the amount of public support that came behind us in the first couple of days.'

Getting rid of Sandline was Enuma's top priority. 'I wanted them out by Wednesday,' he said. He was worried about what might happen if the Government succeeded in freeing Tim Spicer. 'As soon as the command element was out they would rally support to try and free the [other] hostages. In the process we would have had a confrontation,' he believed. 'We would have definitely had a shoot out. The quickest way to de-escalate the whole situation was to get them out of the country.' He was also unsure what Sandline's subcontractor, Executive Outcomes, might do if the drama dragged on. However, the officer given the task of arranging flights disappeared. 'That really pissed me off,' Enuma said. Some tickets had been found in the East Boroko residence. These were given to the 2IC Murray Barracks, Major William Bartley. 'I was given a bundle of Qantas tickets by Major Toropo,' Bartley told the Los Inquiry. 'I was told by Major Enuma that these people needed to go out quickly so ... I made reservations for [them to] travel via Singapore to Johannesburg.'

That flight, PX 392, a joint Air Niugini–Singapore Airlines service, would leave at 3.25 p.m. the next day, Wednesday 19 March. It was time to bring Spicer back to shore. He had been held on the HMPNGS *Buna* out at sea since Sunday night and had been given a rough time. Spicer later told the London *Telegraph* that when they came for him at about midday Tuesday, he feared he was about to die. He said a small boat pulled up alongside the *Buna*. Captain Namah, wearing a black singlet, combat trousers and running shoes led armed soldiers on board and ordered Spicer to the end of the landing craft. 'I thought, "This does not look good." Then I saw the boat. He said, "Get into it." He tied a combat jacket around my head as a blindfold. I really thought this was the end—they're going to take me out to a small island and shoot me. Nobody would have known,' he told the London *Telegraph*. 'We sailed out for an hour. Then I sensed we were changing course. My blindfold had slipped, and out of the side, I eventually saw we were coming down a creek into land.' They had taken the sea route to Bootless Inlet behind Taurama Barracks, avoiding any trip through the streets of Port Moresby.

That afternoon Sir Julius Chan called in the media to announce that his Government was 'in absolute control'. He accused Singirok of 'gross insubordination, bordering on treason' claiming that 'you could conclude ... he was attempting a coup'. He would be 'dealt with' by the law. Sir Julius said there were 'unanswered questions' behind what he called 'this attempted destabilisation of the Government'. And he postulated an astonishing theory that Singirok was part of an international conspiracy to manipulate the world price of copper. 'The Commander's initial assertion that the relevant issue was Sandline,' he said, 'may be a convenient front for other more sinister motives.' Chan's evidence was 'research, not yet complete' that three copper mines had been hit by trouble in the late 1980s forcing up the copper price. Perhaps someone was worried, he speculated, about Panguna reopening. There was a second claim, equally fantastic, that Sir Julius made that afternoon. 'According to all the reports, all the appraisals, all the readings that I've got up to just a few minutes ago,' Sir Julius said, '[Colonel Aikung] enjoys popular support among his peers.'

Sir Julius may have been rattled. He admitted to being extremely tired. But at about the same time as his news conference was ending he was getting support from a quarter that had been criticising him over the Sandline issue for three weeks. John Howard was on his feet in the House of Representatives in Canberra. 'I would therefore make it very clear on behalf of the Government and I believe on behalf of every Member of the House,' the Australian Prime Minister said, 'that we utterly deplore the attempts by the former chief of the PNGDF to defy the authority of the duly elected Government. In the circumstances the action taken by Sir Julius Chan to remove the head of the Defence Force was both understandable and justified.' Later, on the ABC's '7.30 Report', Howard rejected a suggestion Chan had made, broadcast on 'AM' on ABC Radio that morning, that Singirok might have been encouraged to do what he did by Australia's reaction to the mercenaries. Howard suggested a better analysis might be that 'instability had been fuelled' by the presence of the mercenaries.

Chan's claims that he was in 'absolute control' of the country and Colonel Aikung was 'in control' of the Defence Force were contradicted on the National EM-TV News at six o'clock that night. Major Enuma appeared live to announce that Operation Rausim Kwik would continue. He said the removal of the mercenaries from PNG had the support of the whole army with the only exceptions being 'some Colonels'. 'Changing the Commander is not the issue,' Enuma stated. 'The issue is Sandline International.' That night there was a meeting at Murray Barracks at which some of the 'exceptions' to whom Enuma referred attempted to reassert authority. Lieutenant Colonel Salamas told the gathering, which included the Commanding Officers of both Murray and Taurama Barracks, that the instruction from the Defence Minister was for Operation Rausim Kwik to cease and for the Sandline personnel to be freed. Captain Kaliop, who was present, quoted Salamas as saying the 'civil police were now after the ring leaders of Rausim Kwik'.

In a radio interview with the ABC that night, Jerry Singirok rejected Chan's world copper price conspiracy theory. 'Yesterday was not a military coup or a takeover,' he said. 'I have absolutely no connections as to who influenced me. [It was] my own conscience as a professional officer to express discontent about what the Government was wanting me to do ... The world is watching. Suddenly, before the election, Sir Julius is going to use Sandline to wipe out the rebels. He believes he can do that and convince the people he can do it militarily. And I'm not prepared as the Commander to do that for him.' In an analysis of the events of that day written some months later, Henry Ivarature, a Senior Research Fellow at the PNG National Research Institute, wrote that: 'Despite international apprehension and the Government's anxiety, Singirok's action received overwhelming public support. Impromptu public opinion surveys conducted by the *Post Courier* on 18 March in two provinces revealed that 90 per cent of the people interviewed supported Singirok.'

Whereas the public demonstration in support of Singirok outside Murray Barracks had been peaceful on the Tuesday, it was a different story on Wednesday 19 March. The foreign media had been pouring into PNG. Cameramen and photographers found to their delight that there was a big and volatile crowd outside Murray Barracks. Singirok's accusations of secret commissions in the Sandline deal were readily believed by a public convinced their political leaders were corrupt. The Governor General, Sir Wiwa Korowi, thought so too. In a provocative full-page advertisement in both national daily newspapers that morning Sir Wiwa warned that 'Papua New Guinea will by destroyed by Papua New Guineans one day through greed, corruption, nepotism, malice, selfishness and manipulation.' He wrote of the 'termites of greed' and claimed 'abuse of office' had reached 'alarming' proportions. 'Yes, I know it and you know it,' the Governor General told the politicians 'we have gone excessively beyond the tolerable levels for national forgiveness from the citizens of this country.' Sir Wiwa wrote directly to Sir Julius Chan that day as well. Chan later claimed the Governor General recommended that it would be in PNG's best interests for him 'not to touch Singirok'.

Inside Murray Barracks there was another, short-lived attempt to halt Operation Rausim Kwik. Defence Intelligence Captain Kaliop told the Los Inquiry that one of the more senior Lieutenant Colonels, Yaura Sasa, called all staff officers from headquarters to the Force Operations Centre that Wednesday morning and told them Rausim Kwik was over. 'As soon as he said that, Major Enuma turned around and asked, "Do you know the ramifications of this action?" And before Colonel Sasa could answer, he stormed out of the office.' Captain Kaliop said that the meeting broke up. About an hour later, he claimed, Enuma returned. 'This time in our armoured vehicle, the SSV, and he came out this time in full battle gear. He had his body armour on, helmet, pistol, and he asked me for the senior officers. I just pointed ... When he came out I was still standing there. He said, "You tell these people they will have to take us on if they want to get these Sandline personnel" ... and he drove off again.'

Major Enuma was given a hero's welcome when he walked through the crowd outside the barracks at about 11.00 a.m. Holding his unloaded 9 mm pistol above his head he passed NGO placards bearing slogans such as 'After Bougainville, We're Next', 'Send the Mercenaries Home' and 'People's Coup'. He walked into the barracks through a broken section of the fence facing the Sir Hubert Murray Highway and addressed a large group of soldiers on the grass under the trees next to the Murray Barracks Australian Rules football oval. 'We will not take the law into our own hands,' he told them. 'We will not do any public demonstrations. That is up to the citizens.' He told soldiers to remain in uniform and he would call on them if they were needed. 'There are some elements in the higher ranks who are against us,' he said 'but you have a moral responsibility to ensure things do not get out of hand.' He told a group of journalists afterwards that the mercenaries who were being held at Wewak's Moem Barracks wanted to go home to Africa but that Chan was stopping them.

The reality was that the Defence Force CASA aircraft which was supposed to transport the Wewak contingent to Port Moresby was having mechanical problems and Chan would not provide a charter. 'Wednesday, I had a lot of problems,' Enuma recalled. Not the least of them was that the citizens' demonstration deteriorated into a riot. Enuma claimed that the Port Moresby Police Commander, Sam Inguba, was under a lot of pressure to suppress demonstrations. Deputy Commissioner Ludwig Kembu told the Los Inquiry that when he arrived at 12.30 p.m. there were 5000 demonstrators. 'I called the Mobile Squad Commanders to prepare themselves for dispersal actions,' he said. Things got out of hand at about 1.30 p.m. when opportunists in the crowd attacked the Taurama self-service supermarket opposite the barracks. MelSol organisers called the mob back but it became a stampede. 'Men, boys and even girls poured into shops, helping themselves to clothing, shoes and electrical equipment,' one of the *Post Courier*'s PNG journalists reported.

Police eventually reasserted control. Kembu said he then spoke to the MelSol organisers telling them the assembly was illegal. 'Police had not given approval for them to be there and I asked them to present their petition within half an hour ... and allow the people to go home.' Two Ministers arrived, Works Minister Peter Yama and Minister for State Paul Tohian. At about 3.00 p.m. the General Secretary of MelSol, Peti Lafanama (who was to win a seat himself in the elections), presented Yama with a petition calling for the resignation of the Prime Minister and the deportation of the Sandline mercenaries within twenty-four hours. After a few speeches the crowd started to disperse. Across town, Port Moresby's Governor, Bill Skate, and his Peoples National Congress Deputy Leader, Simon Kaumi, told a news conference that the Governor General should be given powers to sack the Prime Minister. Skate said he had met with Chan for more than an hour the previous day and was 'disgusted'. 'The Prime Minister should step aside,' he said, 'and allow for a public inquiry.'

During the afternoon, John Howard rang Chan assuring him that Singirok's sacking had Australian support and asking whether Sir Julius would receive a personal emissary. Sir Julius agreed. But they gave different interpretations of what the emissary's mission would be. Howard told the Australian Parliament that the 'reasonable alternatives' he had discussed with Chan at Kirribilli House ten days earlier remained on the table. 'I continue to hold the view,' he said, 'that it is not in the interests of PNG, it's not in the interests of the region, certainly not in our interests, to see what I described last night as the sordid use of mercenaries in our part of the world.' At his third news conference in as many days, Sir Julius said he appreciated Howard's call. 'I want to say that you don't know who your friends are until you have a situation like this.' A news release issued later said Sir Julius wanted to focus on rectifying 'the destabilisation' Singirok had caused and that revised aid and defence relations would be discussed.

'I do not want to be premature in predicting a specific outcome,' the statement quoted the PNG Prime Minister as saying, '[but] I believe Australia may finally realise the terrible toll that Bougainville has placed on Papua New Guinea.' Sir Julius's expectations seemed to be that Australia might be prepared to duplicate at least part of the Sandline arrangements—to provide the PNG Defence Force with counter-insurgency training, hardware and electronic warfare capabilities that would enable him, in Tim Spicer's words, 'to negotiate from a position of strength'. Howard's 'personal emissary' turned out to be a three-member delegation—led by the head of the Australian Foreign Affairs Department, Phillip Flood. The other members were a former Australian High Commissioner to Port Moresby, Alan Taylor, and a Deputy Secretary of Defence, Hugh White. Their brief was to convince a seriously weakened PNG Prime Minister that he had no option left but to abandon the Sandline deal. They left Canberra on a RAAF VIP flight and arrived in Port Moresby at 8.20 p.m.

At his news conference Chan had addressed the two issues raised in the NGO petition. 'The question of resignation you can forget about,' he said. 'No one group has any authority to ask the Defence Minister and the Deputy Prime Minister or even myself to resign ... The cancellation of Sandline as demanded by the petition will be considered by Cabinet,' he said. But then, under intense questioning, Chan backtracked, denying this meant PNG might pull out of the contract. 'I didn't say I was prepared to terminate the contract ... They won't get out of the contract. We've paid the money and we expect the results,' he said. Sir Julius did concede that the proposed military operation on Bougainville might have to be modified because of all the publicity. Colonel Aikung sat with him at the news conference. But Chan protected his new Acting Commander from having to answer any questions, cutting in when a question was directed to the Acting Commander, saying that it was 'totally inappropriate' to ask Aikung his attitude to Sandline.

Aikung's most loyal follower, Acting Chief of Operations Walter Salamas, took matters into his own hands to secure the release of Sandline's key Command and Control Group. First, he went to the house at East Boroko, ordered the soldiers guarding it to leave and installed a cook to prepare a meal for Spicer, Van den Berg and the others to eat when he brought them back. 'I was instructed by the Defence Minister, Mr Ijape, to find out where the Sandline executives were and [return] them to their residence,' Lieutenant

Colonel Salamas told the Los Inquiry. He drove out to Taurama Barracks. 'I went and met with Brigadier Van den Berg who was living in the Commanding Officer's flat ... I mentioned to the CO of the 1st Battalion, Lieutenant Colonel Kanene, that the Minister had asked me to come and [release] the Sandline executives ... he said he was going to talk to Major Enuma ... I had to apply some pressure ... they eventually gave in and gave me a vehicle ... As we drove down to the Taurama main gate, we were then challenged at gunpoint.'

Major Enuma said he turned up at Taurama Barracks with Major Toropo just by chance to check on the prisoners. He described the scene in an interview some months later:

> I was surprised to find, when I got there, Tokam Kanene and all the officers were just sitting around. It was supposed to be a Command Post ... and I said, "What's happening here?" "Oh, sir, the Chief of Operations is releasing the prisoners." I asked, "Who did he get the orders from?" "He's using his rank." And I said, "Nobody is going to release any prisoners. Do you realise what you are up to. The moment these guys get out we are going to have a bloody shit fight on our hands. These are the Command and Control Element... They may call for reinforcements. They've no doubt got contingency plans both internal and external. Do you realise what you guys are up to?" So I told the Commander 1PIR, "Nobody is leaving." When Salamas came out, I said, "What's all this story about releasing the prisoners. Do you realise what you are doing?" "I realise, I know the consequences," he said. "I'll wear it."
>
> Because CO 1RPIR was the CO there and I didn't want to overrule his command I said, "CO, if the Colonel has to talk to one of them then make it one-on-one, Colonel to Colonel. The rest of the guys stay." And Colonel Salamas pushed his rank and said, "No. Everybody's going. I'm the Chief of Operations. Tokam Kanene," he shouted down at Tokam. Kanene naturally snapped to attention. I said, "Stuff this!" I told Gilbert, "Let's get the hell out of here." We drove out past Taurama gate, past the "death road", and I said, "No! We just can't let these guys out." So we turned around and came back. We told the guards on the gate, "If these guys come out, stop them here."

Major Toropo was asked at the Los Inquiry if it was true the Sandline executives had been manhandled. 'I cannot say manhandled,' he said, 'because we stopped the vehicle and opened the door for them to come out. We turned the vehicle around and we took them back to Taurama Barracks Officers Mess.'

'There was a frightful scene,' is how Tim Spicer described it to the British journalist, Andrew Lycett, in London seven months later. 'A lot of jabbing and punching. I think they did it deliberately to intimidate. I got hold of the Commanding Officer of the barracks and told him I was not going back to that cell, I was not a political prisoner.' Lycett wrote that Spicer's argument 'cut no ice' and he went back to his cell. The reason Spicer was in a cell and Van den Berg was in the CO's flat is that Spicer had tried to escape when he had been locked in an ordinary room in the Single Officers quarters after being brought ashore from the landing craft. 'I had retained a knife [the pocket knife he had pushed up his anus]. So in an effort to escape, I began cutting through part of the door,' he told Lycett. 'What I didn't realise was that there was a guard outside. A pistol was put to my head and I was taken to a real jail—eight foot by ten—where I was eaten alive by mossies.' But his treatment was still better than on the barge. One of the soldiers even slipped him a packet of cigarettes.

Lieutenant Colonel Salamas was not the only one who allegedly attempted to rescue Tim Spicer from his Taurama Barracks cell that day. Soldiers from the 1st Battalion 'captured' two employees of the security firm, Network International Security Services, part-owned by Sir Julius Chan's son, Byron. The soldiers claimed the two security officers, John Butler and Richard Alden, were on a mission to find and free Spicer. Butler and Alden were handed over to the police along with a pistol and ammunition allegedly found in their car. The Commander of the 1st Battalion, Lieutenant Colonel Kanene told Neville Togarewa of the *Post Courier* that both men had gone to Murray Barracks on two consecutive days and were arrested at the officers quarters close to where Spicer was being held. The incident added to Singirok's suspicion that there was a blossoming connection between Sandline and Byron Chan's company and that they planned to go into business together to provide a security force for the Panguna mine once it resumed operations. Byron Chan dismissed the speculation. Some of Sandline's aircrew did leave Papua New Guinea that Wednesday. They went on the Air Niugini–Singapore Airlines flight, PX 392, to Singapore and made connections through to Johannesberg.

Tell the lads

Sandline's Financial Controller, Michael Grunberg, was in Hong Kong right through this hectic period, frantically trying to keep in touch with developments. An amateur electronics buff who had his own communication scanning equipment called the ABC office one day and when I met him at a location of his choosing, he gave me a large envelope with tapes and transcripts of a number of Grunberg's conversations with mobile telephone users.

'We've been here in Hong Kong all week and we've been talking directly to Julius Chan and his team,' Grunberg says on one tape, apparently recorded when he was able to speak to Johnny Maass, the Sandline Colonel in charge of the training team in Wewak. 'Hopefully it will all come to an end soon. I've got lots to tell him. Tell the lads, tell all the lads that we've been very concerned and that we've been keeping a close watch on the situation, literally day and night, Johnny. And the Prime Minister has been superb. I've been speaking to him literally every three hours over the past two days.'

In one call Grunberg tells the PNGDF Chief of Staff, Colonel Jack Tuat, he saw him on the TV News. 'You looked like a movie star.' In another he suggests to a PNG Government Minister that they might have to resort to a 'dirty tricks' campaign against Singirok. One of Grunberg's major concerns was to get an undertaking from the PNG Government that it would cover Sandline for the costs of keeping the giant Antonov 124 with its cargo of helicopter gunships on stand-by in Thailand. He kept asking for a letter guaranteeing that PNG would meet any additional costs caused by the disruption of the contract.

On the Friday, when most of the mercenaries were at the Port Moresby airport about to be deported, Grunberg was understandably keen to ensure that publicity was kept to a minimum. 'Johnny, I want you to pass the word amongst the boys to give no comment to the press. No comment to the press. Because it's possible when you get to Hong Kong there'll be a lot of journalists—if they manage to get into the transfer lounge. Okay? So just say, "I'm very sorry, you'll have to talk to my company, Sandline International. The contract is with Sandline and only Sandline can comment." Okay? And I'd like you to spread that word.'

The whole of Port Moresby virtually shut down on the Thursday. Chaos reigned in the streets outside Murray Barracks. The crowds returned bigger than ever, taunting the mobile police squads and retreating into the grounds of the barracks whenever the police moved against them. There were by now gaping holes in the fence fronting the Sir Hubert Murray Highway and the demonstrators and looters knew the police had no desire to move into the barracks and take on the army. For the police it was an extremely frustrating day. The looting continued. One security guard located inside one of the stores under attack retaliated. As a looter reached in to grab what he could the security guard chopped off his hand with a machete. The PNG Business Council later estimated the losses from looting and foregone trade that day amounted to more the K300,000. 'The whole of Thursday you could hear all this firing of tear gas and weapons,' Major Enuma remembered. 'It was worse than Bougainville.' The Operation Rausim Kwik Commander spoke to the NGO leaders.

'I gave a very strong warning to all those organisations,' he claimed. 'I told them, "I don't want any more looting. Okay? You're going to lose the plot. Looting and chaos doesn't achieve anything. In fact, it's the opposite. Those opposing us want it to go on so they can blame the chaos and anarchy on those who instigated the trouble and they will water down the whole issue of corruption."' Trouble spread to other PNG centres and a few foreign business interests panicked. BHP, for one, shut its Port Moresby steel processing centre and evacuated Australian employees and their families. In Lae, BHP's deserted warehouse was burnt down the following week. British Petroleum was another to order its people to flee PNG. Fred Haynes, BP's PNG boss, asked his superiors in Australia what they would do about his wife, a PNG citizen. 'She's certainly not going to leave.' The British High Commissioner, Brian Lowe, was asked by the Foreign Office whether he should send his wife out for her own safety. 'What sort of a message do you think that will send to the 1000 or so Brits here?' he asked London.

Lowe had been attempting to negotiate Spicer's release into his protection. When that became known, demonstrators gathered outside the British High Commission. The Commission, unlike Murray Barracks, is not near any shops so those who came together there were genuine anti-Sandline protesters. While it was noisy, there was no violence. Back at Murray Barracks, however, the long-anticipated clash between the police and the military almost happened late in the afternoon. After a tense day, mobile police pursued some protesters towards the Hohola gate, the one Corporal Alan controlled. Some tear gas canisters fired after the fleeing protesters landed in the barracks, one at the feet of the Chief of Staff Tuat. Rubber bullets had also been fired and some soldiers, thinking they were under police attack, tried to break into the armoury and get weapons. Prominent amongst those who stopped them was 'Terminator' Alan who jumped in front of soldiers trying to kick down the armoury door, warning them back with his pistol.

Colonel Tuat had been about to address several hundred soldiers who had that morning signed and presented a petition to the Defence Secretary, calling for Singirok's reinstatement and for the mercenaries to be deported within twenty-four hours. That night, officers from most barracks pledged their loyalty to Singirok. (And, in a complete about turn from his pledge to Chan three nights earlier, the President of the Police Association, Aloysius Aviaisa, said the police union now backed the sacked Commander.) In a pathetic letter acknowledging he had no control, Colonel Aikung pleaded with Singirok to help him. 'It is with utmost concern that I am writing to you. The situation within Murray Barracks is that the CO has lost control of his command. The gates into Murray Barracks [are] manned by servicemen who are unauthorised and armed to the teeth. The wives and children do not feel secure. They have run out of food ... I am under siege unnecessarily ... General, I seek your understanding and kind assistance, especially to get the word to the troops to leave the gates alone.'

Brigadier Singirok did not reply. He and his legal adviser, Peter Donigi, were busy trying to convince the police to lay criminal charges against Spicer. Donigi, a lawyer who had been prominent in PNG public life for years (amongst other things he had been PNG's Ambassador to Brussels), had offered his services to Singirok a day or so into the crisis at the request of Sir Barry Holloway, a friend of Singirok's and a former policeman. Deputy Police Commissioner Kembu told the Los Inquiry that he had gone that afternoon to Flagstaff House at Singirok's invitation. 'Singirok pulled out a bag and he opened it and showed us some cash in US dollars and said, "There is half a million US dollars in there."' The money had been found in a safe the soldiers had taken from the East Boroko residence and cut open. 'Donigi then told us, "We want an investigation to be done as to how the money was allowed ... into the country."' Kembu said Donigi suggested Spicer should be charged with breaching foreign exchange regulations. 'The Brigadier then showed us a pistol.' They also wanted Spicer charged with possessing an unlicensed firearm.

Prime Minister Howard's 'special emissary' group had a tough, four-hour session with Sir Julius Chan. Their blunt message was that if he did not abandon the use of mercenaries on Bougainville then Australia would take what were described as 'dramatic and drastic measures that would harm PNG'. These measures would involve both the annual $A300 million

Australian aid package and the $A12 million Defence Cooperation Program. Australia would give PNG the six months notice required under the aid treaty of its intention to cut aid. Chan was reluctant. He stressed PNG's contractual obligations and tried to bargain. Would Australia buy the military equipment Sandline had acquired? The answer was no. Sir Julius had hoped the meeting would help reinforce his authority in the face of Singirok's revolt. But the Australians were taking advantage of the destabilisation. 'In all our discussions,' Chan said somewhat bitterly later, 'the question of rebels was never addressed ... Representatives of the Australian Government threatened to withdraw financial and non-financial assistance to the Independent State [of PNG] because of the engagement of Sandline.'

The meeting broke up with the Australians unsure of the outcome. Chan would see them again on Friday morning. Sir Julius consulted with two of his own Ministers who had been to see Singirok that evening to seek a compromise—the Foreign Minister, Kilroy Genia, and Provincial Affairs Minister Barter. In a news release issued that night, Sir Julius announced the suspension of the Sandline contract and the setting up of a judicial inquiry with one term of reference: 'to inquire into the circumstances surrounding the engagement of Sandline International'. The inquiry would not be given much time to carry out its investigations and public hearings. It would be required, Sir Julius said, to report to Cabinet within two weeks. 'I believe it is the only way to dispel all allegations against the Government and set the record straight,' the PNG Prime Minister's statement said, adding 'We have listened to the wishes of our people.' The PNG *Post Courier* the next morning headlined the story: 'Singirok Wins'.

The arrangements for the deportation of the mercenaries were also put in place late that Thursday night. Enuma was up at Flagstaff House with Singirok when Sandline's Financial Director, Michael Grunberg, rang. 'Walter,' Singirok had said, 'this is one of the Sandline Directors ringing from Hong Kong.' 'I picked up the phone,' Enuma said, 'and I told him, "You will organise two aircraft. One out of Wewak to Moresby and one from Moresby to Hong Kong. Get your men out!" I said, "Don't give me any bullshit because you have the capacity, the capabilities, the contacts. Just do it. Get your men out of here. At the earliest by Friday, tomorrow. The latest by Saturday." Grunberg said, "I want to talk to the General and the Prime Minister." I told him, "The Prime Minister hasn't got your men. I've got your men! You've got to talk to me. The General? The General hasn't got your men. I've got your men! You've got to talk to me. You've got to do what I say. You've got one hour to come back to me." So he called me back one hour later and said, "Yes, it's done. There'll be one aircraft from Wewak to Moresby. And one aircraft from Singapore to Moresby." I said, "Fuck that! You get an aircraft from Moresby out, not from outside in! You've got that." So he said, "Yes, okay, we'll get an aircraft from Moresby out."'

The police were out in force early Friday mounting roadblocks to prevent demonstrations. The newspaper headlines of Chan's suspension of the contract helped ease the public mood and Port Moresby was relatively calm all day. Even the banks felt confident enough to open, and queues stretched out the doors into the streets. Student leaders at the university organised a protest forum inside the university grounds. But when the Education Minister, John Waiko, who had been Professor of History at the UPNG, turned up to accept their petition, they refused to give it to him. Later, they did hand it over to the two PPP Ministers, Yama and Tohian, who had received the NGO petition outside Murray Barracks earlier in the week. The Australian emissaries found their second meeting with Sir Julius Chan far more to their liking than the first. He told them that the mercenaries were leaving. He was chartering an Air Niugini airbus to fly them out to Hong Kong that afternoon. They would all go, Chan told them, with the exception of Spicer, who would stay for the inquiry.

As the newspaper headline said, Singirok seemed to have won. But the Brigadier was determined to go further and bring Sir Julius Chan down. He called a news conference at Flagstaff House that Friday and set a new deadline. 'At the beginning of this saga,' he said, 'I asked for only three things to happen. One, the Sandline contract must be terminated and the personnel be repatriated from PNG. Two, an independent Commission of Inquiry. Three, I wanted the Prime Minister and the two Ministers who are implicated to resign.' While the first condition was being met he was not happy with the announced inquiry. He wanted it headed by a Papua New Guinean Judge, not the Australian, Justice Warwick Andrew. And he claimed it would not be impartial if it was reporting to a Cabinet including the three implicated Ministers. He gave them until Tuesday, when the Parliament would begin its final session, to resign. Singirok also handed out copies of the Sandline contract and invited the public to judge whether Chan, Haiveta and Ijape 'have been telling you the truth all along'.

Deputy Police Commissioner Kembu gave evidence that he had been asked to go to Flagstaff House a few hours before that news conference. He claimed Donigi wanted him to lay criminal charges against Chan, Haiveta and Ijape. 'He went to the printer, the computer printer, and he pulled out a piece of paper and he handed it to me ... Donigi explained that it was a crime under the Criminal Code for any person to organise [a private army] ... and he handed me the copy of the Sandline contract and he said,

"If you look at the Sandline contract, what the Prime Minister and Deputy Prime Minister and Defence Minister have done is a crime under the Criminal Code. These are the sections that you will have to charge them under."' Kembu claimed he began to get uneasy. 'I began to feel that Singirok was trying to control the Police Force as well.' He said he made no further visits to Flagstaff House partly because the Police Commissioner became suspicious of him after the TV News that night had shown him standing with Donigi at the Commander's residence.

A small but vocal crowd gathered at Jackson's International Airport to see the mercenaries leave. Farewell was not quite the public sentiment. One placard read: 'Sandline Piss Off'. A few of the mercenaries from Wewak seemed oddly out of place. They were carrying woven baskets and artefacts, gifts from members of the SFU. Their Air Niugini F28 flight from Wewak had been delayed that morning and the SFU had taken them into town on a shopping trip. The Sandline personnel they met up with in Port Moresby had been far more closely guarded. The men held at Taurama and Kiki Barracks were brought together at the Air Transport Squadron and then escorted to the commercial terminal by heavily armed troops. Spicer was not with them. 'I made a last-minute decision not to deport him,' Enuma told the Los Inquiry, claiming evidence had turned up sufficient for criminal charges to be laid against him. The mercenaries boarded the Air Niugini Airbus late in the afternoon but refused to allow the crew to take off. They said they would not leave until Spicer was aboard. But after a while they relented and the Airbus took off for Hong Kong. Major Enuma turned to a TV camera and said, 'We've won. Sandline's leaving.'

The fact that Spicer had not boarded took a number of people by surprise, including Defence Intelligence Captain Ben Sesinu who had been given Spicer's leather briefcase to return to him. The case, which had been confiscated when Spicer was detained, contained his passport, a ticket and $US10,000 in cash. Sesinu said he knew that Brigadier Singirok had removed a cheque for K24 million from the case. That was the cheque from Roadco that Spicer had been given as 'comfort' pending the transfer of the first $US18 million to Sandline's bank account in Hong Kong. It had ceased to have any value when the transfer was made but Singirok wanted it for evidence before the Sandline Inquiry. However, Captain Sesinu never knew it was worthless and he had decided not to give the briefcase to Spicer until the very last minute because he did not want a scene. 'When the plane was about to depart,' he told the Los Inquiry, 'I gave the bag to one of the Air Niugini staff to hand it over in the aircraft.' Once Sesinu realised Spicer was not on board he had it retrieved.

Captain Sesinu held onto the briefcase. The next day he exchanged some of the US currency for kina at the Lamana Hotel. Soldiers loyal to Singirok picked him up there in the hotel's exclusive club, the Gold Room, on Saturday night, after he had been drinking for several hours, and accused him of stealing $US10,000 from Spicer. Sesinu admitted to the Los Inquiry he did take some of the money. 'There was a bundle of money ... I took $US700 out and I did tell the Foreign Affairs personnel because I was not given any operational allowance for my job with intelligence ... I said the Intelligence Bureau is going to pay for it.' The Foreign Affairs person he told was Simon Namis–his drinking partner. Asked what had happened to the $US700, Sesinu claimed it had all been spent. 'I used it up on my work-related matters on intelligence.' The reason for being in the Gold Room, he said, was because that was where he did a lot of his intelligence work. Sesinu complained to the Los Inquiry that he had been taken back to Murray Barracks and locked up for the rest of the weekend.

The British High Commissioner was another who found out at the airport that Spicer was being held back in PNG. 'After Spicer was abducted, I tried all week to arrange consular access,' High Commissioner Lowe related. 'They would not let us see him. Jerry Singirok kept saying, "Yes, yes." But he was not doing a thing to make it happen.' On the Friday, Lowe was told about the deportation flight and he went out to the airport. 'I saw Nick Van den Berg and asked him where Spicer was. "They took him away about half an hour ago," he said.' Eventually somebody referred the High Commissioner to Walter Enuma. 'I told Enuma I needed to speak to or see Spicer, that he was a British citizen and I had consular responsibility for him. Enuma said, "He'll be facing currency charges." "I have to speak to him," I said. Enuma arranged it that night. He was also allowed to ring his wife ... That Friday night, I spoke to Singirok again and he said, "We'll be giving him to the police." "Give him to me," I said. "Tomorrow," said Singirok.'

Colonel Muso RIP

'At around 8 p.m.,' Colonel Alfred Aikung said, 'two soldiers came to my house [at Murray Barracks] and at gunpoint demanded the car keys for the Disciplined Forces Institutional Housing Project vehicle, the Muso. Members of my family were terror stricken ... They were all crying ... my second eldest daughter had a fit and almost choked herself to death, but fortunately her uncle revived her by way of mouth-to-mouth resuscitation.'

It was Friday night, 21 March. Colonel Aikung had been Acting Commander of the PNG Defence Force for not quite four days. 'Because they cocked the gun on me, I said, "Fair enough. Is that all? Anything else?" And they said, "No, we will just get the key and go." So I got the key to the vehicle and I gave it to them.' Aikung told the Los Inquiry he recognised one of the two soldiers. He was a Private attached to the transport workshop at Murray Barracks. The other soldier was masked.

The soldiers did not take the Muso far. They drove it outside the Hohola gate and set it ablaze in front of one of the barracks that had been built by the Malaysian contractor under the Institutional Housing Project. The vehicle had been the subject of gossip within the Defence Force ever since Aikung had taken possession of it as Chief of Logistics and Chairman of the Housing Project Committee. The Muso had been supplied to the PNGDF by the Malaysian contractor. The next day, Saturday, somebody affixed a sign to the burnt out wreck: 'Colonel Muso, 1995-1997, R.I.P.'

Colonel Aikung and his family fled from their home in Murray Barracks soon after the armed soldiers had driven away. They crept to the fence adjoining the PNG Electricity Commission compound on the Hohola suburb side of the barracks and clambered over. Aikung told the Los Inquiry that all nine of them, his wife, himself and seven children, climbed the fence. 'Outside of the barracks, yes. [It was] very, very dangerous.'

What tenuous authority Chan's Acting Commander, Colonel Alfred Aikung, might have had evaporated that Friday night after his vehicle was confiscated and set on fire, and he and his family fled from Murray Barracks in fear for their lives. The man who Sir Julius had proclaimed just days before to have enjoyed 'popular support among his peers' had to be fetched from an Electricity Commission employee's house where he had sought temporary refuge. 'At the Parliament House, I briefed the Prime Minister and his Cabinet Ministers on the events of the day,' Aikung said. One thing they wanted to know was whether the Government should appeal to another country to send in troops to take on the PNGDF. 'The government was in a position to do that [try to suppress the revolt] but they were advised not to do anything, to avoid the confrontation ... I was asked whether we could use a neutral force to try and get the control back into Murray Barracks and knowing the situation on the ground, I advised that it was impossible.'

The Australian troops in Townsville had been in a heightened state of readiness as a Ready Reaction Force since Thursday. Despite Aikung's advice, the subject of whether Australian soldiers could be sent to PNG to help the Chan Government restore its authority was raised with Canberra. Australia never really responded. Australia's Opposition Leader, Kim Beazley, said the Australian Government was adopting a cautious approach, which he believed was appropriate. 'There is always a reservation by every Australian Government,' he said, 'that if Australian citizens are in some way or another in trouble, and we can do it, then we're prepared to use our armed forces to do it. It's appropriate. Anything further than that would be entered into with exceptional reluctance.' The Australian Democrats Senator, Andrew Murray, warned about how any response by Australia might be viewed. 'What you have is a lot of civil unrest and rioting,' he said, 'and I don't think that's a time for us to act as a colonising power. Let the independent state look after its own affairs.'

The burning of Colonel Aikung's Housing Project vehicle vividly emphasised the point that, in any conventional sense, the PNGDF was leaderless. Enuma, who had seen his first mission through—the expulsion of Sandline—decided there was a need for someone to exert authority over the junior ranks. He held a news conference at Murray Barracks on Saturday morning. His comments were misinterpreted by some international newsagency journalists who reported that this Major had declared himself the new leader of the PNG army. The words Enuma actually used were, 'We are not in command, but we are in control.' He did elaborate. 'There is no way the guys in headquarters have control over the troops,' he said. 'That is evident.' The Major said he had ordered the soldiers to stay in the barracks until the political crisis was resolved. On the burning of Aikung's vehicle he said he did not approve of the action of the troops but claimed they were provoked by Chan's comments that Colonel Aikung was in control.

Spicer had spent his last night as a prisoner of the PNGDF. Soldiers took him to the Port Moresby Metropolitan Police Station at Boroko. 'I was very glad to get into police custody,' Spicer said when he spoke to the media a few days later, 'very glad to be back in what I would call a proper system.' Singirok rang the British High Commissioner telling him Spicer was at the Boroko cells. He could go and get him. 'When I turned up, I was surrounded by this motley group of soldiers,' Brian Lowe said. 'One was particularly aggressive—he had on a bandanna, camouflage pants, he had a big gun and was wearing a Cardiff football guernsey. I could see and hear Spicer demanding to see the British High Commissioner. "I'm here," I said, tapping him on the shoulder. They had removed his belt and had him locked up in a cell. I spoke to the Metropolitan Superintendent, Sam Inguba, about releasing him. Inguba said they were charging him with an alleged firearms offence but that the police were concerned for his safety if he left with me. The soldiers were still around. Spicer told him, "I'll take my chances with the British High Commissioner."

'I went down the stairs to sort out the bail. "This will have to be Magistrate's Bail," they said. But there was no Magistrate around and we probably would not have been able to get one until Monday. "Inguba said it would be Police Bail," I told them. But Inguba had driven out. So a very cooperative Sergeant got in touch with Inguba on the police radio. "It's Police Bail," he said. "K200." I didn't have that on me so I asked if they would take a cheque. "No." I had to go home to look for K200. It was Saturday and no banks were open. But as I drove out I thought that if I could not find the K200 I'd go to the Papua Club and do a whip-around!' But Lowe did have K200 at home. 'When I got back and paid the bail, there were still soldiers about not wanting to see Spicer released ... Then Walter Enuma turned up and went into a meeting. After half an hour, he came down the steps, smiled and said the police had explained everything and that I would be responsible for making sure Spicer turned up for his court appearance. And that I could take him.' It had taken five hours.

Deputy Police Commissioner Kembu claimed Enuma put a lot of pressure on the police to hold onto Spicer and not release him into Lowe's care. 'But we explained to Enuma that he was entitled to bail just like anybody else and we were intending to release him to the British High Commissioner.' Kembu said Enuma claimed that Spicer might escape. The police placed six armed policemen around the High Commissioner's residence. Lowe was amused by this because while the military saw it as keeping Spicer in, Spicer was thankful it kept the soldiers out. But the High Commissioner, a Scotsman, was not so amused at Spicer's wit. 'The night we got him out, after he'd cleaned up and showered, we were having a gin and tonic on the verandah and I asked, "How do you get into the Scots Guards, Tim? There's nothing Scottish about you." And the cheeky bugger replied, "Well, you know, High Commissioner, all our colonial troops need white officers!"'

Chapter Fifteen

Parliament Under Siege

*The Military Maintain the Pressure; The
Parliament Backs Chan; An All-night Blockade;
Chan Steps Down
23–27 March 1997*

'Don't make me angry!' Brigadier Singirok snapped at a group of foreign journalists and television cameramen. 'There is absolutely no coup!' The media had clustered around him following a combined church service at Murray Barracks for soldiers, officers and families on the morning of Sunday 23 March. A number of prominent PNG citizens attended the church service and photos of one of them, Sir Paulius Matane, hugging Singirok appeared in the PNG media the following day. Expelling evil foreigners in the form of the mercenaries, taking a self-righteous stand against corruption and praying to God make up a potent mix in Papua New Guinea, where the power of the Christian faith as taught by the missionaries should never be underestimated. On that Sunday there were many PNG Christians thanking God and praying for Jerry Singirok.

One of the most visible Christians, the Governor General, Sir Wiwa Korowi, held a news conference at Government House announcing that he would be calling a meeting the following day, Monday, of Constitutional Office Holders to 'discuss the crisis' and to advise the Prime Minister on possible actions 'to take the heat off' himself. Sir Wiwa himself turned up the heat, raising doubts about the technical legality of the Sandline contract because contracts of that size, $US36 million, required the Governor General's signature and he had never seen nor signed it. And under questioning, he commented that Chan, Haiveta and Ijape were 'not indispensable'. The Speaker of the National Parliament, Sir Rabbie Namaliu, one of the 'Constitutional Office Holders' Sir Wiwa referred to, was by this stage playing a far less public but undoubtedly more productive role trying to defuse the crisis. A former Prime Minister himself and well respected by all sides in PNG politics, Sir Rabbie had received a call from the Prime Minister's office asking him to return to Port Moresby. Chan told the Los Inquiry that the suggestion of approaching 'a middle-man' came from the Secretary General of the Commonwealth, Chief Emeka Anyaoku, who had rung him from London and who was about to visit Australia.

'I was asked to come back from Rabaul that weekend,' Sir Rabbie recalled in an interview some months later. The request was for him to act as a neutral party to establish dialogue with the Brigadier General. 'Sir Julius asked me to come to Parliament. I asked if I could get some background from the Ministers concerned. So I sat down with Mathias Ijape. John Giheno [the Mining and Petroleum Minister] joined us a little later in my office along with Peter Barter. They took me through what had happened during the week. And then Chris [Haiveta] came and spoke to me. They put to me that since it was difficult for any of them to talk to the former Commander directly they wondered whether I could act as an intermediary. After our meeting I then met with Sir Julius and he put it to me formally and gave me the mandate to speak to Singirok. He gave me the terms of reference of what I should say to him.' This was that the first two of Singirok's three demands were being met. The commission of inquiry would happen and the Government would be prepared to terminate the contract. Sandline was gone.

'On the question of resigning, Chan told me to tell Singirok that he would find it very difficult to do that because of the constitutional implications and the fact that it would set a bad precedent. But, he said, "Tell him that if it is the wish of the Parliament—to have me step aside—I will accept the decision of Parliament." With those terms a meeting was set up for me to go to Murray Barracks which I did on Sunday.' Before Sir Rabbie went to his appointment with the Brigadier he met with a group of distinguished individuals (none of whom, it must be said, were strong Chan supporters) who had taken on the role of offering counsel to Singirok. All four of them knew him well. They were: Sir Barry Holloway, a former Speaker; Meg Taylor, a lawyer and former Ambassador to the USA; John Pasca, the General Secretary of the PNG Trade Union Congress; and Richard Kassman, a leading PNG insurance broker who was on the Board of Transparency International (PNG).

'I had breakfast with Holloway, Taylor, Pasca and Kassman,' Namaliu said. 'They took me through that side of it because they had obviously been helping Singirok. They wanted to ensure that [whatever way it was resolved] the Constitution be upheld.' In fact, Taylor, Pasca and Kassman had already had one private audience with Chan, on the previous Thursday in his Parliament House office. Chan told the Los Inquiry that they urged him to 'accommodate' some of Singirok's demands. Namaliu drove to Murray Barracks. 'Just as we turned past the lights at the intersection outside the barracks,' Namaliu recalled, 'the Military Police, who were expecting me, met us and they took me up to the gate.' There they were stopped by armed soldiers. But the message had been sent down to let the Speaker through. They drove up to Flagstaff House which itself was well guarded by armed soldiers. 'I spoke to Singirok. Peter Donigi was with him. I told him what my mission was. He responded that he was glad that the Government had agreed to set up an inquiry and he would cooperate with it. Secondly, he was glad the contract was terminated. On the question of resignation he obviously would have liked the Prime Minister to resign but he would accept whatever the decision of the Parliament was.

' "But," Singirok said to me, "I want you to convey to the Prime Minister that I have no control whatsoever over the public out there and what they are likely to do. I may still have some influence over the soldiers but outside of this barracks I have none." They wanted to show me the money [$US400,000] they had taken from Spicer and I said, "No, I believe you." I came back to Parliament and told Sir Julius the outcome of the discussions. I then indicated to him my thoughts. I told him that I'd go away and try to put something on paper. In the evening, I got back together with Meg, Barry, Richard and John in my office. We went though the issues and the Constitution.' Namaliu wrote out several options and at midnight went to Barter's house. 'I just wanted to run it past Peter because Peter and [Foreign Minister] Kilroy Genia had been sent by the PM during the week to see Singirok.' The brief was delivered to Chan the next day, Monday. 'One of the options was: "You don't have to resign but you can step aside." That gets around the problem of Parliament having to elect a new Prime Minister,' Namaliu said he informed Chan. 'It would be up to the Cabinet to select an Acting Prime Minister.'

Other people, too, were working that weekend on ways to ease the crisis. Senior officers of both the Police and the Defence Force met and agreed to cooperate to prevent looting and other problems. Colonel Aikung was in hiding at his brother's residence on the University of PNG campus and did not attend. Deputy Police Commissioner Kembu, who did, said a major worry was the complete loss of authority from the Commander's office. 'We were concerned about the breakdown of command and control in the army barracks, and one of our efforts was to see if we could re-establish command and control.' Aikung had to go. It was obvious, Kembu told the Los Inquiry, that the Acting Commander was unable to control the Force. The most likely senior officer to command respect was the Chief of Staff, Colonel Jack Tuat. 'I spoke to Mr Tuat to see if he could accept the job,' Kembu said. 'Jack Tuat accepted ... with some reservations ... I briefed the Prime Minister on that.' Cabinet met that Sunday, revoked Colonel Aikung's appointment and appointed Colonel Tuat as the substantive Commander.

The Cabinet also directed the Police Commissioner to ban all marches and public demonstrations during the session of Parliament beginning on Tuesday. Reports from Madang, Singirok's home province, said 3000 demonstrators had turned up to an anti-Government, anti-corruption rally that weekend. The previous day there had been rioting and looting in the provincial capital of the Simbu Province in the Highlands, Kundiawa. NGO groups in Port Moresby were talking about organising a big march on the Parliament. Port Moresby Governor Bill Skate announced he would move a motion on Tuesday calling on Chan to resign. Defence headquarters sent out a signal to all unit Commanders. 'Be advised that certain non-government organisations are planning public protest marches against government corruption,' the signal said. 'As unit Commanders and OCs of sub units [you] may be requested to participate ... The headquarters PNG Defence Force official position is that, as the PNG Defence Force ... is an apolitical organisation ... units are not to be involved in the activities.'

In the circumstances it was no great surprise to anybody when Speaker Namaliu postponed the annual prayer breakfast at Parliament scheduled for the Monday morning. Tuesday's Parliamentary proceedings became the focus of an apprehensive nation's attention. While Singirok's ominous public ultimatum on Friday had been for the three Ministers to resign before the Parliament met on the Tuesday—with consequences he would not specify if they did not—the weekend discussions, with Namaliu as go-between, shifted the emphasis onto what would happen in Parliament after the sitting began. Technically, Chan was in a strong position. A successful no-confidence vote would simply bring on an election and Chan could remain as Prime Minister during the campaign. The writs for the scheduled election were to be issued in a few days time anyway, on Thursday. 'Although we cannot force him [to resign] constitutionally,' John Momis told a news conference called by the Opposition parties, 'we expect to force him morally and politically.' Paias Wingti drew much laughter when he suggested the PPP, Chan's party, now stood for the 'People's Pockets Party'.

Operation Rausim Kwik turned its attention to applying pressure on the Parliamentarians to vote against Chan. Official minutes taken by the Military Assistant to the Commander, Lieutenant Colonel Fabila, of a 'crisis' meeting within Murray Barracks which Major Enuma was invited to address reveal the strategy. Enuma told the officers, all of whom were senior to him in rank, that 'the force must be seen to exist as a force'; that the aim was to help Members of Parliament work within 'the constitutional framework to have the PM, DPM and the Defence Minister removed from office'; and that the army should 'not use force to make the change—the public has been rallied, they will take up the issues of corruption to the government'. Enuma stressed the importance of the PNGDF making 'one stand as one force from the most junior private to the [most] senior officer'. He said the 'Opposition parties have met—Bill Skate, Roy Yaki and Sir Michael Somare are ready with a motion'. The minutes note that 'Major Enuma stated that the overall effect of our action is to totally change the trend of politics in Papua New Guinea'. The crisis meeting delegated considerable power to Major Enuma. 'Lieutenant Colonel Pinia proposed,' the minutes say, 'that Major Enuma be in charge of all current operations relating to the crisis but [he] must keep the office of the Chief of Staff informed. And all agreed.'

Singirok's last parade

'I am no Messiah,' Brigadier Singirok shouted. 'I am only an instrument.' Dressed in civilian clothes and speaking through a megaphone that he held to his lips, the sacked PNGDF Commander was once again addressing 'his' troops. 'I humble myself. I don't intend to get this glory. But I cannot put up with corruption.' The parade at Murray Barracks on Monday 24 March 1997 took on the atmosphere of a revival crusade. The new Acting Commander, Colonel Jack Tuat, had invited Brigadier Singirok down from Flagstaff House to address the parade. Tuat claimed to the Los Inquiry he had hoped Singirok would calm the troops.

If that was his hope it was not realised. Striding back and forth across the dais, Singirok fired the men up. 'I have a serious, serious loyalty problem with Chan and Haiveta,' he barked out to the assembled troops. 'I cannot say yes to them any more.' Several times Singirok bellowed: 'The Defence Force is intact!' Sandline, he claimed, would have destroyed the PNGDF. 'They are international terrorists as far as I'm concerned. They go to third world countries, banana republics, they make national forces totally useless. That's what they nearly did here.'

The Brigadier's portrayal of himself as the anti-corruption saviour of Papua New Guinea might not have had the same impact that morning if the soldiers had known about Singirok's Visa Card account in London.

But news of the £30,000 (K70,000) that the military clothing manufacturer and arms agent, Sidney Franklin, had deposited in the young General's account was not to break for several months. Singirok presented his actions as having preserved PNG's integrity. And the troops wanted to see it that way. 'The Force must continue to protect [PNG's] sovereignty and defend it's people. Right?' he asked them. 'RIGHT!' they yelled.

'I saw his speech as inciting,' Colonel Tuat told Justice Los's Inquiry. 'I think there was a lot of, obviously there was, a sound of jubilation ... The troops responded.' Tuat was, by this stage, Acting Commander. The Cabinet had rescinded its decision of the previous day to appoint him full-time Commander. Sir Julius Chan's Cabinet figured this was not the time to make a permanent appointment.

The Fabila minutes of the PNGDF crisis meeting reveal that Enuma was concerned about a possible confrontation with the police. Cabinet had ordered Police Commissioner Nenta to halt public demonstrations but the Rausim Kwik strategy now was to facilitate them. Major Enuma described a clash as 'the worst case situation ... [which] must be avoided at all cost.' He told the meeting there was a split in the Police Force with many policemen sympathetic. 'In fact,' the minutes say, 'Mobile Squads at McGregor Barracks were going to put down their arms and come and support the PNG Defence Force. Major Enuma informed the meeting that he went out this morning and told the Mobile Squads we thanked them for their support but they must continue to maintain [their] constitutional duties.' Deputy Police Commissioner Kembu gave a different version to the Los Inquiry. He said he had heard that Enuma went seeking support. 'I proceeded straight to McGregor Barracks and assembled all the Police Mobile Force personnel ... and informed them the consequences of ... them trying to deviate from the role as the law enforcer.'

However, Enuma claimed Kembu was acting on misinformation. 'I went there very early, at about six o'clock in the morning, to McGregor Barracks when I learnt that the police there were not going to go out and do their job,' he related in a lengthy interview in September 1997. 'I went there and asked, "What's all this?" And they said, "Sir, we've stuck together for the last few years on Bougainville. Why should we stand back and let you guys cop all this shit. We're together." I said, "Yes, we are together but you have to go out there and carry out your constitutional duties." "Sir," they said, "we want to leave our weapons and go out there without our weapons to show you guys that we are with you." I said, "No, you will take your weapons and you will do your job and we will support you. And we will control the crowd." I had breakfast with them. When Mr Kembu and Mr Inguba heard that I was in McGregor they drove out there like mad and rocketed everybody.' This account by Enuma is backed up by the Murray Barracks crisis meeting minutes.

'So we had an understanding already, the frontline guys out in the streets,' Enuma said. 'We had our network already in place. We knew that we would not confront each other. Except the senior officers did not know. They were shaky.' The hardships the policemen and soldiers had shared on Bougainville had broken down much of the traditional animosity between the two disciplined forces which had led to legendary street battles in the 1970s and 1980s. On Bougainville Police Mobile Squad members had been absorbed into army units. Of the five hostages taken at Kangu Beach and still then in BRA captivity, three were soldiers and two were policemen. Operation Oyster put their lives at risk. 'Perhaps the only opposition [to the new camaraderie] you will find,' Enuma maintained, 'is amongst the officers, the young ones who have never been in operations and the senior officers who have always been up there. But the soldiers and the policemen they know. They see these men in the other uniform as their friends. They've been together now on Bougainville for years. I have saved a couple of policemen myself, physically gone in there and got them out when they were surrounded.'

A new signal was sent out from PNGDF headquarters cancelling Sunday's message to all units to stay clear of protest demonstrations. It authorised several for Tuesday. '[You] are informed that only units in [the] Port Moresby area will march to the Parliament House,' it said, 'servicemen in Igam Barracks area [Lae], Moem Barracks [Wewak] and Lombrum [Manus] will conduct a sit-in protest as arranged by unit COs.' Singirok claimed to the Los Inquiry that this was not his doing. 'I was quite surprised when I saw the contents of this signal ... released by the Acting Commander then, Jack Tuat, authorising soldiers to march to the Parliament House. It is not proper under the Constitution and under the Defence Act for soldiers to participate in political protest marches.' While this sounds disingenuous the evidence shows that those most closely involved with Rausim Kwik did prevent any march of soldiers on the Parliament the next day. The police, however, had been informed by Tuat's office and approved a route for the march, catering for it in their operational plan Lukautim Siti ('look after the city').

The event that attracted most media attention that Monday was Tim Spicer's appearance in court. The crush of television cameramen, sound recordists, newspaper photographers and journalists quite overwhelmed staff at the Boroko District Courthouse. The court documents showed that Spicer, forty-four, married with four children, of Wandsworth in England, whose occupation was given as Sandline Project Coordinator, was charged on two counts. One was possessing an unlicensed firearm, a Makarov pistol, and the other possessing forty-one rounds of 9 mm ammunition. Onlookers booed and shouted insults. Spicer pleaded 'not guilty' and was granted bail. But the magistrate refused an application for his passport to be returned to enable him to travel to Hong Kong for medical reasons and to collect documents for the Sandline Inquiry. A few hours later, he told a news conference at the British High Commission that he would be happy to testify at the Andrew Inquiry. Sandline had acted 'in good faith', he said. Asked if Sandline's PNG foray had been a disaster, Spicer smiled and replied, 'It hasn't been a roaring success.'

Tuesday 25 March began with both national dailies reporting overnight desertions from the Chan Cabinet. Sir Albert Kipalan, the Deputy Leader of Sir Julius's Peoples Progress Party, was quoted as speaking on behalf of three Ministers from the PPP, himself as Lands Minister, Works Minister Peter Yama, and Agriculture Minister David Mai. 'We have decided to step down as Ministers while still remaining loyal to the party,' he was reported as saying, 'to enable the Prime Minister and other Ministers implicated to follow suit.' Parliament was scheduled to begin its session at 2 p.m. and the three Ministers gave Chan until noon to follow their lead with the implication that if he did not, they would vote against him. Both papers also reported that Provincial Affairs Minister Barter was prepared to vote against Chan on the Sandline issue. Apprehension gripped the capital. Shops, banks and schools shut. A thousand police were out early on the streets and Metropolitan Superintendent Sam Inguba told the public: 'I will not tolerate any looters.'

The Commonwealth Secretary General, Chief Emeka Anyaoku, flew into Port Moresby that morning on a chartered aircraft from Cairns in Australia in an attempt to play a mediating role. Chief Anyaoku had asked the Australian Government to provide him with an RAAF VIP jet to make the trip to PNG. He was told one was not available. Interviewed on the Monday night while still in Australia, he said he was 'very worried' that developments in PNG were challenging the 'fundamental values of the Commonwealth ... democracy, constitutionality and good government'. Australia's attitude was that on each of those scores PNG was doing better than Anyaoku's own country, Nigeria. While the Commonwealth Secretary General was making his own way to PNG, the British High Commission rang Murray Barracks to explain the purpose of the trip after a rumour spread that this African chief was on a mission to rescue Spicer. Anyaoku met Chan, Korowi, Singirok and Enuma and flew back to Australia that afternoon. Sir Julius was the one who took most encouragement from the encounter. 'We discussed the question of parliamentary supremacy,' Chan said. 'That I intended to uphold.'

Justice Warwick Andrew convened his Commission of Inquiry for a preliminary hearing. A lawyer appearing for Singirok foreshadowed a request to extend the terms of reference and the Inquiry adjourned for a week. Sandline was represented but the company was more interested that day in getting a chartered Antonov 124 full of military helicopters, rockets and other weaponry off its hands. The giant Russian cargo transport had been held up for a week, first in Thailand, then in Malaysia, and the delay was costing Sandline $US100,000 a day. Sandline's Financial Director, Michael Grunberg, called Acting Commander Tuat asking if the Antonov would be allowed to land the following day, Wednesday 26 March. 'The A/Commander advised that the aircraft must return to Russia until the current situation is resolved,' the Murray Barracks daily log records. 'The arrival of the aircraft ... would only add fuel to aggravate the current situation,' the log explains, adding that it would be 'wrong and improper for the PNGDF to accept the equipment before the Inquiry is completed'.

That same log records that journalists who rang Murray Barracks that morning (and even well on into the afternoon) were informed that an 'orderly' march of soldiers to the Parliament would be going ahead. Port Moresby Police Commander Inguba had been quoted in the morning press as saying he was aware that 'all elements of the Defence Force will march in uniform to Parliament... We have been advised that they will be marching peacefully. We have also been guaranteed that they will be unarmed. We agreed that they will be taking the shortest route in their march to Parliament [so as] not to inconvenience the public.' But such a march did not fit in with the plans of Operation Rausim Kwik. It would look too much like orchestrated military intimidation. After a week of having defied Colonel Aikung, Major Enuma now found himself having to deal with the consequences of having an Acting Commander only too willing to placate the rank and file.

SFU Commander Gilbert Toropo told the Los Inquiry of how Enuma had to confront the men who had supported him so enthusiastically up until then. 'Major Enuma went down and addressed [the men in] the car park towards the gate and he said, "We will not march to Parliament House! Let the civilians go themselves because they have their own agenda. We do not want to be seen to be mixing together with the civilians." And I can recall very correctly there were soldiers who were there [who demanded] of Walter Enuma: "We have come this far! Why are we not going to go to the

Parliament House?" And Major Enuma said, "We will not allow it guys. Cool down."' Enuma believed a march by the military would have played into Chan's hands. 'The Government wanted it,' he claimed months later. 'For obvious reasons—to cause a fiasco, looting and everything. Divert the whole issue from Sandline to a bunch of renegade soldiers causing problems and inciting public disorder. That was the strategy. My counter strategy was do absolutely nothing, don't march. And control the group.'

The other strand of the strategy was to make sure plenty of civilians demonstrated. At 10 a.m., the Boroko Police Station advised PNGDF HQ that some soldiers were travelling into settlements asking people to join the protest outside Parliament. Assistant Commissioner Kembu told the Los Inquiry he rang Enuma. 'I spoke to him on the mobile phone trying to find out why he was sending his men to escort these people in and then he asked me if I could meet him up at the army barracks.' They met in the Chief of Staff's office. 'Enuma asked me if I could relax all my operations ... and I told him, "Are you trying to interfere with my work?"' Kembu said he warned Enuma he could be charged with treason over Operation Rausim Kwik. Enuma agreed he told Kembu to ease off. 'I said, "Hey, you are going to have to change your mode of dealing with this from suppression to control because the whole city has gone up. The whole country is about to march. You'll end up with a situation where you and the Government are on one side and the military and the civilians are on the other." So I said, "Change the concept. Change your mode from suppression to control and we will help you to control it."'

Two hours before the session was due to begin, large and vocal crowds had gathered outside Parliament House. Police attempts to stop students travelling to the Parliament were thwarted by soldiers who escorted them in from the university. Shortly after 12.30 p.m., Enuma rang headquarters to complain that police were trying to disperse the crowd. Colonel Tuat rang Assistant Commissioner Inguba and asked him to reconsider. As Members turned up for the session there were thousands of people at both the front gate—the public entrance, which had been closed—and the rear gate—the Members' entrance, which was heavily guarded by parliamentary security guards and armed police. There were hundreds of police, many of them formed up inside the Parliament grounds. Major Enuma had successfully kept most soldiers in the barracks. He had about sixty deployed on the operation to facilitate the demonstrations. MelSol organisers were delighted with the turnout.

Televising Parliament

Throughout Papua New Guinea television sets were switched to EM TV. It had to be the largest television audience the station had ever had at two o'clock in the afternoon. For the first time in PNG's history, the Speaker of the National Parliament had granted permission for television cameras to broadcast the proceedings of a session live. The Parliament was not set up for direct television broadcasts. So half the Press Gallery was taken over as a television outside broadcast control booth. The mass of television cables running out to the cameras meant the door could not shut.

Following prayers, three Members tabled public petitions relating to the Sandline issue. Normal business was then set aside to allow the Governor of Port Moresby, Bill Skate, to move his motion that 'Parliament resolves that the Prime Minister now stands resigned and the Office of the Prime Minister is now vacant.' His motion was seconded. As Skate spoke there were rowdy interjections. 'On 22 February, when I first called this Government's intention an act of madness,' he began, 'and called on the Prime Minister to resign, little did I or anyone else know how much of a monumental disaster this exercise was.'

Skate called the Sandline deal a 'crazy plan to wage war' which 'was always doomed to fail'. The Member for Koroba Lake Kopiago, Herowa Agiwa, loudly called a point of order. The Speaker, Sir Rabbie Namaliu, acknowledged him and asked Skate to sit down. 'You and the former Prime Minister, Mr Wingti,' Agiwa said to the Speaker, 'every one of you fucked up this country. Do not blame anyone.' Sir Rabbie, who had been Prime Minister from 1988–92, glanced with concern at the television cameras, ruled that Agiwa's point of order was out of order and invited Skate to continue. Throughout the nationally televised debate, which was to go on for almost five hours, tempers flared and insults and curses were exchanged but fortunately perhaps, from the Speaker's point of view, the altercations were verbal not physical.

Outside Parliament, both at the front gates and the rear, noisy protests continued. A huge cheer went up when a PNGDF Iroquois clattered less than a thousand feet over the roof of Parliament House. While foreign television crews had been denied their march on Parliament this equally dramatic evidence of military intimidation was shown around the world.

Colonel Tuat told the Los Inquiry he had directed the helicopter to move from the airport to Murray Barracks to be on stand-by for possible medical evacuations. 'We found out later that somehow that helicopter was diverted and flew around the Parliament House at low level,' he said. The pilot, Charlie Andrews, was a good friend of Jerry Singirok's. He had given up a better paid commercial pilot's job when Singirok, after becoming Commander, had appealed to him to return to the Force. At 3.45 p.m. on this perhaps the most tense day in PNG's history, New Zealand's Defence Attache, Wing Commander Athol Forrest, rang Murray Barracks to inquire about PNGDF nominations to a Defence Seminar in New Zealand. 'A/COS advised,' the Murray Barracks log notes dryly, 'that due to the current situation, training ... would be deferred until further notice.'

Most attention was on the debate in Parliament. The longest serving Member, Sir Pita Lus, who is the only PNG politician to have won at every election since the very first in 1964, opposed Skate's motion that Chan resign. 'I do not support the Prime Minister but I am upholding and defending the Constitution and the democratic process ... I don't want the Defence Force to give orders to this Parliament for the Prime Minister to resign ... They have no right ... We must look after the interests of our people and protect the democracy of this country rather than allowing the army to demand the Government resign at gunpoint.' Even strong supporters of Skate's motion disassociated themselves from the soldiers. 'Let us be clear about one thing,' the Member for Wewak, Bernard Narokobi, said, 'we must not bow down to the military.' But, he said, Chan should voluntarily step aside. 'It is the honourable thing to do.' Opposition Leader Roy Yaki argued that Members would rightly reject changing the Government 'under the barrel of a gun' but the issue was not the installation of an alternative government, he said. It was the Sandline deal.

Chan's Health Minister, Philemon Embel, attacked individuals 'like the Governor General' for 'scaring the people by telling them that this country is in chaos. They panic and take the law into their own hands.' He argued that the 'people' of PNG could not understand 'complex issues'. The Defence Minister, Mathias Ijape, defended himself and Sandline. He said 200 soldiers and 50 policemen had died on Bougainville and he claimed Australia and New Zealand were partly to blame. 'We told them that we were not able to quell [the] Bougainville uprising if we did not have the helicopters that are fitted with rockets ... ships that could fire rockets, if we didn't have the intelligence network [to] hear conversations on the island ... So this private company was contracted and we asked them to provide us with the training and capabilities to tackle Bougainville ... Those capabilities [would have solved] ... the Bougainville problem in no time.' Sir Michael Somare successfully amended Skate's motion, dropping the resignation demand so that it simply asked Chan to step down for the period of the Inquiry.

Sir Michael began speaking quietly. 'Bougainvilleans are our people and we should not hire other people to kill them.' But he soon became riled and snapped back at one interjector: 'I am not like you who gets money from the leader every month, you pig.' Somare questioned the background of Sandline's South African associate, Executive Outcomes, 'because for 300 years they have been killing black South Africans. And these are the kind of people that the Government invites to come and intimidate Papua New Guineans?' The Manus Governor, Stephen Pokawin, asked Members to look at the issue from the soldiers' perspective. '[If I was] a soldier who was sent to Bougainville and while on duty in Bougainville I have had no rice to eat, no sugar for my tea, no bullet for my gun and upon my return to the barracks, I find that the same situation applies and that the Government has no money to pay my allowances. Suddenly, the Government pays a huge amount of money to hire foreigners to do my job. Will I not be very angry? If I was a soldier, I will definitely be very angry.'

Governor Pokawin urged Members to 'pause for moment and listen to the voices out there'. He said the army had not staged a coup. 'They have not removed us from office, they are appealing and petitioning the Parliament to do something ... I do not think the Constitution is at stake. Had the Constitution been at stake, we all would have been removed by the soldiers when this affair became public!' Chris Haiveta claimed the Sandline issue should never have become public. 'We have to change our laws,' he said, 'because everything in this country is an open secret.' He complained that the State could do 'nothing to protect itself'. Narokobi interjected: 'If the Deputy Prime Minister is suggesting an open, transparent democracy is not acceptable, we have a lot to be concerned about.' The ambivalent attitude of many was well summed up by Paias Wingti, who was worried about the army making demands as to who should or should not be Prime Minister. 'If they are allowed to do it to Sir Julius Chan, they will do it tomorrow to another Prime Minister. Our Constitution should not be tampered with in that way.'

Sir Julius Chan, the ultimate deal maker, let it be known around the parliamentary corridors that if Members supported him he would step aside anyway. By voting down the motion they would preserve the integrity of Parliament. Neither the crowd outside nor the public watching on television had any inkling of this when Sir Julius rose as the last speaker in the debate. 'We must never compromise the Constitution of this country,' he said. Chan rebuked Bill Skate, claiming that the Port Moresby Governor had come to him for a confidential briefing and he was shocked when some of the information appeared in the paper the next day. 'Next time,' he said, 'we will never believe you ... I am surprised that he should be the one to move this motion after getting all the information from me and using it as ammunition to knock me.' Skate jumped to his feet claiming that the reason he had gone public was that Chan had told him lies. At 6.45 p.m., after more than four hours of debate, the amended motion was put. The Parliament voted by a solid majority, fifty-eight to thirty-nine, against calling on the three Ministers to step aside.

The Ministers who had reportedly quit Chan's Cabinet–Kipalan, Yama and Mai–all voted with him. The only Government Minister amongst the thirty-nine who supported the motion was Peter Barter. 'While I remain a staunch supporter of the current Government,' Barter explained that night, 'I feel that standing aside was the best option for the Prime Minister in the light of the civil unrest in the country.' He said he had written to Chan explaining how he would vote and why. 'I have no regrets and I will stick by my decision even if I am sacked.' As soon as the result was announced, the Leader of Government Business, Andrew Baing, moved that Parliament adjourn. Some Members who had agreed to vote against the motion because they had been told that Sir Julius would voluntarily step aside were angry. 'When that did not happen immediately,' Sir Rabbie Namaliu said later, 'some of the Members came to me and said, "Hey, this is what we had agreed to do. He agreed to step aside. But he hasn't done it."' Namaliu said this was the first he had heard about the step-aside promise.

Outside the gates there was fury. The crowd at the rear entrance was particularly angry. Over the Parliament intercom came a message advising everyone within Parliament to stay inside as cars leaving were being stoned. The police, who had tried unsuccessfully to get the crowd to disperse before 6.00 p.m., had a contingency plan to whisk the Prime Minister and the Deputy Prime Minister away. Barely moments after the Parliament rose, Chan and Haiveta were taken to the basement car park, given police overalls to pull on and driven out in police vehicles. Sir Rabbie Namaliu said that when he got back to the Speaker's office, he was advised by the police that no Members of Parliament were to leave until the all-clear signal was given. He was told that Chan and Haiveta had already left. They got away just in time. By 7.20 p.m., Assistant Police Commissioner Mula rang Murray Barracks to report that armed soldiers outside the Members' gate were searching police vehicles trying to leave. 'Major Enuma was directed to control the soldiers and not to cause any problems,' the daily log records.

Parliament was blocked off. The number of soldiers was not large but those who were there were armed with M16s. And they were backed by thousands of civilian demonstrators cheering them on. The siege continued and some inside started to panic. A journalist from the PNG English-language weekly, the *Independent*, reported seeing some Members who had tried to leave via the back gate running back towards the Parliament telling bystanders as they ran that there was a military coup underway. He went and asked the soldiers at the gate who told him, 'No. We are just going to prevent any Members leaving.' One Member went to his car, got a gun and brought it back inside the Parliament. The *Independent* reported that a Government Minister was seen carrying a box of what appeared to be 9 mm bullets. 'As he was walking up the stairs from the Members' entrance another Minister with a hand gun visibly stuck in his pants asked for some and they shared the bullets. Another Member brought in a long object covered in red material.' An ABC Radio journalist, Marius Benson, got out but the vehicle he was in was searched by eight soldiers.

At least seven Members of Parliament attempted to escape by climbing over the Parliament's three-metre-high steel spike fence. Some did elude capture but others were not so lucky. 'A number of them tried and ended up straight in the hands of the Defence Force,' Namaliu related in an interview in September 1997. 'I did not know that until the next day when one of them rang up my office from wherever they were, it must have been Murray Barracks, asking though my Executive Officer if I could help, talk to the Commander, so they could be released to come back to Parliament. I never got the number exactly but the number that was given to me was four or five. One of them was William Wi, the Member for Angalimp South Wahgi. They climbed over the two fences. After getting over the first they had to deal with the second where the security forces were waiting. Some succeeded in getting away, Minister Michael Nali was one,' Namaliu said. 'I got onto the Clerk to ring the Police Commissioner and the Acting Commander and those Members were released and allowed to come back to Parliament for the Wednesday afternoon session.'

But most members remained inside for the night, fearful of what might lie ahead. 'There was a lot of fear in this building that night,' Namaliu recalled, 'and most people thought that not only was the Defence Force ready to move in but that they would come in here and have the whole lot of us arrested. That was what was going through the minds of everybody in this building. There were a couple of Members who had guns here. I did not know that until afterwards because Members are not supposed to carry guns into the building. One of them was Michael Nali, he had a gun. And he was waving it around here, apparently. By the time I found out he had already escaped. I was not prepared to ignore the possibility that we might have had a military takeover on our hands.' This was not to be. But Sir Rabbie Namaliu confided months later his worries about the precedent of intimidation that was set. 'The fact that it's happened once does give the people in the military the excuse that having done it once they could do it again. To that extent it has set a very bad precedent.'

That Tuesday night, however, PNG's democracy prevailed. 'Later that evening,' Namaliu related, 'the former Commander got in touch with me through Peter Donigi and Barry Holloway. They asked if the former Commander could speak to me. They wanted to know whether it would be possible for Walter Enuma to come up to Parliament to address the Members. I said, "That is fine but I want to know the following things. One, is he coming by himself or with other soldiers?" The answer was, "No, he's coming by himself and he may be accompanied by Peter Donigi." Secondly, I asked if they were coming unarmed. They assured me they would not be carrying any weapons. And then, thirdly, I asked what he was coming to talk to us about. They told me that he was coming to give us the assurance that they had accepted the decision of Parliament, that they respected the fact that the people's rights had been exercised on the floor, that they would uphold the Constitution and PNG's parliamentary democracy and that we should not be too concerned about any intention to take over the Government.

'So I said, "Okay, that's fine." After that conversation, I went back to the Speaker's lounge where many Government Members had gathered and I announced the request I'd received and told them of the conditions. They were not too sure about it. And I said, "No, I have got the assurance that they won't be armed." Some still wouldn't believe me. Because of the reservations I said, "Well, those of you who are not too sure, don't have to come. Those of you who are coming, follow." And I led the way up to the Conference Room attached to the Prime Minister's Office on the fourth floor. Quite a few Ministers chose not to come. The Defence Minister was one. I could understand that. He obviously felt vulnerable.' The Speaker then went to invite the Opposition. But they did not want to mix with Members of the Government. 'Emotions were running high and the Opposition put the blame squarely on the Government for having engendered this situation. They were pretty angry at being held up in the Parliament. And so I said, "I'll bring them down to the Opposition Conference Room as soon as they come."'

At about 11.15 p.m., Enuma, Donigi and Toropo all arrived at the back gate to Parliament House in a two-vehicle convoy accompanied by two SFU motorcycles. 'They arrived like cowboys, sort of wild people on a bike,' Deputy Commissioner Kembu claimed to the Los Inquiry. 'They just arrived and the tension built up.' Kembu said he thought that he and his men were going to have to take on the soldiers and the crowd. 'I sensed that the takeover of Parliament was imminent because the excitement had increased ... I stood in front of them and I told them to stop and I directed the policeman to block off the road ... I told them, "You stop or we will confront you. We are prepared to die for democracy."' Major Toropo said Kembu misunderstood what their purpose was. He said Enuma and Donigi were not on bikes. Those were ridden by two of his SFU soldiers. 'Ludwig Kembu was not aware that Major Enuma was going to go and talk to the politicians,' Toropo told Justice Los. 'He thought that we were mobilising ... so that is when he got so aggressive.'

The editor of the *Independent*, Dominic Karkas reported that Enuma ordered the soldiers to withdraw. 'The men were hesitant, some even refused to move. Major Enuma repeated the order. Some soldiers could be heard saying, "Lets just go in and get them." The Major quietened his men.' Karkas said Enuma told the men they were there to uphold democracy and that if they took over the Parliament they would be making themselves hypocrites. 'One of the men disagreed and Enuma called him over. Major Enuma looked the soldier in the eye and asked, "Do you respect me?" We could not hear what the soldier's reply was but he withdrew with the others.' Enuma had applied the pressure all day on the Parliamentarians to dump Chan, Haiveta and Ijape but he accepted the result. 'By storming into the Parliament what are we going to achieve?' he asked, reflecting on the night months later. 'I may have done it for good intentions but what about the next guy? You know what happens when guys are intoxicated by the power that they gain. They promise you an election next year and then they say, "Oh, the following year." That's your democracy out of the window. So what have we become? Another Banana Republic? Another African country?'

Kembu escorted Enuma and Donigi through the gates and up into Parliament House. 'When they turned up,' Namaliu said, 'I took them into the Prime Minister's Conference Room and introduced them. Then I asked Major Enuma to address the MPs. It was what they had promised on the phone. "We respect the decision of Parliament. You have made the decision. We may not necessarily agree with it but we accept it. We have sworn as soldiers to uphold the Constitution and we respect parliamentary democracy. And I want to assure you that we have no intention of taking over the Government." Although some didn't believe him, you could hear the sighs of relief. Everybody burst out in applause. The final thing Enuma said was, "I will now go out there and order my soldiers to go back to Murray Barracks but you have to give me about an hour to do it because I need to go out there and cool them down and demobilise them. And after that it should be possible for the Members to leave Parliament and go home. The police will advise you." Then I took them down to the Opposition Conference Room in B Wing and it was the same.' It was just past midnight.

Returning to the back gate of Parliament, Enuma and Kembu faced a tense situation. Kembu claimed the armoured car drove up to the gate and there was a man in the turret with a gun. 'There was a sudden build up of the military outside,' he told the Los Inquiry. MelSol's General Secretary, Peti Lafanama, who had been prominent in the protest all day told those cramming around the gate that the issue was not resolved. Karkas reported in the *Independent* that one of the soldiers yelled, 'Open the gates and let us go in!' 'However, Major Enuma, Major Toropo and Mr Kembu stood their ground and told the soldiers no one was going in,' Karkas wrote. 'Major Enuma ordered his men to retreat but not one soldier moved back. He then repeated his message to other soldiers who had come up. "We are here to uphold the Constitution and democracy, not destroy it. Let us not be hypocrites." The ordinary protesters had by then moved closer to the gates.' Karkas said that when the soldiers eventually obeyed and stopped the public advancing further, an angry NGO representative shouted out, 'Rank and file, your officers have compromised themselves.'

Major Toropo told the Los Inquiry that he and Major Enuma were abused by a civilian protester who was urging the soldiers to disobey them. '[When] we came out of the [back] gate, the crowd closed in ... And when we told them to move back [to allow] for the politicians to move out, one of the guys just told me and Walter Enuma, he said, "You officers are slack!" We had some heated argument and then Walter Enuma and I got the civilian leaders together to try to tell the civilians to make way for the politicians to move out ... they said, "No, we are not moving!" ... no one wanted to listen to Major Enuma.' Deputy Commissioner Kembu said that after Enuma and Donigi had explained to the NGO leaders what they had said to the Members in Parliament–that it was all over and they should go home–the civilian leaders held a separate meeting by the side of the road. 'Enuma came and told me, "It looks like they are going to stay on." So with Enuma we tried to explain the situation to them but they insisted that they stay on until the Parliament changes its decision.'

Waiting for the blockade to lift

Papua New Guinea's beautifully appointed Parliament, opened by Prince Charles in 1984 (and since cared for better than any other public facility in PNG), was not designed for overnight accommodation. On the night of 25–26 March 1997 it had several hundred unexpected overnight guests. As well as ninety or more politicians, there were senior bureaucrats, ministerial advisers, journalists and parliamentary staff—all unable to leave because of angry crowds blocking both gates. Most of those inside were not very pleased. A few were terrified.

The Speaker, Sir Rabbie Namaliu, had been waiting for two hours since Major Enuma had assured him and other MPs that there was no military coup and that he would be going out to order the sixty or so soldiers interspersed through the crowd back to their barracks. 'At about 1.00 a.m. we still had not heard anything from the gate,' Sir Rabbie said, 'and we knew it must have been a difficult situation. There were thousands of people out there.' It was well after curfew and the crowds knew they had broken the curfew laws. If the soldiers left, the police might move in and arrest them.

'We waited and waited and waited,' Namaliu said. 'At about 2.00 a.m., Somare got word. The police sent somebody up to tell him that Enuma was having a difficult time getting the soldiers back to the barracks because the people refused to allow the soldiers to go. And they asked if Somare and the Speaker could go out there and address the crowd. Somare rang me up at my office and I said, "That's okay by me." The advice to us was that we shouldn't go, there was no guarantee that we'd be safe out there. In the end, Somare and I decided, "No, we must go. If it's going to help defuse the situation we must go."

'It was obvious that the leaders of this demonstration were the leaders of MelSol, Melanesian Solidarity. They addressed us first, saying, "We are not going to allow you to leave the precincts of Parliament until this decision of Parliament is changed. We want you to take this message to the Prime Minister. We want him to step aside or resign." Somare then addressed them and I spoke. The gist of what we were saying was that the Parliament had made its decision. Somare told them how he and Bill Skate had sponsored the motion. It had been lost. There was nothing he could do because that was the wish of the majority. We would take the message back but we didn't know where the Prime Minister was. We then came back in.' They stayed in the Parliament building for the rest of the night. Outside, the demonstrators lit bonfires and sang 'We Shall Not Be Moved' and other protest songs through to the morning.

Only a limited number of people knew where Sir Julius Chan was. He spent the night at a friend's house not far from the Parliament. When Chan's Media Director, Mark Lillyman, suggested to a producer from Channel Nine's 'A Current Affair' that the Prime Minister had gone 'far away', there were erroneous reports carried by various sections of the media that Chan had fled the country. The protesters who had spent the whole night holding Parliament under siege were reinforced as the new day began. Police numbers had thinned out dramatically after the 'protesters council' had spoken to Somare and Namaliu but they built up again around 6 a.m. The exact number of soldiers in the vicinity of Parliament that Wednesday morning was hard to determine but it appeared to be fewer than sixty. Some began searching all cars heading for the Parliament. Police Commissioner Nenta complained to Murray Barracks that soldiers had taken up 'strategic positions' around the main city police station at Boroko. But a quick check revealed this apparently sinister development 'was recruits from Goldie Training Depot trying to do their banking'.

During the morning Governor General Sir Wiwa Korowi made a televised national address appealing to all soldiers to leave the streets. He said the whole country had to respect the Parliament's vote. 'If PNGDF members go against this decision, through defiance and ultimatum, it is unconstitutional,' Sir Wiwa said, 'and I appeal to the soldiers to return to their respective barracks immediately.' He said that under PNG's system of parliamentary democracy, once the Parliament had voted on an issue, 'we cannot change it through the barrel of a gun or by force ... I am asking soldiers to return to normal duties and work under your newly appointed Commander without delay.' At 10 a.m., the Parliament session resumed but Chan, Haiveta and Ijape never took their seats. 'On the morning of the 26th we were under extreme pressure from the Members of both the Government and Opposition to locate the Prime Minister and bring him back,' Deputy Police Commissioner Kembu said. 'And so we had to come up with plans to bring him back ... It was very dangerous.'

Kembu told the Los Inquiry that both he and the Metropolitan Superintendent, Assistant Commissioner Inguba, were in the vehicle that took Sir Julius back to Parliament through the soldiers and the crowd. Chan was not recognised. Soon after arriving Sir Julius directed that he wanted to have a meeting with Major Enuma. 'He requested to see us,' Major Toropo told Justice Los. 'One of his aides called for us and so we went in on his request ... and he told us he was going to step aside and he pleaded with us ... to go back and work together with the police to make sure that the civilians go back [home and] do not destroy properties or installations.' Sir Julius told the Andrew Inquiry that Major Enuma made an implied request that the troops involved in Operation Rausim Kwik be granted a pardon. 'I replied that there was no charge at present,' Sir Julius said, 'that I cannot interfere with the normal carriage of justice nor had the power to direct Constitutional Office Holders. However, if such charges were laid and the situation arose, then I would consider his request sympathetically.'

Enuma said he believed they reached an understanding on the amnesty issue. 'I met with the Prime Minister a couple of minutes before he stood down. And this is exactly what I told him: "Mr Prime Minister, I am very sorry that we have come this far. For a military man in uniform to face the Prime Minister of the day in the circumstances which we are facing, I hope this is the first and the last time. Your advisers, your staff, the various institutions that are supposed to provide advice to de-escalate the problem have allowed it to come this far. I have managed to control the situation up to now. I'm going to wash my hands. Whatever you are going to say when you go out there the onus is on you." So he told me, "Can you guarantee me–both me and my family–their safety? Can you people go out and perform your constitutional duties as soldiers of the PNGDF?" And I said, "I want the same guarantee. That you allow me to go out and carry out my constitutional duties, not as a rebel, but as a member of this force?" He gave me that guarantee. "You will go out and your first constitutional duty is to help the police get the crowd home after I make my decision." I said, "That will be done." So that guarantee was given, man to man. I live by my word and my honour.'

The Speaker said Chan informed him that he wanted to make a statement. Other Members had already told Sir Rabbie of the deal made the day before that if they voted to defeat the motion Chan would step aside pending the outcome of the Inquiry. 'I was told that was the undertaking he had given on Tuesday,' Namaliu said, 'but until he came back to Parliament on the Wednesday I was not sure he was going to do it.' At 3 p.m., Sir Julius Chan was given leave by the Parliament to make a statement. 'The Parliament has voted and parliamentary democracy is preserved,' he said. 'And that is all I stood for. I must now look at the perception outside ... This statement is made without any pressure ... I have chosen to defuse the situation to hopefully allow the due process of the law to take its normal course ... To force the Prime Minister to resign under pressure and duress would be wrong.' It was a lengthy, quite rambling statement and the strain of the ten days of havoc that the engagement of Sandline had loosed upon PNG was evident in his eyes.

'The people have shown and perceived that there is something wrong,' Sir Julius went on, 'and I think the best way for us to preserve that, is for them to express now through the ballot box ... So, Mr Speaker ... for the good of our country and in order to defuse the situation I consider to be a little bit explosive outside, I will direct the Deputy Prime Minister and the Minister for Defence to step aside. I myself will step aside. And I will have the NEC consider and appoint an Acting Prime Minister to continue to lead this Government into the elections and as long as the Commission of Inquiry [takes to] complete its exercise independently, without any interference from the three of us; that is the Minister for Finance, the Minister for Defence and myself who were responsible for this particular animal, the Sandline contract, that has ... caused a lot of confusion in the land ... [We] have gone through these tough times, with the foreign media painting us as rascals. They can condemn this country [for] losing democracy [but] they forget we did not fire a shot. That by itself is proof of the tolerance and the ability of Papua New Guineans to solve their problems in their own way.'

The crowds around Parliament went crazy with delight. At the front gate soldiers were hoisted onto the shoulders of civilians and carried around to chants of 'Singirok! Singirok! Singirok!' The daily log at Murray Barracks recorded that 'servicemen and the general public were jubilant and celebrated the "news".' Walter Enuma shook hands with his men, the Operation Rausim Kwik team. 'My first constitutional duty was to go out there and announce that the Prime Minister had stepped aside and that the Inquiry was to proceed,' he said. ' "And everybody is to go home peacefully," I told them. "The soldiers will remain to make sure everybody goes home." And the crowd just disappeared without any problems. I asked everybody to go home. And they did. And that shows the people's concern, the reason that they came and stood around the Parliament. Once they achieved what they wanted, they just went home. There was no looting. That was a credit to the people. That should be a very strong message. The people were fed up with corruption. They simply went home. Within minutes they were all gone.'

Back at Murray Barracks the man who had held sway over all comings and goings for the previous two weeks, the controller of the gate, Corporal Alan 'Terminator' Nangurumo, told Wally Hiambohn of the PNG *Post Courier* of his sense of achievement. 'I contained all the soldiers. The top hierarchy had no option but to come down to me. We are the backbone of the army,' he boasted. 'It was a fight against corruption ... we felt like any other citizen of the country about this issue. Some of our own people are here for their own interests. This is typical of the Defence Force. They knew something was wrong but they couldn't stand up because it was their bread and butter.' Corporal Alan revealed to Hiambohn the 'code names' of four other people central to the success of Operation Rausim Kwik. Singirok was known as 'Renegade', Enuma as 'Ace', Toropo was 'Eagle' and Captain Belden Namah was 'Skull'. Nangurumo claimed the key to their success had been discipline. 'We knew we were fighting brains so we had to be smart too. We really contained ourselves.'

After the Parliament rose, Sir Julius Chan drove to Government House to speak to Sir Wiwa Korowi. 'I had some very strong private discussions with the Governor General,' Sir Julius said in his written statement to the Los Inquiry. 'I pointed out to him that by his many remarks in the media and in becoming involved in the politics of the situation, he had inflamed the crisis ... He did not respond.' Chan was convinced there was a conspiracy against him and that his life was threatened. 'There were even fears of a rocket launcher being used from Flaghouse to destroy my house.' The Commander's official residence and Chan's home are more than a kilometre apart on separate hills. Chan also complained that the National Intelligence Organisation refused to keep him briefed. 'Beginning from 17 March 1997 national intelligence reports from the Chief of the National Intelligence Organisation seemed to disappear and became dormant up until after I stood aside on March 26,' he told Justice Los. 'I was not receiving my usual regular reports from the NIO during this period.' Very little of what happened in PNG was usual or regular during those ten days of havoc.

The morning after Chan's announcement that he would stand aside, on Thursday 27 March, the roaming Antonov 124 finally found a dumping ground for the Mi-24s, Mi-17s, rockets and other hardware it had been trying to drop off for a fortnight. It touched down at the Tindal RAAF base in Australia's Northern Territory. An agreement had been reached between Sandline's Michael Grunberg, PNG's Foreign Minister Genia and Australia's Alexander Downer that Australia would store the helicopters and arsenal until the situation in Port Moresby stabilised. A spokesman for the Australian Defence Minister, Ian McLachlan, said the PNG Government had been 'concerned about the delivery of this material to PNG in the uncertain circumstances and asked Australia to receive it and store it. We have agreed to do so.' Twelve months later, the dismantled helicopters and weaponry were still stored at Tindal while Sandline and Bill Skate's PNG Government squabbled over ownership. A PNG delegation which visited Tindal in April 1997 reported that the transport helicopters were earlier models than those PNG had been charged for and that the rockets were in 'poor condition' and 'weeping'.

The 1992-97 Papua New Guinea Parliament ended its final session on that Thursday before the 1997 Easter long weekend. The writs for the 1997 national elections were issued that day too. When the Parliament rose, the Members still did not know who the Acting Prime Minister was going to be. The Cabinet had trouble choosing a temporary replacement for Sir Julius. The PNG Press Gallery had assumed that the job would go to the next most senior member of Sir Julius Chan's People's Progress Party, Sir Albert Kipalan. But Sir Albert had not endeared himself to Sir Julius by having gone public with his claim on the Monday night that he would quit the Cabinet to set an example for Chan to follow. The Pangu Pati, whose leader, Chris Haiveta, was also stepping aside, quickly nominated John Giheno, the Mining and Petroleum Minister, as Pangu's choice for the Acting Deputy Prime Minister's job. The PPP eventually decided that its temporary leader should be the Forests Minister and Leader of Government Business, Andrew Baing. Baing could not command the same respect as Giheno and so the roles switched—Giheno became Acting PM and Baing his Acting Deputy.

It was not until Thursday evening that this was all sorted out. At the swearing in at Government House Sir Julius explained why Giheno had been chosen. 'I think the country needed a strong leader. He is the right leader.' Acting Prime Minister Giheno told journalists at the ceremony that he was 'just looking after the job for the time being'. He said he was not going to intervene if there was any legal action taken against the troops who had participated in Operation Rausim Kwik. 'With regard to the soldiers, the mutiny, you know, you've broken the law—you expect the consequences.' 'So you won't guarantee immunity?' he was asked. 'No! No!' Sir Julius Chan had a message for those who had moved against him. 'Stand for the election. Don't pretend to be in Government when [you] are not, [when you have] not been given a mandate to govern. So I invite all these people, all these dissident groups of people to go to the election to support their candidates or get themselves in.' Peti Lafanama, for one, took up his challenge and became the Governor of the Eastern Highlands. Singirok did not.

Chapter Sixteen

Consequences

*The Andrew Inquiry; Papua New Guinea Votes;
Skate Elected PM; The Australia–PNG
Relationship; Ceasefire on Bougainville
April 1997–April 1998*

Justice Warwick Andrew began hearing evidence in the first Sandline Inquiry on the Tuesday following the Easter long weekend, 1 April 1997–the same day that had been nominated as D-Day for the aborted Operation Oyster. Tim Spicer was the first to appear and was in the witness box for three days. Police dropped the criminal charges against him and, after his evidence was completed, he was allowed to return home to the United Kingdom. Jerry Singirok was next to appear and with a flourish he handed over to the Judge a canvas bag containing the $US400,000 that the soldiers had recovered from the safe taken from the Sandline residence in East Boroko. However, Singirok could produce no specific evidence that would allow the Judge to make a definite finding of corruption against any of the three Ministers forced to stand aside. He was interrogated for a week, finally losing his temper when Marshall Cooke QC, representing Sir Julius Chan, Chris Haiveta and Mathias Ijape, accused him of being a liar. Singirok refused to answer any further questions until Cooke apologised, which Cooke would not do. Justice Andrew, who was working under a considerable time constraint and still had many witnesses to hear, let Singirok go.

Towards the middle of April it was clear that the first deadline for Andrew's report could not be met. The Acting Prime Minister, John Giheno, extended the Inquiry by another six weeks, setting a new deadline of the end of May. That was just two weeks before voting in the national elections would begin. Chan's election campaign strategy had been wrecked by Operation Rausim Kwik but he was confident he would be cleared by the Inquiry and wanted to face the voters back in charge as Prime Minister.

Giheno rejected a request by Singirok's lawyer, Peter Donigi, to extend the terms of reference. And the day before Chan was to appear as a witness (23 April), the Acting Prime Minister turned down a recommendation from the Judge that the State meet Singirok's legal costs. Donigi withdrew. With no cross-examination Chan's evidence was over in less than two-and-a-half hours. Leaving the Inquiry, Sir Julius claimed he had been vindicated.

Giheno took delivery of Justice Andrew's report on Thursday 29 May. But he refused to make the findings public immediately. 'People need to be patient,' he told the media after posing with the Judge. In an interview with the ABC Giheno said he would 'need time to actually look at the recommendations' and suggested it could be 'two to three weeks' before he would be in a position to decide what to do. Voting was to begin on 14 June. For the first time since the Sandline deal had been exposed Julius Chan and Jerry Singirok were in agreement. Both wanted the report released. 'I think there are a lot of very anxious ordinary Papua New Guineas out there who are all anxious to know the outcome ...' Singirok said from Flagstaff House, the PNGDF Commander's residence which he was still occupying. 'So I think it is in the best interests of the nation that the Acting Prime Minister makes a decision about the Inquiry.' Chan's staff obtained a copy of the report and began a selective leaking operation. It went badly wrong when Nicos Violaris, the business 'friend' of Chan's who had disappeared during the public hearings, invited Singirok to a room at the Airways Motel on Saturday 31 May and showed sections of it to him in a clumsy attempt to set up a deal under which the Brigadier would be offered a diplomatic or study posting overseas.

'We're now able to see Sir Julius Chan's associates are still at work in Papua New Guinea,' Singirok claimed at a news conference he called at Flagstaff House on Sunday 1 June, '[acting] with impunity and utter disregard for the procedural law of this nation'. Singirok had been to see the Acting Prime Minister to protest that Violaris had seen the Judge's report when he, the one who had demanded the inquiry and who had subjected himself under oath to a relentless grilling, had not. 'I have just returned from Mr Giheno's office,' Singirok said, 'and he is absolutely disgusted.' The next day the nation was in complete confusion as to who was leading it. That Monday, 2 June, the media was called to two Prime Ministerial news conferences. Acting Prime Minister Giheno held the first one at the Prime Minister's office in the Department of the Prime Minister at Morauta House. 'As of now I think I am still the Acting Prime Minister,' he said and suggested there was a need to further explore concerns which Justice Andrew had raised but which were outside his terms of reference. 'What I want to do is get another investigation set up into areas the Commission could not go into,' Giheno said. But at the second news conference, held two hours later in the Prime Minister's office at Parliament House, Sir Julius said he had informed the Governor General that he had resumed the leadership. 'There is only one elected Prime Minister of PNG,' Chan said. 'I am that person.'

Chan ordered the immediate release of Justice Andrew's findings, which were that there was 'no credible evidence upon which a finding of personal corruption or impropriety' could be made against Chan or Ijape. The Judge was very critical of Haiveta saying he had not told the truth and that the Commission remained 'suspicious of Mr Haiveta's actions and motivations'. But again he concluded that there was 'insufficient evidence upon which a finding of personal corruption could be made against' Haiveta. Justice Andrew also criticised Singirok. 'The Commander has admitted in evidence,' he said, 'that he had no evidence of corruption but only a suspicion of corruption.' He also claimed Singirok had been 'enthusiastic about the benefits of the engagement' of Sandline. In attempting to ascribe motives for Singirok's actions the Judge concluded that 'he became increasingly irritated and then resentful and finally hostile by what he saw as Sandline personnel, in particular Mr Spicer, usurping his authority as Commander'. Singirok claimed the report was a 'whitewash' and called for a new inquiry. But Chan, back in control, took his revenge.

The first decision Chan's Cabinet took after his return was to appoint Singirok's greatest enemy in the military, Colonel Leo Nuia, Commander of the PNG Defence Force. The legitimacy of Nuia's appointment was later to be tested in court because he had been dismissed from the PNGDF in 1996, retrenched by Singirok. He was not recommissioned before being promoted to Brigadier General and made Commander. Nuia ordered Singirok out of Flagstaff House. A month later, by notice in the *Government Gazette*, Singirok was sacked from the force. Walter Enuma was arrested by the police in late July and held in the Boroko police cells on charges only marginally related to the events of March. Captain Bola Renagi, second-in-command of the Special Forces Unit, then led a raid on the cells, freeing Enuma and placing Nuia under house arrest for twelve hours. Enuma and four others were later court-martialled for mutiny and sentenced to terms in prison of between five and ten years. Enuma, who deserved a medal for the extraordinary control he had exercised over the troops in March, was out on bail appealing against the sentence when this book went to publication. The Chan Government had announced that Singirok would face trial for alleged sedition but by mid-1998 the trial had not begun. By then, it was a very different government in power.

Neither Chan nor Giheno survived the 1997 election. Giheno's loss was not totally unexpected. Although admired by the private sector and generally regarded as one of the best performing Ministers in government, John Giheno was from a relatively small language group in his Henganofi electorate in the Eastern Highlands. Viviso Seravo had beaten him in the 1992 elections but Giheno won the seat back narrowly in a by-election after he had successfully contested the result in the Court of Disputed Returns. Seravo, from a more populous area, had worked hard in the intervening five years to unseat Giheno and succeeded. Chan's loss, however, was a major upset. He was beaten by the candidate representing Sir Michael Somare's new National Alliance, Ephraim Apelis, who outpolled Sir Julius by a mere 110 votes. Amongst the other losers were Mathias Ijape and Peter Barter. In fact six of the nine Ministers who had attended the 15 January National Security Council meeting, which approved the hiring of Sandline, lost their seats. The morning after Chan's loss was announced somebody hung a banner along the fence outside the Murray Barracks residential quarters proclaiming, 'The Monster Is Dead.' Asked at his final Prime Ministerial news conference if he believed the Sandline crisis had led to his defeat, Sir Julius replied: 'You can say that, yes.'

The most prominent member of the Opposition defeated was Paias Wingti. He lost his Governorship of the Western Highlands to one of the leading anti-corruption campaigners, a Catholic priest, Father Robert Lak. It was the first time any Prime Minister or ex-Prime Minister had been rejected since Independence and two of the four men who had led PNG were dumped at the one election—Chan and Wingti. Somare won his seat easily and Rabbie Namaliu was returned in the seat of Kokopo in East New Britain. Haiveta survived but his chances of winning the Prime Ministership were slim and dealt a further blow when Namaliu announced he would not support his Pangu Pati leader for the nation's top job. Namaliu had tried to convince Pangu to quit its partnership with Chan's People's Progress Party but failed. 'Unquestionably the people of Papua New Guinea voted for change,' Namaliu said. 'They did not vote for a continuation of what we've experienced and endured over the last three years.' It seemed that Michael Somare had the inside running for a third turn as PM.

However, forming a government in PNG is never straightforward. The frantic scramble for numbers began well before all results were known. Chan's PPP had the most Members returned of any party, sixteen (down from thirty-two). Haiveta's Pangu had thirteen. Wingti's now leaderless People's Democratic Movement had nine; Somare's National Alliance, seven; and the party led by the Governor of Port Moresby, Bill Skate, the People's National

Congress, won six. Seven other parties shared eighteen seats. But by far the biggest block of winners were Independents, forty of them—thirty-three elected for the first time. Michael Somare gathered his forces in Wewak. Bill Skate linked up with Wingti's PDM and also, in one of those confounding PNG political twists, with a group of Independents who had gathered around the priest who had defeated Wingti, Father Lak. An Australian businessman, Mujo Sefa, offered Skate advice and security services and he helped arrange for those supporting Skate to gather together at a tourist lodge at Tufi in the Oro Province. He also took their measurements and ordered suits for them all from a tailor in Port Moresby, Luk Poy Wai.

The Tufi Camp, as it became known, included many of the most vitriolic critics of the Chan-Haiveta Government. Peti Lafanama from Melanesian Solidarity who had led the anti-Sandline, pro-Singirok public demonstrations in Port Moresby was there supporting Father Lak. Skate chartered an aircraft and he and Lak visited Somare in Wewak to discuss forming a coalition. But there was disagreement over who should be Prime Minister. The Manus Governor, Stephen Pokawin, was prominent in the Wewak Camp and he convinced all around Somare that the leadership of the incoming government was not negotiable. Somare must be the one. Then, in a breathtaking development that left much of the country stunned and many PNG political observers cynical, Skate started dealing with Chan and Haiveta. The day before the vote was to be taken by the newly elected Parliament, Skate met with Chan and Haiveta at Paias Wingti's house in Port Moresby. When the Parliament met on Tuesday 22 July, Skate was elected Prime Minister easily defeating Somare seventy-one votes to thirty-five. 'Politics is a funny game,' Skate told the Parliament after his victory. Haiveta, the man most heavily criticised by Justice Andrew, stayed on as Deputy Prime Minister.

It was not the government Australia might have wished for. Indeed, as it was being formed, Australia's disparaging official view of PNG, and of Haiveta in particular, became glaringly and embarrassingly public. An AUSTEO (Australian Eyes Only) briefing paper prepared for Australia's Treasurer, Peter Costello, for a meeting of South Pacific Forum Economic Ministers in Cairns had been left lying around outside the meeting and was picked up by a journalist from Reuters newsagency. 'Haiveta is an ambitious and self-confident minister but his prospects have been severely damaged,' the briefing claimed, 'at least for the time being, by the Sandline affair and the electoral backlash against corruption and poor government. Despite his strong background in policy and administration, he has not shown sound political instincts and good judgement as finance minister and Pangu Party leader. He has a brutal streak and has disappointed hopes that he would, as a leader from a new generation, herald a new and less self-serving style of national leadership. To the contrary, he has immersed himself in jobbery and money politics.'

In an extraordinary misreading of Haiveta, the paper went on to describe him insultingly as 'Chan's lickspittle'. 'In good part,' it claimed, 'Haiveta's problems arose because he was too beholden to Chan, failing to assert himself in Cabinet and protect his party's interests.' Haiveta rarely failed to assert himself and his party position was assured because of the solid support he had from Pangu strongman, Sir Pita Lus. The document claimed Haiveta's arrogance had antagonised many and predicted he might lose the party leadership and even his seat. Three strikes and three misses: Haiveta won his seat; he retained the Pangu leadership; and, rather than having his prospects 'severely damaged', he was back as Deputy Prime Minister. 'Well, I would expect Australia to say that anyway,' Haiveta said in Port Moresby when the comments about him were widely publicised. 'I haven't seen the report itself but I've seen the press comments and they see me as a combative person towards Australia. If it's a report from Australia', he shrugged, 'what do you expect?' Sir Julius described the assessment as 'very shallow'. Asked if he thought it had damaged the relationship, Chan replied: 'Of course it has.'

It was the tone of superiority, as much as the misinterpretations, that did the damage. Professor Ted Wolfers, Professor of Politics at Wollongong University, who has worked very closely for years with senior administrative and political figures in PNG, wrote in the *Sydney Morning Herald* about how the 'dismissive, almost contemptuous way, in which the brief described regional leaders' was indicative of an attitude long suspected by those in the Pacific with whom Australia dealt. 'Anyone who has attended official hearings and presentations on Australian aid to Papua New Guinea must have observed the increasing disregard for local sensitivities displayed by Australians who criticise conditions there,' he wrote, 'including alleged corruption and mismanagement. They offer advice with a degree of presumption that they would not dare to display towards South-East Asian countries, for example.' He concluded his article with the observation that an 'Australian government that encourages others to practise good governance by increasing transparency' might 'well wish that its own lack of interest and sensitivity in relation to neighbouring countries had not been put so transparently on display ...'

The AUSTEO paper highlighted one of the biggest problems Australia has in dealing with Papua New Guinea. Too many Australians who know too little about the country tend to believe they have the solutions for PNG's problems. After briefly discussing some of these problems—'weak public sector management', 'high costs', 'law and order problems' and 'landowner claims'—the paper suggested that the 'World Bank program and Australia's shift to program aid should help to address [them]. But progress will be grandual at best and will require a strong presence on the ground including from Australia,' it said, predicting that despite this heavy Australian presence 'thorough reform will be difficult, politically and administratively'. 'Leaders will respond best,' it suggested in a tip to Costello on the way he should deal with the 'combative' Haiveta, 'if they can be persuaded to look at the longer term and understand that better basic services would help them politically. And the prospect of better services gives Australia the opportunity to build, through program aid, popular pressure for reform on a reluctant elite in Port Moresby.'

This patronising tone has been around for years. In 1994, Michael O'Connor of the Australian Defence Association, wrote about how pessimism about PNG had become 'almost *de rigueur* in Australian public discourse'. At the time he was questioning an 'extravagantly gloomy' report on PNG by the Joint Standing Committee on Foreign Affairs, Defence and Trade. O'Connor suggested that the 'media, academic seminars and respected commentators bewail the condition of what the Department of Foreign Affairs and Trade has suggested could become a "broken-backed" state'. He said the fifty-six recommendations in the committee's report 'were based on this view as well as on the somewhat condescending attitude that Australian wisdom could solve all PNG's problems'. At a subsequent seminar organised by the same parliamentary committee (held in November 1996 in Canberra) Professor Hank Nelson from the Australian National University told the following story to illustrate how Australian consultants and experts advising on PNG were often the ones going through the learning process.

> *Imagine the Victorian police force had a problem and an agency said, 'Look, we have got a Javanese policeman, he is an extremely good policeman, his English is only fair, though, and he may have difficulty communicating with a lot of the Victorian police, but he will get by. He has never been to Australia. He cannot come and live in Victoria but we are going to fly him over eight times, and he will stay in Victoria about a week at a time. He will get around the country, he will have an hour in Manangatang, two hours somewhere else and he might overnight in Mildura.' At the end of the two years that he has been monitoring the Victorian police he puts in his report. He goes back to Bandung and at a conference*

> *in Bandung he is absolutely sparkling. He has got a whole lot of anecdotes about what he found out about the Victorian police, about the scones that he was served in Manangatang and so on, and he really is, in Bandung, an expert on the Victorian police. What has happened is that there has been a transference of knowledge about the Victorian police force to this Javanese expert and he is now extremely well informed and can talk authoritatively about the Victorian police force. What do you think has happened about the report he put in on the Victorian police and the perception that those Victorian police have on that report from that Javanese outsider?*

It is a telling comparison. Australia's non-military cooperation aid to Papua New Guinea averages about $A300 million a year. Up until the late 1980s most of that aid was provided to PNG in cash as support for the PNG budget. Under the current agreement, which Australia insisted be adopted following criticism by the Australian Auditor General, this annual grant is being transformed rapidly into aid for mutually agreed, specific programs and projects. Mutual agreement is at least the principle. By the year 2000 the spending of the entire $A300 million will be under the supervision of Australian bureaucrats working for AusAid. In November 1993 AusAid's predecessor, AIDAB, organised a two-day forum in Brisbane to explain this big switch in aid from cash support to program aid. The forum was attended by 400 hungry-eyed Australian consultants and representatives of non-government organisations all with ideas on how to get in on the action. A year or two prior to this AIDAB had set up 'joint' committees called Sectoral Working Groups covering the agreed sectors into which the Australian money would be channelled—health, education, infrastructure, renewable resources, law and order, and the private sector.

The chairmen of these Sectoral Working Groups presented their reports to the forum on what was planned in their area of expertise. It was stunning just how much basic policy on fundamental issues, such as the future of education and health in Papua New Guinea, had been appropriated by these committees. Admittedly they did have representation from PNG Government Departments ('line agencies' is what the bureaucrats called them). But given the shortages of skills in the PNG bureaucracy and the multiple demands on talented manpower it was inevitable that the Australian 'experts' dominated these committees, working under the imperatives of deadlines set by the Australian aid authorities. Chan, who was Finance Minister at the time and a constant critic of the switch in aid, told the ABC during the forum that it was 'a very cumbersome, very tedious, very unnecessary load of work'. Australia's then Development Cooperation Minister, Gordon Bilney, put the alternative argument. He said in his address that the untied aid arrangement agreed to at Independence out of 'respect' for PNG's sovereignty might not have been the right decision.

'Would it have been better in hindsight,' Bilney asked, '[for Australia] to have remained engaged in some way? Would it have been better to use Australia's more developed technical and human resources to work together with Papua New Guinea to develop their country? Would that have ensured more rapid and more equitable development?' Chan's answer to each of Bilney's questions was no. 'We are concerned,' Sir Julius told the forum, 'that the decreasing real value of support could lead to be of less and less tangible benefit if it is frittered away on too many projects and programs which have excessive bureaucratic and administrative costs.' He was particularly concerned about the rake-off to consultants. 'I must emphasise,' he also said, 'that PNG must have direct control on where and how project and program aid funds are spent. We are not prepared to return our sovereign rights back to Canberra.' The then Secretary of the PNG Prime Minister's Department, Brown Bai, after hearing the presentations by the Australian chairmen of these committees, expressed surprise at the amount of work the teams had done on planning PNG's future. 'I am supposed to be the PNG Government's chief adviser,' he said, 'but I know nothing about this.'

Bai was not necessarily complaining about the quality of the work done. He said he had found some of the presentations 'excellent'. 'But I want to ask you,' he said from the floor during one question and answer session towards the end of the forum, 'with all this twenty years, thirty years, ten years planning that you are now proposing under these programs, how would that accommodate any changes that would arise as a result of new policy initiatives coming out of the government of the day?' The feeble answer was that Papua New Guineans had been involved as members of the committees. But these committee members were bureaucratic, often relatively junior, representatives of the 'line agencies'. Professor Wolfers raised a similar point while speaking to the Australian joint parliamentary committee forum in late 1996. He said the Australian Government needed to be 'sensitive to the contradictions' in its policy of doing away with budget support while criticising PNG's system of government. 'Bearing in mind that accounting is not the same as accountability,' he said '[Australia] should also be conscious of the potential for conflict between political pressures and bureaucratic plans, especially in a democracy... The problems of accountability to the electorate are at least as important as problems of accountability to aid donors [and] international financial institutions and they are very real problems in the management of Papua New Guinea.'

AusAid is in a difficult position. It is required to have all the $A300 million linked to specific programs by the year 2000. Each year another huge lump of the aid ceases to be cash support and comes under AusAid's rigorous accounting guidelines. AusAid Deputy Director General Bruce Davis told the Canberra forum about some of the agency's problems. Quoting from the joint committee's 1991 report, which said 'negotiating projects and programs involves great administrative complexity and absorbs a large amount of scarce high level management capacity,' Davis said AusAid was 'learning on a daily basis how true this statement' was. 'Within our own system the volume of program aid had grown much more rapidly than the resources that we have available in Canberra and Port Moresby have grown to administer it.' If AusAid, which had set up the new administrative requirements, has been struggling with them, imagine how the PNG bureaucracy has coped. Reiterating Wolfer's point that 'accounting is not accountability', Anthropology Professor Maev O'Collins, who has often been hired by AusAid as an adviser, said she had found she could identify different priorities once in the field. 'By the time I go through the AusAid bureaucratic process and I do the mountainous paperwork to get the little program changed, the person has died, or I have moved on ... I think Australian aid needs to be brave enough to be a bit more flexible.'

The change in the aid program is creating huge problems for the overall Australia–PNG relationship. With increasing numbers of Australian officials and consultants delving into all these areas of PNG Government responsibility the range of points of irritation has grown exponentially. There is a terrible temptation facing Australians who work on these aid projects to push the Papua New Guineans aside and take over the problem to effect a quicker result. But it is self-defeating. '[We] in this country have been inclined to be too prescriptive about what Papua New Guinea should be doing,' according to Michael O'Connor, 'putting ourselves in a position of being the experts rather than neighbours and friends ... I would add that given the PNG experience of Australian solutions to PNG problems, it might not be too much to argue that solutions contrived by sophisticated Australians could be presumed to be wrong in the PNG context.' O'Connor went as far as to claim that Australian 'intervention' was 'an important element of the problem rather than the solution'.

Australia also can not avoid the occasional contrary accusation that in its rush to spend this money it gets caught up in helping PNG politicians pander to their electorates. Several years ago, the then head of AIDAB,

Phillip Flood, announced two major road projects had been approved in consultation with the PNG Government. Flood dismissed the suggestion, when it was put to him, that both projects were extremely political and that Australia was open to criticism of helping the longer-term electoral prospects of the two PNG Ministers most heavily involved in the discussions. Both projects were to improve sections of the Highlands Highway. One was in the electorate of the then Minister for Transport, Roy Yaki, and the other in the electorate of the then Finance Minister, Masket Iangalio. Both roads, Flood announced, would be completed in 1997. Work went ahead. Seats in the Highlands have the highest turnover rate in the country. More than sixty per cent of Highlands Members (twenty-four out of thirty-nine) lost their seats in the 1997 election. But Yaki and Iangalio both defied the statistics and won.

While there is an increasing number of Australian officials being sent to live in Papua New Guinea there seems to be less and less social contact between those Australians and ordinary Papua New Guineans. Several years ago the Australian Government sold off all its stand-alone houses in Port Moresby that accommodated High Commission staff and moved them into compounds. There are now several of these Australian compounds in the city—the largest jokingly referred to as Fort Moresby. Although part of the reason for abandoning homes in the general community was to provide the Australians with better guarantees of security, the paranoia about crime has grown. Some of the dependants living in these compounds never leave unless in convoys. Crime is a serious problem in the PNG capital but it is not so bad that everybody has to hide twenty-four hours a day behind high concrete walls topped with razor wire. A ghetto mentality has unavoidably developed. PNG's Foreign Affairs Department was outraged in November 1995 when the High Commission officially advised 'all Australians in Papua New Guinea' of the possibility 'that there may be an attack this weekend on Australian expatriates as "payback" for the shooting of a PNG citizen, Mrs Helen Merkle, in Wodonga'. Merkle had been shot dead by Victorian police. Despite the fears raised no Australian was attacked.

During the height of the Sandline drama in Port Moresby Australia's Shadow Foreign Minister, Laurie Brereton, earned himself an entire editorial of condemnation in the *National* newspaper when he suggested that all Australian Defence Force staff in PNG should take refuge in the Australian High Commission. 'It was all in the great tradition of the famous headline in the *Rabaul Times*,' the *National* claimed, 'that trumpeted "No White Woman Safe!", after a minor incident in that town. The headline was published in 1929, and much of Mr Brereton's explosive rhetoric belongs in the same era.' The PNG media, which takes a lot more notice of Australia than the Australian media takes of PNG, carried some excellent cartoons lampooning Australia during the crisis. One had an Australian Government official banging a desk and yelling at the PNG military, 'Mercenaries, killers, bunch of bloodhounds, get them out of PNG now!!' While over his shoulder he is saying to the Australian military, 'Now that the mercenaries are gone prepare to send our troops to rescue the Australians.'

In a separate article on the PNG-Australia relationship the *National* criticised the Australian media for ignoring the region of the world in which Australia is geographically placed. 'Part of the Australian media blindness,' the paper argued, 'stems from that country's apparently endemic identity crisis. Who are the Australians? Are they a lost tribe that has strayed from its ethnic and cultural roots in distant Britain and Europe?' Australia did not do its relations with the PNG media much good when, in 1996, the Foreign Affairs Department, in an economy drive, abolished the only diplomatic position in the High Commission held by a journalist, the First Secretary, Information. These jobs were eliminated in other places too but a few were retained, for instance in London and Washington. In PNG's case it was a mistake of considerable significance. The First Secretary, Information in Port Moresby (if he was any good—as Grant Thompson, the then incumbant, was) had an almost daily influence on what appeared in the PNG media. Australia and what it does is big news in PNG. And it was not only the public relations that suffered. Australia's severing of its daily diplomatic contact with the media meant a whole range of information flowing to the High Commission stopped. That loss had real implications for the Australian Government's understanding of what was going on in February-March 1997.

The Australian Foreign Affairs Department spends a considerable amount of money trying to keep abreast of events in PNG. However, questions should be asked about whether Australia is getting value for money. The Department seems to have an institutional difficulty taking the country seriously. Despite the money spent there appears to be no encouragement for anybody to specialise. The diplomats tend to stay for two years (or three at the most) and almost never return. It is as though spending a term in Port Moresby is a penance to be endured before they can qualify for some more desirable posting well away from Australia. The result is no corporate memory. The political staff race around while they are in PNG collecting screeds of information but by the time they come to be in a position to assess it they are gone. It is not only Foreign Affairs that seems to have this problem. The Office of National Assessment (ONA) in the Prime Minister's

Department advertised for a PNG analyst in 1997. The man who won the job is undoubtedly a fine and intelligent person. But he had no PNG experience whatsoever. His most telling qualification seemed to be that he had done a thesis on Fiji.

It is no great accident therefore that Australia was caught so off-guard by the Chan Government's hiring of the mercenaries. ABC TV's 'Four Corners' devoted a program to the question of whether Australia's security intelligence services had let the country down. In Port Moresby those most caught out were the defence staff at the Australian High Commission. Relations between them and Singirok had reached a sorry point, and in the case of the Deputy Head of Australian Defence Staff, Lieutenant Colonel Gary Hogan, of personal animosity. On 3 March Hogan became very upset in Singirok's office, demanding an explanation as to why Australia had not been kept informed on the Sandline deal. Singirok, who regarded Hogan as arrogant and disrespectful, considered deporting him. Michael O'Connor stated in 1996 that he believed the tension between the Australian and PNG Defence Forces had become an institutional problem. 'While Australia should stand ready to assist Papua New Guinea resolve some of its security problems,' he maintained, 'our capacity to do so is limited by what I would regard as an institutional ignorance of Papua New Guinea and a predisposition to an increasingly offensive paternalism.'

Australia's Foreign Minister, Alexander Downer, acknowledged the problem in an address to a breakfast for businessmen in Port Moresby in August 1997. 'I think we do have a record of sometimes being too patronising and paternalistic,' Downer said, 'and we've got to get away from that.' In an interview for this book, Downer claimed that he regarded the outcome of the Sandline crisis as quite a victory for Australian diplomacy. Australia had certainly put a lot of pressure on Chan. But any interpretation that Australian opposition to the mercenaries gave Singirok the confidence to move against them is a plain misreading of the situation. If anything the Australian pressure won public support in PNG for Chan. And Australians should be aware of how hypocritical, viewed from a Port Moresby perspective, the subsequent Australian stance appeared to be. Australia demanded the mercenaries be removed and then condemned the man who did it, Singirok, by supporting Chan's sacking of him. In the circumstances it probably had no choice. But it is a little much to claim in retrospect what a triumph for Australian diplomacy the whole affair was. In the end Jerry Singirok's motivation for doing what he did certainly did not include any consideration of what might please Australia. His own explanation that he had a crisis of conscience is probably close to the truth although there were undoubtedly other factors involved.

What is indisputable is that Singirok's actions in terminating the Sandline deal provided a welcome circuit-breaker to the war on Bougainville. Fortunately New Zealand had just the man who could make the most of the opportunity. John Hayes, the former NZ High Commissioner to PNG, who had helped arrange the first substantial peace talks in 1990 on board the warship *Endeavour*, was directed by New Zealand's Foreign Minister, Don McKinnon, to apply himself to the Bougainville problem once more. Hayes flew into Port Moresby during the election campaign on a so-called 'fishing holiday'. He met with Giheno and with Chan and renewed his contacts with the secessionist leaders. The outcome was an agreement that New Zealand would host preliminary, all-Bougainvillean talks at a New Zealand defence base, Burnham, near Christchurch, in early July. Hayes spoke directly by satellite telephone with Francis Ona but could not convince Ona to attend. On 4 July Hayes flew into the mountains of central Bougainville on a chartered civilian helicopter to pick up Bougainville Revolutionary Army delegates. Near Guava, Ona's village, the helicopter was shot up and forced to make an emergency landing on the west coast. Nobody was injured but the message from Ona was clear. He was still opposed to a negotiated settlement.

However, the Chairman of the secessionist Bougainville Interim Government, Vice President Joseph Kabui, and the Military Commander of the BRA, General Sam Kauona, were willing to negotiate. They met at Burnham with Premier Gerard Sinato, and other members of his Bougainville Transitional Government, and the newly elected and re-elected MPs for Bougainville in the PNG Parliament. John Momis, who had been taken hostage by one BRA group loyal to Ona in early June, only to be released ten days later, attended, as did the new Member for Central Bougainville, Sam Akoitai. Akoitai was the recognised leader of all the Resistance Groups on Bougainville. In a major breakthrough, the secessionist leaders who attended the Burnham talks arranged on their return to Bougainville for the release of the five PNG security force members still held hostage following the Kangu Beach massacre. Welcoming the five, who travelled with Hayes on a New Zealand Air Force Hercules back to Port Moresby, Skate, now Prime Minister, declared it was 'a great start for reconciliation' on Bougainville.

Skate followed up that positive start by appointing Akoitai to his Cabinet as Minister for Bougainville Affairs. A second round of talks held later in 1997, also at Burnham, led eventually to a truce. Those second Burnham talks involved scores of young BRA and Resistance Group commanders from almost all areas on Bougainville. In January 1998 Prime Minister Skate flew to New Zealand and met with Kabui and Kauona. He authorised the man he had appointed as a bipartisan State Negotiator, the Member for Rabaul,

Sir John Kaputin, to sign what became known as the Lincoln Agreement. This set out a process that would lead to the formation of a Reconciliation Government for Bougainville by the end of 1998. At the end of April a permanent cease-fire was signed in Arawa. General Kauona declared the war was over. Ona still held out but appeared to have been effectively marginalised. Neither Kabui nor Kauona had given up on secession. But, they said, the resolution of the political issues would be achieved through negotiation not through gunfire. By mid-1998 peace had settled over most of Bougainville and a multination Peace Monitoring Group made up of unarmed soldiers and civilians from Australia, New Zealand, Fiji and Vanuatu were on the island observing it.

A senior British diplomat with some experience in Africa said after the Sandline crisis had subsided that if a similar uprising against a mercenary group had occurred in Africa, then Spicer, at least, and possibly some of his more senior white associates, would have been killed. 'He did get messed about a little,' the diplomat said. 'But if this had been Africa he would not have lived.' One of the mercenaries, just before he left PNG, said they had been surprised by what happened because their experience in Africa had not prepared them for the complexity of the relationship that exists in Papua New Guinea between the military and the civilian government. 'A lot of things can go bad when you are dealing with African countries and governments,' he said. 'But then, if it does go bad, you just get out of your volition. Here ... ? Well, what happened here could not have happened in Africa.' At his news conference on 17 March, explaining the previous night's revolt against the mercenaries, Jerry Singirok drummed his forefinger on the desk in front of him. 'This is not Africa,' he said emphatically. 'This is Papua New Guinea.' Papua New Guinea will go on fulfilling its promise to perplex outsiders as the Land of the Unexpected.

Index

Adson Holdings, 28
Agiwa, Herowa, 319
AIDAB, 92, 340
Aikung, Colonel Alfred, 67, 68, 78, 284–95, 287–88, 296, 301, 305–16, 311
Akoirai, Paul, 47
Akoitai, Sam, 104, 346
Alatas, Ali, 266
Amet, Sir Arnold, 274–76
Anderson, Warren, 26
Andrew, Justice Warwick, 27, 35, 144, 149–50, 181, 192, 196–207, 200–202, 204, 211–13, 217–18, 244, 333
Andrew Inquiry, 27–28, 34, 119, 170, 184–85, 191–92, 199, 302–303, 317, 333–35
Angolan civil war, 29–30
Anis, Thomas, 107
Anyaoku, Chief Emeka, 310, 316–17
Apelis, Ephraim, 157, 336
Apis, Dennis, 68
Arawa Peace Conference, 54
Arek, Hudson, 168
Armour Holdings, 87
Aropa assault, 132–35
Ashworth, Michael, 244, 265–66
AusAid, 92, 99, 251, 340, 342
AUSTEO paper, 337–39
Australia
  aid to PNG, 92, 110, 136, 255, 262, 340–43
  parliamentary delegation to Bougainville, 50
  reaction to Sandline, 221–23, 226, 234, 238, 251–55, 264–66, 300–302, 306–307
  relations with PNG, 15–17, 137–38, 164–65, 228, 235–36, 337–45
  storage of Sandline hardware, 331
Australian Police Assistance project, 98, 100–101
Australians on attachment to PNGDF, 282
Aviaisa, Aloysius, 284, 301

Bai, Brown, 341
Baing, Andrew, 145–47, 322, 332
Ballesteros, Enrique Bernales, 31–32, 33–34
Barlow, Eeben, 30–32, 35, 143
Barter, Peter, 151, 177, 180, 205, 221, 239, 322, 336
BCL (Bougainville Copper Limited), 39–40
  share price increase, 215–18
  takeover plan, 210, 245–47, 256–57
Beattie, Peter, 254

Benson, Marius, 323
Berapu, Lieutenant Colonel Seke, 134
Bika, John, 45
Billy-Hilly, Francis, 51–52, 130
Bilney, Gordon, 341
Bougainville, 37–56
  blockade, 48–50
  origins of war, 36, 38
  peace, 346–47
  unrest, 102–104, 106–108
Bougainville Interim Government, 46
Bougainville Revolutionary Army (BRA), 37, 43–44, 167
Bougainville Transitional Government, 55, 221, 223, 239, 346
Branch Energy, 30, 35–36, 112–13, 172
Branch Minerals, 172
Bredmeyer, Justice, 70
Brereton, Laurie, 126, 226, 261, 264, 281–82
Brukim, Skru, 275
Buckingham, Anthony (Tony), 29, 31, 34–35, 112–13, 123, 138–39, 143–44, 160–61, 168, 172, 212–13
Buka Liberation Front, 48–49, 107
Burt, Christopher, 188–89, 194, 242–43

Cairns peace meetings, 56, 102–103, 129
Calkins, Richard, 187
Chamber of Mines and Petroleum, 88–90, 93, 95
Chan, Byron, 172, 298
Chan, Sir Julius, 26, 108, 177, 252, 254
  agreement to step aside, 321–22, 329–30
  appointed Singirok as Commander, 79–81
  attitude to Sandline, 113–14, 122, 136, 144, 156, 172–73, 232–34, 264
  on Australia, 130, 136–38, 224–25, 227, 341
  criticism of, 255–56
  elected Prime Minister, 52
  journey to Marshall Islands, 177–78
  letter from Singirok, 280
  lifting of cease-fire, 109
  meeting with Alexander Downer, 222–23
  meeting with Australian emissaries, 301–302, 303
  meeting with John Howard, 261–62
  meeting with Tim Spicer, 171, 173–74
  plan for peace keeping force, 51, 52–53
  reaction to Rausim Kwik, 284, 288, 292, 295–96
  report on Defence spending, 64–65
  return to Prime Ministership, 335

348

statement on Bougainville, 205-206
  on takeover of BCL, 245-46
  on World Bank, 114-15, 146-47
Choiseul Bay incidents, 124-27
Clifford Report, 23
Codyre, Major Peter, 95, 99, 100
Cooke, Marshall, 86, 119, 157, 214, 249, 272, 275, 333
corruption, 23-24, 77-78, 293-94
CRA (Conzinc Rio Tinto Australia), 42
  buy out, 183, 193-94, 210-211, 213, 239-41, 245-47, 256-57

Dademo, Brigadier General Bob, 66, 69, 79
Damen, Damien, 43
Daniel, Amos Emos, 156-57
David, Lieutenant Colonel John, 67-68
David, Lieutenant Michael, 282
Davis, Bruce, 342
Deats, Karl, 11-12, 268-70
Defence Board of Inquiry 1989, 70-71
Defence Cooperation Program, Australian, 44, 63, 136, 141, 158
Defence Systems Limited (DSL), 82-101, 105-106, 112
Defence White Paper 1996, 61-64
De La Billiere, Sir Peter, 28, 150-51
Destination Papua New Guinea, 24-25
Diamond Works, 35
Dinnen, Sinclair, 88-93, 96-100
Diro, Brigadier General Ted, 59, 78
Diro, Captain Siale, 162, 270-71, 281
Donigi, Peter, 301, 303, 311, 324, 334
Dorney, Sean, 114, 244-45, 265-66, 279-80
Downer, Alexander, 110, 123, 129-30, 133, 136-37, 221-25, 227, 234-35, 255, 261, 264, 267, 331, 345
Downer Constructions, 93, 94
Dusava, Gabriel, 254

East, Colin, 61
Ehava, Sergeant John, 58
Eka, Peter, 162, 179, 182, 199, 208-209, 285
Embel, Philemon, 320
Endeavour Accord, 47
Enuma, Major Walter, 70
  commander of Rausim Kwik, 259-61, 266-67, 269-72, 279, 285-86
  court martial, 335
  Defence Force protest march, 317-18
  directive control of army, 11-14, 287-89, 290, 291, 293-94, 297, 300, 305, 307-308
  dispersal of protesters, 329-30
  Murray Barracks crisis meeting, 313-15
  speech to Parliament, 324-26
Evara, Roy, 109, 155
Executive Outcomes, 10, 27-28, 32-35, 113, 172, 266
  involvement in Africa, 29-32

Fabila, Lieutenant Colonel Joseph, 274, 312
Fischer, Stanley, 241-42

Flood, Phillip, 296, 343
Forrester, James, 194-96, 203-204
Foundation for Law, Order and Justice, 157
Franklin, J&S Ltd, 69-70, 104
Franklin, Sidney, 69, 104, 116, 118-121
Fridriksson, Gudmundur, 24-25

Gabi, Sao, 179, 193
Geai, Corporal, 58
Gelu, Zacchary, 193-97, 199-200, 203, 243-45
Gemel, Cecilia, 42-43
Genia, Jack, 91
Genia, Kilroy, 177, 228-29, 257, 261, 302, 331
Geno, Ila, 92, 95
Geno, Makena, 24, 26
Germania Club incident, 73-74
Giheno, John, 211, 332-35
Goulet, Yves, 29, 30, 34-35
Grunberg, Michael, 34, 35-36, 117-18, 161, 179-80, 188-89, 194, 197, 198, 200, 208, 212-13, 299, 302, 317, 331

Haiveta, Chris, 26, 144, 168, 204, 263, 282-83
  Andrews finding, 335
  arranged Spicer's first visit to PNG, 158-59
  AUSTEO view of, 337-38
  on CRA buy-out, 247
  first meeting with Tim Spicer, 149-50
  funding for Sandline, 174, 179-84, 188, 190, 192, 195
  Hong Kong meeting, 210-15, 220
  meeting with Alexander Downer, 267
  mini budget, 146-47
  signed Sandline contract, 10, 202-203
  World Bank dealings, 145
Hambros group, 87
Hamidian-Rad, Pirouz, 114-15, 146
Hannett, Leo, 39
Hasluck, Sir Paul, 16-17, 27
Havini, Moses, 103, 124, 135, 206, 250-52, 257, 265
Hayes, John, 346
Head, Ian, 247-48
helicopters, 62, 142, 163, 197-98
  iroquois, 44-45, 62, 103, 115-16, 125, 131-33, 137-38
Heritage Oil and Gas Ltd, 34-35, 143
Hesse, Archbishop Karl, 226
Hogan, Lieutenant Colonel Gary, 345
Holloway, Barry, 324
Honiara Commitments, 52, 54
Honiara Declaration, 48
Howard, John, 110, 222-23, 252-53, 261-62, 292-93, 295-96, 301
Huai, Brigadier General Tony, 71, 78-79
human rights violations, 50, 103

Iamo, Vele, 116, 119, 184-86, 188-90, 194-96, 199-201, 203, 242-44
Iangalio, Masket, 95, 101, 343
Ijape, Mathias, 124, 129, 170-71, 173-75, 178, 180, 248-49, 282-83, 289, 296, 336

Hong Kong meeting, 220–21, 214, 218–19, 220
proposal for police Rapid Deployment Unit,
    88–91, 93–94, 102
reprimanded by Chan, 158
on Sandline, 82–83, 230, 237, 320–21
search for military help, 102, 104–105, 107–108,
    110–111, 121–23, 138–140
Individual and Community Rights Advocacy Forum
    (ICRAF), 258
Indonesia, 266
Inguba, Sam, 277, 295, 307–308, 316–18, 328
Internal Revenue Commission (IRC), 202–203
Internal Security Act, 99, 102
International Business Company Limited (IBCOL),
    163
Irvine, David, 130, 180, 223
Ivarature, Henry, 293

Jakis, Sergeant Francis, 237–38, 281
Jardine Fleming, 150–51, 184, 210, 240, 248
Jess, Tim, 215

Kabua, Amata, 169
Kabui, Joseph, 40, 45, 47–48, 53, 55–56, 102, 167,
    210, 346
Kalang Pty Ltd, 212
Kaliop, Paul, 285, 290, 293–94
Kanene, Lieutenant Colonel Tokam, 258, 297–98
Kangu Beach hostages, 154–56, 162, 346
Kangu Beach massacre, 140–42, 180
Kaputin, John, 347
Karkas, Dominic, 325
Katingo Pty Ltd, 26
Kaumi, Simon, 295
Kauona, Sam, 43–46, 48, 52–56, 130,
    133–34, 154–55, 167, 210, 251, 346
Keleto, Captain John, 272
Kembu, Ludwig, 274–77, 286, 295, 301, 303–304,
    308, 311, 314, 318, 325–26, 328
Kipalan, Sir Albert, 316, 322, 332
Kipo, Lieutenant Colonel Daniel, 67–68
Kongara Valley mission, 130, 132, 135
Korowi, Sir Wiwa, 155, 274–76, 286, 293–94,
    309, 328
Kove, Matthew, 41

Lafanama, Peti, 291, 295, 326, 332, 337
Laguai, Bougainville, 159–60
Laidlaw, Richard, 15
Lak, Father Robert, 336–37
Lamont, Jim, 240–41
Lapun, Sir Paul, 47
Lepani, Charles, 232
Levi, Noel, 136, 143–44, 157, 162, 179, 200, 202,
    211–12
Lillyman, Mark, 170, 257, 262
Lincoln Agreement, 347
Liria, Yauka, 18, 44–45, 72–73, 75
Littlemore, Stuart, 86, 218–19
Lohia, Renagi, 277
Lokinap, Brigadier Rochus, 78, 157

Loko, James, 179, 182–84, 186, 188, 189–190,
    201, 216–17, 232
Los, Justice Sir Kubulan, 27, 104, 193
Los Inquiry, 27, 67–69, 119, 170, 172, 212, 219,
    272
Lowe, Brian, 143, 300, 307–308
Lowing, Peter, 193, 247
Luitingh, Lafras, 35
Lus, Sir Pita, 283, 320
Lycett, Andrew, 142

Maass, Johnny, 207, 238, 299
Mai, David, 316, 322
Makau, Sylvester, 152
Malasang village incident, 108
Mamae, Brigadier Gago, 78
Mamaloni, Solomon, 111, 170, 257
Manning, Bishop Kevin, 155
Maras, Colonel Joe, 73–74
Marsungan Island incident, 106–107
Matane, Sir Paulius, 309
McCowan, Rupert, 144, 148–51, 183–85, 189–90,
    193–96, 204, 210, 240–41, 248
McLachlan, Ian, 110, 142, 331
Melegepa, James, 67, 104, 114, 122, 158, 161–62,
    195–96, 199, 201
MelSol (Melanesian Solidarity), 291, 295, 318,
    326–27
military hardware purchase, 191–92
Minerals Resources Development Company
    (MRDC), 184–86
Mirigini Charter, 54–55
Miriki, Andrew, 180
Miriori, Martin, 103, 124, 142
Miriung, Theodore, 38, 54–56, 81, 103, 130–31,
    136, 142
    assassination, 151–54, 194
Molloy, Ian, 84–86, 120, 199–200, 203, 218–20,
    243–44
Momis, John, 37, 39, 156, 162, 283–84, 312, 347
Moore, Bishop Desmond, 257
Moramoro, Moseley, 193–94, 210
Morrison, Alistair, 84, 87, 91, 95, 102, 105–106,
    112
Mount Kare incident, 90–91
Mulina, Rupa, 185, 188–92, 194, 203–204
Murdoch, Lindsay, 251

Nali, Michael, 323–24
Namah, Captain, Belden, 12–13
Namaliu, Sir Rabbie, 43, 45, 91, 94, 309–312,
    319, 322–24, 327, 336
Namis, Simon, 206
Nangurumo, Alan 'Terminator,' 290–91, 301,
    330–31
Narokobi, Bernard, 23, 47, 56, 108, 162, 235,
    256–57, 320–21
National Security Council (NSC), 176–77
N'diaye, Wally, 128
Needham, Bob, 95
Nelson, Hank, 339

Nenta, Bob, 101, 129, 169-70, 273-76, 283-84, 314
Network International Security Services, 172, 298
New Zealand, 47
  peace talks, 346-47
  reaction to Sandline, 230, 238-39
Noga, Ken, 78, 234-38
North Fly Highway Development Corporation see Roadco
Nuia, Colonel Leo, 44, 46, 79, 170, 335

O'Callaghan, Mary-Louise, 44, 119, 121, 223-25
O'Collins, Maeve, 342
O'Connor, Michael, 255, 339, 342, 345
O'Grady, Bishop Bernard, 127
Ok Tedi copper mine, 185-86
Ona, Francis, 37-38, 40-41, 43, 46-48, 53, 55-56, 136, 165, 167, 177, 210, 246-47, 251, 256, 346-47
Operation Electric Shock, 78
Operation High Speed I, 51, 80, 165
Operation High Speed II, 109, 115-16, 121, 123, 124-36, 157
Operation No Mercy, 136
Operation Oyster, 11, 14, 209-10, 220, 280-81
Operation Rausim Kwik, 10-14, 263, 268-86
  cancelled, 287, 293
Orogen Minerals, 144-45, 147-48, 184-85, 187, 231-32
Orogen Roadshow, 144-45, 148

Pacific Islands Regiment, 57-60
Pacific Paradise Corporation, 67-68
Palm, Nico, 31, 35
Panguna copper mine, 39-40, 105, 165, 167, 172, 183, 193, 246
Panguna Landowners Association, 41-42
Pato, Rimbink, 257-58, 263
Pentanu, Simon, 24, 154
Philp, Noel, 87-88, 105
Pil, Stanley, 100-101
Pinoko, Father Peter, 159-60
Plaza 107, 34-35, 112, 113, 117, 143, 175
PNG
  Constitution, 18-19, 60-61, 200, 263-64, 276
  independence, 17
  political parties, 19-20
  press reaction to Sandline, 229
  society, 17-18
  voting system, 20-21
PNG Banking Corporation (PNGBC), 185, 187-88, 190, 203
PNG Defence Council, 104-105, 108
  Cairns Hilton meeting, 112-14
PNGDF (Papua New Guinea Defence Force), 57-81
  collapse in discipline, 59-60, 70-76
PNG Parliament, 19, 22-23
  debate and blockade, 316-30
  1997 election, 336
  protest demonstrations, 315, 318-19
Pokasui, James, 71, 78

Pokawin, Stephen, 321, 337
Police attitude to Operation Rausim Kwik, 283-84
Police Tactical Force (PTF), 96-101
Porgera gold mine, dispute, 95-96, 102
Posou, Michael, 69
Proctor, Murray, 255
Project Beacon, 250-51
Project Contravene, 117-18, 121-23, 161-62, 164-68, 171-72, 198
  costs, 175-76
  four options, 166-67
Project Oyster, 198, 250, 253-54, 263
  public demonostrations, 291, 293, 295, 300, 303, 315, 318-19, 329-30
Public Finances (Management) Act, 186, 199-200, 202
Public Officers Superannuation Fund (POSF), 26, 216-17

Ragi, Ereman, 217
Rangit, Tom, 67, 68
Raphael, Stephen, 174
Rapid Deployment Unit, Police, 88-95, 102
Regan, Anthony, 55-56
Renagi, Captain Bola, 238, 263, 284, 358
Resistants, 49
Reynolds, J. P., 42
Roadco, 185-86, 188-89, 194, 231, 242-44
Rubin, Elizabeth, 36

Sabumei, Benias, 83-86, 220
Salamas, Colonel Walter, 12, 237, 258, 268-69, 272, 287, 293, 296-98
Samuel, Sergeant Petueli, 159
Sandline International, 10, 27-28, 144, 158-59
  Cabinet submission, 174-75, 177-79, 196, 199
  draft contract, 179-81, 196-99, 202-203, 220, 225-26, 229
  funding of, 161-62, 175, 178-79, 182-204, 242-44
Sandline merceneries
  admitted to PNG, 206-208
  deportation, 304
Sarei, Alexis, 39
Sasa, Lieutenant Colonel Yaura, 142, 294
Sefa, Mujo, 337
Seravo, Viviso, 336
Serero, Perpetua, 41-42, 43
Sesinu, Captain Ben, 269-70, 272, 304-305
SFU (Special Forces Unit), 58, 207, 208-209, 237-38
Siaguru, Anthony, 20
Sierra, Leone, 30-31, 36
Sinato, Gerard, 131, 226, 256, 346
Singirok, Brigadier Jerry, 160-61, 165, 169-70, 182-83, 194-96, 197-98, 202, 206, 220
  Address to the Nation, 277-79
  appointed as Commander of PNGDF, 79-81
  army career, 59
  attitude to Sandline, 174, 208-209, 248-49
  author of Defence White Paper, 63-64
  before Andrews Inquiry, 333-35

criticism of, 156–58
decision to get rid of Sandline, 258–60
demands, 301, 303–304, 310–12
dismissed, 284, 288, 335
last parade, 313–14
news conference, 281
on Operation High Speed II, 125–26, 132–35
Operation Rausim Kwik, 269–70, 272–74
Singapore/London trip, 116–19
Visa card account, 69, 119–21, 314
Singirok, Weni, 6
Singkai, Bishop Gregory, 39, 42, 45, 47, 154
Singko, James, 56
Siroi, Captain Chris, 283, 289
Skate, Bill, 20, 83, 221, 226, 295, 312–13, 319, 324, 336–37, 346
Smales, Gus, 15–16
Sode, David, 202–203
Solomon Islands, 51, 111, 124–26, 236
Somare, Sir Michael, 17, 47, 162, 180, 252, 313, 321, 336
Sosori, Paul, 158
South Bougainville Interim Authority (SBIA), 126
Special Forces Unit (SFU), 168, 171–72, 178
Spicer, Tim, 28–29, 31, 143–44, 179–80, 182, 184, 188–94, 198, 203–204, 251–52, 262
  before Andrews Inquiry, 333
  approaches to Chan and Ijape, 135–36, 139–40
  arrest and imprisonment, 12–13, 268–72, 291–92, 298, 305, 307–308
  Cairns Hilton meeting, 112–13
  consultancy report, 164–69
  court appearance, 315–16
  first meeting with Haiveta, 149
  first visit to PNG, 158, 160–63
  Hong Kong meeting, 212
  meeting with Chan, 171–75
  presentation of Project Contravene, 117–18, 122–23
Steinsson, Jon, 25
Strategic Resources Corporation, 31–32, 34
Suntheralingham, Justice Thirunavukkarasu, 151–52, 194

Tamalanga, Lieutenant Colonel Michael, 258, 281
Tanao, Avusi, 95, 99–100
Tarata, Koiari, 182, 186–87, 192
Tarii, Thomas, 155–56, 180
Temu, Ila, 184, 186
Thompson, Grant, 344
Toarama, Ishmael, 103, 106, 125, 131, 167
Togarewa, Neville, 74, 132–33
Tokam, Henry, 95, 98–101
Toropo, Major Gilbert, 162, 237, 262, 270–71, 286, 289, 298, 317, 324–26, 328
Transparency International (PNG), 192–93
Triton, Sal, 191
Tuat, Colonal Jack, 153, 174
Tuat, Colonel Jack, 299, 301, 312, 315, 317–18, 320
Tulo, Sam, 47–48, 128

Ume, Miria, 179
Unicorn International Pty Ltd, 104–105, 116, 121

Vagi, Veali, 206
Vaki, Geoffrey, 93
Van den Berg, Brigadier Nick, 10–12, 194, 202–203, 237–38, 253–54, 268–70
Vendrell, Francesc, 129
Violaris, Nicos, 211–12, 282, 334

Wagambi, John, 254
Watawi, Joe, 46–47
Wi, William, 323
Wingia, Joseph, 216–17
Wingti, Paias, 50–52, 94–96, 101, 312, 321, 336
Wolfers, Ted, 338, 341–42
World Bank, 114, 146, 174, 187
  Structural Adjustment Program, 114–15, 145, 147, 175

Yaki, Roy, 81, 108, 226, 235, 254, 313, 320, 343
Yama, Peter, 295, 316, 322